Opposing Power

WEISER CENTER FOR EMERGING DEMOCRACIES

Series Editor
Dan Slater is Professor of Political Science,
Ronald and Eileen Weiser Professor of Emerging Democracies,
and Director of the Weiser Center for Emerging Democracies (WCED)
at the University of Michigan. dnsltr@umich.edu

———————

The series highlights the leading role of the University of Michigan Press, Weiser Center for Emerging Democracies, and International Institute as premier sites for the research and production of knowledge on the conditions that make democracies emerge and dictatorships endure.

———————

The Dictator's Dilemma at the Ballot Box: Electoral Manipulation, Economic Maneuvering, and Political Order in Autocracies
    Masaaki Higashijima

Opposing Power: Building Opposition Alliances in Electoral Autocracies
    Elvin Ong

The Development of Political Institutions: Power, Legitimacy, Democracy
    Federico Ferrara

Aid Imperium: United States Foreign Policy and Human Rights in Post–Cold War Southeast Asia
    Salvador Santino F. Regilme Jr.

Opposing Democracy in the Digital Age: The Yellow Shirts in Thailand
    Aim Sinpeng

Normalizing Corruption: Failures of Accountability in Ukraine
    Erik S. Herron

Economic Shocks and Authoritarian Stability: Duration, Financial Control, and Institutions
    Victor C. Shih, Editor

Electoral Reform and the Fate of New Democracies: Lessons from the Indonesian Case
    Sarah Shair-Rosenfield

Campaigns and Voters in Developing Democracies: Argentina in Comparative Perspective
    Noam Lupu, Virginia Oliveros, and Luis Schiumerini, Editors

Opposing Power

Building Opposition Alliances in Electoral Autocracies

Elvin Ong

UNIVERSITY OF MICHIGAN PRESS

Ann Arbor

Published in the United States of America by the
University of Michigan Press
Manufactured in the United States of America
Printed on acid-free paper
First published May 2022

A CIP catalog record for this book is available from the British Library.

Library of Congress Cataloging-in-Publication data has been applied for.

Library of Congress Control Number: 2022931217

ISBN 978-0-472-13300-0 (hardcover : alk. paper)
ISBN 978-0-472-03888-6 (paper : alk. paper)
ISBN 978-0-472-90272-9 (open access e-book)

DOI: https://doi.org/10.3998/mpub.12001520

An electronic version of this book is freely available, thanks in part to the support of libraries
working with Knowledge Unlatched (KU). KU is a collaborative initiative designed to make high
quality books Open Access for the public good. More information about the initiative and links to
the Open Access version can be found at www.knowledgeunlatched.org.

The University of Michigan Press's open access publishing program is made possible thanks to
additional funding from the University of Michigan Office of the Provost and the generous
support of contributing libraries.

Cover illustration: Philippine opposition leaders protesting against the Marcos administration in
Quezon City, September 27, 1984. Photo courtesy of Jacinto Tee.

Contents

Acknowledgments   vii

List of Figures   xi

List of Tables   xiii

Part I. Introduction, Theory, and Research Design

1 | The Challenges of Building Opposition Alliances   3

2 | Coordination Problems, Regime Vulnerability,
and Interparty Dependence   32

3 | Studying Cases in East and Southeast Asia   57

Part II. Perceptions of Mutual Dependency

4 | Opposing Marcos: Opposition Alliance Formation in
the Philippines   73

5 | Opposing Roh: Opposition Fracture in South Korea   104

Part III. Perceptions of Regime Vulnerability

6 | The Divergent Party Systems in Malaysia and Singapore   133

7 | Constructing Opposition Alliances in Malaysia, 1965–2018   156

8 | Failing to Build Opposition Alliances in Singapore,
1965–2020   206

9 | Conclusion   228

Notes   241

Bibliography   259

Index   285

Digital materials related to this title can be found on
the Fulcrum platform via the following citable URL:
https://doi.org/10.3998/mpub.12001520

Acknowledgments

This book began as a dissertation project when I undertook graduate studies at Emory University's Department of Political Science. I am grateful to my dissertation committee for their long-standing guidance and mentorship, both during its inception and at its later stages. My dissertation cochairs, Richard Doner and Jennifer Gandhi, were always generous, patient, and kind with their feedback and comments. Adam Glynn provided useful feedback on key aspects of the design, implementation, and interpretation of surveys I conducted in Malaysia, which have since grown into extensions beyond this book project. During my time at Emory, other faculty in the department also subtly molded my thinking about the practice and research of politics. Nuggets of insights from Dan Reiter, Thomas Remington, Jeff Staton, Eric Reinhardt, Danielle Jung, Andra Gillespie, and Thomas Lancaster can be found scattered throughout this book. Without the sharp training under their wings, this book would not have been possible.

Outside of Emory, I am indebted to the professional advice from numerous senior scholars at various stages of the book-writing process. Many of them are involved in the Southeast Asia Research Group (SEAREG) and have read and provided feedback on numerous shorter and longer versions of this book. They include Dan Slater, Tom Pepinsky, Allen Hicken, Eddy Malesky, Amy Liu, Kai Ostwald, Steven Oliver, Erik Kuhonta, Risa Toha, Paul Schuler, Jacob Ricks, Bridget Welsh, Meredith Weiss, Kikue Hamayotsu, Netina Tan, Lynette Ong, Lee Morgenbesser, Aim Sinpeng, Aries Arugay, Jean Hong, Jai Kwan Jung, Yuko Kasuya, Hidekuni Washida, Rachel Riedl, Michael Wahman, Adam Ziegfeld, and Leonardo Arriola, among others. In their numerous ways, they helped shape the book into what it is now. Dan, in particular, was instrumental and generous in hosting a book workshop for the completed manuscript. It turned the book into a much more focused piece of research, making it a steep improvement from its previously muddled versions. I am particularly appreciative of Michael Wahman, Adam Ziegfeld, Hanisah Abdullah Sani, and Masaaki Higashijima, all of whom gave their precious time and feedback during the book workshop.

In Malaysia and Singapore, especially at National University of Singapore (NUS), the book benefited from my numerous conversations with fellow colleagues. I would like to thank Terence Lee, Ian Chong, Sooyeon Kim, Deepak Nair, Bilveer Singh, Hyejin Kim, Mohamed Nawab, Donald Low, Kenneth Paul Tan, Wong Chin Huat, Terence Gomez, Joel Moore, Lee Hwok Aun, Tricia Yeoh, Shaun Kua, and John Donaldson. Terence Lee and John Donaldson deserve special mention. John started my political science training when I was a budding undergraduate at Singapore Management University. His shadow can be found lurking on numerous pages. Terence plucked me from relative obscurity while I was in my third year of graduate studies. He piled me with opportunities that turbocharged the research for this book, and advocated for me when I found myself at a dead end. My local research assistants, Immanuela Asa Rahadini, Angela Lim Pei Rong, Esther Lam, and Sabrina Hardy, were all resourceful, independent, and brilliant. I could not have asked for a better team. Thiyaghessan Poongundranar provided invaluable assistance at the eleventh hour.

Graduate studies and book writing can be a lonely endeavor. I am immensely grateful to have found peer support from Kirsten Widner, Kevin Brown, Nancy Arrington, Steven Webster, Drew Wagstaff, Travis Curtice, Josh Fjestul, Lizzy Weiner, Sebastian Dettman, Maryhen Jimenez Morales, Ryan Tans, Jared Bok, Walid Jumblatt Abdullah, Kay Key Teo, Lin Hongxuan, Su Jun Jie, Angela Poh, Jack Chia, Hanisah Abdullah Sani, Wei-Ting Yen, Carmen Jacqueline, Minjung Kim, Nhu Trong, Jessica Soedirgo, Harvey Cheong, Eitan Paul, Dani Nedal, Alec Nash, Caiwei Huang, Mark Youngyuen, Tommy Koh, Clare Kim, Isabel Chew, Nathan Peng Li, Stanley Chia, Edgar Liao, Louisa-May Khoo, Vanessa Banta, Shravan Krishnan, Nila Utami, Constant Courtin, Lui Xia Lee, Salihin Subhan, and Teilhard Paradela. Some of them opened up their homes to me when I needed short-term accommodation. Others directed me to particular empirical sources. We commiserated with each other over numerous meals at school, at our homes, at conferences, in the field, and at the airport.

I would also like to thank various institutions for providing the funds, space, and network to facilitate different parts of the research in this book. They are the Institute of Southeast Asian Studies, the University of Malaya, Emory University's Laney Graduate School, SEAREG, the NUS' Overseas

Graduate Scholarship, Overseas Postdoctoral Fellowship, and Development Fund, the Dan David Prize Scholarship Committee for Defending Democracy, the Ronald Reagan Presidential Library and Museum, and the Centre for Southeast Asia Research (CSEAR) at the University of British Columbia. Both SEAREG and CSEAR warrant special credit. SEAREG approved a USD$5,000 pre-dissertation grant funding at the initial stages of my dissertation research, and provided a platform to solicit critical feedback as a Young Southeast Asia Fellow. SEAREG's funding, in particular, allowed me to "soak and poke" in the region, giving me the time to learn the sensibility of navigating the treacherous waters of field research. SEAREG is also one of the most welcoming academic communities in political science research, ensuring that its junior members never feel alone in the long hard slog of academic publishing. My time as a postdoctoral fellow at CSEAR and Vancouver gave me the perfect space and time to complete the vast majority of the writing and revisions of the book. I am particularly thankful to CSEAR's Director, Kai Ostwald, for being a warm and generous host.

In shepherding the book manuscript through the review and production process, the team at the University of Michigan Press has been very kind and patient with this first-time book author. I am particularly grateful to Elizabeth Demers and Haley Winkle for all their guidance in the early stages of the process. Additionally, I would like to extend my sincerest gratitude to Filipino photographer Jacinto Tee for contributing his hitherto unpublished photographs for the book cover and in chapter 4. When I first saw his photographs of drenched Philippine opposition politicians protesting against the Marcos regime in 1984, I immediately thought that they accurately captured the spirit of the opposition in this book—courageous resilience and determination even while under pervasive repression.

Last, but definitely not least, I am forever grateful to my wife Phoebe Luo, my parents, and my in-laws for their quiet support over the many years spent researching and writing. I drew strength and resolve from the knowledge that they are always there for me. Nothing would have been accomplished without their blessing and encouragement.

Figures

1.1. A Theory of Opposition Alliance Formation in
Electoral Autocracies 24

4.1. Water Cannons Used against Philippine Protestors at the
Welcome Rotunda, Quezon City, September 27, 1984 79

4.2. Philippine Opposition Leaders Protesting against the Marcos
Administration at the Welcome Rotunda, Quezon City,
September 27, 1984 79

7.1. Allocation of Electoral Districts in the 1999 Malaysian
General Elections 169

7.2. Allocation of Electoral Districts in the 2013 Malaysian
General Elections 169

7.3. Clause 5 of the Pakatan Harapan Alliance Agreement 172

7.4. Proportion of the Different Types of Articles Appearing in
The Rocket 188

7.5. Example of "Negative Image" and "Justify Non-cooperation"
Article in *The Rocket* 189

7.6. Example of "Positive Rival" Article in *The Rocket* 190

7.7. Cover Page of *The Rocket* in January 2012 191

7.8. T-shirt for Sale Printed with the Pakatan Harapan Manifesto 199

7.9. Tun Dr. Mahathir Mohamad Campaigning during the
2018 General Election in the Lembah Pantai Constituency 201

7.10. Candidates of Hulu Langat Constituency on Nomination Day
for the 2018 Malaysian General Election 204

8.1. Proportion of Electoral Districts with Coordination Failure
in Singapore Elections, 1968–2020 209

8.2. Proportion of Electoral Districts with Walkover in Singapore
Elections, 1968–2020 210

8.3. PAP's Performance in Singapore Elections, 1968–2020 216

Tables

2.1. Lack of Opposition Coordination in Geographically
Segregated Elections   35

2.2. Opposition Coordination in Geographically
Segregated Elections   35

3.1. Location of Empirical Cases in the Theory   59

4.1. Timeline of Key Events in Philippine Politics in the 1970s
and 1980s   75

5.1. Timeline of Key Events in South Korean Politics in the 1970s
and 1980s   106

6.1. Malaysia's Major Political Parties   143

6.2. Singapore's Numerous Political Parties   153

7.1. Timeline of Key Events in Malaysian Politics from 1965 to 2018   158

7.2. Average Number of Candidates per Constituency across
Elections, 1974–95   166

7.3. Interviews with Malaysian Opposition Party Leaders   171

7.4. Malaysia's Many Pre-electoral Opposition Alliances   175

8.1. Timeline of Key Events in Singapore Politics from 1965
to 2020   208

8.2. Interviews with Singapore Opposition Party Leaders   218

Part I

Introduction, Theory, and Research Design

1 | The Challenges of Building
Opposition Alliances

At 11:00 p.m. on December 11, 1985, a mere one hour before the midnight deadline for filing nomination papers to contest in the upcoming Philippine presidential elections, Corazon Aquino and Salvador Laurel finally agreed to a compromise and filed for their joint candidacy.[1] Corazon Aquino would be the presidential candidate for the opposition alliance known as the United Nationalist Democratic Organization (UNIDO). Salvador Laurel would be her vice-presidential candidate. Over the next few weeks, they would campaign together against Ferdinand Marcos, the autocratic and irrepressible president who had ruled the Philippines for the past 20 years. They would give speeches around the country adorned in yellow and green—yellow was associated with Benigno Aquino, Corazon's late husband, who was assassinated in August 1983, while green was the party color of UNIDO, Laurel's political party. Later in the election, held on February 7, 1986, one marked by various electoral irregularities, the pliant electoral commission declared Marcos the winner by more than 1.5 million votes, while external election observers declared Aquino the winner with more than half a million votes. In the ensuing impasse, millions of Filipinos poured onto the streets to protest against the Marcos regime in the now-famous "People Power Revolution." The Philippine military defected from Marcos, throwing their support behind the protest movement and the two opposition leaders. Finally, on February 25, 1986, Ferdinand Marcos fled to Guam with his family after being airlifted aboard two U.S. Air Force transport airplanes, ending two decades of dictatorship.

The shocking and humiliating collapse of the Marcos regime inspired other opposition leaders and movements across the world, none more so than those in South Korea. Opposition leader Kim Dae Jung declared the country's autocratic military leader, Chun Doo Hwan, a "second Marcos"

3

and the possibility of the country becoming a "second Philippines." Sure enough, just over a year later, on July 1, 1987, the South Korean military regime capitulated in the face of massive street protests. They agreed to release all political prisoners, liberalize the media, guarantee civil rights, and, most importantly, hold direct presidential elections in December of that year. In the ensuing months, interparty jostling and negotiations between the two main opposition leaders, Kim Dae Jung and Kim Young Sam, intensified over who would be the opposition's sole presidential candidate contesting against the incumbent regime's nominee, Roh Tae Woo. To everyone's horror, two young opposition supporters even protested against opposition disunity by committing suicide.[2] But their deaths were to no avail. In the elections on December 16, 1987, Roh cruised to victory with 36.6 percent of the votes. The anti-regime vote was split among three opposition candidates—Kim Young Sam won a 28 percent vote share, Kim Dae Jung 27 percent, and Kim Jong Pil 8.1 percent.

This stark divergence in opposition unity and electoral outcomes between the Philippines and South Korea mirrors similar variation in opposition pre-electoral cohesion and its consequences in other electoral autocracies around the world. In Africa, the most famous opposition pre-electoral coalition[3] was the National Rainbow Coalition (NARC) formed in Kenya in 2002 (Arriola 2013; Kadima and Owuor 2006; Ndegwa 2003). The coalition's Mwai Kibaki secured victory with 61 percent of the votes against the long-dominant Kenya African National Union's Uhuru Kenyatta, who had only 30 percent of the votes. NARC also won 125 out of 210 contested legislative seats. In postcommunist Eastern Europe, the triumphs of the Slovak Democratic Coalition in Slovakia in 1998, and the Social Democratic Party–Croatian Social Liberal Party coalition in Croatia in 2000, served as models for opposition party cooperation and subsequent opposition victories throughout the region (Bunce and Wolchik 2009, 2011). From 2005 to 2015, opposition parties in Venezuela deepened their cooperation progressively into an all-inclusive Democratic Unity Roundtable alliance. The alliance won a supermajority in parliamentary elections in 2015, the first time since Hugo Chávez took power in 1998 (Morales 2018). Overall, global data on electoral autocracies reveal that when opposition parties form alliances in the run-up to autocratic elections, they are more than twice as likely to defeat dominant incumbents compared to elections where they contest alone (Sato and Wahman 2019).

By contrast, when opposition parties fail to coordinate and coalesce into a coherent pre-electoral alliance, then electoral authoritarianism is much more likely to persist. Kenya's Daniel arap Moi, for instance, was able to win the country's presidential elections in 1992 and 1997 with less than an outright majority of votes because the rest of the votes were split between at least three other major opposition candidates. The similar failure of Turkey's opposition parties to coordinate behind a single opposition candidate in the country's 2014 and 2018 presidential elections also strengthened the long-ruling Recep Tayyip Erdoğan (Çarkoğlu and Yildirim 2018; Selçuk and Hekimci 2020; Yardımcı-Geyikçi and Yavuzyilmaz 2020). Both times, their pre-electoral fracture allowed him to win with a majority of votes in the first round of elections, thereby avoiding a second-round runoff. In Tunisia, the recurring failure of the opposition parties to coordinate with each other throughout the 2000s arguably allowed the autocratic Zine El Abidine Ben Ali free rein to consolidate his rule (Haugbølle and Cavatorta 2011).

That building opposition pre-electoral alliances could result in monumental consequences—continued repression under an autocratic incumbent or a regime transition—motivates a deeper, more perplexing question: under what conditions will opposition parties and their leaders build pre-electoral alliances? Answering this question is crucially important insofar as the opposition parties are one of the "specific collective actors that are doing the hard work of demanding, forging, and sustaining democracy," and are therefore "usually key to democratization's fate" (Bermeo and Yashar 2016, 2). A united opposition can mean maintaining pressure for continued liberalization or erecting a bulwark against democratic erosion (Bermeo 2016; Dresden and Howard 2016; Gandhi 2018; Levitsky and Ziblatt 2018; Lührmann and Lindberg 2019; Mechkova, Lührmann, and Lindberg 2017; Waldner and Lust 2018). Autocrats recognize that if their opponents coordinate to attempt to oust them, their days at the top of the pyramid are numbered (Howard and Roessler 2006; Bunce and Wolchik 2011; Teorell and Wahman 2018; Donno 2013; Wahman 2013; Stepan 2016). Conversely, if opposition parties remain divided, then there are scant prospects for constructing or preserving democracy (Magaloni 2006; Ziegfeld and Tudor 2017; Lust 2004, 2005; Svolik 2019; Gamboa 2017).[4]

In order to understand and explain when opposition pre-electoral alliances are built, this book first emphasizes clarity on two distinct, but oftentimes conflated, tasks that such alliances accomplish. At the outset, opposition alliances *coordinate and select opposition candidates* contesting against the dominant incumbent. When there are too many opposition candidates, anti-regime votes will be split, and the incumbent can run away with victory. When opposition alliances minimize the number of candidates running against the incumbent in executive or legislative elections, opposition parties maximize the chances of incumbent defeat. In addition, opposition alliances *coordinate joint campaigns* against the dominant incumbent. These joint campaigns can include campaigning together using a common alliance name, logo, and color, endorsing each other's candidates, committing to a common manifesto clarifying the policy agenda of an opposition-controlled government, or even a pre-electoral declaration of what a post-electoral cabinet will look like. Taken together, these joint campaigns work to maximize anti-regime vote share, again helping opposition parties to maximize their chances of victory.

But negotiating and coordinating candidate selection and joint campaigns in opposition alliances entail highly uncertain benefits and costs to opposition parties and their leaders. Opposition party leaders need to delicately assess a broad range of factors that impact their decision-making. This book argues that two key variables most decisively sway their efforts and actions—their *perceptions of regime vulnerability* and *perceptions of mutual dependency* for opposition victory. If party leaders detect that the incumbent regime is still overwhelmingly dominant and that they have a near zero chance of winning, then building full alliances is likely to be considered a futile endeavor. No party leader will want to invest in the costly efforts and compromises required to coordinate to achieve negligible returns. Even if they do attempt some form of coordination, they will only attempt partial coordination over candidate selection and allocation for the multiple districts in legislative or local elections at best. However, if party leaders perceive that an incumbent is on the edge of a precipice, then they will be galvanized to construct full-fledged alliances to maximize their chances of pushing the autocrat over the edge. The tantalizing lure of potential victory motivates party leaders to redouble their negotiation efforts to mute their differences and secure the ultimate prize of incumbent defeat. Additionally, during the process of inter-party negotiations, opposition party leaders must also assess whether they really do need the help of their rivals to achieve victory. Where opposition party leaders judge that their parties are not at all dependent on each other to seize victory, they will likely eschew building alliances. Instead, they will be more likely to drink their own Kool-Aid: self-rationalize that they have a path to winning on their own without relying on others at all. Alternatively, if party leaders judge that their respective parties must depend on each other's help in order to win, then they will be more willing to expend costly resources and effort to construct pre-electoral alliances.

To be clear, this book's focus is different from the existing voluminous literature examining the variety of pathways toward democratization. The specific phenomena I am interested in explaining are when and how opposition parties and leaders build pre-electoral alliances. Such alliances increase the chances of, but do not guarantee, incumbent defeat (Bunce and Wolchik 2011). Nor does alliance formation and incumbent defeat guarantee democratization (Wahman 2013; Sato and Wahman 2019). What we do know, however, is that the process of democratization is a long-term, careening process played by frequently vacillating characters (Schedler 2002b; Slater 2013; Teorell and Wahman 2018; Ziblatt 2017). Opposition parties and their leaders are one of these major, but oftentimes neglected, characters. Demystifying how they strategically interact with each other can provide more analytical clarity surrounding the circumstances in which democracy ultimately rises or falls.

The Challenges of Building Opposition Alliances under Electoral Authoritarianism

Since the end of the Cold War, electoral authoritarian regimes are now one of the most common regime types in the world (Gandhi 2015; Gandhi and Lust-Okar 2009; Morse 2012; Schedler 2006). In 2021, Freedom House coded 30 percent of 195 countries as "Partly Free" hybrid regimes, alongside 42 percent "Free" democratic countries and 28 percent "Not Free" autocratic countries (Freedom House 2021). The most recent report from the Varieties of Democracy (VDem) project indicates that there were 62 electoral authoritarian regimes in 2021, more than the 60 electoral democracies, 32 liberal democracies, and 25 closed autocracies (Alizada et al. 2021). Modern electoral autocracies include Vladimir Putin's Russia, Nicolás Maduro's Venezuela, Yoweri Museveni's Uganda, Recep Tayip Erdoğan's Turkey, and Hun Sen's Cambodia (Esen and Gumuscu 2016; Handlin 2016; Izama and Wilkerson 2011; Reuter 2017; Strangio 2014).

The primary characteristic of such hybrid regimes is that they combine the facade of democratic elections with autocratic repression (Diamond 2002; Levitsky and Way 2010). Even as they permit opposition parties to contest in national elections, their dominant incumbents manipulate state institutions and resources to tilt those elections in their own favor (Magaloni 2006; Pepinsky 2007; Slater and Fenner 2011). Common tactics include creating a partial election commission to implement biased electoral rules, strategically deploying the state's coercive forces to repress and intimidate the opposition and their supporters, controlling the media environment to stifle dissenting voices and propagate an aura of dominance, and buying support through extensive patronage (Greitens 2016; Lehoucq and Molina Jiménez 2002; Rajah 2012; Schedler 2002a; Stockmann and Gallagher 2011). The result is an institutionalized and stable form of autocracy that typically outlasts other autocracies such as monarchies, military juntas, or one-party states (Gandhi 2008; Geddes 1999; Wright and Escribà-Folch 2012).

Building opposition pre-electoral alliances in such hybrid regimes is deeply challenging for a number of reasons, reasons that originate from the recurring features undergirding the regime's longevity. At the outset, dominant incumbents typically occupy the broad middle section of a unidimensional ideological spectrum, to the extent that there exists ideological spatial competition even in autocratic elections.[5] In line with Downsian expectations, the regime implements policies and generates public goods that appeal to the vast majority of moderate median voters, thus pushing opposition parties to either end of the ideological spectrum (Magaloni 2006; Greene 2007). Additionally, to pay off and mobilize the large groups of elites and supporters in the ideological middle, incumbents require vast amounts of material and symbolic resources which they extract from and deploy via the state (Slater 2010; Slater and Fenner 2011). For fellow elites, autocrats can share material rents from state contracts and coffers, along with the selective invitation to participate in the legislature to negotiate policy concessions (Gandhi 2008; Gandhi and Przeworski 2006, 2007). For the masses, autocrats selectively distribute patronage through a state-imposed "punishment regime," rewarding those who acquiesce and punishing those who rebel (Diaz-Cayeros, Magaloni, and Weingast 2003; Magaloni and Kricheli 2010; Blaydes 2011). Ultimately, the longevity of an autocratic, dominant, ruling party turns, to a large extent, on its ability to systematically organize the cyclical process of resource extraction and redeployment to secure the necessary control over state and society (Svolik 2012).

Consequently, the twin dominance of autocratic incumbents in terms of ideological orientation and resources means that opposition parties find themselves ideologically marginalized and resource-starved (Rakner and van de Walle 2009). Without the necessary financial inducements to reward the upward mobility of its members, an opposition party can only recruit ideologically devoted candidates and activists from the ideological fringes of society. In this way, opposition parties in electoral autocracies typically become "niche" parties—emerging from and producing platforms that appeal to specific geographical regions, ethnoreligious groups, or extreme ideological positions (Wahman 2017; Bischof 2017; Greene 2007). Islamic opposition parties within the Middle East and North Africa, for example, generally first arise from niche sources of support from marginalized conservative social movements, such as the Muslim Brotherhood (Albrecht 2010, 2013; Wegner 2011; Wickham 2002, 2015). Similarly, in Mexico, the centrist dominant ruling Partido Revolucionario Institucional (PRI) that had governed the country between 1946 and 2000 encountered opposition from its ideological flanks (Greene 2002; Magaloni 2006). The conservative Partido Acción Nacional (PAN) and the liberal Partido de la Revolución Democrática (PRD) both competed from their ideological ends to attempt to win votes and seats against the centrist PRI, squeezing the PRI in a pincer-like movement.

The Challenges of Ideological Compromise

The "original sin" of resource-starved and ideologically niche opposition parties presents a first key stumbling block for building opposition preelectoral alliances. In general terms, the intuition is that parties on the progressive left, or those representing the niche interests of one ethnic, religious, or geographical group, cannot bear to work with their ideological rivals on the conservative right, or those representing the niche interests of other competing minority ethnic, religious, or geographical groups (Golder 2006; Greene 2002, 2007; Wahman 2017). That is, opposition parties care about competing against each other as much if not more than competing against the autocrat (Przeworski 1991). Viewed differently, an autocrat's dominance of the ideological middle embodies a divide-and-rule strategy. Riker's analysis of multipartyism in the Indian legislature noted that "Congress in the center has usually been able to keep the opposite ends from combining against it" (Riker 1976, 104). Similar conclusions were also drawn from observing the lack of cooperation between the Islamists and secularists in Tunisia and Egypt (Haugbølle and Cavatorta 2011; Shehata 2010), and between the PAN and the PRD in Mexico (Magaloni 2006). In all of these cases, the blame was placed squarely on ideologically divided opposition party leaders for not being able to bridge their ideological chasms.

But beyond party leaders, ideological divisions among the masses also potentially hinder opposition coordination on two levels. First, an opposition party's members may chafe at cooperating with their ideological rivals, even if their party's leaders may desire to do so. After all, they have joined the party to advance specific ideological causes. But interparty coordination in joint campaigns, such as campaigning using a common manifesto, requires their party to forsake some of these causes. An Islamic party, for example, may be compelled by its secular allies to drop its demand for implementing sharia law in a coalition manifesto. Correspondingly, the Islamic party may also demand its secular partners compromise by staying silent on their position on religion's place in the country. In fact, these were exactly the kinds of quid pro quo concessions observed in Yemen's Joint Meeting Parties (JMP) opposition coalition (Browers 2007, 577–81). In a joint election platform for reform circulated by the JMP in 2005, there was "the lack of a single mention of Islamic law" despite the fact that the two largest component parties in the alliance were Islamist and socialist opposition parties (Browers 2007, 581). But if opposition party leaders anticipate that their party members will not tolerate such ideological compromises, then they are likely to abandon alliance formation altogether. Opposition party leaders are wary of frustrated party members who can potentially mount an internal coup against the party leadership if they disagree vehemently with the compromises forged, reasoning that their party leaders are "sell-out[s] to a party that they perceived as diametrically opposed to their preferences" (Greene 2007, 223).

Second, an opposition party's mass supporters can also abandon their own party if it makes too many compromises to their ideological rivals that are inimical to their own preferences (Gandhi and Ong 2019). In Malaysia's 1999 general election, for example, the Chinese- and Indian-backed Democratic Action Party (DAP) formed an alliance with Malay-Islamist Parti Islam Se-Malaysia (PAS) together with the multiethnic Parti Keadilan Rakyat. The alliance, known as Barisan Alternatif, did not emphasize ethnic minority issues that were important to Chinese and Indian voters. Instead, its election platform chose to focus on the liberal democratic reforms that the opposition coalition would implement if it was victorious against the long-dominant Barisan Nasional (BN) ruling coalition. The DAP lost a significant portion of its supporters as a result. In a stunning setback demonstrating their own miscalculation, the DAP's leaders, Lim Kit Siang and Karpal Singh, lost their own electoral races (Abbott 2000; Felker 2000; Khoo 2000; Mutalib 2000). If the party leaders had more accurately anticipated that their own mass supporters would not follow them in their gamble, then they might not have collaborated at all. In the final analysis, we cannot assume the supporters of opposition parties are necessarily "stackable voting blocs that can be used to manufacture popular majorities" (Wahman 2016, 5).

The Challenges of Electoral Systems

In addition to ideological differences splintering the opposition, certain features of electoral systems also pose formidable coordination challenges for selecting opposition candidates and managing joint campaigns. For presidential systems, in particular, forming pre-electoral alliances requires opposition elites to choose one single opposition candidate to contest against the regime. This is an extremely treacherous bargaining process generally known as the strategic entry problem (Cox 1997, 151–78). If there are too many opposition candidates running against the incumbent, anti-regime votes will be split, and the chances of victory will be reduced. But uniting behind one single opposition candidate also entails selecting one leader to compete for a single indivisible prize (Fearon 1995; Gandhi 2014; Hassner 2009). The numerous opposition party leaders withdrawing their own candidacy in favor of another opposition party leader give up a golden opportunity to become the president of their country. This personal cost to their own electoral ambition may prove difficult to swallow (Arriola 2013).

In other types of autocratic elections with multiple, geographically segregated electoral districts, such as legislative and local (i.e., gubernatorial, mayoral, or municipal) elections, there is no single indivisible prize for being the sole opposition nominee. Instead, forming pre-electoral alliances entails interparty bargaining over allocating which opposition party's candidate or teams of candidates run in which electoral district. Anti-regime voters can most easily identify and consolidate their vote for the opposition if there is only one opposition candidate in each electoral district contesting against the ruling party's candidate. Similarly, in electoral autocracies with closed-list, proportional representation systems, opposition parties need to coordinate fused lists of candidates to pool all anti-regime votes. Interparty bargaining subsequently occurs over which party's candidates are ranked higher or lower on that list.

But regardless of the type of electoral system used, interparty coordination for these kinds of elections can still quickly escalate into a nightmare. Opposition party leaders need ample information to decide their relative standing in each electoral district or their relative positions in a list. Many resort to rhetorical bluster to misrepresent their relative strength and claim a larger share of districts to compete in (Ong 2016). The single, nontransferable vote (SNTV) system also piles on more problems, to result in the most painful of coordination headaches (Cox 1997, 238–50;

Batto and Kim 2012; Buttorff 2015). Over and above selecting candidates to contest in particular districts, party leaders also need to mobilize and instruct voters on how to vote so that all opposition candidates have enough vote share to win against the ruling incumbent party's candidates. If opposition voters do not know how to vote and whom to vote for, then their votes are wasted. In countries that used or are using the SNTV, such as in Taiwan, Japan, and Jordan, resource asymmetry between the incumbent and the opposition mean that the former is simply more capable of overcoming these coordination challenges. Recent empirical research also suggests that dominant incumbent autocrats frequently change electoral rules to make it more difficult for opposition parties to make sense of how to best coordinate with each other (Ostwald 2013; Posusney 2002; Tan and Grofman 2018).

Lastly, all alliances coordinating candidate selection across any electoral system entail at least some potential opposition candidates withdrawing or shifting their candidacy in favor of other candidates. These maneuvers can generate potential intraparty revolt. Disgruntled party members may abandon the party and refuse to campaign for the alliance. Party leaders withdrawing their own candidacy must explain to their party members and supporters why they are giving up a chance at seizing executive office and what compensation they are receiving in return for supporting another candidate. If they are unable to persuade their followers that supporting an alternative candidate for president is in the party's best interests, then they risk making a costly sacrifice for the disintegration of their own party. Even more, party leaders negotiating concessions across an electoral map over multiple districts are also likely to risk the wrath of their local party activists. These local activists who expect to be nominated as the opposition candidate in their own districts may refuse to swallow the bitter pill of making way for another party's candidate. They may already have invested a great deal of time and resources in the election off-season cultivating grassroots support. Allowing another opposition party's candidate to contest in their district nullifies their efforts. Come election time, these disgruntled local activists may decide to go ahead and contest on their own anyway, thus undermining any alliance's original intent of reducing the number of opposition candidates. When the United National Front for Change opposition coalition contested in the Egyptian legislative elections in 2005, for instance, many local candidates ignored the instructions of their national leaders to withdraw from their respective districts (Kraetzschmar 2010, 108–11). They contested in the elections using their own personalist campaigns and their own individual party label, ignoring their party leader's instructions to use the opposition coalition's common name, logo, and manifesto. To persuade their fellow party members to stand down, party leaders must either provide them with material side payments or threaten to expel them from the party. Either way, opposition party leaders deplete their already meager reservoir of material and symbolic resources.

The Challenges of Credible Commitment

To overcome interparty ideological differences and intraparty objections surrounding the withdrawal of candidacies, clearly more popular opposition leaders, also known as coalition formateurs, can promise to share power with their weaker allies after the opposition coalition is victorious (Arriola 2013). Absent the financial resources to adequately compensate their weaker allies before elections, promising to share post-election spoils is likely to be the dominant strategy for coalition formateurs. Specifically, they can promise to appoint alliance members as cabinet members, or enact legislation and implement policies favorable to their coalition partners. Their weaker allies can attempt to hold coalition formateurs to their promises by publicly declaring the power-sharing agreement and potential policy concessions, threatening to shame them if they renege. Approaching Tanzania's 2015 general elections, for instance, the component parties of the opposition coalition, Ukawa, publicly signed a memorandum of understanding to cement the interparty cooperation between them.[6] The document not only committed the parties to field only one single opposition candidate for all levels of elections throughout the country (executive, legislative, and local), it also detailed a power-sharing agreement in a future government if they won the elections (Roop and Weghorst 2016). Subsequently, Ukawa also launched a combined manifesto, promising to prioritize adopting a new constitution that the ruling party had abandoned, among other socioeconomic reform initiatives.[7]

Yet this intertemporal bargain—pre-election compromises for post-election spoils—is rarely reached because the coalition formateur cannot always credibly commit to share post-election spoils. The coalition formateur's credible commitment problem is likely to be inextricably deep for a number of reasons. First, no third party exists that can enforce the intertemporal agreement reached between a victorious opposition nominee and his coalition partners (Staton and Moore 2011; Svolik 2012). In other words, no actor can compel the newly elected leader to abide by his pre-electoral promises. As Arriola (2013, 20) writes, "Coalition partners

understand that they will have no means of enforcing pre-election promises once the formateur is installed in office." Indeed, even the threat of
public naming and shaming for reneging on his promises remains highly
uncertain. The newly elected leader is likely to escape sanction if he is able
to invent some convenient excuse for delays in fulfilling his promises.
These rhetorical excuses can include the need to implement policies satisfying his own supporters first, authoritarian legacies in various state institutions preventing the successful implementation of new policies, or the
lack of resources available to implement all his pre-electoral promises.

Second, while the coalition formateur may tie his own hands by publicly promising to share post-election spoils, the incentives to renege after
elections are likely to be equally powerful, particularly in presidential systems with outsized power residing in the executive office (Fearon 1997;
Gandhi 2014). Newly victorious leaders may care less about rewarding
their pre-electoral allies than about securing the loyalty of new actors who
may threaten their ascent to executive office. The military, for instance,
may require adequate compensation for their post-electoral acquiescence.
Pre-electoral bills incurred by a newly elected leader's close supporters
also need to be paid with freshly gained post-electoral resources. There
may be little left to go around to reward coalition allies once those
resources run out.

Third, even if the weaker opposition leaders withdraw in favor of the
coalition formateur, the selected nominee's victory over the dominant
incumbent is not guaranteed. If the dominant incumbent prevails, which
is the typical expectation in the face of unfree and unfair autocratic elections, then the withdrawing opposition leaders' sacrifices would be for
naught. A pre-electoral commitment to share post-electoral spoils
requires at least some level of certainty that those spoils are attainable in
the first place.

The Challenges of Autocratic Interference

Finally, what makes the difficulty of opposition coordination under electoral authoritarianism a uniquely *autocratic* story is the ability of the dominant incumbent to actively employ various strategies to divide and rule.
The incumbent, for instance, can rely on the legislature to co-opt some of
his opponents at the expense of others (Lust 2005). Co-opted opposition
members in the legislature are allowed to bargain with the regime for
minor policy concessions, perpetuating a facade of regime largess and
democratic competition (Gandhi and Przeworski 2006; Gandhi 2008). In

order to preserve their "special access" to the regime and the spoils of power, co-opted opposition parties are less likely to create alliances with non-co-opted opposition parties. In Morocco, the national leadership of the Socialist Union of Popular Forces (USFP) consistently declined to cooperate with the Islamist Party of Justice and Development (PJD) throughout the 2000s (Wegner and Pellicer 2011). It appeared that USFP's leaders desired to retain their cabinet positions more than they were interested in political liberalization and democratic change (Wegner and Pellicer 2011, 321). Their co-optation thus dramatically reduced their incentives to form alliances with the staunchly anti-regime PJD.

An autocratic incumbent's institutional manipulation to divide the opposition can also manifest through electoral manipulation (Birch 2011; Lust 2006; Posusney 2002). When autocrats first take power, they frequently craft electoral rules to perpetuate their dominance (Lust-Okar and Jamal 2002). As their dominance erodes over time, dominant autocrats can shift the electoral rules to shore up their own support and to throw new sand into the opposition's wheels. Singapore's dominant ruling party, the People's Action Party, created supersized multimember group representative constituencies to replace numerous single-member constituencies from the late 1980s onward, allegedly in response to its declining vote and seat shares (Tan 2013; Tan and Grofman 2018). The election commission, institutionally accountable only to the prime minister's office, also changes the electoral boundaries every electoral cycle purportedly in response to "population shifts" (Open Singapore Centre 2000). By raising the barriers of entry for each individual opposition party and changing the lines of contestation for every single election, the ruling party effectively creates new obstacles to opposition interparty coordination every five years. Rather than preparing to negotiate with each other on established rules, opposition party leaders have to wrangle anew with each other on which opposition party is more popular in which district across the electoral map and therefore earns the privilege of contesting in whichever electoral district it chooses (Ong 2016).

Lastly, autocratic incumbents can also resort to strategic repression to deter opposition coordination (Bhasin and Gandhi 2013; Escribà-Folch 2013). By targeting the most important opposition leaders for repression, dominant autocrats nip in the bud any attempts at collective action. Without a clear opposition leader to coalesce around, opposition forces find it difficult to mobilize supporters to turn out into the streets or to vote against the autocrat at the ballot box. That is why rising stars among opposition forces are frequently targeted for arbitrary arrest and incarceration.

In 2018 and 2019, the Ugandan opposition Member of Parliament Robert Kyagulanyi, better known as the pop-star Bobi Wine, was arrested and charged for illegally organizing mass protests.[8] Apparently, his growing popularity and intention to contest in the 2021 elections against Yoweri Museveni was deemed too much of a threat. Similarly, in late 2019, Thanathorn Juangroongruangkit, leader of Thailand's Future Forward Party, was disqualified as a parliamentarian as a result of breaking specific electoral funding rules.[9] His newly created party, which placed third in the March 2019 general elections, was too much of a threat to the military-backed political establishment. To be sure, such elite-focused repression also has the secondary effect of signaling autocratic dominance and spreading fear among ordinary voters that they too will be targeted (Shen-Bayh 2018). When faced with a choice of participation and arrest versus nonparticipation and safety, some voters may choose the latter. Overall support for the opposition can collapse as a result. Better still, such "calibrated coercion" spreads fear without incurring too much backlash (George 2007). Indiscriminate repression by state security forces generates widespread resentment among the populace, narrowing the autocrat's potential sources of support (Curtice and Behlendorf 2021).

Existing Explanations of Building Opposition Alliances under Electoral Authoritarianism

Ideological differences, complex electoral systems, the credible commitment problem, and autocratic interference appear to be four significant reasons explaining why building opposition pre-electoral alliances is so challenging and rare in electoral authoritarian regimes. Opposition parties must not only navigate the shifting goalposts imposed by dominant incumbents but must also overcome their own interparty and intraparty impediments to coordination. Yet these obstacles do not explain why and when coalition formation occurs, and even if they occur, why and when they occur among ideologically heterogeneous opposition parties. In the existing literature, at least three theories provide some important insights.

The first explanation is a pecuniary one. In explaining why a multiethnic opposition coalition formed in Kenya in 2002 but not in Cameroon in 2004, Arriola (2013) argues that the Kenyan coalition formateur, Mwai Kibaki, had access to financial resources, whereas his Cameroonian counterpart did not. Mwai Kibaki could utilize the extensive finances that he had amassed from donations from the liberalized private business sector to pay off his fellow opposition elites to secure their withdrawal and their endorsements for his candidacy. His fellow opposition elites did not have to rely on his noncredible promises to share rewards after the elections, but simply acquiesced with his pre-electoral payment. In other words, money solved the credible commitment problem. It also helped his cause that his fellow opposition elites were heavily indebted from earlier electoral campaigns. In Cameroon, by contrast, no single opposition leader had an outsized financial advantage over the other. Both Fru Ndi and Ndam Njoya lacked the requisite resources to pay off each other or their supporters. Limited campaign donations from a small private business sector also could not tip one side over the other.

A second explanation for opposition alliance formation is also based on a close examination of African presidential autocracies. Van de Walle (2006) argues that formations of opposition coalitions are "tipping games" that involve rapid power transition from one coalition underpinning autocratic stability to another coalition securing opposition victory. He, like Wahman (2011), proposes an endogenous explanation for opposition alliance formation based on structural conditions. He argues that regime defection and subsequent "opposition cohesion become[s] more likely when an opposition victory appears more likely" (van de Walle 2006, 86). This perception of opposition victory and incumbent defeat is in turn influenced by a variety of factors such as political institutions, history and culture, ethnic fragmentation, and socioeconomic development, as well as international factors such as international pressures for democracy and expatriate support for the opposition. Economic crises, for example, generally encourage regime defection, while sanctions from international institutions and election observers increase the costs of regime repression and embolden the opposition (Hyde and Marinov 2014; Reuter and Gandhi 2011; Levitsky and Way 2010).

A third and final set of scholarship emphasizes the nature of the democracy-authoritarian cleavage (Ibenskas 2016; Selçuk and Hekimci 2020; Tudor and Ziegfeld 2019; Wahman 2011). Simply put, the greater the intensity and salience of the cleavage between the dominant incumbent and the rest of the opposition parties, the more likely opposition parties will form pre-electoral alliances, even if they themselves are ideologically divided. Selçuk and Hekimci (2020), for instance, demonstrate that increasing frustration and antipathy with autocratic repression in Erdoğan's Turkey galvanized ideologically disparate opposition parties and leaders to deepen their efforts at pre-electoral coordination over time. Within five years, Turkish opposition parties from across the ethnic and ideological spectrum managed to coordinate candidate selection for legislative and subnational local elections across the entire country. They even coordinated joint campaigns with cross-party endorsements and common manifestos against Erdoğan's dominant Justice and Development Party (AKP). While they were not able to depose Erdoğan himself, they did manage to deny the AKP a parliamentary supermajority and win local offices in four out of the five largest cities in Turkey.

Assumptions in the Existing Literature

Yet these various explanations of opposition coalition formation make at least two important assumptions about the perceptions of opposition party leaders and their followers. The first assumption is that both opposition elites and the masses who are sympathetic to the opposition's cause are all similarly certain about the autocratic regime's vulnerability. This implies that they all agree on the degree to which electoral victory is possible and that alliance formation is one of the final steps they can take toward boosting their chances of defeating the incumbent. Yet *the true popularity and vulnerability of an autocratic regime is usually highly uncertain and oftentimes in dispute*. The government-controlled mass media are likely to project regime dominance and control, even when the dominant incumbent is under stress (Dimitrov 2017; George 2012; Stier 2015; Stockmann and Gallagher 2011). Preference falsification and self-censorship among citizens due to the fear of repression are also likely to muddy the waters on the true level of public support for the regime (Kuran 1991; Ong 2021). As Bunce and Wolchik (2011, 244) caution about the persistent "political fog" of electoral autocracies,

> Mixed regimes are fluid formations that send out contradictory and ever-changing signals. This means that it is very hard for citizens and opposition groups to read the strength of a mixed regime and to adjust their behavior accordingly. At the same time, regimes that straddle democracy and dictatorship provide very poor information about the extent of public support for the regime and opposition groups.

Uncertainty about the regime's vulnerability inhibits opposition alliance building in a number of ways. From the elite perspective, high uncertainty about the prospect of regime change generates inter-elite disagreement about the prospective payoffs to cooperation (Kadivar 2013).

Opposition leaders who believe that the regime is truly vulnerable and electoral victory to be within their grasp will calculate a positive payoff from cooperation. They will be more willing to accept costly compromises in coordinating to construct pre-electoral alliances. By contrast, leaders who continue to believe that the regime is still dominant and that building alliances is futile will reckon that the overall payoff from cooperation is negative. They will therefore exert minimal effort to find acceptable mutual concessions in candidate selection or in joint campaigns. Ultimately, intra-elite disagreement leads to varying and divergent levels of effort and motivation to coordinate. The result is inefficient and ineffective bargaining, shallow compromises, and half-baked outcomes.

Likewise, from the voters' perspective, uncertainty about regime vulnerability is likely to condition their responses toward opposition alliances. Voters who perceive the regime to be still dominant are unlikely to defect to an opposition coalition. Risk-averse voters will stick with the regime to continue receiving its benefits and for fear of repression (Diaz-Cayeros, Magaloni, and Weingast 2003; Magaloni 2006). Moreover, as Bunce and Wolchik (2011, 245) also highlight, citizens oftentimes "disliked the opposition and doubted that it either could or should win office," even if they rejected the dominant incumbent. When opposition elites sense that voters sympathetic to the opposition are split or undecided, they are likely to forsake negotiations to create alliances altogether. Few will want to make costly concessions if they anticipate that not all of their supporters are behind them.

But even if everyone agrees with each other that the incumbent regime is on its last legs, the existing models also make a second assumption—that *all opposition parties are mutually dependent on each other for potential victory*. For instance, when Mwai Kibaki, an ethnic Kikuyu opposition leader, was contesting against the incumbent regime's candidate, Uhuru Kenyatta, in Kenya in 2002, he had the ex ante expectation that he could not win on his own (Arriola 2013, 200–205). Relying on his own coethnics to vote for him would not be enough to deliver victory. Hence, a pre-electoral alliance with Kijana Wamalwa, an ethnic Luhya opposition leader, was crucial to boosting his chances of winning. In forging his alliance with Wamalwa, Kibaki further made the assumption, or had a high degree of confidence, that Luhya voters who had previously backed Wamalwa would be willing to "hold their noses" to vote for him if Wamalwa endorsed him. On the other hand, Wamalwa relied on Kibaki to deliver pre-electoral financial resources to pay down his debts incurred from earlier elections. Furthermore, Kibaki had promised Wamalwa the vice presidency if Kenyatta was defeated. The mutual reliance of Kibaki and Wamalwa thus helped seal their quid pro quo deal, even as the two opposition leaders represented different ethnic groups from different regions of Kenya.

Now consider the counterfactual. If Kibaki had assessed that he could win against the incumbent Kenyatta on his own, or if Wamalwa had no debts to clear, then neither of them depended on each other. Kibaki would foresee little gain from paying Wamalwa for his acquiescence, and Wamalwa would not be desperate enough to seek a financial arrangement with Kibaki. Since neither party relied on the other for a deal to work, we can surmise that little effort would be spent on coordinating to build a pre-electoral alliance. Both Kibaki and Wamalwa could have been belligerent opposition leaders insisting on their superior candidacies in the absence of mutual dependency. For this reason, perceptions of mutual dependence for victory are a key assumption we must recognize in the alliance-building process.

The Argument in Brief

This book begins with a simple proposal: opposition alliances consist of two different types of coordination between opposition parties. The first type of coordination involves candidate selection or allocation. In presidential elections, this involves opposition elites selecting one single opposition candidate from among themselves to contest against the autocratic incumbent. In legislative or local (i.e., gubernatorial, mayoral, or municipal) elections, coordination involves opposition parties negotiating with each other regarding whose candidate should contest in which district in countries with district-based plurality systems. Opposition parties contesting in legislative elections with proportional representation bargain with each other over which party's candidate should occupy which specific position in a joint list of opposition candidates. In all cases, the intuition is to maximize opposition vote share and the prospects of victory by reducing the number of or sets of opposition candidates competing against the autocrat (Cox 1997; Duverger 1954).

But intra-elite coordination among the opposition is not enough to qualify as a full-fledged opposition alliance. Defeating the dominant incumbent in autocratic elections requires mobilizing a majority of voters to support the opposition. In other words, opposition voters must be persuaded to vote strategically to support the nominee no matter the candidate's partisan affiliation. To do this, opposition alliances must coordinate joint electoral campaigns against the autocrat. This is the second type of coordination required in opposition alliances. Examples of joint campaigns by opposition alliances typically involve opposition parties and leaders campaigning together using a common coalition logo, name, or manifesto. It can also involve opposition elites publicly endorsing the selected opposition candidate(s) or announcing what a post-election cabinet might look like. Such joint campaigns persuade voters to vote strategically via three mechanisms. First, by emphasizing the opposition's joint unity against the regime, they enhance the salience of the anti-regime cleavage, thus persuading voters sympathetic to the opposition's cause to prioritize regime change over their policy differences. Second, joint campaigns highlight the ideological compromises that opposition parties have made with each other. These compromises can persuade the ideological purists in each niche opposition party to "hold their noses" to vote strategically for the selected coalition candidate(s). Third, joint campaigns can also clarify the material and policy benefits that regime change will bring, reducing the uncertainty of what an opposition-controlled government might entail. When an opposition coalition announces the prospective makeup of a post-election cabinet, for instance, voters have less uncertainty about the substantive policy agenda of the opposition. This can help reassure voters who are wary of the uncertainty in policy changes should the opposition be victorious.

Because these two forms of coordination entail very costly compromises among opposition parties, they emerge only under unique conditions. Whether opposition parties build alliances is a function of their leaders' *perceptions of the regime's vulnerability, as well as their perceptions of the opposition parties' mutual dependence.* These two variables are, in turn, conditional upon the autocratic environment.

First, when party leaders assess their chances of winning in the forthcoming election, they look for explicit and public signals of regime vulnerability. The existing literature on electoral autocracies suggests that economic crises, regime defections, or mass street protests are all signs of a weakening incumbent (Casper and Tyson 2014; Haggard and Kaufman 2016; Pepinsky 2009; Reuter and Gandhi 2011; Reuter and Szakonyi 2019; Sato and Wahman 2019). Nonetheless, when dominant incumbents experience these debilitating setbacks in isolated episodes, they are unlikely to generate widespread cognitive updating and agreement about the regime's faltering authority among the opposition. However, *when the incumbent regime encounters an accelerating series of*

regime-debilitating setbacks within a short period of time, then party lead-
ers are much more likely to update their assessments of the regime's vulner-
ability. A surprising intra-regime defection, a deepening economic crisis, recurring massive street protests, or startlingly weak election results
all occurring within a few months or years is more likely to portend the
regime's impending downfall. Consequently, the enticing prospect of
potential victory galvanizes opposition party leaders to find innovative
solutions to overcome their mutual animosities and coordinate to push
the regime over the edge of its precipice.

Second, even if opposition party leaders all agree on the incumbent
regime's accelerating vulnerability, they must also assess if their eventual
victory is dependent on their mutual dependence with each other. *Such*
perceptions of interparty dependence pivot on at least two variables: (1) ex
ante information about the parties' relative strengths and weaknesses, and
(2) party leaders' expectations of the degree of strategic cross-party voting
that will occur among their supporters. In both instances, party leaders can
be informed by numerous sources, such as past electoral results, polling
data, or reputable third parties. Regardless, when opposition party leaders
clearly know their relative strengths and weaknesses, then interparty
negotiations on which candidates to select and the form of compromises
acceptable in joint campaigns will be less fractious. There is very little rhetorical room to exaggerate one's superiority or inability to accept any compromises if all parties have similar information telling them those claims
are untrue. Also, if party leaders have strong ex ante expectations that
their supporters will engage in strategic cross-party voting to support the
nominated alliance candidate(s), then they will be more likely to assess
that they can depend on their rival to maximize their vote share and
chances of winning. Conversely, if opposition party leaders are very
uncertain of who among them is more popular, more organized, or has
more resources, then everyone will have incentives to misrepresent themselves and be belligerent about their relative chances of winning. Similarly,
if party leaders possess low expectations that their supporters will vote
strategically for the nominated alliance candidate(s), then they will hesi-
tate to make costly investments to compromise on candidate selection or
joint campaigns. Under such circumstances, negotiations to coordinate in
pre-electoral alliances are more likely to fail.

To be sure, hope is not lost even when an autocratic incumbent is
judged to be so dominant as to make full-fledged national-level opposition alliances useless. A minor, less interesting side story can still occur.
When opposition elites evaluate their chances of capturing national govern-

ment to be low, opposition interparty coordination can sometimes still occur, albeit only at a lower level of coordinating the allocation of opposition candidates for elections with geographically segregated electoral districts, without joint campaigns. By coordinating to reduce the number of opposition candidates competing against the incumbent ruling parties' candidates in each district, opposition parties act in their own self-interest to maximize vote share and their associated probability of victory within those negotiated electoral districts. They can focus on campaigning in those subnational districts on their own, and do not necessarily need to invest costly time and effort in forging joint campaigns at the national level. Accordingly, *whether parties are successful in dividing up the electoral map is dependent on the availability of ex ante information about the relative popularities of the different parties* (Fearon 1995; Ramsay 2017; Reiter 2009). Clear information about which opposition party is stronger or weaker in particular geographical areas leads to less fractious negotiations about which opposition party should contest where. A clearly less popular and inferior opposition party has less incentives and legitimacy to insist on a right to contest in a district vis-à-vis a clearly more popular opposition counterpart. In contrast, where there is a lack of information and high uncertainty about the relative geographic popularities of different opposition parties, opposition leaders are more likely to be belligerent in refusing to give way to each other. Figure 1.1 illustrates the causal logic and potential outcomes that I have just explicated in the preceding paragraphs.

Core Contributions

This book makes at least three different contributions to the growing literature on opposition alliances under electoral authoritarianism. In clarifying the inner workings of opposition alliances, it first expands and renders more accurately the empirical range of potential outcomes we study. Existing scholarship on opposition alliances typically operationalizes alliance formation as a binary measure—whether alliances are formed or not. For example, Arriola (2013, 8) defines an opposition pre-electoral coalition as "an electoral alliance in which politicians from different ethnic or regional groups endorse a single candidate for executive office." Similarly, Sato and Wahman (2019, 1423) define "opposition coordination as a situation where opposition parties or candidates unify under one banner to challenge the incumbent, rather than running alternate campaigns." In both instances, coordination on *both* candidate selection and joint cam-

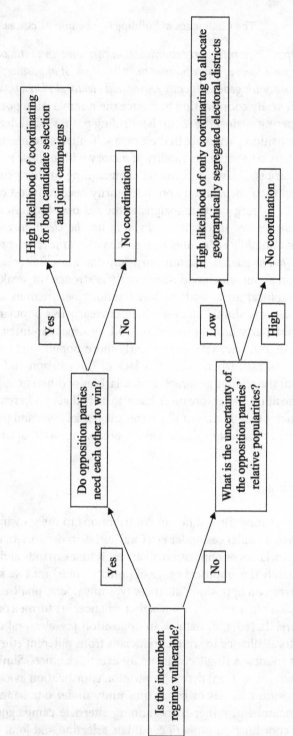

Fig 1.1. A Theory of Opposition Alliance Formation in Electoral Autocracies

paigns is necessary for inclusion as a pre-electoral coalition. In contrast, Gandhi and Reuter (2013, 147) define an opposition pre-electoral coalition as "a public statement of mutual support or a division of electoral districts for each party to contest." Their conceptualization views fulfilling *either* criterion qualifying a coalition as an opposition alliance. More curiously, Howard and Roessler (2006, 371) define opposition coalitions as "multiple opposition groupings, parties, or candidates joined together to create a broad movement in opposition to the incumbent leader or party in power." This definition is an expansive one, covering everything from electoral coordination to social movements. Regardless, this medley of definitions risks conceptual stretching and a corresponding loss in analytical and empirical precision (Sartori 1970).

Eschewing this binary and inclusive approach to operationalizing opposition alliance formation, this book's proposed *ordinal* measurement focuses more narrowly on electoral contestation. Above the absence of alliances lies an intermediate stage where opposition parties coordinate candidate selection and allocation for legislative or local elections that have multiple geographically segregated districts, but do not run joint campaigns. These arrangements are what scholars studying opposition coordination in the Middle East and North African region have frequently alluded to as "tactical alliances" containing "non-competition agreements" (Browers 2007; Kraetzschmar 2010, 2011; Shehata 2010, 83–89). Thereafter, opposition parties coordinating both candidate selection and joint campaigns at the national level can be considered full-fledged opposition alliances. This ordinal approach provides scholars with greater theoretical and analytical specificity on the coordination problems that opposition parties encounter and how they go about solving them. Future scholarship comparing cross-national instances of pre-electoral alliances can then rely on deep case-specific knowledge to identify what particular kinds of coordination opposition parties engage in. This will facilitate a more rigorous and fine-grained examination of the causes and effects of opposition collective action in the future.

Second, in specifying the conditions under which perceptions of regime vulnerability and mutual dependency arise, this book complements and extends the existing pecuniary, endogenous, and cleavage-based explanations of opposition alliance formation. All three explanations have a vulnerable regime at the heart of the opposition coordination decision-making process. This is an oftentimes implicit but necessary condition that motivates alliance formation in the first place. Indeed, multiple scholars have assessed the causal impact of individual regime-debilitating events, such as economic crises, on increasing regime vulnerability and impending collapse (Pepinsky 2009; Reuter and Gandhi 2011; Reuter and Szakonyi 2019). In contrast, this book widens the temporal lens to examine multiple, likely related, regime-debilitating events occurring prior to autocratic elections (Hale 2013). This attention to a broader span of time then provides new theoretical leverage to suggest how a cascade of regime-debilitating events can pierce the foggy aura of regime invincibility, prompting opposition elites and masses to update their expectations of potential victory and rethink their strategies in an upcoming election.

In the same vein, the attention on the factors that inform perceptions of mutual dependency also suggests an important caveat to the existing scholarship that emphasizes how ethnoreligious or ideological differences between opposition parties hobble alliance formation (Golder 2006; Greene 2007; Magaloni 2006). What this book suggests and demonstrates is that neither ethnoreligious nor ideological difference is destiny. On the contrary, polarized parties appealing to niche groups of supporters can actually complement each other by bringing together different sets of voters to build a majority against the dominant incumbent (Greene 2002; Beardsworth 2016). So long as the masses prioritize regime change over their partisan differences, ethnically or ideologically divided opposition supporters can combine forces to push a faltering regime over the edge. In this scenario, what opposition elites do to persuade their supporters to back an alliance's nominee(s) is crucial. Coordinated joint electoral campaigns broadcasting the benefits of regime change can work to cajole and persuade reluctant supporters to prioritize achieving democracy over partisan bickering. The potential gains from democratic reforms through prospective regime change can prove irresistible to long-weary opposition supporters. Of course, even when the incumbent is dominant and not vulnerable, polarized opposition parties can still coordinate "tactical" candidate allocation across electoral districts in service of their own self-interest—maximizing vote shares in the districts where they want to contest in. Possessing prior information about their relative popularities and associated chances of winning helps grease interparty negotiations and mitigate tendencies to be belligerent.

Third and finally, the book's arguments enlighten a growing debate in the literature about the theory of democratization by elections. Proponents of the theory argue that multiparty autocratic elections, even if such elections are unfree or unfair, have democratizing effects. Recurring multiparty autocratic elections provide opportunities for opposition parties to pressure the incumbent regime for reforms (Lindberg 2009; Schedler

2002b; Teorell and Wahman 2018). They also allow citizens to learn liberal values and how to deliberate on important topics among themselves, as in a modern democracy (Edgell et al. 2018). In contrast, the theory's opponents contend that recurring elections are actually a stabilizing force for autocrats (Knutsen, Nygård, and Wig 2017). Even if we observe some autocratic elections leading to the downfall of dominant incumbents, we must conclude that they signal the end of democratization rather than its beginning (Morgenbesser and Pepinsky 2019). But as much as both sets of researchers have contrasting takes about the effect of recurring autocratic elections, almost everyone highlights the importance of opposition collective action potentially challenging dominant incumbents as a key factor in influencing the trajectory of democratization. Yet scholars still oftentimes stay silent on exactly *what* ends opposition collective action entails, and *when* they actually arise.

This book's theoretical and empirical account pushes the debate in a new direction by shifting the level of analysis from the macro-level concepts of elections and democratization, to the meso-level analytical units of opposition parties and their respective leaders. By specifying the difficult and uncertain strategic choices that these key actors confront, the theory underlines the conditional causal relationships connecting autocratic elections and democratization. While most autocratic elections provide recurring opportunities for the incumbent regime to refresh its legitimacy and maintain its dominance over the long run, some autocratic elections in the short run inadvertently expose the autocrat to opposition challenges when they occur alongside other regime-debilitating events (Schedler 2013). Opposition parties bide their time until such "regime-subverting" autocratic elections occur, and then quickly seize the opportunity to coordinate and challenge the incumbent. From this perspective, opposition parties are opportunistic actors, unable to decisively alter the status quo over the long term, but ever ready to take advantage of cracks in the autocrat's armor once exposed in the short term.

Plan of the Book

In chapters 2 and 3, I elaborate the book's theory alongside the book's empirical focus on cases in East Asia. In particular, in chapter 2, I specify exactly what opposition interparty coordination around candidate selection or allocation entails, as well as what coordination for joint electoral campaigns means. I then explicate how varying perceptions of regime vulnerability and interparty dependence affect the propensity of alliance formation. Most importantly, I discuss how multiple regime-debilitating events accelerating within a short period of time, the possession of ex ante information about the parties' relative strengths and weaknesses, and prior expectations about strategic cross-party voting, all work to motivate alliance formation. Chapter 3 discusses and justifies the research design involving the process tracing of two pairs of controlled comparisons juxtaposing opposition alliance formation in the Philippines and South Korea, and in Malaysia and Singapore. I pay particular attention to how close similarities within the two pairs eliminate rival explanations of alliance formation, and also how the variety of sources of quantitative and qualitative empirical evidence I use triangulate to enhance causal inference.

The rest of the book details the empirical evidence. To first demonstrate how varying perceptions of mutual dependency affect opposition party leaders' assessments on whether to forge alliances, Part II of the book undertakes a cross-national controlled comparison between successful opposition alliance formation in 1986 in the Philippines and failed coalition building in 1987 in South Korea.

Chapter 4 process-traces the successful formation of an opposition alliance between Corazon Aquino and Salvador Laurel in the run-up to the February 1986 snap presidential elections called by Philippine autocrat Ferdinand Marcos. It describes how Benigno Aquino's assassination in 1983, a deteriorating economy, the gradual reduction in support for Marcos within the US Department of State, and the declining health of Marcos all converged to foreshadow regime collapse. Additionally, clear knowledge about their relative popularity and organizational strengths led to little doubt about who was the leading coalition formateur. Corazon Aquino, who was clearly the more popular among the masses, had the backing of a large number of opposition elites and among the general population, while Salvador Laurel, who had the better-organized party machinery to turn out voters, sought to extract post-electoral concessions from her. The fact that the elections involved a joint ticket with candidates for president and for vice president further ensured their mutual dependency and created a high degree of confidence that their supporters would vote strategically for their joint ticket. All these factors induced Salvador Laurel to acquiesce to be the vice-presidential candidate and throw his party's support behind Corazon Aquino as the opposition flagbearer. Similarly, Corazon Aquino also grew to accept Salvador Laurel as a running mate and make a series of post-election promises to secure his pre-electoral acquiesce.

Chapter 5 demonstrates the counterfactual of the absence of perceived mutual dependency. It process-traces the failure of Kim Dae Jung and Kim Young Sam to mutually agree to coordinate behind one candidate to contest against the military regime's Roh Tae Woo in the run-up to the December 1987 South Korean presidential elections. Similar to the Philippines, a variety of factors from the Kwangju massacre, to recurring massive street protests, to the reduction in American support for the South Korean government also indicated impending regime collapse. Despite the repeated pleas of their supporters to unite behind one anti-regime candidate, however, high levels of uncertainty over the relative strengths and weaknesses of the two Kims meant that no one acquiesced during interparty negotiations. The fact that they had their own sources of mass support from different regions of the country—Kim Dae Jung being the celebrated son of Jeolla province in the southwest of Korea, and Kim Young Sam having his support base in Gyeongsang province in the southeast—also fostered significant doubts whether their supporters would vote for any one selected opposition candidate against Roh. Consequently, the two party leaders ultimately came to believe that they could defeat Roh Tae Woo on their own without depending on the support of each other. Both remained belligerent about their own chances of winning right up to the eve of election day.

But constructing opposition alliances is also dependent on opposition elite assessments that the regime is ready to fall in the first place. Because the Philippines in 1986 and South Korea in 1987 both possessed this initial condition, its causal effect must be illustrated via other empirical cases. Part III of the book, containing chapters 6, 7, and 8 demonstrates the temporal variation in regime vulnerability and its effect through a second controlled comparison between Malaysia and Singapore between 1965 and 2020.

Chapter 6 provides an empirical guide toward understanding divergent party systems in the controlled comparison of Malaysia and Singapore from 1965 onward. It describes how different party systems were established in the two countries, despite their similar British colonial origins. This chapter first accounts for how ethnic mobilization in the aftermath of World War II in Malaysia resulted in ethnoreligious political parties—a multiethnic, dominant BN ruling coalition in the middle squeezed by the secularist, non-Malay DAP on the left, and the Malay, religious PAS on the right. By contrast, the absence of ethnic mobilization in the decolonization process in Singapore resulted in the growth of personality-based opposition parties flailing against a dominant People's

Action Party (PAP) that emphasized multiracial peace and pragmatic economic development.

Subsequently, chapter 7, on Malaysia, demonstrates how electoral alliance building among ethnically and ideologically polarized opposition parties can occur repeatedly over four decades whenever the opposition detects heightened episodes of regime vulnerability. In particular, the chapter details how interparty coordination between the DAP and PAS took on two distinct forms over four decades. First, during the period of BN regime dominance in the 1970s and 1980s, opposition party leaders initially floundered, but began to learn that interparty coordination of allocating electoral districts helped all parties maximize vote share and their chances of winning in each district against the BN. Self-interested opposition party leaders thus progressively institute rules and mechanisms for resolving interparty differences over district allocation in Malaysia's plurality single-member district parliamentary system. Second, Malaysia's opposition party leaders further coordinated beyond candidate selection to develop joint pre-electoral anti-regime campaigns, but only in 1990, 1999, 2013, and 2018. Prior to those election years, surprising intraregime elite defections combined with mass street protests and economic crises led opposition leaders to perceive that the BN was increasingly vulnerable. They thus upgraded their coordination with joint coalition campaigns to boost their overall chances of electoral victory. Even more, the opposition alliances of 2013 and 2018 saw far more sophisticated campaign strategies to persuade voters to abandon the autocratic BN than the ones in 1999 and 1990. The common manifestos put forth by the alliances were more substantive, the campaign messaging was sharper, and a common logo was adopted to signal their joint fate. In the rest of the electoral years, 1986, 1995, 2004, and 2008, however, opposition party leaders declined to campaign jointly. The incumbent BN was far too dominant for any coordination in joint campaigns to make any gains.

Chapter 8 reveals how opposition parties can still coordinate under circumstances of persistent incumbent dominance, albeit only at the stage of allocating subnational electoral districts in legislative elections. Specifically, I show Singapore's opposition party leaders learned over time with greater information to institute rules to efficiently coordinate to reduce the number of opposition candidates in each electoral district contesting against the PAP. They came to the same conclusion as Malaysia's opposition party leaders: coordinating to allocate only one opposition candidate or teams of candidates in each electoral district maximizes their chances of winning against the ruling PAP candidate. Yet, unlike Malaysia, Singaporean opposition parties never upgraded their coordination to include joint anti-regime electoral campaigns. Costly compromises surrounding party identity and organization were prohibitive for opposition party leaders. Even more important was the perception that there were few or unclear benefits from joint electoral campaigns under the PAP's consistent dominance. The PAP's unrelenting grip over Singapore's media, legal, and economic institutions also provided little new information over the decades that changed their minds about how stable the incumbent PAP regime was.

The concluding chapter 9 summarizes the book's most salient insights and is divided into two sections. The first describes the book's implications for researchers. In doing so, it considers its contribution to the theoretical literature on comparative democratization and democratic erosion, particularly its lessons for taking temporality and endogenous learning much more seriously. The second section then considers the book's implications for a broader general audience of policy practitioners invested in understanding democratization, democracy promotion, and democratic consolidation. It highlights how policy practitioners can aid democracy by helping opposition actors learn to innovate their strategies over time, and how public opinion surveys can play a crucial role in revealing voter preferences and choices in an information-deficit political environment.

2 | Coordination Problems, Regime Vulnerability, and Interparty Dependence

When opposition parties and their leaders choose to participate in autocratic elections, they encounter a vast sea of challenges. They have to evade the autocrat's repression, circumvent the biased media, raise funds from miserly donors, and build their grassroots organization. Additionally, they are confronted with at least two different types of coordination problems. On the one hand, opposition elites have to coordinate to select or allocate candidates to maximize their chances of winning against the autocrat. Thereafter, they have to coordinate joint electoral campaigns to mobilize ordinary citizens to support the nominated candidates on election day. To resolve these two coordination problems, rules and procedures are developed to structure interparty negotiations. These rules and procedures, together with the final coordinated outcomes to the respective coordination problems, represent the overall institutional architecture of pre-electoral opposition alliances in electoral autocracies.

Bargaining to Coordinate Opposition Elites

The opposition's initial coordination problem of selecting or allocating candidates varies significantly depending on whether the elections are for a single nationwide executive office, or for multiple political offices that are geographically segregated in legislative and other subnational elections (e.g., gubernatorial, mayoral, or other local elections). This can have important consequences for the speed and ease in which opposition elites coordinate with each other against the autocrat. To begin with, in presidential electoral autocracies such as Uganda and Venezuela, the executive office is typically helmed by a single autocrat who is typically elected in presidential elections by plurality rule. Usually a personalist dictator or a military general backed by the armed forces, the autocrat has veto power over policy implementation and overall governance in the country. While legislatures in presidential systems may play additional roles in extracting policy concessions or by providing information to guide governance, the autocrat is the single most important executive figure (Gandhi 2008; Reuter and Robertson 2015; Schuler and Malesky 2014; Svolik 2012). Come election time, there is little doubt that the autocrat or his handpicked successor will be the incumbent regime's presidential candidate.

When faced with one powerful incumbent candidate elected by a plurality of the popular vote, fragmented opposition elites have very low chances of victory if they contest alone (Rakner and van de Walle 2009; Wahman 2014; Ziegfeld and Tudor 2017). Multiple opposition presidential candidates splinter the anti-regime vote with divided loyalties, allowing the autocrat to stroll toward victory. Besides, a divided opposition can also dishearten erstwhile supporters and depress turnout. Opposition followers may be less likely to turn out to vote for their leaders if they perceive that the incumbent's almost-guaranteed victory renders their vote meaningless (Frye, Reuter, and Szakonyi 2018; Letsa 2019a). To maximize their chances of toppling the incumbent, opposition leaders need to coordinate behind a single opposition alliance candidate for president. A clear opposition flagbearer becomes an embodiment of the entire opposition movement, and focuses the attention of the voting public by setting clear expectations about who exactly will replace the one single autocrat, should the opposition prevail. This collective act of inter-elite bargaining and coordination to decide who is the opposition flagbearer is known more generally as the "strategic entry" problem (Cox 1997, 151–78). That is, parties must strategize with each other to decide who enters the electoral arena to contest against the dominant incumbent.

In other types of elections in autocracies, such as legislative and subnational elections, electoral districts are geographically segregated and distributed across an electoral map. Therefore, interparty coordination is not about bargaining over who will be the opposition's sole flagbearer. Instead, if we make a simplifying assumption that the winner in each geographically segregated electoral district is elected by plurality rule, then interparty bargaining and coordination takes on a different form— opposition parties must coordinate to allocate only one opposition candidate (or teams of candidates in multimember districts) in each electoral district. This reduces vote splitting at the district level, potentially aggregates all anti-regime votes within each district, and maximizes the chances of the opposition alliance's candidates winning their respective districts. Multiple candidates from different opposition parties in each electoral district only serve to split the opposition votes, allowing the ruling party's candidate in that district to win with less than an outright majority of votes—a logic not unlike that in presidential elections. But because electoral office is divided into multiple pieces across the country's electoral map, opposition parties can develop multiple ways to decide how to split the electoral map.

Substantively, nationwide elections in parliamentary electoral autocracies such as Ethiopia and Malaysia function in a manner similar to legislative elections in presidential autocracies. Both involve geographically segregated electoral districts. Opposition parties contesting in parliamentary autocracies therefore encounter the same coordination problem as their counterparts confronting legislative elections in presidential autocracies. They need to coordinate to allocate a candidate from a particular opposition party (or teams of candidates) in each local electoral district across the electoral map. If they fail to coordinate candidate allocation, then incumbent ruling party candidates are more likely to have an easier time campaigning and winning against a divided opposition.

To better illustrate the differences between coordinating over candidate selection in national-level elections for a single executive office and other types of elections where electoral office is geographically segregated, consider the following hypothetical example. Assume that an opinion poll on an approaching election in a hypothetical electoral autocracy indicates that the ruling incumbent party will have a vote share of 40 percent, with opposition parties A and B polling 30 percent each. Let us further assume that these vote shares are evenly distributed throughout an entire country. In a presidential election with plurality electoral rules, the incumbent autocrat can run away with victory under these circumstances. Indeed, that is exactly what occurred in South Korea in 1987. Roh Tae Woo, the incumbent candidate affiliated with the military, won with a nearly 40 percent vote share. Kim Dae Jung and Kim Young Sam polled close to 30 percent each. Because the opposition did not coordinate behind one single candidate, Roh Tae Woo won the election. If Kim Dae Jung or Kim Young Sam had coalesced behind one candidate beforehand, however, the selected candidate could have won, assuming all the votes of one opposition leader were transferred to the other selected opposition candidate.

In elections with geographically segregated districts, though, consider table 2.1 and table 2.2. Each cell represents an electoral district where the

TABLE 2.1. Lack of Opposition Coordination in Geographically Segregated Elections

Ruling Party Candidate Opposition Party A Candidate Opposition Party B Candidate	Ruling Party Candidate Opposition Party A Candidate Opposition Party B Candidate
Ruling Party Candidate Opposition Party A Candidate Opposition Party B Candidate	Ruling Party Candidate Opposition Party A Candidate Opposition Party B Candidate
Ruling Party Candidate Opposition Party A Candidate Opposition Party B Candidate	Ruling Party Candidate Opposition Party A Candidate Opposition Party B Candidate
Ruling Party Candidate Opposition Party A Candidate Opposition Party B Candidate	Ruling Party Candidate Opposition Party A Candidate Opposition Party B Candidate

TABLE 2.2. Opposition Coordination in Geographically Segregated Elections

Ruling Party Candidate Opposition Party A Candidate	Ruling Party Candidate Opposition Party B Candidate
Ruling Party Candidate Opposition Party A Candidate	Ruling Party Candidate Opposition Party B Candidate
Ruling Party Candidate Opposition Party A Candidate	Ruling Party Candidate Opposition Party B Candidate
Ruling Party Candidate Opposition Party A Candidate	Ruling Party Candidate Opposition Party B Candidate

winner is decided by a plurality rule. The labels in each cell represent the candidates selected by their respective parties to run in those districts.

In table 2.1, opposition parties A and B are unable to reach a mutually acceptable compromise over an agreement to allocate the electoral districts. Both have eight candidates contesting in all eight districts within the country. Since opposition votes in each district are split evenly between the two party's candidates, we can expect the incumbent ruling party's candidates to be victorious in all eight districts with only a 40 percent national vote share. In short, a 40 percent national vote share for the incumbent produces a 100 percent seat share. This scenario clearly demonstrates the majoritarian nature of single-member district plurality electoral systems, all else equal.

In table 2.2, by contrast, a pre-electoral alliance sees opposition parties A and B agree to coordinate candidate allocation for each electoral district. Each opposition party agrees to field only four candidates in four selected districts, avoiding conflict in the location of districts they contest in. If we further assume that the vote share for both parties is aggregated within each district, then the four candidates each from both parties A and B will win their respective races with vote shares of 60 percent. The ruling incumbent that will have no seats, even with a 40 percent national vote share. In this manner, a coordinated opposition can turn its fortunes around, from a complete wipeout to secure an overwhelming victory against the incumbent.

Interparty bargaining over candidate selection for a single opposition flagbearer and interparty bargaining over allocating multiple geographically segregated electoral districts are clearly not identical to each other. The indivisible prize of being the nominated opposition in a presidential election is likely to engender a much more intense and protracted bargaining process between competing opposition elites (Fearon 1995; Hassner 2009; Gandhi 2014). If opposition elites detect that the incumbent is ready to fall, few will want to give up the chance of displacing the autocrat and reap the gains of total control. But when opposition parties bargain with each other to allocate electoral districts in geographically segregated elections, the multiple ways of dividing up the overall electoral pie are likely to result in less acrimonious and swifter negotiations. Angst at losing the opportunity to contest in one electoral district can always be compensated by the opportunity to contest in another electoral district.

To be sure, there is another benefit of coordinating candidate allocation for geographically segregated electoral districts that enhances its efficiency. After negotiations conclude, an opposition party is likely to contest in a smaller number of districts than what it would otherwise like to claim it can contest in. For a resource-starved opposition party, such an outcome is not altogether unwelcomed (Ong 2016). The party can make use of its scarce resources more efficiently in terms of mobilizing voters for a smaller number of candidates. Conversely, if a resource-starved opposition party spreads its resources too thinly across the electoral map or across too many candidates, then it may not actually mobilize enough votes to maximize its chances of victory for all its candidates. The focus should be to mobilize the greatest number of opposition votes in the most optimal number of districts or candidates that is conducive for maximizing vote share and seat share.

But even as the benefits of interparty coordination to select and allocate candidates are quite intuitive, the costs and difficulties of such coordination are equally visceral, as there are both short- and long-term consequences. Over the short run in presidential elections, public withdrawal of one's candidacy to step down in favor of another leader's candidacy means completely giving up the opportunity to contest for executive control. Even if a party leader may accept such a sacrifice, his followers may detest his acquiescence and abandon their support for him. Likewise, when party leaders have to order their potential candidates to withdraw from contesting in certain electoral districts in legislative or local elections, they will have to face the immediate wrath of angry party members who resent having to give way to other opposition parties. Ultimately, opposition leaders and parties who acquiesce one way or another will also have to endure the public perception that it is a smaller and weaker opposition party relative to other opposition parties.

Over the longer term, one's acquiescence in the initial round of negotiations can be seen as a leader's fatal weakness, generating expectations of future acquiescence in future negotiations. Suppose that the alliance topples the autocrat and forms the next government. If opposition party A wins more legislative seats than opposition party B by virtue of party A having contested in more districts, then it relegates opposition party B to a minor role in any coalition government. The same is true for a victorious opposition alliance in a presidential election where the flagbearer appoints cabinet members from his own party to important cabinet positions rather than to his coalition partners. In both cases, pre-electoral acquiescence by any opposition leader or party solidifies the imbalance of power among opposition parties, which in turn influences future material outcomes (Knight 1992; Fearon 1994). Opposition elites who care about the imbalance in future gains may therefore demur from coordinating their candidate selection and allocation.

Finally, note that regardless of whether opposition parties are coordinating to select candidates for a single office or allocate them across multiple geographically segregated districts, the ideological content of the respective parties does not necessarily matter in interparty negotiations. Even if two opposition parties are ideological enemies, they encounter the same coordination problems as two opposition parties who are ideological twins. To maximize their own respective chances of winning, one side must necessarily give way to another, their ideological positions notwithstanding.

Campaigning to Coordinate Opposition Voters

Suppose that opposition party leaders do indeed coordinate their candidate selection and allocation for whatever type of elections they encounter. Can they make the assumption that all the supporters of the opposition will want to vote for the nominated opposition candidate from a particular opposition party? To what degree will the nominated opposition candidate peel support away from the incumbent autocrat and his ruling party? Doubts over the answers to these two questions reflect the difficulty of coordinating the masses against the autocrat, even if opposition elites have resolved their own coordination problem (Cox 1997; Haggard and Kaufman 2016; Sato and Wahman 2019; Tucker 2007).

First and foremost, ideological positions now matter. The leaders of ideologically diverse opposition parties cannot take their supporters for granted and assume that the anti-regime vote shares will be aggregated in each electoral district, or for the single presidential candidate. In particular, supporters who have a strong partisan affiliation to their niche opposition parties will be very wary of voting for candidates from other opposition parties who are their ideological rivals. We can imagine, for instance, that long-standing supporters of an Islamic opposition party advocating for the imposition of Islamic law will be reluctant to vote for alliance candidates from a secular opposition party who promote the opposite (Kraetzschmar 2013; Shehata 2010; Stepan 2018). Similarly, to reinvoke the case of PRI-dominated Mexico, we can imagine that PAN supporters will be unwilling to support PRD's presidential candidate or their affiliated subnational candidates for legislature. Although both parties are indeed opposed to the dominant incumbent, a significant segment of opposition voters care about policy more than they care about defeating the dominant incumbent (Gandhi and Ong 2019; Svolik 2019). Therefore, to overcome the barrier of ideological differences among opposition voters, party leaders must somehow persuade their supporters to engage in cross-party vote transfers. In practical terms, this means that opposition supporters must reduce the salience of their ideological attachments and weigh their joint commitments as anti-autocrats more heavily. As Magaloni (2006, 199) writes about PAN and PRD opposition voters potentially coordinating against the PRI,

In order to defeat the PRI, opposition voters need to put aside their ideological differences, strategically supporting the opposition party most likely to defeat the PRI. Ideological divisions can prevent the opposition from coordinating if most opposition votes rank the PRI second. In order for the opposition to be able to coordinate, most opposition voters must possess a preference ranking whereby any outcome is preferable to the PRI—there should be more "tactical" than "ideological" opposition voters. (emphasis added)

Stepan (2018, 45) writes likewise about the necessity of persuading ideologically divided opposition voters in the Middle East and North Africa region to coordinate against the dominant incumbent:

It is possible that there are both secularist and Islamist citizens in some Muslim-majority countries who actually lean toward democracy as their preferred solution but cannot cooperate with one another against a dictatorship given the intensity of the secular/Islamist divide. If this is so, *it is vitally important for the emergence of democracy that such citizens, via dialogue, doctrinal evolution, and mutual accommodation, come to the shared conclusion that they hate the dictatorship more than they hate and fear one another.* (emphasis added)

Not only do pre-electoral ideological differences among the opposition cripple mass coordination against the autocrat, post-electoral policy uncertainty also undermines mass turnout, particularly for ideologically diverse opposition parties (Gandhi and Ong 2019). When once-rivalrous parties unexpectedly cooperate publicly with each other, voters become perplexed over what ideological position the new alliance represents and what policies a new opposition-controlled government will implement. In other words, voters sympathetic to the opposition's cause can be unclear on what they are voting for, even if they already know what they are voting against. Even more, parliamentary systems are likely to induce more policy uncertainty as compared to presidential systems (Bargsted and Kedar 2009). In presidential systems where the opposition coalesce behind a single candidate, the policy position of a future opposition-controlled government is relatively clearer. Voters will expect the winning opposition candidate to implement policies that his party has long advocated while giving minor attention to the policy demands of his coalition partners. In a parliamentary system with either majoritarian or proportional electoral systems, voters are uncertain about which party in the opposition alliance will win the greatest number of seats and who will occupy executive office. Even if one opposition party successfully negotiates for a larger share of seats to contest as compared to other component parties in the coalition, there is no guarantee that the party will be able to win a larger share of seats or obtain executive control.

Finally, uncertainty over the material consequences resulting from an opposition-controlled government can also lead to opposition-sympathetic voters withholding their support. By definition, opposition parties in electoral autocracies have little or no experience governing at the national level, even if some of them may be successful at subnational local governance. Voters are likely to have doubts about whether they will be able to control the national bureaucracy, continue providing public goods, and protect the country against external enemies through robust national security and foreign policies. Sound economic management, in particular, is likely to be a most salient and important issue for moderate voters, especially during times of economic crisis, when dissatisfaction against the incumbent regime is likely to be highest (Murillo and Calvo 2019; Pepinsky 2009; Reuter and Gandhi 2011; Shih 2020; Teorell and Wahman 2018). It is during such times of economic downturn that moderate voters look for alternatives to the autocratic incumbent and will most likely consider supporting opposition parties. If opposition parties and their alliance cannot somehow project at least some level of confidence in their economic management skills, then they run the risk of not being able to persuade voters that their material lives will remain intact or even improve. To be sure, opposition parties with some success governing at the local subnational level may be able to make a case for similar competency at the national level (Lucardi 2016; McLellan 2019). But these claims can always be undermined by a dominant incumbent in numerous ways, such as biased reporting from state-controlled media. In this manner, voter uncertainty about the material consequences of a victorious opposition is maintained.

These three obstacles to voter coordination—pre-electoral ideological differences among opposition parties, post-electoral policy uncertainty, and uncertainty over the material consequences for voters—all potentially contribute to a depressed vote share for the opposition, independent of what the autocrat might do. So how do opposition leaders try to resolve all three issues? Much will depend on the campaign strategies that opposition leaders undertake. Within their own parties, we should expect party leaders to communicate to their supporters about the need for short-term compromises. Leaders must at least clarify the prospective policy consequences and benefits of opposition victory, such as the implementation of their niche policies as part of a future opposition alliance government. An Islamic opposition party, for instance, will want to tout to its own supporters the increased chances of implementing sharia law in certain parts of the country, or increased funding for mosques and religious programs. An economic leftist party leader will want to argue to its own supporters that the prospects of increasing the national minimum wage are better as part of a future government, rather than an empty promise when in perpetual opposition. Furthermore, we can also expect opposition leaders to try to paint their fellow allies in a positive light by highlighting their commonalities in fighting for democracy (Stepan 2018). Reduced corruption, increased governance transparency, and electoral reforms are outcomes that all opposition parties desire. Highlighting commonalities increases the salience of the opposition's joint antiauthoritarian commitments, and decreases the salience of perceived ideological differences between opposition parties, thereby potentially increasing the degree of cross-party strategic voting.

But perhaps more important than intraparty rhetoric is overt opposition interparty coordination on joint electoral campaigns. This can involve opposition parties campaigning together using a common coalition name, slogan, and logo. Some opposition parties may even exhibit their unity by campaigning using a common coalition color. By coordinating on these joint campaigns, opposition parties and leaders within a pre-electoral alliance signal their unity in opposing autocracy, thereby increasing the salience of the anti-regime cleavage while suppressing the salience of their ideological differences. In this manner, these joint campaigns encourage opposition supporters to "hold their noses" to vote for nominated alliance candidates who may be from a different opposition party than the one they support. That is, joint campaigns persuade opposition supporters to engage in cross-party strategic voting.

To be sure, such rhetorical symbolism can be easily dismissed as "cheap talk" (Farrell 1987; Farrell and Rabin 1996). Other potentially more substantive joint campaign strategies in the opposition's "playbook" involve campaigning using a common coalition manifesto (as in Tanzania in 2015),[1] public endorsements by opposition leaders of the candidates from other parties (as in Kenya in 2002), or openly declaring the prime ministerial candidate or cabinet positions of the prospective opposition-controlled government even before elections are held (as in Malaysia in 2018).[2] These strategies are likely to be more costly for each individual opposition party and are therefore likely to be less common. Yet, because they are so rare, they are likely to be more persuasive in mobilizing voters to vote for opposition alliance candidates.

Campaigning using a common alliance manifesto, for example, may involve articulating certain policy compromises that opposition leaders may be reluctant to make. But clarity on what policies an opposition-controlled government will implement also increases the salience of the anti-regime cleavage and reduces post-electoral policy uncertainty at the same time. In particular, an alliance manifesto that details the institutional reforms to the judiciary and election commission, proposes policies for economic growth, and articulates national defense and foreign policies clearly reassures voters about what are the prospective policies that they are voting for. Similarly, a pre-electoral pronouncement of the cabinet positions of a future opposition-controlled government necessitates intense bargaining to negotiate the costly withdrawal of claims to cabinet positions and government leadership. But the rewards of such a strategy, if they are achieved, are likely to be significant in increasing opposition vote share and eroding incumbent support (Abdullah 2019). Nominating a charismatic prime ministerial candidate ahead of parliamentary elections, for instance, can assure voters that there is a steady captain at the helm of the ship. The joint candidate works to galvanize the anti-regime troops, reduce post-electoral policy uncertainty, and project confidence in the new opposition-controlled government's governing abilities.

Certainly, no single document or person readily embodies all the policy positions of an opposition alliance. Ideologically polarized opposition parties may be forced to leave some contentious policies "off the table" when negotiating over the precise terms of a manifesto. A secular opposition party may be compelled by an Islamic opposition party not to articulate its position on religion. An ethnic-based opposition party may be told by its coalition partners that they do not want to sign on to a manifesto that discusses protections for particular ethnic groups. Theoretically, by leaving their niche contentious policies off the table, each alliance component party can potentially attract the votes from the supporters of other opposition parties. That is, supporters of opposition party B will be induced to hold their noses to vote strategically for candidates from opposition party A when they observe that party A stayed silent on its niche policies. Vice versa, when opposition party B makes similar compromises, then the supporters of opposition party A will be induced to hold their noses to vote strategically for party B's candidates. In this manner, by strategically staying silent, ideologically polarized opposition parties can paradoxically stimulate cross-party strategic voting for each other.

In any case, the probability of observing joint electoral campaigns by an opposition alliance is likely to vary subtly across single-office executive elections and multi-office geographically segregated elections. Where and when opposition leaders have decided to unite behind one candidate in nationwide executive elections, that candidate has to campaign to the entire country's voting population as one single electoral constituency to maximize his winning chances. If, for some reason, a unity candidate does not campaign jointly with his alliance partners, then the electoral credibility of that candidate is undermined. Voters will doubt whether that nominated candidate really has the backing of other opposition leaders. In other words, in a presidential election, candidate coordination necessitates coordinated electoral campaigns.

This logic is dissimilar for a parliamentary autocracy or other geographically segregated elections, however. Once opposition parties successfully bargain and allocate subnational electoral districts to compete in, they can always focus on their own campaigns to maximizing turnout in those districts. There is no necessary requirement to mount a national-level electoral campaign. For example, consider the "tactical" coordination among Egypt's opposition parties in the country's 1984, 1987, and 2005 legislative elections (Shehata 2010, chapter 4). The secularist Wafd Party and the Islamist Muslim Brotherhood coordinated with a joint list of candidates for the proportional representation electoral system in the 1980s, and allocated electoral districts in the plurality electoral system in 2005. When it came to electoral campaigns, however, "The two groups campaigned separately for the election, raised distinct slogans and banners, and drafted separate election programs" (Shehata 2010, 87). If they could maximize their chances of winning in their own allocated districts through their own efforts, there was no reason to undertake costly compromises by campaigning with their ideological rivals. And as we shall see in the Malaysian and Singaporean cases, opposition leaders also frequently coordinated on allocating electoral districts but disavowed joint electoral campaigns frequently under conditions of persistent regime dominance over five decades.

In essence, therefore, opposition pre-electoral alliance formation occurs in an ordinal fashion, ranging from (1) no coordination at all, to (2) partial coordination for candidate allocation in parliamentary or other geographically segregated elections only, to (3) full-fledged coordination for both candidate selection or allocation with joint campaigns. And in pursuing different forms and combinations of coordination at different times, opposition party leaders instinctively recognize the tremendous costs of compromises required. Withdrawing their own candidacy, setting aside their long-avowed policy goals, and publicly campaigning together with their erstwhile ideological rivals are actions impinging on the very core of their credentials as leaders of their niche opposition parties. Hence, if opposition interparty coordination is so costly, then under what circumstances will it be worthwhile doing so? In other words, when does the perceived benefit of coordinating to build alliances outweigh its significant costs?

Building Full-Fledged Opposition Pre-electoral Alliances

This book proposes that opposition party leaders assess two crucial variables when they decide whether the costs of building full-fledged alliances are worthwhile: (1) their perceptions regarding the incumbent regime's vulnerability and their associated chances of victory in an upcoming election, and (2) their perceptions about their parties' mutual dependency. These perceptions vary over time and across space, depending on the particular historical and informational environment that opposition party leaders find themselves in.

Uncertainty and Certainty about Incumbent Vulnerability

In the first instance, the authoritarian-controlled information environment that opposition party leaders are embedded in make them highly uncertain about the true vulnerability of the dominant incumbent. This makes assessing the opposition's chances of winning with or without a pre-electoral alliance an exceedingly tricky and risky task. Autocratic regimes are deeply invested in maintaining an aura of invincibility. They manipulate elections to achieve supermajoritarian victories to demonstrate dominance (Simpser 2014). They use the law to silence dissenters, inducing ordinary citizens to falsify their preferences or to self-censor (Kuran 1991; Shen-Bayh 2018; Ong 2021). They control the media to make sure that pliant journalists do not ask inconvenient questions undermining their legitimacy and authority (George 2012; Stockmann and Gallagher 2011; Dimitrov 2017). Furthermore, government-controlled mass-media platforms are often vague, biased, and unreliable (Stier 2015; Oates 2013; King, Pan, and Roberts 2017). Often exhorting the superlative qualities of the country's charismatic leadership, officially sanctioned media outlets shun covering the opposition, demean their efforts, distort assessments of their support, and criticize them for destabilizing society. That is why opposition activists, parties, and their leaders rely so much on relatively more liberal new media technologies, such as alternative news outlets and social media, to propagate their message (Duong 2017; Gainous, Wagner, and Ziegler 2018; Howard and Hussain 2013; Reuter and Szakonyi 2015; Tapsell 2019).

On occasion, new and surprising regime-debilitating events may occur indicating that the incumbent's armor contain some serious chinks. These events may occur as a form of exogenous shock or emerge endogenously within the autocratic regime. For example, surprising gains by the opposition in subnational elections, a corruption scandal in a government-linked company, a startling spontaneous mass protest in the city center, or the unexpected sacking of a cabinet minister can do more than rouse the imaginations of a few jaded journalists reporting for the government-controlled mainstream newspaper. When these events occur, some opposition leaders may be tempted to update their answers about whether alliance building is worthwhile (Fudenberg and Levine 2009, 2014, 2016; Little 2017). They may assess these shocking events as reflective of regime weakness and its growing vulnerability to an opposition challenge. But even then, each individual opposition leader may still be uncertain about what other opposition leaders really think. No one individual opposition leader has perfect information about the political calculations of other opposition party leaders. As a result, there is likely to be continued disagreement among the opposition about the incumbent's vulnerability. Intense disputes among party leaders and their followers will persist over whether the costs of pre-electoral compromises are worthwhile for uncertain gains. Deep disagreements narrow the acceptable range of compromises that party leaders are willing to bear and prolong interparty negotiations, likely leading to coordination failure.

Conversely, when several alarming, public, regime-debilitating events striking at the heart of an incumbent regime's legitimacy occur rapidly in close succession, we can expect far less disagreement about the regime's shaky foundations (Gerschewski 2018; Hale 2013; Slater and Wong 2013). Unclear public speeches of a propped-up, sickly dictator (as in the Philippines), a major corruption scandal with clear ties to the autocrat (as in Malaysia), or massive street protests culminating in concessions from the autocrat (as in South Korea), when combined with a crippling economic crisis or unexpected defections from previously high-ranking regime insiders, prompt opposition leaders to jointly update their opinions of how vulnerable the regime truly is (Reuter and Gandhi 2011; Bak and

Moon 2016; Reuter and Szakonyi 2019). In other words, *multiple public regime-debilitating setbacks occurring within a short period of time create common knowledge of the regime's weakness* (Angeletos, Hellwig, and Pavan 2007; Chassang 2010; Chwe 2003; Shadmehr and Bernhardt 2011; Shurchkov 2016). They serve as clear signals suggesting that "now is the time" for opposition elites and their mass followers to coordinate and mount a united attack. Party leaders are more likely to reason that a pre-electoral coalition will be the final knife that secures the autocrat's inevitable death. Those who hold up interparty negotiations will be derided as spoilers when electoral victory is perceived to be within their grasp. Costly compromises within an alliance in such circumstances will be deemed necessary costs to be paid for securing prospective regime change.

This book's emphasis on multiple regime-debilitating events occurring within a short period of time speaks to its focus on the *temporality* in which such events occur (Thelen 2000; Büthe 2002; Pierson 2000, 2004). Rather than a linear decline in a regime's dominance, a nonlinear *acceleration* in regime vulnerability is more likely to update and converge the subjective perception of opposition elites (Grzymala-Busse 2011; Kadivar 2013). To be more explicit, I hypothesize that *multiple public regime-debilitating events occurring within a short period of time signal accelerating regime vulnerability, compelling the public and opposition leaders to update their expectations about the probability of electoral victory*. Consequently, the enticing aroma of victory leads opposition party leaders to assess the benefits of constructing pre-electoral alliances to outweigh their costs, ultimately motivating them to swallow their mutual animosities to spur alliance formation. Take, for instance, Malaysia's political experience in the late 1990s (Weiss 2006). Anwar Ibrahim's public sacking as the deputy prime minister of Malaysia in late 1998 was undertaken in the midst of the 1997 Asian financial crisis. It was quickly followed by unprecedented mass rallies in Malaysia's economic capital, Kuala Lumpur. Protestors demonstrated against Anwar's sacking and his suffering while under police detention, calling for increased government transparency and an end to nepotism. This led opposition leaders to significantly revise upward their assessments of the incumbent BN's weakness and the potential size of their potential support at the ballot box, subsequently spurring them to form the first-ever comprehensive electoral coalition in Malaysia.

Among the universe of potential regime-debilitating events that may occur, two types are particularly important for engendering opposition alliance formation. The first is high-ranking defections from the incumbent. Regime defections are harbingers of escalating regime vulnerability from several perspectives. Defections by the military, for example, are clear indications of autocrats losing control over their coercive apparatus (Albrecht and Ohl 2016; Kim 2013; Lee 2015; Svolik 2013). When autocrats cannot successfully maintain their monopoly over the state's means of violence, the opposition is emboldened. Public demonstrations challenging the regime's legitimacy are more likely when the military refuses to clamp down on the demonstrators. The opposition should also expect the state's security forces to perpetuate less electoral manipulation and election-related violence (Bhasin and Gandhi 2013; Fjelde and Höglund 2016; Gehlbach and Simpser 2015; Hafner-Burton, Hyde, and Jablonski 2018). Opposition leaders have higher confidence that opposition-inclined voters will turn out to vote for invigorated opposition parties, conditional upon alliance formation. Additionally, surprising defections from a regime's inner circle, such as a cabinet minister or a close deputy, also indicate that the regime's power-sharing agreement is fraying at the seams (Reuter and Gandhi 2011; Reuter and Szakonyi 2019; Svolik 2012). When the incumbent can no longer secure the allegiance of key elite allies, then the masses are more likely to defect as well. Finally, in regimes with weak opposition leaders, high-ranking defections to the opposition can potentially provide a new alternative focal point for the opposition voters to rally around. Opposition supporters and moderate voters who have previously rejected voting for weak opposition leaders may be enticed to vote for a new opposition alternative who preserves governance stability as an former regime insider, but is not the autocrat himself.

Unrelenting, recurring, massive street protests are a second important type of regime-debilitating event encouraging opposition pre-electoral alliance formation (Casper and Tyson 2014; Kuran 1991; Little 2017; Little, Tucker, and LaGatta 2015; Tucker 2007). The fear of election-related violence and widespread electoral manipulation in autocratic elections can depress opposition voter turnout (Birch 2010; Carreras and İrepoğlu 2013; Simpser 2012). Whether voters will turn up and vote for the opposition is also likely to turn on their perceptions of the opposition's relative winning chances (Letsa 2019a). When some citizens do not perceive a forthcoming election to be a clearly meaningful one, they would rather stay home. It makes little sense to participate in an election with a foregone conclusion. But recurring massive street protests directly challenging autocratic rule, especially those that involve protestors from a wide range of groups in society, are likely to dispel doubts that the population is turning its back on the incumbent. If an election is indeed held, moderate, independent voters should have stronger confidence that a majority of their fellow citizens prioritize regime change and are ready to turn out to vote for a united opposition alliance (Kuran 1991).

To be more specific, whether a particular event or a specific episode is a "regime-debilitating event" is contingent on the empirical and historical context. More generally, *an event is most likely to be "regime-debilitating" if it is historically unprecedented.* The first historically unprecedented intra-regime defection of a cabinet minister is likely to surprise political observers. But subsequent defections are unlikely to shock anyone. Similarly, a mass protest is unlikely to be perceived in the same way across countries and across time. In Singapore, where large-scale protests are extremely rare, a historically unprecedented four-thousand-person mass protest in 2013 appeared to be a strong and clear signal of dissent against the government's policies.[3] In contrast, a pro-Marcos rally five times larger in downtown Manila in April 1986 protesting Ferdinand Marcos's ouster hardly drew a whimper.[4] This simple comparison hints that a purely quantitative assessment of events is not enough. What is required for causal inference is a close attention to the historical sociopolitical context in which these events occur in order to assess their causal effect (Lustick 1996; Falleti and Lynch 2009; Gerring 2012). In this regard, the main strategy of this book is to triangulate assessments of political events from a variety of empirical sources, such as the secondary literature, newspapers, diaries and autobiographies of opposition leaders, diplomatic reports, and field interviews. Multiple sources from different perspectives help verify the empirical significance of the events and their perceived momentum, strengthening the inference that one can make regarding its causal link to updating opposition elites' expectations of their chances of victory and subsequent motivation to build alliances.

Uncertainty and Certainty about the Opposition Parties' Mutual Dependence

Widespread agreement about the accelerating vulnerability of the regime is not the only critical variable affecting pre-electoral alliance formation. If party leaders are confident of their own chances of victory when they contest alone, then they are likely to forgo building alliances altogether. No party leader who already thinks that he has a good chance of winning against a flailing incumbent autocrat will want to pay the costs of compromise. Therefore, to be convinced that paying the costs of compromise in building pre-electoral alliances is worthwhile, opposition party leaders *must also recognize that that their parties need each other to assure victory.*

In turn, perceptions of mutual dependency rest on two related variables—(1) *ex ante information about the parties' relative strengths and weaknesses*, and (2) *party leaders' expectations of the degree of cross-party strategic voting that will occur among their supporters.*

Following Lebas (2011, chapter 2), I operationalize opposition party strength as consisting of three major attributes—their resources, their organization, and their outcomes. In terms of resources, opposition parties can vary in terms of the financial resources that they possess, the number of permanent, skilled party organizers that they have, the existence of a party newspaper and the extent of its distribution, the number and geographical coverage of their local branches, and the size of their dues-paying membership. With regards to organization, opposition parties can vary in terms of the strength of their communication across different levels of party organization; the existence of rules to resolve intra-party conflict; the depth, breath, and complexity of their linkages with the broader society, such as trade unions and civic associations; and their ideological coherence. Finally, regarding outcomes, an opposition party can be deemed stronger or weaker in terms of its electoral success, the perceived size and loyalty of its mass support, its longevity as a cohesive party, and its ability to mobilize supporters to protest against the incumbent for a particular cause.

Canonical models of interstate bargaining suggest that when there are high uncertainties and information asymmetries over the capabilities, intent, and resolve of dueling states and leaders, coordination is more likely to fail (Fearon 1995; Powell 2002; Reiter 2003, 2009; Ramsay 2017). In a similar vein, we can anticipate that *if opposition party leaders lack information about and have high uncertainty about the relative strengths and weaknesses of each opposition party, then opposition party leaders will disagree with each other on whether they really need to depend on each other to win.* Imagine, as in our earlier toy example, that there is no clear and reliable pre-electoral polling indicating a 40-30-30 vote share split between the incumbent and the two opposition parties. There is also a lack of clear and public information about the prospective size of an opposition party's mass support simply because elections have been suspended for a long period of time. Even more, opposition party leaders may also be unclear, due to a lack of clear information from inadequate past electoral experience, which opposition party is more organized, has more resources, or can mobilize more voters. When opposition parties encounter such a "fog of uncertainty," deep disagreements will arise over who exactly is the coalition formateur who will lead interparty negotiations and provide the material incentives for other party leaders to step aside (Arriola 2013). With no clear leader to coalesce around, opposition elites are more likely to be belligerent about their own chances of winning, resulting in opposition fracture.

Opposition fracture in Uganda in 2015 illustrates this point vividly (Beardsworth 2016). At that time, Uganda's opposition disagreed over who should be the alliance's sole opposition candidate contesting against Yoweri Museveni, the country's ruler for almost three decades. Anti-regime elites were split between Kizza Besigye, the opposition's longtime leader, and John Patrick Amama Mbabazi, Uganda's former prime minister and a new defector from Museveni's dominant ruling party, the National Resistance Movement. Besigye's perceived declining popularity after numerous failed elections and Mbabazi's sizable election war chest led many to believe that the latter was a stronger candidate than the former. Mbabazi's status as a former regime insider, particularly among the security forces, also raised hopes that his candidacy could persuade a significant number of government bureaucrats to defect. Yet, because there was no clear indicator and agreement of Besigye's and Mbabazi's relative electoral chances, no conclusion could be drawn on who should give way to the other. The fact that Mbabazi had no experience competing in executive elections on his own led to discounts on his claims of superior electability. Both parties then remained belligerent about their own chances of winning, believing that they did not need to rely on the other's acquiescence to win against Museveni. In the end, with the party machineries of Besigye and Mbabazi pitted against each other, Museveni strolled to victory with a 61 percent vote share in Uganda's 2016 presidential election. Besigye obtained a 36 percent vote share, while Mbabazi trailed far behind with just over 1 percent of the votes.

Consequently, we can hypothesize that where there is *clear information and low uncertainty on the strengths and weaknesses of different opposition parties, opposition elites are more likely to see their mutual dependence for potential victory as justifying alliance formation.* For instance, clear recognition of party A's strength in disciplined organization can be complemented with party B's ample endowment of financial resources to maximize everyone's chances of winning. Similarly, party A's strong support in certain geographical areas or among certain groups of voters may also be potentially aggregated in support of party B's popularity in other geographical areas or among other social groups, conditional on successful joint campaigns. Clear knowledge and appreciation of mutual dependence significantly reduces the ability and incentive to be belligerent about one's own chances of victory (Fearon 1995; Reiter 2003; Walter 2009; Ramsay 2017). When everyone knows everyone else's strengths and weaknesses, claims to want to contest in a larger number of districts or to accept fewer compromises in a common manifesto are scarcely credible.

Another necessary background condition for opposition party leaders' recognition of mutual dependency is their *ex ante expectation that the vote shares of opposition parties in a potential alliance will be aggregated if an alliance is formed; that is, a high degree of cross-party strategic voting will occur among their supporters.* This underlying assumption is oftentimes left undeclared and undefined. Even if party leaders have very good information about their relative strengths and weaknesses, they must also have high prior confidence that their supporters will follow the cues of their joint campaigns to vote strategically for the nominated alliance candidate(s) against the dominant incumbent. Only then will they assess that making costly compromises within the alliance is worthwhile to maximize their chances of winning. Conversely, if opposition party leaders have little confidence that their supporters will heed their cries of unity to vote for the nominated alliance candidates, then they are likely to abandon any costly alliance-building efforts altogether, even under conditions of low uncertainty of their relative strengths and weaknesses. They will not want to indulge in making costly compromises if they do not expect that their reluctant supporters will follow them. For these resource-starved opposition parties, the time, resources, and energies not spent in forging costly compromises can be better expended elsewhere to fight the dominant incumbent.

At this point, then, we are left asking where opposition party leaders and their supporters can obtain the necessary information to assess their mutual dependency. One important source of public information is past electoral results (Miller 2015; Pop-Eleches and Robertson 2015). At the onset of autocracy, when there are no past electoral results to lean on, an opposition leader's claim to be the front runner of the anti-regime pack will always be in doubt. But even when they are the product of unfree or unfair conditions, past electoral results are a signal of the regime's and the opposition's relative levels of mass support. Aggregate vote share numbers are particularly useful for establishing some ex ante expectations of a hierarchy of opposition parties. They are simple and convenient proxy measures of which party is more popular and more capable of mobilizing voters toward the opposition's cause. A leader can more easily justify his position as the most prominent opposition leader and coalition formateur if his party had the highest vote share in the most recent election. Alternatively, when past electoral results indicate that some opposition parties are weaker, leaders of those parties will find it difficult to misrepresent their relative electoral strength vis-à-vis the coalition formateur. They will have little choice but to support the coalition formateur, even if withdrawing their candidacy comes at a cost to themselves. Obstinate insistence on being the sole opposition nominee even though one is the less popular candidate invites public ridicule and criticism, diminishing the opposition's chances of gains at the upcoming polls.

Disaggregated electoral results by electoral districts, moreover, are especially useful for opposition parties. First, they can provide some indication of the geographical strongholds of each opposition party. Coordination to allocate electoral districts and candidates for the next election is easier as party leaders acknowledge each other's geographical strongholds (Wahman 2017). Intense bargaining and debate will then occur over who should contest in the incumbent's strongholds (Ong 2016). For instance, Beardsworth (2016, 763) submits that in Kenya, "relatively reliable ethnic voting produces somewhat more predictable outcomes depending on turnout levels in ethnic strongholds." Opposition parties are therefore better able to negotiate candidate allocation for electoral districts by using the geographical distribution of ethnic groups as a convenient proxy for estimating winning chances against the incumbent. Second, not all electoral districts are equal. Some urban districts, such as the areas surrounding the capital, are generally perceived to be better barometers of overall population sentiment than rural electoral districts. Opposition success in those areas can signal which opposition party or leader is the front runner of the opposition pack. In June 2019, for instance, Ekrem İmamoğlu, the opposition candidate in the district of Istanbul, won a rerun in the mayoral elections against the government's candidate backed by the autocratic Reccep Tayyip Erdoğan.[5] Because of Istanbul's strategic importance as the economic metropolis of Turkey, İmamoğlu's victory was seen as a major blow to Erdoğan's popularity. It also solidified the reputation of the Republican People's Party, of which İmamoğlu is a member, as the leading opposition party in the country. Erdoğan's ominous remark, "Whoever loses Istanbul loses Turkey," will likely galvanize the opposition against his rule.[6]

Beyond publicly available electoral results, opinion polls and third-party mediators can also inform opposition party leaders' perceptions of mutual dependency. Reliable polls conducted by universities, newspapers, or civil society organizations can guide elite and mass expectations about the hierarchy of opposition parties. Although these surveys cannot provide granular details of an opposition party's strengths and weaknesses, their aggregate popularity numbers can indicate where popular sentiment is. But perhaps more interesting is the role of third-party mediators. Prominent third parties in democratizing electoral autocracies include religious authorities such as churches and international powers such as the United States (Cheng and Brown 2006; O'Rourke 2018; McClendon and Riedl 2019). These third parties can reduce information asymmetries between dueling opposition leaders to the extent that they are frequently considered to be impartial mediators (Chernykh and Svolik 2015; Kleiboer 1996; Kydd 2003). By providing crucial information from the outside about the perceptions of the relative strengths and weaknesses of competing opposition parties or about their supporters' willingness to vote strategically, they provide an external reality check for party leaders, encouraging cooperation rather than continued conflict. As we shall see later in this book about opposition alliance building in the Philippines in the 1980s, the influential Catholic Church and staff from the American embassy both acted as crucial third parties highlighting mutual dependency among the Philippines' opposition leaders. They strove to convince Corazon Aquino and Salvador Laurel that a coordinated alliance was a necessary condition for having a chance at overthrowing Marcos at the upcoming election. Neither could win without the other.

Partial Candidate Coordination under Persistent Incumbent Dominance

But what if an autocratic incumbent is perceived to be stubbornly dominant? Under conditions of persistent incumbent dominance (see the bottom branch of figure 1.1 in chapter 1), full-fledged pre-electoral alliances with both candidate coordination and joint campaigns are unlikely to be forged at the national level. High levels of press censorship and self-censorship among the citizenry make discerning the population's sentiments about regime change highly uncertain. Opposition elites will not coalesce if they cannot be sure about their supporters mobilizing behind the alliance. They will also have a very difficult time trying to assess their relative strengths and weaknesses. Negotiations over who should give way and who should lead are likely to be intractable. What is more, incumbent autocratic preponderance also makes the co-optation of opposition elites more likely. When co-opted opposition parties refuse to coordinate in nationwide alliance-building efforts, voters remain split and confused, dampening the chances of non-co-opted opposition parties. Ultimately, opposition elites will see little gain to be made through costly compromises in joint campaigns or through coordinating behind any single opposition candidate.

Yet this does not mean that opposition parties completely lack agency or rest on their laurels. Opposition leaders frequently still strive to make the best out of a bad situation. The opportunity arises where there are geographically segregated elections, such as legislative, gubernatorial, or local municipal elections. Opposition parties are interested in contesting in this type of elections because control of local electoral offices brings new resources and voters, helping the opposition party prepare to challenge the incumbent autocrat in the next cycle of executive elections (Lucardi 2016; Resnick 2014; McLellan 2019). Additionally, as alluded to earlier, because electoral office is split among multiple districts across a map, opposition parties can campaign in their own districts against the incumbent once coordination on candidate allocation is accomplished. They do not have to engage in costly national-level joint campaigns against the incumbent. The objective is to maximize their probability of winning in their own subnational districts.

Generally, when coordinating to allocate candidates to different districts under conditions of persistent regime dominance, opposition parties want to safeguard their geographical strongholds first, and will thus want to avoid multiple opposition parties contesting in those areas (Beardsworth 2016; Letsa 2019b; Resnick 2011; Wahman 2017). Safeguarding strongholds consolidates support, ensuring the opposition party's survival for the longer term. In other districts where the incumbent is historically strong, opposition parties want to amplify their probability of winning by offering the sole opposition candidate in any one district. Parties and candidates typically dislike wasting precious resources by waging futile campaigns against the incumbent and against each other. Opposition-sympathetic voters will also be turned off by intra-opposition fracture when they encounter multiple opposition candidates in their district.

From this perspective, successful coordination on candidate allocation in subnational elections is largely dependent on one main variable—*ex ante information about the relative popularities of opposition parties, which indicates which party stands the highest chance of winning in the electoral district* (Fearon 1995; Ramsay 2017; Reiter 2009). Unlike assessments of mutual dependence where granular knowledge about relative strengths and weaknesses is crucial, party leaders can coordinate on allocating electoral districts simply based on aggregated information about the respective parties' level of popularity across the electoral map. Party leaders will more likely back down from contesting in certain electoral districts if they know that their party is less popular, in exchange for contesting in other electoral districts where their party is more popular. For instance, opposition party A, representing ethnic group A, will be more willing to withdraw from contesting in districts where the proportion of ethnic group B voters is high, in exchange for contesting in districts where there is a large proportion of ethnic group A voters. Similarly, opposition party B, representing ethnic group B, will want to contest where the proportion of ethnic group B voters is high, in return for withdrawing from districts with a large proportion of ethnic A voters. In so doing, both parties reduce the number of opposition candidates contesting in their negotiated districts and maximize their chances of winning those particular districts. By contrast, where there is a lack of information or high uncertainty about which opposition party has the better odds of defeating the incumbent regime's candidate in particular districts, more intense negotiations are likely. If opposition leaders are sufficiently belligerent about their winning chances, then coordination failure is to be expected.

Scope Conditions

Of course, the theoretical arguments elaborated in this chapter are circumscribed by a set of scope conditions. These conditions can be thought of as the necessary assumptions built into this book's model of preelectoral alliance formation (Diermeier and Krehbiel 2003; Gehlbach, Sonin, and Svolik 2016). The assumptions make the model minimally tractable to empirical reality, while allowing for enough flexibility to explain a range of coordination outcomes.

First, opposition parties and their leaders must be in the "participation" equilibrium of autocratic elections rather than in the "boycott" equilibrium. For a variety of reasons, opposition parties may sometimes choose to boycott autocratic elections (Beaulieu 2014; Beaulieu and Hyde 2009; Buttorff and Dion 2017; Smith 2014). The elections may be too manipulated or the risk of electoral violence too high, for instance, so as to render participation meaningless. When boycott is chosen, whether opposition parties form alliances is not a valid question to consider. Even more, opposition parties may choose to cooperate with civil society to mobilize citizens to protest on the streets in addition to their choice of electoral boycott. But explaining the dynamics of protest and cooperation with civil society is beyond the theoretical and empirical scope of this book.

Second, the number of opposition parties and their leaders coordinating in an alliance should be small, not co-opted, and include, at the minimum, all the major opposition parties. When too many party leaders jostle with each other over candidate selection and joint campaigns, the efficiency of negotiations and the effectiveness of coordination are impeded (Olson 1965). High transaction costs on top of the already substantive costs of coordination make the alliance-building process protracted and complicated. Co-opted opposition parties can also sow discord among the opposition, depressing the likelihood of interparty coordination. Finally, if a pre-electoral alliance is formed only among minor opposition parties or includes only a limited number of the major players, then it cannot be reasonably assessed as a "full-fledged" pre-electoral alliance. For theoretical parsimony, assuming that a small number of non-co-opted, major opposition party leaders are engaged in constructing alliances means setting aside questions about the transaction costs of coordination.

Third, and perhaps most importantly, I assume that autocrats' intervention to manipulate the electoral environment in their favor is endogenous to opposition party leaders' perceptions of regime vulnerability and mutual dependency. That is, opposition party leaders' assessments about whether and how to coordinate with each other take into account how the dominant incumbent shapes the electoral environment. No assumption is made about the autocrat being a static actor. Hence, whatever coordination outcomes are observed are a result of opposition elite calculations that include the consequences of autocratic maneuvering. Indeed, this is what we observe in the South Korean case as I elaborate later in the book. Even as the military government under Chun Doo Hwan capitulated to recurring massive street protests to allow direct presidential elections in 1987, it also insisted that all candidates would run independently with no joint vice-presidential candidates. By setting the rules of the game in this manner, the military regime further depressed any ex ante expectation that the supporters of Kim Dae Jung and Kim Young Sam would aggregate their votes and vote strategically for one of the two if the other had given way. This expectation thus contributed to the divide between the two Kims and subsequent coordination failure.

3 | Studying Cases in East and Southeast Asia

As the third wave of democratization rolled across Latin America, Eastern Europe, and Africa, East and Southeast Asia was not spared from its path (Huntington 1993). In Taiwan, for example, Chiang Ching Kuo and Lee Teng Hui paved the way for the island's democratization under the close watch of the dominant party, the Kuomintang (Cheng and Haggard 1992; Rigger 1999). In Indonesia, President Suharto's resignation in May 1998 marked the start of a gradual, sequenced democratization of the world's most populous Muslim country (Liddle 2000; Horowitz 2013). The region's political, social, and cultural diversity has motivated a wealth of scholarly research examining the multiple tortured paths that countries have taken toward democratization (Lee 2002; Croissant 2004; Hao and Gao 2016; Slater and Wong 2013).

Leveraging the region's manifold historical experiences with democratization, this book illustrates the divergent trajectories of opposition alliance formation through two pairs of cross-national comparisons in East and Southeast Asia. The first comparison consists of a controlled comparison of opposition pre-electoral coordination in the Philippines and South Korea in the late 1980s (Fearon 1991; Mahoney 2000; Slater and Ziblatt 2013; Tarrow 2010). Specifically, this comparison demonstrates how two similarly vulnerable presidential electoral autocracies—the Philippines under Ferdinand Marcos and South Korea under Chun Doo Hwan—developed very different perceptions of mutual dependency among the opposition leaders. In the Philippines, clear recognition of the mutual dependencies of their respective candidacies led the leading opposition leaders of that time, Corazon Aquino and Salvador Laurel, to eventually coalesce into a united front against Marcos in the 1986 presidential elections. In South Korea, however, opposition leaders Kim Dae Jung and Kim Young Sam were highly uncertain and unclear about their mutual dependency. As a result, both of them were persistently belligerent about their own chances of winning, and eventually mounted independent campaigns to contest against the military regime's candidate, Roh Tae Woo.

The second comparison involves a longitudinal comparative historical analysis of multiple episodes of opposition pre-electoral alliance building or nonbuilding in Malaysia and Singapore—the world's two most robust electoral autocracies—between 1965 and 2020 (Slater 2012; Weiss 2020). Malaysia's recurring experiments with full-fledged opposition alliances in the 1990, 1999, 2013, and 2018 general elections vividly exemplify how efforts to build national-level alliances occur under fluctuating perceptions of heightened incumbent regime vulnerability. At all other times, however, these two country cases also demonstrate how coordination in allocating opposition candidates at the subnational level can still occur even under persistent incumbent regime dominance. Opposition coordination over candidate allocation only emerged in the 1986, 1995, 2004, and 2008 general elections in Malaysia, and in the vast majority of general elections in Singapore.

To more clearly indicate how the two comparisons help to illustrate this book's theoretical framework, table 3.1 matches the empirical observations of opposition coordination and their various forms across the four country cases with the expected coordination outcome predicted by the theory. As the keen reader will recognize, assessing the long-term trajectory of opposition coordination in Malaysia and Singapore over multiple decades has the added benefit of increasing our number of observations in the sample. This ensures that the full ordinal range of opposition coordination types is theoretically and empirically accounted for. In the rest of this chapter, I elaborate on why the similar conditions between the two pairs of country cases increase the increase the internal validity of the theory while eliminating rival explanations. Moreover, I describe the multiple sources of empirical evidence that the book relies on to buttress causal inference.

Comparing the Philippines and South Korea in the Late 1980s

The Philippines–South Korea cross-case comparison is crucial for a number of reasons. Two key features of the comparative exercise reinforce the internal validity of the book's theoretical arguments. First, process tracing within the two cases empirically verifies the sequence of events connecting the independent variable of mutual dependency to the dependent variable of building full-fledged opposition alliances, while also establish-

TABLE 3.1. Location of Empirical Cases in the Theory

Causal Condition 1	Causal Condition 2	Expected Coordination Outcome	Empirical Case
Perceived High Regime Vulnerability	Perceived High Mutual Dependency	National-Level Candidate Coordination and Joint Campaigns	1986 Philippines 1990 Malaysia 1999 Malaysia 2013 Malaysia 2018 Malaysia
	Perceived Low Mutual Dependency	None	1987 South Korea
Perceived Low Regime Vulnerability	Clear Relative Popularity of Opposition Parties	Allocating Geographically Segregated Electoral Districts Only	1995 Malaysia 2004 Malaysia 2008 Malaysia 1976 Singapore 1980 Singapore 1984 Singapore 1988 Singapore 1991 Singapore 1997 Singapore 2001 Singapore 2006 Singapore 2011 Singapore 2015 Singapore 2020 Singapore
	Unclear Relative Popularity of Opposition Parties	None	1978 Malaysia 1982 Malaysia 1986 Malaysia 1972 Singapore

ing the counterfactual causal process (Beach and Pedersen 2013; Bennett 2010; Collier 2011; Mahoney 2012; Falleti and Lynch 2009; Ricks and Liu 2018; Goertz 2017). In South Korea, high levels of uncertainty about opposition leaders' strengths and weaknesses as well as the degree of cross-party strategic voting fermented deep, intense disagreements among the competing party leaders, resulting in failed bargaining and coordination. In the Philippines, however, low levels of uncertainty provoked only shallow disagreement between rivalrous opposition leaders, encouraging them to acquiesce to each other's demands within a grand coalition bargain. Second, triangulating multiple sources of empirical evidence helped to fortify the internal validity of this process tracing. Data was collected from the wealth of secondary literature, newspaper articles, diaries and autobiographies of the opposition leaders, transcripts of congressional hearings regarding American foreign policy toward the two countries, as well as a trove of declassified foreign policy documents from the Ronald Reagan administration. These include diplomatic cables from the American embassies in Seoul and Manila, National Security Council meeting minutes, Department of State briefing memos, and Central Intelligence Agency (CIA) intelligence reports.

Among the various types of empirical evidence that I draw on, the data from the thousands of pages of declassified American foreign policy documents are of particular import. These documents, all previously classified secret or top secret, were assembled from the Digital National Security Archives,[1] the CIA Freedom of Information Act Electronic Reading Room,[2] and the archives at the Ronald Reagan Presidential Library and Museum in Simi Valley, California.[3] They provide unprecedented insight into the rapidly evolving political situations in both countries insofar as their authors—all agents of a foreign power with crucial national security interests in both countries—were trying to accurately assess what was actually going on. These documents can be relied upon to provide accurate third-party assessments of actual facts on the ground based on both public and private sources of information at those particular points in time.

Most importantly, these American foreign policy documents highlight the striking similarities between the Philippines' and South Korea's relations with the United States. On the one hand, both countries shared intimate histories with the United States. America had fought the bloody Korean War between 1950 and 1953, where more than 30,000 American troops died pushing back the North Koreans and the Chinese to defend South Korea. The Philippines was an American colony for more than four decades in the first half of the twentieth century and adopted many of America's modern democratic institutions. On the other hand, pragmatic military relations during the Cold War bonded the two pairs of countries. Both the Filipino and South Korean autocratic regimes relied on the United States for international and domestic legitimacy as well as military and financial support. In return, American national and security interests in East Asia and the Pacific were secured. The 40,000 American troops stationed in South Korea in the 1980s formed the pointed tip of America's defense strategy in East Asia against North Korean and Soviet communism. Clark Air Base and Subic Bay Naval Base in the Philippines were America's two largest overseas military installations at the forefront of America's projection of military power in the Pacific. In particular, Subic

Bay Naval Base was the main support base of the US Seventh Fleet patrolling Pacific and Indian waters, while Clark Air Base was home of the Thirteenth Air Force. If America had lost control of the two bases, it would entail "an immediate and drastic decline in U.S. power in the western Pacific, Southeast Asia, and the Indian Ocean" (Munro 1984, 187).

Although worsening autocratic repression by Chun Doo Hwan and Ferdinand Marcos had tested America's patience with the two countries, its security interests forced the Reagan administration to generally maintain a pragmatic policy of tacit approval of incumbent stability in its first term (Pee and Schmidli 2019). But into Reagan's second term, both Chun and Marcos were slowly pressured into implementing political and economic reforms. Indeed, in Reagan's second term, American foreign policy toward both countries progressively shifted to one encouraging "quiet diplomacy" in the pursuit of gradual democratization (Fibiger 2019; Work 2019). As late as February 20, 1985, Ronald Reagan signed and endorsed a secret National Security Decision Directive stating clearly America's policy toward the Philippines. It declared that although the United States was not out to intervene in Philippine politics to replace Marcos, it was invested in preserving "the stability of a key ally by working with the Philippine Government and moderate elements of Philippine society" in order to "assure both a smooth transition when President Marcos does pass from the scene and longer-term stability."[4] Similarly, at a congressional hearing on June 30, 1987, on South Korea's democratic opening, the assistant secretary of state for East Asian and Pacific affairs, Gaston Sigur, stated, "We support no particular system and no individuals or parties, but have no hesitation about supporting and encouraging the democratic process."[5] Both statements indicate that Ronald Reagan's second administration disapproved of outright repression in both the Philippines and South Korea, and supported free and fair elections in both countries in 1986 and 1987 respectively (Owen and Poznansky 2014). Accordingly, there was little difference between the two countries in terms of external intervention in driving regime change: both experienced US pressure to democratize (Levitsky and Way 2010). The critical point for the controlled comparison is that this similarity between the two countries eliminates variation in foreign intervention as a rivalrous explanation of opposition alliance formation.

In addition, remarkable similarities in the domestic situations of both countries also help to eliminate alternative explanations of divergent opposition alliance-building outcomes. In terms of institutional and structural conditions, the two countries exhibit broad similarities. The countries shared a similar type of electoral system in the late 1980s—single-round presidential elections elected via plurality rule. Moreover, both countries were, and still are, ethnically homogenous. In terms of the respective autocratic grip on their societies, the two electoral autocracies slowly but surely were passing the "apex of their dominance" (Slater and Wong 2013). In South Korea, the assassination of the military dictator Park Chung Hee in October 1979, alongside the Kwangju uprising in 1980, signaled the beginning of the gradual decline of the military's involvement in politics (Greitens 2016). President Chun Doo Hwan, a military general, shed his uniform for civilian clothes, ruling South Korea as the head of the Democratic Justice Party. Likewise, Ferdinand Marcos's failing health, as indicated by his alarming televised speeches and declining number of public campaign appearances, entrenched common knowledge that the end of his era was near.

The similarities across the two countries extend to the nature of the opposition movements. The two regimes confronted massive street protests throughout the 1980s and immediately prior to their respective elections. Led by the two pairs of opposition leaders in each country, crosscutting mass movements consisting of various societal groups from different economic classes, ages, occupational backgrounds, and education levels turned out onto the streets to signal their dissatisfaction with authoritarianism. Catholic Church leaders in both countries were among the key symbolic actors encouraging their followers to turn against the regimes. In addition, all opposition candidates were equally repressed by the incumbent autocrats and received no preferential treatment as compared to their rivals. This meant that there was little variation in animosities toward the autocratic incumbent among opposition leaders in the respective countries that could potentially forestall cooperation (Lust 2004, 2005; Gandhi and Reuter 2013). Although there were minor policy differences between the two opposition leaders, these gaps did not correspond to the deep ideological divisions observed in other countries that impede alliance formation, such as contests over ethnicities, religion, or economic redistribution (Arriola 2013; Greene 2007; Magaloni 2006; Wahman 2011, 2014). In fact, as the subsequent empirical chapters will show, the rivalrous pursuit of power, not ideological differences, fostered resentment between opposition leaders.

To be sure, at least two key differences did exist between the two countries. The main difference was their contrasting economic fortunes. South Korea was undergoing massive transformation, having experienced near 10 percent real annual GDP growth for close to three decades. The Philippine economy, conversely, was in the economic doldrums, with more than half of the population under the official poverty line. Munro's (1984, 178) stark comparison is striking: "In 1965, the year Marcos was elected president, the value of Philippine exports was four times that of South Korea. By 1982, the situation was reversed. South Korea's exports were four times those of the Philippines." Moreover, in the 1960s, the Philippines "had one of the highest per capita incomes in the region—higher than South Korea, and more than double that of Indonesia and Thailand" (Hill 1986, 240). But by 1985, South Korea's GDP per capita in constant 2010 US$ was almost four times that of the Philippines, and its overall GDP in constant 2010 US$ was almost three times that of the latter.[6] Another important difference between the two regimes was the strength of their ruling parties and their associated state apparatus. The existing literature suggests that variation in ruling party strengths is a key variable affecting divergent pathways to democratization (Handlin 2016; Riedl et al. 2020). In the Philippines, it was widely acknowledged that Ferdinand Marcos's ruling party, the Kilusang Bagong Lipunan, was generally weak in terms of organization, relative to Chun Doo Hwan's ruling party, the Democratic Justice Party (DJP) (Brownlee 2007; Doner, Ritchie, and Slater 2005; Hellmann 2018; Slater 2010). The former was a narrow patronage-based and electorally inexperienced ruling party, whereas the latter was a persistently dominant ruling party comprising of military, economic, bureaucratic, and intellectual elites.

While clearly extraordinary, these significant differences in economic development and ruling party strengths do not undermine the controlled comparison and internal validity of the theory. First, neither variation in economic outlook nor ruling party strength engendered variation in the magnitude of public opposition to the respective regimes. In South Korea, some analysts even argued that the country's rapidly expanding and better-educated middle class led the charge for democracy (Bellin 2000). Because both professional capitalists and labor decreased their dependence on state patronage as the private sector economy expanded, widespread social fear of resisting autocracy and repression eroded, driving open embrace of democracy. By the mid-1980s, the DJP was winning only a slim majority of legislative seats through only one-third of the popular vote (Slater and Wong 2013, 725). In the Philippines, the middle class too provided broad support to the opposition, but for the opposite reason. An appalling reduction of about 15 percent in per capita GDP over the two years between 1984 and 1985 precipitated pervasive dissatisfaction with the country's disastrous economy (Hill 1986). Filipinos turned against Marcos out of economic desperation as much as they desired to topple the autocratic status quo. From this perspective, then, both sets of opposition party leaders could be reasonably confident that the masses would turn out at the polls to indicate their dissent. What was unclear and uncertain, as the empirical chapters will reveal, was how much popular support each opposition leader had, and whether one's popular support could be transferred to another if a sole candidate were nominated to be the opposition flagbearer.

Second, differences in the economy and ruling party strength did not affect opposition party leaders' access to financial resources and their strategic calculus about opposition alliance formation (Arriola 2013). While variation in access to material incentives can produce different coordination outcomes, opposition leaders in the Philippines and South Korea were equally starved of campaign finances. Kim Dae Jung lamented in his autobiography that in the run-up to the elections, when he was deciding whether to form a coalition with Kim Young Sam, he and his party "were short on everything, including time, organization, and funds" (Kim 2019, 345). Similarly, Salvador Laurel complained in his diary six months before opposition coalition talks, "I will have to raise funds. My friends are helping but not enough to support a presidential campaign. . . . I will have to tap friends in Japan and U.S.,"[7] which was followed by another diary entry three months later: "Our problem is, as expected, *funding*."[8] His despair over his financial situation was corroborated in an American embassy report a year earlier. It observed that candidates from the United Nationalist Democratic Organization (UNIDO), Laurel's party, had to finance its local parliamentary campaigns on its own for the most part because "UNIDO's central fund-raising capability has been near zero."[9] Another report in February 1985 concurred: "A fundamental problem the opposition has in facing elections is limited financial resources."[10] It appears that no matter whether the economy was booming or diving, or whether the ruling party was strong or weak, it is a norm for opposition leaders in autocracies to be financially strapped.

Comparing 1965–2020 Malaysia and Singapore

The second controlled comparison in this book is a comparative historical analysis of opposition alliance formation between Malaysia and Singapore spanning more than five decades from 1965 to 2020. Apart from demonstrating temporal variation in regime vulnerability and coordination outcomes while increasing the number of observations in our sample, this second Malaysia-Singapore comparison also serves at least two more useful purposes. First, it demonstrates how accounting for variation across presidential and parliamentary electoral systems leads to new insights about the ordinal range of opposition coordination outcomes. Rather than assuming that opposition alliances simply build full-fledged alliances or not, Malaysia's and Singapore's parliamentary systems reveal how coordination in opposition alliances takes on an ordinal, rather than a dichotomous, form. At the start of autocratic elections, when information about relative popularity is scarce, opposition parties and their leaders remain belligerent and refuse to coordinate in any manner whatsoever. But as uncertainty about the opposition parties' relative standing decreases over time through recurring cycles of elections, Malaysian and Singaporean opposition parties "pause" at an intermediate stage of coordination—interparty candidate allocation for electoral districts only. Finally, as the Malaysian case will further reveal, opposition party leaders can sometimes "upgrade" their coordination into full-fledged alliances with joint campaigns when they sense that the regime is vulnerable, innovating and deepening these joint campaigns over time as they gain incremental experience about what sort of electoral strategy works best to maximize turnout.

Second, rather than drawing causal inferences only from historical evidence, as in the Philippine–South Korean comparison, the longitudinal comparison between Malaysia and Singapore allows me to rely on more contemporary empirical evidence to validate this book's theoretical arguments. In particular, I draw on multiple episodes of fieldwork conducted in both countries conducted over five years—dozens of field interviews with contemporary opposition leaders, participant observation of electoral campaigning in Malaysia's 2018 general election and Singapore's 2020 general elections, and exclusive access to the archives of an opposition party's internal newsletter. These sources comprehensively reveal how elites and the masses perceive incumbent regime vulnerability and mutual dependency, and react to the uncertainties of autocratic electoral competition as the theory predicts.

Once again, important similarities between Malaysia and Singapore make their comparative historical analysis a sound research design strategy. The two countries share similar colonial and postcolonial experiences under the British, and adopted similar British institutions and electoral systems after their respective independence. The British parliamentary system with first-past-the-post plurality electoral rules were adopted in both countries after their respective independence. Additionally, the two countries have similar ethnically and religiously diverse populations (Slater 2010; Liu 2015). Historically, Singapore and the Malaysian ports of Malacca and Penang were midway points for merchant ships connecting British India with the Dutch East Indies and British Hong Kong. These three coastal cities were governed under the same Straits Settlements administrative structures in 1826 under the East India Company, and then reorganized under full direct control of the British colonial authorities in London as a crown colony in 1867 (Mills 1966; Turnbull 1972; Webster 2011). The Straits Settlements' openness to trade, combined with Peninsular Malaya's demand for cheap labor for the rapidly expanding tin mines and rubber plantations, drove massive inward immigration (Chai 1964, chapter 3; Parmer 1960; Lees 2017). Joining the local Malays were wealthy trade merchants hailing from the Arabian Peninsula, from western Indian regions such as Gujarat and Punjab, from southern Chinese provinces such as Guangdong and Fujian, and from the surrounding Dutch East Indies archipelago. Massive waves of poorer laborers also arrived from China and India, particularly the Tamil Nadu region. After gaining self-governance from the British following the end of World War II, a short and unhappy merger between Singapore and Malaysia from 1963 to 1965 ended with their divorce. There is little doubt that their similar rich immigrant soil of societal diversity cross-cut by ethnicity, religion, language, and class made the two countries and their dominant party regimes "look like no others in the world—except for each other" (Slater 2012, 19). The latest statistics show that Malaysia is three-quarters Bumiputera-Malay, with substantial Chinese and Indians minorities.[11] By contrast, Singapore is 75 percent Chinese, with substantial Malay and Indian minorities.[12]

Since 1965, both electoral autocracies have also seen rapid economic development resulting in burgeoning middle classes, with neoliberal open economies and close ties with Western countries—all factors that the existing literature suggests influences variation in democratization trajectories (Lipset 1959; Arriola 2013; Levitsky and Way 2010; Goldring and Greitens 2020). While Singapore, with a per capita GDP just above USD$56,000 (in constant 2010 US$), is much more economically developed than Malaysia, which has a per capita GDP of USD$11,600, the two nations are still the two most economically developed countries in the Southeast Asia region.[13] Singapore's urbanized cityscape is not dissimilar to Malaysia's, where more than three-quarters of the population live in urban areas (Hasan and Nair 2014; Yeoh 2015). To be sure, Singapore's population of 5.6 million people squeezed into a geographical area just 5 percent of metropolitan Los Angeles pales in comparison with Malaysia's 32 million people distributed over an area three-quarters the size of the state of California. But if high-density living in closer proximity makes collective action more likely, then Singapore's lack of full-fledged opposition alliances over five decades poses a puzzle that beckons serious investigation. Overall, despite their similar parallel extended experiences with electoral authoritarianism, cross-case temporal variation in coordination outcomes between Singapore and Malaysia suggests that other important variables remain unexplored.

Of course, the single most important difference between Malaysia and Singapore lies in the foundations and nature of their party systems. Although both countries have had long-dominant parties with similar grassroots-driven politics—the Barisan Nasional (BN) in Malaysia and the People's Action Party (PAP) in Singapore—the core ideological premises from which the two parties derive their ideological legitimacy and dominance could not be more different (Weiss 2020). In Malaysia, interparty political competition is primarily driven by ethnoreligious cleavages (Gomez 2016; K. M. Ong 2015; Wong, Chin, and Othman 2010). The BN maintains its dominance because it practices Bumiputera-Malay-dominant consociationalism (Lijphart 1969). This means that Bumiputera-Malays, who are almost all Muslims, are provided with special rights for government contracts, recruitment into the civil service, and university admissions, and maintain overall control of the political system, while Chinese and Indian minorities, who mostly profess other religions, are provided with significant policy autonomy in education and language. The United Malays National Organization is the principal actor within the BN, exercising veto power over its more junior partners—the Malaysian Chinese Association and the Malaysian Indian Congress. In stark contrast, interparty political competition in Singapore is primarily based on valence considerations (Oliver and Ostwald 2018, 2020; Ong and Tim 2014; Tan 2008, 2012). The multiethnic PAP rhetorically justifies authoritarianism in exchange for a highly educated, elite, bureaucratic, and political class that maintains multiethnic and multireligious harmony, produces economic growth, and supplies high-quality public services for the masses. As a result, the PAP has been able to secure domineering victories every election cycle, with more than 90 percent seat shares throughout five decades.

Because the two parties govern their respective countries and win elections so differently, opposition parties across the two nations diverge tremendously in their ideological content, their positioning, and their resultant strategy for competing against the incumbent. Indeed, as I document and explain extensively in chapter 6, opposition parties in Singapore are generally devoid of ideology and highly personalistic. Few opposition parties have been able to find and field highly educated and qualified political candidates that can match the PAP's slate. And even when they have done so, most propose similarly progressive policies that are on the left of the PAP's unique brand of center-right socioeconomic conservatism, with generous state subsidies for housing and education. Opposition parties in Malaysia, in contrast, have found limited success based almost entirely on their polarized ideology on an ethnoreligious left-right spectrum. The Democratic Action Party (DAP) is on the left of the centrist BN, advocating for an end to Bumiputera-Malay special privileges and equal treatment of all ethnicities and religion. On the other hand, the Parti Islam Se-Malaysia (PAS) is on the right of the centrist BN, promoting the idea that Malaysia should be transformed into an Islamic state. From such a perspective, interparty competition in Malaysia is analogous to the left-right spectrum of the progressive PRD and the conservative PAN contesting against the centrist PRI in Mexico (Greene 2007; Magaloni 2006).

Could such differences in party systems and the nature of opposition parties across the two countries lead to variation in opposition coordination outcomes? Theoretically, yes. The existing literature predicts that ideological polarization between the DAP and PAS in Malaysia should inhibit alliance building, while opposition ideological similarity in Singapore should foster cooperation (Golder 2006; Wahman 2011; Kraetzschmar 2013). But in reality, we see the exact opposite. Singapore opposition parties consistently eschew building full-fledged opposition alliances with joint campaigns, while Malaysia's opposition parties have repeatedly experimented with such alliances in at least four instances over the past three decades. So why do their political experiences so bizarrely contradict what the prevailing literature predict will occur? The rest of this book provides the answer.

Generalizing beyond East and Southeast Asia

These two pairs of controlled comparisons in East and Southeast Asia amplify the internal validity of the proposed theoretical framework to a large degree because they are highly similar (within pairs) in terms of their electoral institutions and regime type. But to what extent is this book's emphasis on opposition elites' perceptions of regime vulnerability and mutual dependency likely to be externally generalizable to other country cases with variation along these two dimensions? One way to answer this question is to first consider the generalizability of the twin problems of coordinating elites and coordinating voters. Indeed, although these two coordination problems may vary subtly depending on the institutional and societal setting, opposition parties and their leaders still have to overcome these coordination problems somehow whenever they confront elections (Lipset and Rokkan 1967; Aldrich 1995; Cox 1997; Kam 2011; Stephenson, Aldrich, and Blais 2018). In the complex and messy process of finding solutions to these coordination problems, their perceptions of how they will benefit from collaborating with each other is pivotal to determining the overall efforts that they invest in interparty coordination. From this standpoint, perceptions of eventual victory and mutual dependency are likely to be highly relevant for opposition parties and leaders in any country, even if those countries have different electoral institutions or social structures.

Consider an electoral autocracy that has different electoral rules, such as the list-proportional representation (e.g., Cambodia or Kyrgyzstan) or the single, nontransferable voting system (e.g., Jordan and Mongolia). In the former system, opposition parties need to coordinate with each other to put up joint lists of candidates and to persuade their disparate groups of supporters to vote for the opposition's list of candidates against the government's list (Croissant 2016). In some of these cases, larger opposition parties may need to persuade their supporters to vote strategically for other smaller opposition parties in the alliance so that these smaller parties can cross a minimum threshold to gain representation in parliament, such as in Turkey (Selçuk and Hekimci 2020). Similarly, in the latter system, opposition parties need to coordinate to select and nominate the appropriate number of candidates to run in each district and to persuade their followers to vote for the specific candidates (Buttorff 2015). But regardless of which system is used, both still require opposition parties and their leaders to make hard compromises to withdraw their own prospective candidates in favor of others and to work with each other to persuade the masses to vote strategically against the dominant incumbent. Whether such difficult and costly compromises are really worth it will depend on their own calculations of the benefits that they will obtain from cooperation and the associated costs and benefits of noncooperation. In the complex trade-offs that opposition party leaders have to confront with each decision that they make, perceptions of regime vulnerability and mutual dependency are likely to be crucial ingredients motivating the decision-making process.

Likewise, the generalizability of the coordination problems mean that this book's theoretical framework can also be extended to explain opposition coordination in democracies, particularly those with dominant ruling parties. In these democracies (e.g., India before 1989 and Japan before 2009), opposition parties too face a difficult electoral environment, albeit less repressive and perilous than in an autocracy. They face an organizationally strong, dominant incumbent whom voters are intimately familiar with, and one who is capable of providing patronage and public goods through control of the state apparatus. Toppling the dominant incumbent likely requires some form of coordination among opposition elites to reduce vote splitting as well as joint campaigns to consolidate voters to vote strategically against the dominant incumbent. Whether opposition parties can anticipate impending electoral victory and whether they need to depend on each other to obtain victory are the same two factors that will likely condition interparty coordination. To be sure, in democracies, the stakes of not building alliances are not quite as high as in autocracies. If opposition parties fail to coordinate, they can always live to fight another day. But in autocracies, opposition parties are, in some ways, always running against time. Electoral failure means renewed repression, persistent economic misery, and perhaps the end of their very lives. Against such a backdrop, the baseline motivation for coordinating to defeat the incumbent in an autocracy is surely higher than in a democracy.

Part II

Perceptions of Mutual Dependency

4 | Opposing Marcos

Opposition Alliance Formation in the Philippines

The central proposition of this book can be summarized simply as follows: *variation in opposition party leaders' perceptions of regime vulnerability and their mutual dependency stimulate different efforts to forge full-fledged opposition pre-electoral alliances.* Empirically verifying such perceptions and tracing their causal effect requires compiling and triangulating a wide range of evidence from a variety of sources. Primary evidence, for instance, can include the autobiographies and diaries of opposition party leaders. Secondary evidence can include observations from journalists, aides to the political leaders, biographers, and other close observers of the political situation. In this chapter, I provide detailed empirical evidence from a variety of sources demonstrating that opposition party leaders in the Philippines in the late 1980s had a keen awareness of the severe vulnerability of the Ferdinand Marcos regime and clear knowledge of the mutual dependency between Corazon Aquino and Salvador Laurel needed to make victory more probable.

As a former Spanish and American colony with over two decades of experience with democratic elections after World War II, the Philippines encountered more than 20 years of autocratic rule with Ferdinand Marcos. First elected in 1965 and then reelected in 1969, Marcos declared martial law in September 1972 and oversaw widespread repression before being overthrown via the People Power Revolution in February 1986. The pre-electoral alliance between Corazon Aquino and Salvador Laurel proved crucial in that its popularity forced the Marcos regime to commit extensive electoral fraud in the elections of early February 1986, splitting Marcos from the military, which threw its support behind the opposition leaders, who disputed the manipulated election results. As millions of Filipinos turned out into the streets to support an Aquino-Laurel government and protest against the recalcitrant Marcos, he was forced to flee to the United States, never stepping back onto Filipino soil.

In this chapter's first section, I reveal how six regime-debilitating events pointed in the same direction, foretelling the regime's impending collapse in the three short years between 1983 and 1986. Mass street demonstrations spurred by Benigno Aquino's assassination at Manila airport, surprising opposition gains in the 1984 parliamentary elections by elites who had defected from the regime, widespread poverty amid a crippling economic crisis, Marcos's obviously declining health, as well as the gradual decline in American support for his rule, were all unprecedented events that suggested Marcos's end was near. Not only does the empirical evidence consistently reveal that domestic political elites concurred that the regime was ripe for collapse, even international observers and foreign allies were making contingency plans for a Philippines without Marcos.

In the chapter's second section, I describe the inter-elite jostling between Corazon Aquino and Salvador Laurel to be the opposition flag-bearer. I focus on how clear information from past electoral experience, and from third parties such as the Catholic Church and the American embassy, made the dueling leaders cognizant of their respective strengths and weaknesses. There was even widespread acknowledgment among their own supporters that Aquino was the more popular and charismatic leader, whereas Laurel was the better organized, with potentially better electioneering capabilities through his strong party machine, the United Nationalist Democratic Organization (UNIDO). The perception of their strengths mitigating each other's weaknesses cemented notions of their mutual dependency for eventual victory against Marcos. Everyone recognized and wanted to avoid the counterfactual scenario—perpetual antagonism with no opposition alliance would invite certain defeat.

Finally, in this chapter's third section, I discuss the empirical evidence demonstrating an important condition underpinning the notion of mutual dependency between Aquino and Laurel—their mutual confidence in vote transfer among each other's supporters and mass support for a potential alliance. Specifically, their joint candidacy on a common ticket would help consolidate support, no matter who was the presidential candidate. Furthermore, the evidence also suggests that various public segments of Philippine society, especially the middle class and the Catholic Church, were not split between the two opposition leaders but were all jointly against the Marcos regime. In the face of such support, the eventual conclusion by Aquino and Laurel was that the only stumbling block in their path to victory against Marcos was each other. Thereafter, despite their

TABLE 4.1. Timeline of Key Events in Philippine Politics in the 1970s and 1980s

Date	Event
September 1972	Ferdinand Marcos declares martial law.
April 1978	First parliamentary elections held under martial law. Marcos's party, the Kilusang Bagong Lipunan, sweeps the polls.
January 1981	Martial law lifted.
August 1983	Benigno Aquino assassinated at the Manila airport as he returns after his self-imposed exile in the United States. A million people turn up for his funeral procession.
October 1983	Marcos issues moratorium on all foreign debt repayments. Philippine economy tanks.
May 1984	First parliamentary elections held outside of martial law. Opposition candidates and the United Nationalist Democratic Organization make surprising, unprecedented gains.
November 1984	Marcos taken ill. Disappears from nightly news broadcasts for two weeks.
November 1985	Marcos calls for snap presidential elections in 1986 on the ABC television show *This Week with David Brinkley*.
December 1985	Official nomination for president and vice president joint ticket closed for upcoming February 1986 elections.
February 1986	Presidential elections are held. National Citizens' Movement for Free Elections endorses opposition victory despite official results showing otherwise. Army defects from Marcos. Marcos and his family flee to Guam.

intense bargaining over the exact nature of their alliance, both sides finally acquiesced to each other's demands, just one hour before official nomination for the presidential elections closed on December 11, 1985. Their coordinated joint president and vice-presidential ticket under a single party banner was the start of almost two months of coordinated cross-country campaigning to mobilize the majority of Filipinos to abandon the autocratic status quo.

Readers unfamiliar with Philippine politics in the 1970s and 1980s may be confused at the exact sequence of the various events that occurred. They may also have trouble evaluating the various pieces of process-tracing evidence for the two variables—perceptions of regime vulnerability and mutual dependency—to which I will repeatedly refer throughout this chapter. Following the advice of Ricks and Liu (2018), I provide a timeline of key events before proceeding with the rest of the chapter. In particular, I identify theoretically relevant events in the run-up to December 11, 1985, when the vexing decision to form an opposition coalition reached a climax for both Aquino and Laurel.

Clear Recognition of the Marcos Regime's Vulnerability

When Ferdinand Marcos declared martial law in September 1972, he did so on shaky claims of national security (Slater 2010, 124–36). The majority of Filipino elites did not take seriously his argument that he was suspending the rule of law in order to protect them from violent communists, southern Muslim regional separatists, and shadowy terrorists (Kann 1974, 618–19). As a result, his regime throughout the rest of the 1970s was institutionally weak, albeit still capable of extensive repression (Slater 2010, 163–80; Greitens 2016, 211–36). Philippine capitalists refused to surrender significant portions of their wealth to the ineffective tax authorities, but instead extracted patronage from Marcos in exchange for their support. The Catholic Church, divided in its opinions of Marcos, generally stayed quiet. The military was only kept in check through luxury inducements and by promoting personal loyalists (Greitens 2016, chapter 4). Students and the middle class also had no love for autocratic rule, especially that of Marcos's variety. But because the general economic outlook was stable— and recognizing at the same time that Marcos was simply a larger, national form of "political banditry in which warlords cowed and exploited political serfs" (Kann 1974, 614–15)—the majority of Filipinos acquiesced to Marcos's rule. They would, however, "prefer martial law without Marcos" (Wurfel 1977, 11–13).

The general stability of Marcos's rule throughout the 1970s weakened by the end of the decade. The first indicator to reflect this general shift was an intra-regime elite defection to the opposition—the defection of the Laurel brothers, who formed UNIDO in August 1980 (Brownlee 2007, 185–90; Thompson 1995, 103–6). In its early years, UNIDO was an informal grouping of anti-Marcos elites, such as the Laurel, Roxas, and Aquino families, backed by radical leftist groups who provided mass street-level mobilization and support. This uneasy combination of elite families and mass groups constituted the first time in Marcos's rule that opposition elite collective action supported by ordinary citizens had emerged. Of the elites, the Laurels were the most important. Previously in tacit support of Marcos, his favoritism of other influential political families and cabinet members prompted them to defect. Jose Laurel Jr., the elder of the two brothers, famously declared, "I am fighting Marcos because I have an investment in him. I was hoping to collect but I have waited long enough" (Thompson 1995, 103). He became coleader of UNIDO alongside Gerardo Roxas. Largely seeking an end to Marcos's regime through peaceful, electoral means, UNIDO was formed at the same time as other more violent opposition groupings, such as the April 6 Liberation Movement and the Light-A-Fire Movement, became prominent. Corsino (1981, 242) noted that, in 1980, "whether related or not, the apparent mushrooming of both violent and nonviolent oppositionists—*on a scale unseen* in previous years of martial law—apparently was a barometer that spelled a rising temperature of protest against the martial law regime." Similarly, in Landé's (1981, 1158) assessment, at the start of the 1980s, "Though some still spoke favorably of the regime and many others had lost interest in politics, prevailing opinion among the educated stratum had *shifted decisively against both the President and martial law*, and a widespread desire to see them go was clearly evident."

The Laurels' stature grew alongside UNIDO's importance as the leading anti-Marcos opposition party between 1980 and 1986. Initially a disparate group simply identified by opposition to Marcos, UNIDO gradually transformed from a Manila-based elite faction without mass local penetration into a nationwide organization with connections to local provincial families throughout the country (Brownlee 2007, 189–93; Wurfel 1985, 265). The party boycotted the June 1981 presidential elections, the first ever to be held after the lifting of the martial law in January that year. Choosing between justifying Marcos's rule and nonparticipation to deny legitimacy to his regime, Gerry Roxas and Jose Laurel Jr. decided to refrain from contesting (Thompson 1995, 103–5). Their belief that the electoral victory was scarcely possible due to Marcos's gross electoral manipulation strengthened their decision to boycott. Ultimately, the boycott resulted in Marcos winning the election with an 86 percent vote share against a token Marcos-approved candidate. But UNIDO's boycott of the 1981 presidential elections left the informal group languishing, with nothing really much to do. A political party that had no elections to contest in is like a boxer with no arena to fight in and no opponent.

Three years later, UNIDO's fortunes lifted when the group decided to participate in the May 1984 parliamentary elections against Marcos's party, the Kilusang Bagong Lipunan (KBL / New Society Movement). This time around, Salvador Laurel, the younger of the two Laurel brothers, was leading the charge, as Gerardo Roxas had passed away two years earlier. Ultimately, the opposition performed "far stronger than anyone predicted" even under conditions of substantial electoral manipulation by the Marcos-biased election commission (Malin 1985, 200).[1] The opposition won 61 seats in the assembly, just under one-third of the total number of seats up for election (Kessler 1984, 1209). UNIDO's victorious candidates, in particular, controlled more than half of the 61 opposition-affiliated seats (Thompson 1995, 132). The party also won 15 out of 21 seats in Metro Manila, "devastating the KBL," and signaling its strong base of support among the middle class in the all-important affluent urban areas surrounding the capital (Kessler 1984, 1221). Overall, the opposition's surprising and unprecedented gains are a second clear indicator of the growing vulnerability of Marcos's regime. Although still a minority, a large proportion of the masses were ready to shift their allegiance to the opposition. In evaluating the results, Munro (1984, 173) pronounced that "*never before has Marcos seemed less able to preside effectively over the government.*" Kessler (1984, 1209) further assessed the results as "a resounding defeat for President Ferdinand E. Marcos' New Society Movement Party," indicating "*the depth of popular displeasure* with Marcos" and giving the opposition "a national political presence."

The opposition's surprising success in the May 1984 parliamentary elections in general, and UNIDO's standout performance in particular, when evaluated retrospectively, can be attributed to growing mass dissatisfaction with the Marcos regime. This was reflected in the tremendous spike in the number and size of street demonstrations, unlike any the Philippines had ever seen before—the third indicator of the Marcos regime's impending collapse. One crucial catalyst of the mass street demonstrations was Benigno Aquino's assassination in August 1983. Gunned down as he stepped onto the airport tarmac upon his return to the Philippines after three years of self-imposed exile in the United States, Aquino's death "provoked a national and international reaction of outrage and dissatisfaction over conditions in the country *of dimensions unsurpassed in the peacetime history of the nation*" (Malin 1985, 198). In half a year, there were close to 300 rallies, marches, and demonstrations (Thompson 1995, 116). The two largest were Aquino's own funeral procession, which involved one million people over 11 hours, and a 75-mile commemoration run supported by an estimated half a million people. Even more importantly, participants in these mass demonstrations came from across the socioeconomic spectrum (Thompson 1995, 115; Slater 2010, 199). "The anger at this brazen killing quickly spread to segments of the population *which were never before politicized*, those both high and low," noted Wurfel (1985, 263). For Marcos, "The killing irrevocably undermined the legitimacy of his

Fig 4.1. Water Cannons Used against Philippine Protestors at the Welcome Rotunda, Quezon City, September 27, 1984. Credit: Jacinto Tee.

Fig 4.2. Philippine Opposition Leaders Protesting against the Marcos Administration at the Welcome Rotunda, Quezon City, September 27, 1984. Credit: Jacinto Tee.

Government," intoned a lengthy *New York Times* report.[2] The CIA concurred, noting in a secret "Special National Intelligence Estimate" report in January 1984 that in the wake of Aquino's assassination, "Marcos is *unlikely ever* to regain his former authority" and that "we rate his chances of staying in power through the end of his current term through 1987 as no better than even."[3] The May 1984 parliamentary elections held less than a year after Aquino's death thus represented the first instance in which popular anger could be expressed in political terms.

The fourth indicator of Marcos's accelerating vulnerability, one that fueled mass dissatisfaction and UNIDO's growth, was the state of the economy. The economy had already begun showing signs of decline at the start of the 1980s. Due to the second worldwide oil shock in the late 1970s as a direct result of the Iranian revolution, Philippine inflation was around 20 percent, while unemployment was upwards of 30 percent in 1980 (Corsino 1981, 246). Foreign debt was at US$12 billion, exceeding 20 percent of gross national product (GNP), alongside a trade deficit of US$1.78 billion (Corsino 1981, 251; Mount 1980, 119). GNP growth rate was at 5 percent, the slowest among Southeast Asian countries. For the next three years, the economy was in free fall, accelerated by capital flight driven by the Aquino assassination. In the two months following Aquino's death in August 1983, more than US$1 billion left the country (Wurfel 1985, 164). In October 1983, Marcos effectively told international debtors that his country was bankrupt, as he placed a moratorium on payments on the Philippines' foreign debt obligations, which had more than doubled to US$25 billion (Munro 1984, 179). The peso was devalued once in the middle of the year by 8 percent, and then again in October by 21 percent (Malin 1985, 204; Wurfel 1985, 264). By the middle of 1984, at the time of the parliamentary elections, inflation was at 50 percent. Although inflation would be tempered in 1985 when presidential elections were called, it was the "only bright spot in a *picture of almost unrelieved gloom*" (Hill 1986, 239). Between 1984 and 1985, the Philippines "experienced a catastrophic decline in per capita GDP of about 15 percent" as the "real earnings of those in wage employment declined by at least 25 percent" (Hill 1986, 240–47). Most remarkably, the Philippines' per capita GNP and GDP in 1985 were at the same level as in 1975 (Hill 1986, 255–56). In economic terms, the country was effectively "back to where it was a decade ago" (Hill 1986, 255). In contrast with the rest of Southeast Asia, which was experiencing record economic growth, "The Philippines continued to remain as Southeast Asia's economic 'basket case'" (Youngblood 1986, 233). Unsurprisingly, therefore, frustrated Filipinos were willing to take a chance with the opposition in the 1984 parliamentary elections and in the 1986 presidential elections. Indeed, a poll taken on the eve of the 1984 parliamentary elections found that more than half of the respondents thought that their quality of lives had deteriorated as compared to a year ago (Hawes 1986, 27).

It is crucial to reiterate just how the opposition's significant gains in winning just under one-third of parliamentary seats in the 1984 parliamentary elections decisively shifted both elite and public opinion. Because previous elections, such as the 1978 parliamentary elections, where Marcos's KBL swept more than 90 percent of the seats, and the 1981 presidential elections, where Marcos won with more than four-fifths vote share, were highly fraudulent, opposition parties were generally split between those who advocated electoral boycott and those who preferred electoral participation. Boycotting would deny Marcos governing legitimacy, whereas participation would legitimize Marcos's rule. This division took on a stark, symbolic form when Agapito "Butz" Aquino, Benigno Aquino's younger brother, split from his family to advocate boycott.[4] In contrast, Corazon Aquino, Benigno Aquino's widow, joined those who preferred participation by campaigning extensively with opposition candidates (Komisar 1987, 57). The May 1984 parliamentary elections were relatively less fraudulent. This was primarily due to the large increase in the number of poll watchers from the National Citizens' Movement for Free Elections (NAMFREL), which was established by businessman Jose Concepcion (Kessler 1984, 1218; Wurfel 1985, 270–71). Effectively organized, NAMFREL's 200,000 poll watchers and parallel counting of ballots prevented egregious electoral misconduct, even if it could not prevent all instances of fraud. NAMFREL would later go on to play a critical role by organizing a quick count of the 1986 presidential elections that declared Corazon Aquino and Salvador Laurel the actual winners. Because of NAMFREL's efforts, the May 1984 parliamentary election was credible enough to be deemed "the first honest test of Marcos' popularity since the 1969 presidential election" (Kessler 1984, 1209). Even Richard Childress, resident Philippine expert in the US National Security Council, in a memo to Robert C. McFarlane, Reagan's national security advisor, concluded that "despite the obvious irregularities, by Philippine standards, the election was a meaningful political event."[5] So whereas previous election results could be viewed as unreliable indicators of the true state of Marcos's mass support, the 1984 results were viewed as a more reliable measure of Marcos's crumbling popularity.

Because of the relatively more credible electoral process and the positive outcomes that followed, the vast majority of opposition elites and the public updated their expectations of the degree to which the Marcos regime was vulnerable and the probability of opposition victory in a future election. Whereas some opposition elites who advocated electoral boycott and violent street protests earlier doubted whether they could win through elections, they now changed their stance to accept the viability of elections as a means to topple Marcos. Those who advocated boycott and mass violence "received at least a temporary setback, as the electorate overwhelmingly reaffirmed its preference for elections over violence as the vehicle for seeking political change" (Malin 1985, 200). The American embassy, detailing a confidential meeting with an opposition insider, corroborated the general shift in attitudes toward electoral participation.[6] The insider mentioned that "the boycotters were devastated." Agapito "Butz" Aquino, who had earlier advocated boycott of the elections, "admitted his mistake and was offering to work with the opposition within the system." The embassy's assessment of the polls further noted, "The elections demonstrated that by an overwhelming margin Filipinos continue to believe in elections. . . . The boycott movement simply never caught on."[7] Correspondingly, although some opposition groups advocating electoral boycotts continued to play down the results, the generally positive outcome meant that "some of the boycotters are returning to the [participation] fold" (Kessler 1984, 1226). Ultimately, the positive results increased elite confidence that mass demonstrations on the streets could be translated into votes, and that Filipinos could be counted upon to turn up at the ballot box to vote against the regime.

Adding to the ascendant opposition and a downward-spiraling economy were questions regarding Marcos's personal health—the fifth indicator for opposition elites of potential victory over Marcos. As early as 1980, "persistent rumors that Marcos himself was in serious ill health and perhaps facing death" swirled among opposition circles (Mount 1980, 113). William H. Sullivan, the American ambassador to the Philippines in the first five years of martial law, wrote after Aquino's assassination in late 1983, "It should not prove difficult for the Reagan administration to reach the conclusion that *the days of the Marcos administration are numbered*" because of Marcos's general loss of support among Filipinos and because "health problems will soon incapacitate the president" (Sullivan 1983, 153). These impressions about Marcos's precarious health were compounded in November 1984 when his absence from nightly television newscasts alarmed and surprised the public. A *New York Times* report, ominously headlined "Twilight of the Marcos Era," reported that although the presidential press office finally revealed that Marcos was suffering from a bout of flu, the more widely accepted version of his health was his affliction with lupus, an autoimmune disease affecting the kidneys.[8] To reassure the public that Marcos's questionable physical state was separate from his mental capacity to govern the country, Defense Minister Juan Ponce Enrile offered the following unpersuasive reply after a security meeting with the president: "He was recovering. His mind was very clear."[9] This reassurance was not effective. Doubts over Marcos's continued health sparked open jostling within the KBL to be next in line (Youngblood 1986, 225–26). Minister of Labor Blas Ople, Minister of Defense Juan Ponce Enrile, and Imelda Marcos, Marcos's flamboyant wife and minister of human settlements, appeared to be the three key actors trying to outmaneuver each other (Wurfel 1988, 289).

In the final analysis, the sixth and last consequential factor that solidified elite opinion on Marcos's impending downfall was the notable shift in the United States' support for his continued rule. Because of America's close historical and security relationship with the Philippines, most opposition elites believed that the longevity of the Marcos regime was primarily dependent on American support. If American backing was withdrawn, then surely the Marcos regime was poised to fall. Landé (1981, 1164) summarized the general perception succinctly as follows: "It is the conviction of the Philippine left—and the charge is echoed by many members of the centrist opposition—that President Marcos imposed his dictatorship with American approval and that he could not maintain it without American support." American ambassador Stephen Bosworth agreed, recalling that "we were on the one hand in the minds of many Filipinos seen as the great Satan of the West. On the other hand, we were seen as the deus ex machina from whom all solutions would come if only we decided that's what we wanted to do. . . . People really thought that Marcos was still there because we wanted him to still be."[10] Hence, American encouragement or disapproval of Marcos's rule was an important cue to which all domestic opposition elites were closely attuned.

In the early 1980s, the Reagan administration generally endorsed Marcos's government, to the general despair of opposition elites (Fibiger 2019; Hawes 1986, 21). Vice President George H. W. Bush was the head of the American delegation at Marcos's inauguration as president after he was reelected in June 1981. The secretary of defense, Casper Weinberger, subsequently visited the country and toured Clark Air Base and Subic Bay Naval Base in April 1982. A wildly successful visit by Marcos to the United States in September 1982 marked the peak of warm relations between the two countries and solidified the personal bonds between Marcos and Reagan.[11] Of course, before Marcos's trip to the United States, Reagan's administration was under no illusions about what Marcos wanted from visiting Reagan. "President Marcos is undertaking his state visit to accomplish a goal he has sought for over a decade: implicit endorsement of his regime by a US administration," declared the first sentence of a top-secret CIA memorandum written before his visit.[12] The bargaining chip Marcos had in his corner was renegotiation of the leases of American bases, Clark and Subic Bay, which were due to expire in 1984. It appeared that the United States reciprocated as Marcos desired. The warm reception accorded by President Reagan was highlighted in a full state dinner as well as the ceremonial presentation of US war medals (the Distinguished Service Cross, Silver Star, and Purple Heart) to President Marcos for his efforts in fighting the Japanese in World War II.[13] Subsequently, Reagan's administration was happy to lend legitimacy and financial aid to Marcos's rule in exchange for general assurance of America's security interests (Fibiger 2019; Pee and Schmidli 2019). After all, stability in Marcos's rule was essential in keeping the Philippine communist insurgency in check. Furthermore, he had followed through by agreeing to extend American use of Clark Air Base and Subic Bay Naval Base in the middle of 1983, albeit at a cost of US$900 million in security assistance from the United States.[14] Theirs was a relationship built on pragmatic exchange of benefits as much as it was about personal ties between the two men (Bonner 1987, chapters 12 and 13).

But American support for Marcos declined rapidly after the middle of 1983 for several reasons, much to the delight of the opposition (Bonner 1987, chapter 14). First, Aquino's assassination in August 1983 prompted President Reagan to skip the Philippines as part of his scheduled tour of Asian countries in late 1983. Although Marcos wrote personal letters to Reagan assuring him of his personal safety and promised a speedy inquiry into the Aquino case, Reagan's advisers thought he should avoid the Philippines.[15] They advised him that "the President's visit could galvanize anti-American interests, thus raising questions about the physical safety of President Reagan and of US servicemen and civilians."[16] American ambassador Michael Armacost was also well aware of such anti-American sentiments at the time. He relayed in a cable back to Washington, "The fact that many very prominent businessmen and families were coming to me to urge that President Reagan not come" suggested that "the polarization of opinion in Manila over the visit would expose the President not only to security dangers, but political backlash here and at home."[17] Eventually, Reagan continued with visits only to Japan and South Korea, blaming legislative work on a tight congressional schedule for him skipping the Philippines. From then onward, senior Reagan administration officials who visited Manila repeatedly emphasized to Marcos the need to hold free and fair elections to enjoy Washington's continued endorsement, as compared to previously unequivocal support for his government (Hawes 1986, 18–19). Gradually, these indicators led to Marcos's growing suspicion of Reagan's true support for him. As Thompson (1995, 113) noted, "By 1983, Marcos began to believe that there was a US-supported conspiracy against his continued rule. Although his fears were exaggerated, the *political winds out of Washington had subtly shifted*." Indeed, CIA's January 1984 report noted that "the Intelligence community is pessimistic about the longer-term prospects for efficient government and stability *regardless of how the succession plays itself out*."[18]

Second, the Philippines' crumbling economy in the rest of 1984 and 1985 stoked growing fears within the American administration regarding the overall stability of the Philippine government as well as its ability to combat and eliminate the communist insurgency (Bonner 1987, chapter 15; Kessler 1986, 47–48). In January 1985, the defense minister reported that the New People's Army (NPA), the military arm of the Communist Party of the Philippines, had been growing annually at an alarming rate 23 percent since 1981 (Villegas 1986, 131). This news accompanied visits to the Philippines in the same month by Richard Armitage, assistant secretary of defense, and Paul Wolfowitz, assistant secretary of state for East Asia and the Pacific (Youngblood 1986, 235). After much internal discussion, in February 1985, a full ten months before opposition coalitions talks between Corazon Aquino and Salvador Laurel, Ronald Reagan finally endorsed a National Security Decision Directive Number 163, "United States Policy towards the Philippines."[19] The directive clarified what the US government had been doing in the past year and would do moving forward. While it noted that the administration's goal was "*not* to replace the current leadership of the Philippines," it clarified that the administration's overall objective was "*orderly succession* that leads to a stable transition." This entailed "supporting the efforts of diverse Filipino leaders to promote revitalized institutions," which included "the Catholic hierarchy, the military professionals, *and responsible members of the democratic opposition*." The aim was "to assure both a smooth transition when President Marcos does pass from the scene and longer-term stability." In August 1985, the Philippine military released figures indicating that the NPA had more than tripled in size in the past six years, while NPA-related violent incidents had increased by 1,830 percent, from 249 in 1978 to 4,809 in 1984 (Youngblood 1986,

230). Two months later, in October 1985, as if to make even clearer the Reagan administration's point regarding the need for Marcos to buck up, the National Security Council agreed to send Senator Paul Laxalt, a friend of President Reagan, as a personal emissary to Manila to try to talk some sense into Marcos.[20] Laxalt carried with him "a letter from President Reagan which is said to contain a blunt warning concerning NPA gains and *the pressing need for genuine political, economic, and military reforms*" (Villegas 1986, 134).

Not only was the White House breathing down Marcos's neck, but the US Congress was also actively questioning and modifying American foreign policy toward the Philippines. Between June 1983 and December 1985, the House of Representatives and the Senate held at least seven separate hearings on various issues concerning the Philippines. Among all the officials, Congressman Stephen J. Solarz, chairman of the House of Representatives Committee on Foreign Affairs' Subcommittee on Asian and Pacific Affairs, was the most active. In the wake of the Aquino assassination in August 1983, Solarz set out to urge the Reagan administration to do more to push the Philippines in the direction of democratization.[21] He introduced and sponsored resolutions in the House calling for the Philippine government to thoroughly investigate the Aquino assassination and to hold free and fair elections. In addition, he leveraged his position as the chairman of the Subcommittee on Asian and Pacific Affairs to modify the Reagan administration's security assistance to the Philippines as established under the joint bases agreement. Specifically, in February 1984, he modified the Reagan administration's request to provide US$180 million in aid to the Philippines, comprising US$95 million in economic aid and $85 million in military aid. Instead, he modified the package to US$155 million in economic aid and $25 million in military aid.[22] In February 1985, he again wielded his pen. He cut the Reagan administration aid request for the Philippines from US$195 million back to US$180 million, and again recommended that the ratio of economic aid to military aid be US$155 million to US$25 million.[23] Even more, in early December 1985, right in the midst of opposition coalition talks, he pressured the Marcos regime by holding hearings on whether the Marcos regime had diverted wealth to purchase real estate assets in the United States.[24]

Opposition elites in Manila were well aware of the overall shift in America's attitudes toward Marcos before their coalition-building efforts in late 1985. They frequently met with American embassy officials as well as officials from Congress and the Reagan administration when they visited Manila. Just days before Aquino's assassination in August 1983, for instance, Congressman Solarz met with Philippine opposition leaders on a tour of Asia.[25] He left the country one day before Aquino's return. Upon hearing about Aquino's death in Bangkok, he immediately scrapped the rest of his travel plans and traveled back to the Philippines to visit Aquino's home, where his body was lying in state. He then had dinner at Salvador Laurel's house with other leaders of the opposition. A month later, in September 1983, US ambassador Michael Armacost also met with Laurel. He "made clear to Laurel that *the U.S. would continue to work to encourage the Government in the direction of free and fair elections*."[26] Similarly, five months later, in February 1984, Laurel met with Vice President George H. W. Bush; the latter emphasized to him "*unqualified U.S. support for free and fair parliamentary elections* in which the opposition has an equitable opportunity to take part" and "U.S. support generally for political normalization in the Philippines." He stated that "*the Administration and the Congress are of one mind* in hoping for a full disclosure of the circumstances surrounding the Aquino assassination and for free and fair elections."[27] Even more, when Senator Paul Laxalt visited the Philippines in October 1985, he "sought to reassure the moderate democratic opposition and reformist elements within the military that, despite Marcos's public assertions to the contrary, *the regime no longer enjoyed the unequivocal support of Washington*" (Youngblood 1986, 235–36). After Marcos called for snap elections in early November 1985, the American embassy, alongside Stephen Solarz and John Kerry, then a freshman member of the Senate Foreign Relations Committee, repeatedly reached out to Aquino and Laurel through various intermediaries to encourage them to get on the same ticket. "These people were bombarded. . . . Absolutely overwhelmed," recounted a Foreign Service officer (Bonner 1987, 391).

Taken together, the accelerating trajectory of unprecedented regime-debilitating events between 1983 and 1985 left little doubt in opposition elites' minds that the Marcos regime was ready to fall. Defecting elites formed a viable opposition party in UNIDO. UNIDO made surprising, unprecedented gains in parliamentary elections. Mass street demonstrations intensified against the regime. The economy was spiraling downward with few signs of recovery. Marcos was in ill health. And the United States had given its tacit support for a Philippine government without Marcos. It was now up to the opposition elites to coalesce "as a *necessary condition* for the opposition to have a chance of defeating Marcos" (Youngblood 1986, 226).

Corazon Aquino as the Popular Leader, Salvador Laurel and UNIDO as the Machine

If there was a clear consensus among opposition elites that Marcos's regime was ripe for the picking, could they work collectively to push a single leader up to bring the regime down? This question was clearly on the minds of opposition elites. As early as November 1984, about a year before the actual alliance formation talks between Corazon Aquino and Salvador Laurel, a "Convenor's Group" (CG) was set up to attempt to institutionalize a selection process for a single opposition candidate to contest against Marcos (Komisar 1987, 61). The CG was headed by Jaime Ongpin, a businessman, Lorenzo Tañada, a respected opposition elder, and Corazon Aquino herself. Eleven potential candidates were invited to sign a declaration of unity. They were Agapito Aquino, Jose S. Diokno, Teofisto Guingona, Eva Estrada Kalaw, Salvador Laurel, Raul Manglapus, Ramon Mitra, Ambrosio Padilla, Aquilino Pimentel Jr., Rafael Salas, and Jovito Salonga (Kimura 1991, 217). Among these elites, only Laurel and Kalaw refrained from signing, as both thought the agreement would constrain their chances of becoming the opposition candidate (Komisar 1987, 61). Not to be outdone, Laurel initiated a separate "National Unification Committee" (NUC) with several opposition parties to try to select an opposition presidential candidate. His aim was to take the wind out of the CG by providing another platform where the selection would be made (Kimura 1991, 217–18; Komisar 1987, 62–63). Eventually, by April 1985, a half-baked compromise truce was struck between the CG and the NUC whereby it was agreed that the sole presidential candidate would be selected from one of five political parties—UNIDO, the Liberal Party, the Nacionalista Party, Partido Demokratiko Pilipino–Lakas ng Bayan (PDP-Laban), and Bagong Alyansang Makabayan.

To seize the initiative and bolster his standing to be the nominated opposition candidate in impending presidential elections, Laurel quickly convened a UNIDO party conference in June 1985 and invited fellow leaders from other opposition parties. During the convention, the party formally and openly endorsed him as UNIDO's candidate for the upcoming presidential election. His primary intention was to establish himself as the front runner ahead of Aquino, whom he viewed as his only other true rival. As his diary on the day of the party convention revealed,

All political leaders identified with the opposition were present. Even Cory came despite attempts of her "advisors" to dissuade her. . . . I am told by old-timers that it was the biggest and fightiest [*sic*] political convention on record—and I was unanimously nominated presidential standard bearer of the opposition. . . . I am confident we will have only one candidate in the opposition. The only other possible candidate is Cory but she has repeatedly told me she is not interested and that she will *never* run for the presidency. She has said this privately and publicly. She *appears* to be sincere. She attended today's convention and even delivered a speech supporting my candidacy. I was told her advisors (Tañada, Doikno, Arroyo) were trying to stop her and she was in tears because she wanted to—and she did. Her advisors obviously have their own agenda. I hope Cory will not become a tool in their hands.[28]

Laurel's move to preemptively announce himself as the opposition's presidential candidate in June 1985 ahead of elections not yet called by Marcos was a response to the aforementioned "advisors" of Aquino. They distrusted Laurel and were actively persuading Aquino to run as the opposition's candidate (Komisar 1987, 64–68). A few months later on October 15, 1985, a new organization in that regard was launched. The Cory Aquino for President Movement sought to raise one million signatures endorsing her candidacy. It was a symbolic populist indicator that could potentially persuade Laurel to step aside. Indeed, three days later, on October 18, 1985, Laurel noted in his diary that opposition leaders from the NUC, now having merged with the Aquino-affiliated CG and having evolved into an organization that he could not control, once again sought his acquiesce:

National Unification Committee representatives (NUC) came to the house this morning to suggest process of selection of common opposition candidate. I told them I am already the official candidate of the only accredited opposition party, UNIDO. I suspect they are eyeing Cory as a candidate. It is possible Cory has intimated to Cecilia Muñoz Palma that she may change her mind about running if she is the common candidate. But Cory has continued to deny this *in public*. I am, however, proceeding with my campaign schedule.[29]

The race between Aquino and Laurel further intensified when Marcos announced on November 3, 1985, early presidential elections on the ABC television show *This Week with David Brinkley*. His announcement caught most Filipinos and Americans by surprise, sending his opponents scrambling.[30] The American embassy in Manila regarded Marcos's decision to organize snap elections as an astute move because the opposition was "still trying to find its organizational feet and seriously fragmented between UNIDO front-runner Doy [Salvador] Laurel, Liberal Party leader Jovito Salonga, and possibly Cory (Corazon) Aquino, waiting in the wings for a draft."[31] Marcos himself relished witnessing the opposition fragment. He mocked the opposition by declaring, "The more the merrier. . . . The poor fellows, they will split the voters and demoralize their followers."[32]

Within a week, however, the majority of opposition leaders quickly coalesced around Aquino.[33] An American embassy cable noted that of the 11 potential candidates previously considered by the CG, all nine of those who had signed the opposition unity agreement endorsed Aquino's candidacy. Only Laurel and Kalaw continued to demur.[34] Yet, despite having the support of the vast majority of opposition elites, Aquino continued to decline to run as Marcos's opponent.[35] She was not a politician, after all, just an ordinary housewife, the widow of a slain martyr (Komisar 1987, chapter 6). But Filipinos gravitated toward her precisely because she was not a traditional Filipino politician. As widow of Benigno Aquino Jr., she had been at the forefront of national consciousness after her husband's brutal assassination at Manila airport just two years ago. Her modest and soft-spoken demeanor during her husband's funeral proceedings made her the preferred candidate for Filipinos, who were eager to break with Marcos's authoritarian methods and his proclivity for crony capitalism. She was everything that Marcos was not (Forest and Forest 1988, 54–58). She was to Filipinos, according to a journalist who traveled extensively with her campaign, "the Joan of Arc who would lead them to salvation" (Goodno 1991, 91). Her credibility as the opposition candidate with the best chance to prevail against Marcos was boosted when the Cory Aquino for President Movement, by December 1, 1985, managed to obtain one million signatures petitioning for her candidacy, less than one month after Marcos's called for elections.[36]

To be sure, notwithstanding the widespread recognition of Aquino's favorable qualities as a clean, nontraditional opposition candidate, they were her major weaknesses at the same time. Not being a traditional politician meant that Aquino was not skilled in machine politics. Her fundraising and organizational capabilities paled in comparison to Laurel's, who was a longtime politician hailing from a political family long before the Marcos martial law era. In the run-up to the official nomination day on December 11, 1985, a *New York Times* report noted that Laurel was "the only opposition candidate with serious nationwide political organization" who had "in place a nationwide network of supporters who await the signal to go into action."[37] His supporters offered the fact that Laurel *commands the only nationwide election machinery apart from that of Mr. Marcos*."[38] A US Department of State Bureau of Intelligence and Research Briefing Paper concurred, noting that "Doy Laurel is the most conservative and organized of the opposition leaders and Cory Aquino the most popular."[39] Indeed, in the aftermath of Benigno Aquino Jr.'s assassination, the American embassy had already identified the Laurel-led UNIDO as the major opposition actor resisting Marcos's rule.[40] The embassy noted that "Salvador Laurel is *the opposition's most experienced traditional political fund raiser and his organization would be an asset* in financing a united opposition."[41]

Laurel's leadership of UNIDO was crucial in solidifying his public credibility as a political leader with a strong organizational network capable of mobilizing substantial support. As an American embassy cable suggested, "Doy Laurel's chances of becoming the sole opposition candidate will depend to a large extent on *the assessment of other opposition leaders as to the real strength of UNIDO*."[42] The perception that UNIDO was an impressive party machine can be largely attributed to its outsized success in the May 1984 parliamentary elections. Before 1984, the opposition was noted for being fragmented among a number of opposition parties, headed by their respective elite leaders. Other than UNIDO, the other major parties were the PDP-Laban, founded by Aquilino Pimentel Jr. and Benigno Aquino, the Liberal Party, led by ex-senators Eva Estrada Kalaw and John Osmena, and the Nacionalista Party, reactivated by ex-senator Jose Roy. All were political parties led by the heads of longtime political families with very narrow bases of mass support. But after May 1984, with more than half of the opposition parliamentarians under its wing, UNIDO publicly and clearly signaled that it was the Philippines' leading opposition party. A post-election report prepared for the US Senate Committee on Foreign Relations opined that in the wake of UNIDO's strong showing, Laurel was "the closest thing to an opposition leader in the Philippines today."[43] Another analyst opined that he was "the biggest winner of the 1984 legislative elections," which "made him the undisputed leader of the anti-Marcos forces" (Thompson 1995, 132–33). Most crucially, *even Corazon Aquino's own supporters conceded* that Laurel had a superior party machinery. When they drew up a list of strengths and weaknesses for both candidates, they noted that Laurel was a "political pro" who had the "support of traditional politicians and UNIDO" and could "fight Marcos tough for tough," thus giving him a "good" chance to win the elections (Javate-de Dios, Daroy, and Kalaw-Tirol 1988, 670–72).

In any case, throughout the rest of November and early December 1985, it appeared that a three-way presidential race between Marcos, Aquino, and Laurel was a likely outcome. Open conflict broke out between the NUC, which was now backing Aquino, and Laurel and his UNIDO party. At stake was whether the NUC or UNIDO would be put forward to be certified by the Philippine election commission as the "dominant opposition party." Whichever party to be certified as such would have the right to place poll watchers at the voting stations, thus augmenting and solidifying its nationwide grassroots presence. Laurel even attempted to enlist the help of the American ambassador at that time, Stephen Bosworth, to try to persuade Aquino to be his vice-presidential running mate. Bosworth recalled that "[Laurel] was constantly besieging me to try to get me an interview with her and persuade her that they should be reversed. The ranking should be reversed, and he should be the presidential candidate."[44]

When Aquino finally announced her intention to run as the opposition candidate on December 3, 1985, she offered Laurel the spot as her vice-presidential running mate. As a quid pro quo for acquiescing to Aquino's offer, Laurel, in turn, demanded concessions. First, he insisted that they contest the elections under the UNIDO party banner, which would make UNIDO the dominant opposition party (Komisar 1987, 74; Thompson 1995, 137).[45] He appealed to her by talking up about UNIDO's strength, suggesting that UNIDO "was the largest and most organized party in the country" and "was accredited as the dominant opposition party," and "its capacity to wage and win a nationwide campaign had been convincingly demonstrated in the 1984 elections when we won one third of the seats at stake."[46] Second, he wanted Aquino to promise that "he be appointed prime minister and be given the cabinet post of his choice, that a quarter of other cabinet jobs go to UNIDO people, that he be consulted on all appointments," among other demands (Komisar 1987, 74).[47] Unsurprisingly, Aquino's advisers balked at these demands. "They're blackmailing us," they cried (Komisar 1987, 74).

Laurel's insistence on running under the UNIDO banner was apparently twofold. In the event that the Aquino-Laurel ticket won, UNIDO's prominence would preserve Laurel's influence over future cabinet appointments. Alternatively, in the event that they lost to Marcos, UNIDO's standing as the dominant opposition party would be preserved for future elections (Cameron 1992, 240). Having understood this logic, Aquino initially spurned Laurel's suggestion and proposed a new coalition called UNIDO-LABAN, LABAN being the former party of her slain husband. This new proposal was, of course, unacceptable to Laurel. At a press conference three days before nomination day, he declared that coalition talks had collapsed. "I can sacrifice myself. I can sacrifice the presidency. But I cannot sacrifice my party and my principles," he lamented.[48]

Yet, even then, the respective strengths and weaknesses of the candidates were hard to ignore. There was *widespread elite and mass recognition* that, while Aquino was popular, she was hamstrung by the lack of an effective party machine. Laurel, on the other hand, had a proven party machine but, as a traditional politician, was mistrusted. They depended on each other to maximize their joint chances of victory. An American special interagency meeting in October 1985 noted that "as many as *85 percent of the opposition appear ready to coalesce* behind one or both of these candidates in an election."[49] A month later, a CIA internal meeting concluded that there was "*agreement among most leaders* that a joint ticket between Corazon Aquino and Salvador Laurel would make the strongest opposition ticket."[50] Another widely circulated CIA report in December 1985, right in the midst of opposition coalition talks, commented that "*most opposition leaders—and many ruling party leaders—*believed that a joint Aquino-Laurel ticket would be the opposition's best hope to defeat Marcos."[51]

Even more importantly, both party leaders had little doubt of their relative strengths and weaknesses when explicitly admonished by Cardinal Sin, the influential and charismatic leader of the Catholic Church in the Philippines. He summarized it aptly to Aquino herself: "Cory, you cannot do it alone. You are a housewife. You have no political party, no poll watchers, no national organization. *You have to join with an existing party, or it will not work*" (Bautista 1987, 166). He then had lunch with Laurel and said, "Doy, you are intelligent. You are experienced in politics. But you are not as attractive as Cory. She holds the heart of the people in her hands. *Join with her and you will win*" (Bautista 1987, 167). Opposition supporters themselves concurred that the opposition's best chances for defeating Marcos rested on an alliance between the two candidates.[52] Brownlee noted that both Laurel's and Aquino's supporters "realized that only a united front could challenge Marcos in such a crucial contest" (Brownlee 2007, 194).

Furthermore, it was clear to both Aquino and Laurel that in the counterfactual scenario where there was no alliance between the two, the votes would likely be equally split, thus eliminating any chance of defeating Marcos (Forest and Forest 1988, 55).[53] This counterfactual was obvious to the public, to the two candidates, and to their supporters (Javate-de Dios, Daroy, and Kalaw-Tirol 1988, 181–89). In their respective meetings with Cardinal Sin, "*Both of them were made to realize that if they were not united, neither would make it"* (Goodno 1991, 90).[54] Cardinal Sin added, "The whole nation was sad. They thought that Cory and Laurel would run against each other. *Everybody knew* that with the Marcos cheating already in place and the opposition divided, Cory and Doy would lose and the Philippines would face more years of Marcos terror" (White 1989, 147). Another opposition insider told the American embassy that "if both Laurel and Mrs Aquino declared for the Presidency Dec 11 (nomination day), then the game is over."[55]

For its part, the American embassy too urged the dueling leaders not to be divided. The American deputy chief of mission, Philip S. Kaplan, recalled that when they met for lunch, he told Aquino, "Look, you're going to be the president, you're going to get elected. The vice president only does what you allow him to do. Keep him [Laurel] in the tent. *And if you don't do it, you're not going to win.*"[56] This recognition about certain defeat if they contested alone was further reflected in the generally conciliatory attitudes between the two candidates, even after the press conference when Laurel announced that opposition unity had collapsed. Aquino told reporters that she would seek a final meeting with Laurel: "I just don't want it to be said that I failed to avail of every possible solution in getting the two of us to unite."[57] For his part, Laurel mentioned, "We are still hoping and praying for unity. God works in mysterious ways, after all."[58]

The game of chicken between the two persisted right up till the morning of nomination day, when both candidates filed papers as presidential candidates. But a mere one hour before the deadline, Aquino and Laurel withdrew their individual nominations and filed a joint nomination as presidential and vice-presidential candidates respectively, both running under the UNIDO party label. In Cameron's analysis, Laurel demonstrated stronger resolve to Aquino to make her agree to run under the UNIDO banner (Cameron 1992, 239–46). He was willing to risk an opposition split, even at the cost of certain defeat and Marcos's continued rule. But for Aquino, a continuation of Marcos's disastrous rule was a far worse proposition than conceding to Laurel's demands. Laurel's own diary entry on the date of the nomination day corroborates this analysis. It reveals that it was Aquino who met Laurel at his son's house to announce that she had changed her mind to agree to run under the UNIDO banner, as well as promise a post-election deal over cabinet appointments.[59] To his credit, Laurel blamed Aquino's advisers for the extended, topsy-turvy negotiations, rather than Aquino herself. "If not for the people around Cory, agreement between her and me would have been reached a long time ago," he remarked.[60] In any case, with this final combination, a *New York Times* editorial noted that Marcos might lose the election because "a bickering opposition agreed to a single slate, teaming the personable but untested Corazon Aquino with the seasoned but wily Salvador Laurel."[61]

Expectations of Cross-Party Vote Transfer and Mass Support on Election Day

In forging their alliance, Corazon Aquino and Salvador Laurel made the decision based on a crucial assumption—that their respective sets of supporters would vote strategically for their joint ticket. If they had little confidence that such an assumption was true, then surely they would not have suffered such intense pressure and put so much effort in trying to find an amicable bargain with each other. They would have reasoned that negotiating compromise bargains with each other was a fruitless endeavor because their followers would be split due to some irreconcilable differences anyway. Yet the historical evidence suggests that both Aquino and Laurel were quietly confident of the overall level of cross-party strategic vote transfer if they formed a pre-electoral alliance.

The level of vote transfers among both sets of supporters was expected to be high for at least two reasons. There were few ideological differences between Aquino and Laurel, for one. Both of them were regarded as members of the centrist, moderate, nonviolent opposition (Wurfel 1988, 278–80). By contrast, the Communist Party of the Philippines and its public face, the National Democratic Front, comprised the radical opposition, invested in violent confrontation with the Marcos regime (Wurfel 1988, 280–81). The only issue that appeared to separate the two—whether the American military bases should be allowed to stay—was more of a mirage than reality. It was widely known that Laurel was generally in favor of America's continued presence in the Philippines. While Aquino was noted for her general public opposition to the American bases, she was privately ready to be flexible for the purposes of securing tacit American endorsement of her candidacy. A CIA intelligence assessment report in November 1985 noted that "almost all opposition leaders have waffled on the future of the US facilities . . . and they occasionally make public statements against them in order to bolster their nationalist credentials," yet "most moderates conceded that the benefits of the bases . . . justify their presence and offset any potential infringement of Philippine sovereignty."[62] Aquino demonstrated her flexibility near the end of December 1985 when she stated that she would allow the US military bases to remain in the Philippines if she was elected president, at least until the end of the agreement in 1991.[63] Regardless, it was not evident that America's presence in the Philippines was a major campaign issue. Filipinos in general were more concerned about getting rid of Marcos the autocrat than about the continued presence of the military bases.

The fortuitous structure of the ballot in having joint presidential and vice-presidential teams of candidates is the second reason why both opposition party elites expected a high degree of strategic voting for a joint ticket. Supporters of both Aquino and Laurel would have little problem voting for a joint ticket where both candidates were on the ballot. Voters who were concerned about Aquino's inexperience in the practice of politics and the pragmatics of governance might be reassured that Laurel would be her vice president and be able to provide at least some guidance. Other voters who were concerned about Laurel's questionable reputation as a traditional politician might be persuaded that Aquino at the top of the ticket moderated a temptation to return to Marcos's cronyism. In other words, their coordinated joint ticket would be able to draw support from both sets of supporters, even if their supporters disliked the other candidate.

Not only were the two sets of supporters not ideologically divided, there was also strong evidence that most voters cared much more about opposing Marcos, including independents and moderates who had previously supported Marcos either tacitly by acquiescing to his rule or actively at the ballot box. In other words, *the authoritarian-democratic cleavage among voters was more salient and important than any intra-opposition divisions.* The strongest indication came from the middle class. As the conventional political science wisdom proposes: no bourgeoisie, no democracy (Moore 1966; Bellin 2000). In the Philippines, the middle class generally refers to the bureaucratic and business professionals working in the Metro Manila area, as well as the upper-middle capitalist class of business owners. Before the crunch coalition talks in December 1985, indications of potential middle-class support for a joint opposition ticket were plentiful. The most overt indicator was middle-class participation in mass protests on the streets. In a meeting with President Marcos himself after the Benigno Aquino assassination, American ambassador Michael Armacost told Marcos that he "had been particularly struck in recent days by the number of middle-class businessmen and professionals in the Makati area who had joined the anti-government demonstrations."[64] Rivera (2001, 239) concurs with this assessment: "The most vivid open protests erupted in the very centers of high commerce and finance involving the professionals, white collar workers, and the anti-crony business personalities." To be sure, the middle class revolted not just because of their outrage at Benigno Aquino's assassination. They were also deeply disappointed by the false promises of economic development that was supposed to emerge from Marcos's centralization of political power. Marcos's rule did not bring stability and broad-based economic growth, even as the middle class gave up their political rights as citizens at the onset of martial law. Instead, Marcos's "provision pact" selectively rewarded certain economic elites in exchange for their support, even as he set out to destroy those who resisted his rule (Slater 2010, 163–80). A member of the Makati Business Club, the premier club representing capitalist interests in Metro Manila, bemoaned the failure to enlarge the middle class.

> Marcos launched a revolution from the center. If it was indeed a revolution from the center, it would have survived. It would have brought a lot of people from below to the middle class. There would have been this broad belt of stakeholders in the new society which would have been its impregnable defense mechanism. This didn't happen. *Anong lumitaw*? [What emerged?] The new oligarchs. So it would appear that the revolution sold out to the Commies. (Bello 1984, 300)

In addition to intermittent street protests, moreover, the middle class also organized collectively into various civil society groups opposing Marcos. For example, at least two civil society groups—the August Twenty-One Movement and Justice for Aquino–Justice for All—commemorated Aquino's death. "Most of these groups were organizations of middle-class professionals, including students and church officials," Kessler (1984, 1211) noted. By 1985, Timberman (1991, 132) estimates, "There were more than 100 mass and sectoral organizations that formed and re-formed ever shifting coalitions." While numerous and generally inchoate, these nonviolent groups had the dual effect of isolating the more violent NPA and of energizing previously apathetic citizens into opposing Marcos. As a journalist recounted, "They drew the younger, formerly uninterested businessmen and technocrats into the political mainstream. The young, in turn, recruited the vitally needed big-business leaders and the top-rank academicians and clergy who had stayed out of the arena" (quoted in Timberman 1991, 134). In any case, there were also no evidence indicating that these civil society groups were split in their support for Aquino or Laurel. All jointly opposed Marcos.

Finally, as previously discussed, one of the strongest indicators of middle-class antipathy toward the Marcos regime was the May 1984 parliamentary elections, where UNIDO won the majority of parliamentary seats in the Metro Manila area. Not only did the vast majority of voters turn up to vote—turnout was estimated at about 85 percent—despite the boycott movement, but they turned out to vote despite the threat of electoral violence and vote buying. Approaching the 1986 elections, these threats were again very real. Thompson's (1995, 141–44) analysis of the records suggest that Marcos had set aside a spectacular sum of half a billion US dollars for buying votes, and had ordered the military and the election commission to collaborate to use violence and spread fear among opposition supporters. Assassinations of candidates and violent intimidation of voters, such as firing guns into the air at polling stations, were commonplace and widely expected during election time. What was more, coordinating the potential electoral violence and manipulation was General Fabian Ver, Marcos's loyal chief of staff of the armed forces. He had been acquitted for his alleged involvement in the Benigno Aquino assassination and reinstated immediately by Marcos as chief of staff on December 2, 1985, the same day that Aquino announced that she was running as a candidate. There would have been little doubt in Laurel's and Aquino's minds that Marcos and General Ver would engage in whatever electoral violence, fraud, and manipulation necessary to try to secure victory.

Yet the results of the May 1984 parliamentary elections proved crucial in updating opposition elite expectations that voters, especially the pro-opposition middle class, could be counted to turn up at the polls. NAMFREL's greater prominence was especially powerful in this regard. Between 1984 and 1986, NAMFREL grew its base of volunteers more than two times and had grown its coverage from two-thirds of country to 85 percent (Thompson 1995, 148–49). It also had the backing of the Philippine Catholic Church in the form of a "marine corps" of local priests and nuns who headed local NAMFREL organizations. They provided the symbolic and moral resistance to the military's electoral violence, thereby delivering confidence to voters to vote (Youngblood 1990, 198). Financial backing was secretly provided by the Americans and the Japanese, who altogether funded NAMFREL to the tune of slightly less than US$1 million (Bonner 1987, 408–9). NAMFREL's enlarged status thus generated confidence among opposition elites that the negative effects of electoral violence and vote buying could be attenuated, even if not completely eliminated (Pascual 1990). Moreover, there is no evidence to suggest that NAMFREL favored either Aquino or Laurel. Arguably, its commitment toward enhancing electoral integrity is indicative of the singularity of its anti-Marcos objectives.

But middle-class support alone would not be enough to push Aquino and Laurel over the finish line. After all, some estimates suggest that the middle class in the Philippines constituted only 10 to 12 percent of the working population near the end of the 1990s (Rivera 2001, 232). The proportion in 1986 would surely be smaller. To win, the opposition had to secure enough votes from the rural areas and from the broad masses. In this regard, the Catholic Church's vast network of parishes, priests, and nuns again played a decisive role. In a country where more than 80 percent of the population are nominally Roman Catholic, with a significant portion of the rest Protestants, the church and its clergy were highly influential in swaying public opinion and voting behavior. Here, the overall empirical evidence suggests that the Catholic Church gradually turned against the Marcos regime and did nothing to split Aquino and Laurel. In fact, the church was decisive in urging its flock to vote for the joint opposition ticket.

At the onset of martial law in 1972, the Philippine churches were not entirely opposed to Marcos's rule. In fact, just one month after the declaration of martial law, the National Council of Churches in the Philippines submitted a resolution signed by eight heads of churches expressing their support for his declaration (Rigos 1975, 127). Another letter, written and signed by Archbishop Teopisto V. Alberto, president of the Catholic Bishops' Conference of the Philippines (CBCP) (Rigos 1975, 127–28) expressed reluctant acquiescence to martial law, provided that it was as brief as possible. Dissent within the church, while present, was in the minority (Slater 2010, 168–72; Youngblood 1990, 72–73). Further, in November 1973, a Church-Military Liaison Committee (CMLC) was set up to resolve differences between churches and the military (Rigos 1975, 131). Participation in this committee signaled the churches' willingness to work with the regime to preserve general law and order despite their reservations. Overall, the atmosphere and relationship between the churches and Marcos can be described as "critical co-operation" (Rigos 1975, 131).

By the early 1980s, however, the relationship had changed drastically. In July 1982, Cardinal Jaime Sin, now archbishop of Manila and overall leader of Filipino Catholics, suggested that Marcos had "lost the respect of the people" and that he should "make way for new leadership" (Youngblood 1984, 211–12). The CBCP then voted to withdraw from the CMLC in January 1983, followed by a pastoral letter in February 1983 "read in more than 3,000 parishes, accusing the government of economic mismanagement, corruption, and repression" (Youngblood 1984, 205). The reasons precipitating such a breakdown in relations were several. The primary reason was the government's increasing repression against church workers. Several high-profile cases of military arrests and killing of church workers on charges of alleged antigovernment activities, possessing subversive documents, and providing safe harbor for communists occurred in 1981 and 1982 (Youngblood 1984, 207–9; 1990, 128–32). These arrests were based on the belief that the Communist Party and the NPA had infiltrated Philippine churches, particularly in rural areas. Fighting back against the NPA necessitated action against radical clergy. Yet a CIA report in March 1983 opined that although there were indeed some Communist sympathizers among the clergy, "the total number of religious radicals in the Church remains small" and that the military's actions were counterproductive because they "frequently ensnare innocent Church workers."[65] Nevertheless, the decision by Defense Minister Enrile to turn a CMLC meeting in November 1982 into a media circus embarrassed and enraged the bishops, leading to their withdrawal from the committee two months later.

A secondary, albeit still important reason, was the growing poverty and inequality. Through the 1960s, 1970s and 1980s, Philippine churches became more invested in social justice work as successive popes spoke out against structural injustices in the economy and politics (Youngblood 1990, chapter 4). As a result, churches increasingly found solidarity with the poor and oppressed, spoke out for them, and organized them in seeking collective solutions to their economic misery. The declining economy under Marcos's rule in the early 1980s brought more and more statements of concern from bishops, pastors, priests, and nuns. In his analysis, Youngblood (1990, 190) concluded, "*These statements and others indicate unequivocally* that by the time of the Aquino assassination in August 1983 and the subsequent collapse of the economy, Philippine church leaders had lost faith in the ability of the Marcos regime's economic policies to create a more just and equitable society for the majority of Filipinos." As the economy plummeted further in 1984 and 1985, church dissent grew. The Philippine church heaved under the burden of tending to the spiritual and materials needs of its flock.

After the Aquino assassination in August 1983, the church became even more outspoken against the Marcos regime. A key symbolic indicator was Cardinal Sin's presiding over Aquino's funeral and calling for national reconciliation (Wurfel 1985, 265–66). In particular, he urged Marcos to hold free and fair elections as a first step in removing the shackles of oppression, which had "reduced the Filipino to being an exile in his own country" (Youngblood 1984, 213). This message for free and fair elections was also delivered to President Ronald Reagan himself. In a September 23, 1984, meeting in the Waldorf Towers in New York, Cardinal Sin told Reagan that "he wanted simply to convey one thing, the importance of restoring democracy to the Philippines."[66] A year later, in September 1985, two months before Marcos called for snap elections and three months before the height of opposition coalition talks, a CIA memorandum concluded that growing public dissent from within the Catholic Church was a key reason for Marcos's declining support:

> The Catholic Church is increasingly disenchanted with the Marcos regime over government corruption and human rights abuses. It is particularly aggravated by the harassment, murder, and disappearance of clergy and lay workers. Cardinal Jaime Sin has repeatedly embarrassed Marcos by his outspoken criticism of the ruling family. In addition, many parish priests are openly admonishing the government from the pulpit, and some radical priests are reportedly involved in supporting the Communist insurgency.[67]

In addition, a second, more pragmatic, indicator of the church's ability to shift mass support toward the opposition was its creation of the Radio Veritas, the church's official radio station, and the *Veritas* weekly newspaper. Both alternative media outlets broke the stranglehold of progovernment news reporting (Gonzalez 1988). Their daily coverage of the Aquino assassination trial allowed for a "diversity of viewpoints that went beyond the official version of events," and "provided opinion leadership in reporting and interpreting events beyond the official story" (Gonzalez 1988, 40–41). Because of their affiliation with the Catholic Church, both platforms also served as informal leaders of the alternative press, such as *Malaya*, a weekly English-language tabloid, and *Philippine Collegian*, a University of the Philippines student paper (Siriyuvasak 2005). They led boycotts of the mainstream presses, causing their sales to drop and forcing them to shift their pro-Marcos editorial stances. With at least some allies in the media, opposition elites could be relatively more assured that their campaign messages would get out to the masses to boost electoral turnout (Rosario-Braid and Tuazon 1999).

Taken together—the lack of an ideological divide, the structure of the joint ticket contest, NAMFREL's strong deterrence against electoral violence, vote buying and fraud, and a clear shift in support from Marcos to the opposition by the middle class and by the Philippine church—all strongly indicated to opposition elites that aggregating votes among the supporters of the two leading opposition party leaders would be a non-issue. Laurel and Aquino, as staunch Roman Catholics and members of the same political class traveling in the same circles as other economic elites, would have been well aware of the robust backing that they would potentially receive if they cooperated with each other. Although any electoral campaign against Marcos's financial and coercive war chest would be a monumental task, cross-party strategic voting was one less doubt they had to contend with.

Conclusion

The opposition's confidence in mass support amid the backdrop of a crumbing Marcos regime was fulfilled during the two-month campaign period in the run-up to the February 7, 1986, presidential elections. The church delivered its support most symbolically via Cardinal Sin, who issued two pastoral letters urging people to vote, as "participation in the election was not just a political act, but was also an act of Christian faith, requiring high standards of honesty and integrity" (Youngblood 1990, 199). NAMFREL's operations and US election observers thwarted the most severe cases of electoral manipulation, although they could not prevent the election commission from padding Marcos's vote totals in regions where they had less access (Thompson 1995, 150–51). Ultimately, the official count gave Marcos 54 percent of the vote, a figure disputed by NAM-FREL, the Catholic Bishops' Conference, and election observers from the United States (Bonner 1987, 410–17). Dispute over the degree of electoral fraud and the legitimacy of the official results resulted in a limbo in politics for the rest of the month of February, until a defection in the Philippine military in late February decisively swung the political momentum in favor of the opposition. The People Power Revolution culminated in the gathering of millions of Filipinos in the streets of Manila in support of the rebel army (Thompson 1995, 155–61). Marcos and his entourage finally fled the Philippine presidential palace on four American helicopters to Clark Air Base, and then proceeded to Guam and Hawaii, where the Reagan administration granted asylum. Marcos would never again set foot in the Philippines.

Such a sequence of events would have been highly unlikely if Aquino and Laurel had not formed an alliance on December 11, 1985. They were able to do so because they recognized that electoral victory was possible and its potential benefits realizable, even if coordination on a joint ticket entailed costly compromises. Their perception of their chances of electoral victory was informed by clear indications of Marcos's accelerating vulnerability, as well as acknowledgment of each other's mutual dependency supported by rich information regarding their relative electoral strengths and weaknesses. Confidence with regard to cross-party strategic voting for a joint alliance enhanced perceptions of the opposition's chances of victory. When weighed against a strong chance of defeating Marcos to revive Philippine democracy and end economic misery, the costs of mutual concessions—for Aquino, running under the UNIDO banner while relinquishing autonomy to nominate a sizable portion of a future cabinet; for Laurel, surrendering the presidency and a chance to be a head of state—paled in comparison. The alternative scenario of no opposition alliance appeared to be a guaranteed disaster. Neither Aquino nor Laurel believed they could win without an alliance.

5 | Opposing Roh

Opposition Fracture in South Korea

The Philippines was not alone in its experience with democratization in East and Southeast Asia near the end of the Cold War. Another country was South Korea. In fact, opposition elites in South Korea were particularly attuned to events unfolding in the Philippines. Afterall, South Korea's autocrat Park Chung Hee had declared martial law in October 1972, just one month after Ferdinand Marcos did so in the Philippines. His move caught the American diplomats in Seoul by surprise just as Marcos's declaration did in Manila.[1] Like Marcos, Park was already sitting president of the country when he declared martial law, having seized power in a military coup in 1961. Also like Marcos, Park dissolved the legislative assembly, suspended elections, and imposed press controls, among other measures.[2] He cited a "rapidly changing international situation" that jeopardized North-South reunification talks as the primary reason for martial law. Yet, unlike Marcos, Park would not see the collapse of his own regime. In October 1979, he was assassinated by the head of his intelligence agency, Kim Jae Kyu. The ensuing power struggle saw General Chun Doo Hwan emerge victorious as the next autocratic South Korean military leader. It is during his rule in the 1980s that we observe the decline of authoritarianism in South Korea and the growing space for opposition collective action.

As this book has argued, opposition elite assessments of regime vulnerability alongside their perceptions of mutual dependency jointly influence calculations about the electoral benefits of coordinating in opposition alliances. This chapter details the plentiful empirical evidence for these two variables in explaining the failure to form an opposition alliance in South Korea for the 1987 presidential elections. The chapter's first section details how opposition elites saw at least four signs of the regime's impending fall, similar to their counterparts in the Philippines. The opposition New Korea Democratic Party's surprising gains in the February 1985 legislative elections; recurring mass protests on the streets backed by the Christian churches; the regime's capitulation in late June 1987, allowing direct presidential elections; and the open support by the United States for free and fair elections, all bolstered confidence that the military regime was ready to be toppled in elections in December 1987.

Yet this chapter's second and third sections detail how, unlike their Philippine counterparts, dueling opposition party leaders found little agreement over their mutual dependency, particularly because of a lack of ex ante information about their relative strengths and weaknesses. The lack of past election results, the absence of polling data, and the inability of mass rallies to draw clear conclusions about the relative electability of Kim Dae Jung and Kim Young Sam fostered their mutual belligerence about being the sole opposition nominee. In addition, because both Kims drew their support from different regions of the country, together with a lack of electoral experience, there was significant uncertainty about the degree of vote transfer that would occur even if one candidate was nominated and the other endorsed him. Consequently, the two candidates insisted on their own superior candidacy. They would both go on to claim that their prospective victory in the presidential elections would not depend on cooperation between them. In other words, each could win on his own. Eventually, the military-backed Roh Tae Woo prevailed in the December 1987 elections with only 37 percent of the votes. Kim Dae Jung and Kim Young Sam obtained 27 percent and 28 percent vote shares respectively.

Just as in the previous chapter on opposition alliance formation in the Philippines, a timeline of key events will help readers familiarize themselves with events leading up to the December 1987 presidential elections. The most critical events that propelled the opposition to pressure Chun Doo Hwan to end his autocratic rule involved Kim Dae Jung's return to South Korea, the opposition party's surprising and unprecedented electoral gains in February 1985, the toppling of the Marcos regime in the Philippines in February 1986, key public instances of American support for political liberalization in February and June 1987, and mass street protests sparked by the deaths of university students in January and June 1987.

Accelerating Regime Vulnerability in South Korea

When Ferdinand Marcos and his family fled the Philippines on four American helicopters at the end of February 1986, South Korea's opposi-

TABLE 5.1. Timeline of Key Events in South Korean Politics in the 1970s and 1980s

Date	Event
October 1972	Park Chung Hee declares martial law.
October 1979	Park Chung Hee assassinated.
December 1979	Chun Doo Hwan emerges as new autocratic South Korean leader.
May 1980	The military represses the Kwangju uprising, leaving hundreds dead.
December 1982	Kim Dae Jung allowed to leave for United States for medical treatment and self-exile.
February 1985	Kim Dae Jung returns to South Korea from the United States. Four days later, legislative elections held in South Korea. The opposition party, the New Korea Democratic Party (NKDP) makes surprising, unprecedented gains.
February 1986	The People Power Revolution topples Marcos in the Philippines.
January 1987	Seoul National University student Park Jong Chul dies in police custody. Mass protests recur.
February 1987	Gaston Sigur, US assistant secretary of state for East Asian and Pacific affairs, gives public speech in support of South Korean democratization.
April 1987	Kim Dae Jung and Kim Young Sam withdraw from the NKDP to form the Reunification Democratic Party (RDP). A week later, Chun Doo Hwan suspends debate on new constitution until after 1988 Summer Olympics. Mass street protests renew.
Early June 1987	Mass protests intensify after Chun Doo Hwan announces Roh Tae Woo as his choice to be South Korea's next president. They also intensify after Yonsei University student Lee Han Yol is seriously injured by a tear gas grenade.
Mid June 1987	Middle-class professionals join in the protests against the Chun Doo Hwan regime.
Late June 1987	South Korean government capitulates and agrees to hold direct presidential elections in concession to the opposition.
October 1987	Within a week of each other, both Kim Dae Jung and Kim Young Sam announce intention to contest for South Korean president. Kim Dae Jung splits from the RDP to form the Party for Peace and Democracy.
December 1987	Roh Tae Woo emerges victorious in the presidential elections with 37 percent vote share.

tion elites saw a hitherto inconceivable scenario for their own country becoming reality in front of their very eyes. They grew excited at the prospect of toppling Chun Doo Hwan's autocratic rule in the forthcoming elections, thereby liberating their people from the grip of a repressive military (Heo and Roehrig 2010, 36). A CIA memorandum surveying and summarizing the latest opinion among South Korea opposition leaders just one month after Marcos's fall bluntly stated,

> Nowhere is attention to South Korean-Philippine parallels more intense than in South Korea itself. . . . Leaders of the staunchly anti-Chun New Korea Democratic Party (NKDP) are openly euphoric over events in Manila. They contend a "domino effect" will soon bring democracy to South Korea. In their eyes, Marcos fell because he was a dictator who did not enjoy the support of the people or ultimately of the United States. Kim Young Sam, who with Kim Dae Jung represents Chun's most prominent opponents, brushed aside US Embassy officers' analysis of the differences between the two situations, stressing that Chun will fall as Marcos did. In a prerecorded rally address on 23 March, Kim Dae Jung urged his countrymen to make South Korea a "second Philippines."[3]

But what exactly were the similarities between the two countries that made South Korean opposition leaders so excited about their chances of electoral victory against the autocratic regime? There were several, in fact (Cumings 2005, 299–301). The first indicator of accelerating regime vulnerability is the opposition's surprising gains just a year earlier in the February 1985 legislative elections, just as the Filipino opposition parties made surprising gains in their May 1984 legislative elections (Choe and Kim 2012). In South Korea, the opposition New Korea Democratic Party (NKDP) won 67 out of the 276 legislative seats, or almost one-quarter of all seats. This was nearly half of the Democratic Justice Party's (DJP) number of seats, and was more than double its own expectations (Kim 1986, 69). Even more surprising, the NKDP managed to obtain a 29.2 percent vote share, which was just six percentage points below DJP's 35.3 percent (Koh 1985, 888). Government-approved and government-affiliated opposition parties won the rest of the votes and seats. The DJP only managed to obtain an outsized number of legislative seats due to a heavily manipulated, mixed electoral system that rewarded the political party winning the largest number of district seats with an oversized share of the proportional representation seats. Regardless, NKDP's *unexpectedly strong showing . . .*

exposed the depth of popular antipathy toward Chun," concluded a CIA report.[4] Koh (1985, 883) opined that the results "*stunned all observers* and may well turn out to be a significant milestone in South Korea's tortuous path to democracy."

Further similarities between South Korea's February 1985 legislative elections and the Philippines' May 1984 legislative elections entrenched the Korean event's status as a significant milestone. As in the Philippines, the elections revealed that a significant section of South Koreans were dissatisfied with Chun's repressive, autocratic rule. These mass dissenters responded enthusiastically to the opposition's blunt calls for an end to autocracy. Their overall enthusiasm for antigovernment campaign rhetoric "surprised all observers" (Koh 1985, 885–86). The intensity of the antigovernment rhetoric was due, in part, to Kim Dae Jung's heroic return to South Korea from exile in the United States just four days before the election. Like Benigno Aquino, Kim Dae Jung had been sentenced to death by the autocratic regime for inciting civil unrest. And like Aquino, he had been allowed to travel to the United States for health treatment and self-exile. Prior to his return, Kim Dae Jung sought to play up his similarities with Benigno Aquino.[5] "I hope not to be another Aquino case," he forewarned at a press conference with Californian senator Alan Cranston.[6] "If they turn me into a second Aquino, they [the Korean government] will have to face the same kind of fate as the Philippines," he cautioned in front of an audience of 5,000 at his farewell speech in Los Angeles (Kim 2019, 311). Ultimately, Kim was not assassinated upon his return, as he was accompanied by at least two American congressmen and senior American diplomatic officials guaranteeing his safety. Still, his triumphant return had a similar effect of boosting mass confidence in the opposition. It further increased Kim Dae Jung's stature as one of the leading opposition dissidents of the country, just as Benigno Aquino's death established his widow as the leading opposition figure in the Philippines.

South Korea's February 1985 legislative election results also revealed the degree to which dissatisfied South Koreans were willing to turn out to vote for a united opposition party against the ruling party. Before, government manipulation of the electoral system and harassment of opposition-affiliated campaign workers meant that the opposition's chances of electoral success were slim. At that time, the majority of existing parties were government affiliated, thereby presenting voters with a false choice at the ballot box. Yet, despite the prospect of little material returns, a substantial number of voters still voted for the NKDP. They could be counted as committed democrats who could be relied upon to stick with the opposition.

Furthermore, these NKDP voters were not just supporters of Kim Dae Jung, who was from Jolla province, nor merely supporters of Kim Young Sam, who hailed from Kyongsang province. NKDP found extensive levels of support in the more urbanized, affluent areas of the country, just as UNIDO garnered most support in the urbanized, affluent areas of metropolitan Manila. It was in this election that the urban South Korean middle class finally revealed its political opposition to the military regime (Bellin 2000; Cheng 1990; Cheng and Krause 1991). In South Korea's five largest cities of Seoul, Busan, Taegu, Incheon, and Kwangju, the NKDP outpolled DJP by a ratio of 4 to 3 (Koh 1985, 891). Most significantly, the capital city of Seoul saw NKDP garner 43.3 percent of the votes, to DJP's 23.3 percent. NKDP's ability to mobilize and capture the votes of South Korea's middle class is perhaps exemplified most clearly in Gangnam district, the most affluent, educated, "upper middle class" district in the country. The NKDP candidate Lee Chul, a dissident activist, placed first, with a 46 percent vote share against the DJP's candidate, Lee Tae Sup, an incumbent government minister with a PhD from MIT, who placed third (Kim 1986, 69; Koh 1985, 890).

Opposition elites drew two lessons from the meteoric rise of NKDP a mere month after its birth. The election results first signaled that there was a potential path to victory even with minimal party organization. After all, the results showed that voters clearly recognized NKDP's status as the "true" opposition party linked to Kim Young Sam and Kim Dae Jung, as compared to the other "government approved" opposition parties. Hence, if opposition leaders were to form new political party vehicles for electoral purposes, they could be confident that voters would be able to recognize the change in party affiliation and change their votes accordingly. New party formation and party switching were exactly what happened two years later in 1987.

Second, the results also suggested that further gains could be reaped with a longer period of organization. In the run-up to the elections, Kim Dae Jung was unable to campaign, as he was still under house arrest. Yet the results for the relatively new and inexperienced NKDP were still very encouraging. Hence, in view of Chun Doo Hwan's pledge to hold presidential elections when his term ended in 1988, better organization by NKDP could mean greater pressure on the government to hold direct elections for the presidency via popular vote, rather than indirect elections for presidency via an electoral college. NKDP thus set out to increase its organizational size and capabilities in the immediate aftermath of the elections, just as Salvador Laurel's UNIDO established its position as the leading opposition party in the Philippines after the May 1984 legislative elections. Toward that end, NKDP's leaders sought cooperation with other antigovernment civil society groups, such as church organizations, student groups, and labor unions in the months following its surprising gains in February 1985 (Choe and Kim 2012; J. Lee 2000; N. Lee 2007). NKDP's organizational prominence in parliament also grew significantly in the months after the elections. The collapse of minor parties and their membership's rapid defection to NKDP saw NKDP-affiliated legislators increase in numbers to more than 100 (Koh 1985, 896).

Following the NKDP's surprising gains, hitherto dormant anti-Chun social groups became reinvigorated. This led to recurring, violent street demonstrations—the second indicator of the regime's accelerating vulnerability. A confidential CIA report concluded, "[Demonstrators] sense that Chun's domestic position is weaker as a result of the legislative elections in February and the return to center stage of several outspoken political opponents."[7] In particular, protests led by university students became much more regular. They formed the vanguard of recurring street protests, reprising their role just half a decade earlier when they led protests against Park Chung Hee's regime (Chang 2015, chapter 3; N. Lee 2007). For the entire year of 1985, "There was a total of 3,877 on-campus rallies, demonstrations, and other disturbances, with 46% or 1,792 of these occurring during the first (spring) semester of 1985" (E. Kim 1986, 71). The spring semester's numbers were most alarming. They were more than eight times that of a similar period in 1984 (E. Kim 1985, 365). Most significant was the student occupation of the US Information Service library in downtown Seoul for four days from May 23 to May 26. The university students occupying the library were commemorating the Kwangju massacre in May 1980, which saw several hundred citizens killed when the military repressed mass protestors in the southwestern city of Kwangju (Ch'oe 2006; Katsiaficas and Na 2006; N. Lee 2007). The students also protested against implicit and explicit US support of Chun's actions during the massacre and for his autocratic regime (E. Kim 1986, 71). As a CIA report in the aftermath of the library's occupation concluded, more and more antigovernment critics were beginning to see America's positive relationship with South Korea as an open endorsement of Chun's autocracy, without which his regime would collapse, just like how Ferdinand Marcos enjoyed American support until his downfall.[8] In fact, a recurrent cycle of antigovernment protests followed by government repression became so frequent in 1985 that the CIA became concerned about potential regime change by the end of the year.[9]

The stunning news of Marcos's fleeing to Guam and Hawaii in February 1986 blew new wind into the South Koreans' opposition sails and forced Chun Doo Hwan to reconsider his strategies in dealing with the opposition. During the Philippine elections just before Marcos's escape, the NKDP had already begun a nationwide signature campaign petitioning the government to amend the constitution to allow for direct presidential elections by a popular vote. The campaign was steadily gaining momentum when news filtered through that Marcos had fled the Philippines. "The ousting of the Philippine dictator was a spring breeze to us," claimed Kim Dae Jung (2019, 321). This shocking event prompted Chun to retreat from his repressive stance of clamping down against the NKDP and the petition's signatories (Shorrock 1986, 1195). In a meeting with opposition leaders, he mentioned for the first time that he was agreeable to constitutional amendments, and that the police had overreacted in placing hundreds of opposition party members under house arrest.[10] A transcript of the meeting revealed that Chun himself referred to the Philippines' woes as the result of protracted and unsustainable one-man rule.[11] Chun's retreat from his previously strident stance of no compromise reinvigorated opposition elites. From then on, the ebb and flow of political protests on the streets would coincide with public perceptions of whether the government and opposition were closer or further away from agreement on constitutional amendments (Shorrock 1988). Pressed by continued street protests in major cities, including a particularly violent one in May 1986 in Incheon, for example, the national assembly formed a Special Constitution Revision Committee in late June 1986 to consider the proposed constitutional amendments (E. Kim 1987, 66).

Marcos's downfall inspired not only opposition elites. The South Korean Catholic Church was also stirred by the prominent role of its Philippine counterpart. In early March 1986 just after the collapse of the Marcos regime, the South Korean Catholic leader Cardinal Stephen Kim Sou Hwan gave a rousing sermon to endorse the opposition's call for constitutional amendments for direct elections.[12] Explicitly receiving the cardinal's endorsement of the opposition were Kim Dae Jung, a Roman Catholic, and Kim Young Sam, a Presbyterian, who were in attendance to hear his sermon in the front row of the congregation. Other Christian groups soon got further involved. A week after the cardinal's speech, a National Alliance for Constitutional Reform was formed that included the Reverend Park Hyung Kyu of the Korea Council of Churches, and Reverend Moon Ik Hwan, president of the United Minjung (People's) Movement for Democracy and Unification (UMDU) (Shorrock 1986, 1205–10). The

UMDU itself was a formidable mass organization, consisting of twenty-three anti-Chun groups that represented everyone across the social spectrum, from farmers to poets, journalists, and unionists.

In any case, the South Korean churches' full-throated endorsement of the opposition should have taken few people by surprise. For years under the previous Park Chung Hee regime, South Korean churches functioned as physical and symbolic refuges for antigovernment dissidents, much as in the Philippines (Chang 2015, chapter 4; Hyug 2006). For example, churches and cathedrals functioned as physical sites for meetings to coordinate anti-regime activities, for prayers for the anti-regime movement, and for actual anti-regime demonstrations (Hong 2009, 189). Because of their images as "sacred spaces," the government's coercive forces hesitated to crack down on anti-regime dissidents at these sites. Myungdong Cathedral, the primary site of Catholic leadership in South Korea, was one of the many such physical spaces. Furthermore, protestors and anti-regime critics working within and around these physical spaces found supportive pastors and bishops who too found the repressive tendencies of Park Chung Hee's autocratic regime unjust. By the early 1980s, "Theological self-examination by evangelical churches gradually led to more concern about sociopolitical responsibilities," particularly after the horrors of the Kwangju massacre (Hong 2009, 190). By the mid-1980s, church leaders and student protestors were working in unison against Chun Doo Hwan.

The relentless waves of street protests escalated rapidly throughout 1986 and reached a climax in the spring and summer of 1987 (Han 1988; Heo and Roehrig 2010, 37). In January 1987, revelations about the death of Seoul National University student Park Jong Chol in police custody sparked a new wave of anti-regime demonstrations.[13] The police claimed that the student had drowned as his throat was crushed against the rim of a tub while being held under water during interrogations. An autopsy showed that blood clots induced from electric shock torture had also contributed to his death. Stephen Cardinal Kim Sou Hwan once again lent symbolic legitimacy to the anti-regime protestors, taking advantage of a memorial service for the student to strongly criticize Chun Doo Hwan's government. Subsequently, in April 1987, fresh street demonstrations led by university students broke out. They were protesting Chun Doo Hwan's announcement that he would suspend all negotiations on constitution revision until after Seoul hosted the 1988 Summer Olympics. Chun did so as he thought was taking advantage of the opposition's momentary internal chaos. News had broke that Kim Dae Jung and Kim Young Sam, the de facto leaders of NKDP, announced that they would split away to form a new party called the Reunification Democratic Party (RDP).[14] They did so in protest against Lee Min Woo, the NKDP's formal leader, who had wanted to usurp the influence of the two Kims in forging a compromise on revision of the constitution with Chun Doo Hwan. With their departure, the two Kims brought along with them more than 73 of the NKDP's 90 legislators, the core of the opposition party that had won the largest number of seats in the 1984 legislative elections. In any case, the previously dormant middle-class professionals also joined the student protests in solidarity (J. Lee 2000, 197). A new umbrella antigovernment organization, called the National Coalition for a Democratic Constitution, was formed in late May 1987 (J. Lee 2000, 183–88). It consolidated and coordinated representatives from the UMDU and NKDP, as well as church activists, in response to shocking findings of Park Jong Chol's death under police detention and torture. In the ensuing street protests that pitted more university students against the police, the subsequent death of a Yonsei University student Lee Han Yol brought even more protestors onto the streets for the next three weeks.[15] Lee was struck in the head by a tear gas canister, causing a fatal skull fracture on June 9, 1987. Further news that the DJP and Chun Doo Hwan openly declared Roh Tae Woo, a Chun confidant, as the ruling party's candidate on June 10 for upcoming presidential elections added fuel to the raging fire. By June 18, 1987, "Downtown Seoul looked like a war zone as tens of thousands of demonstrators took control of the streets, overpowering entire units of riot policemen who had run out of tear gas."[16]

Under massive pressure from the recurring and violent street protests, the South Korean government finally capitulated on June 29, 1987. Roh Tae Woo, seizing the initiative as the prospective successor to Chun Doo Hwan, announced a comprehensive package of concessions to the opposition. To the opposition, this was the third clear indicator of the military regime's accelerating vulnerability. Roh agreed to hold direct presidential elections via the popular vote by the end of the year, restored the political rights of Kim Dae Jung to participate in politics, and agreed to restore freedom of the press, among other concessions. This landmark event established the start of a period where the opposition could meaningfully participate in politics and compete against the ruling party, albeit under somewhat biased conditions. As Congressman Stephen Solarz, chairman of the US House of Representatives Subcommittee on Asian and Pacific Affairs, remarked about the South Korean situation at a hearing in the middle of 1987, "It definitely demonstrates, as did the triumph of 'People Power' in the Philippines a year and a half ago, that peaceful political change is possible, and that those who believe they suffer from repression can successfully bring about a real improvement in the political conditions of their existence."[17] A headline from the *New York Times* read, "Bombshell in Seoul: 'People Power,' Korean Style."[18] Frank C. Carlucci, Reagan's national security advisor, concurred. In a memo written for a hastily convened National Security Planning Group meeting one week later among Reagan and his top lieutenants, Carlucci referred to Roh Tae Woo's concessions as "a surprise decision" and "a miracle."[19] Furthermore, he concluded that "the government and the opposition are moving toward the moderate middle ground," and in order to overcome the numerous obstacles to ensure peaceful and orderly democratic transition, "our job is to keep them there."

In the final analysis, as in the Philippines, it was the United States that dealt the decisive blow to South Korea's autocratic regime during the spring and summer of 1987 (Heo and Roehrig 2010, 38–39; D. J. Kim 2019, 336–38; Oberdorfer 2001, 199–210). This was the fourth and final indicator of the regime's accelerating vulnerability. Prior to this period of intensifying mass street protests, the Reagan administration was generally content with using "quiet diplomacy" to gently nudge Chun Doo Hwan toward political liberalization (Nix 1988; Work 2019). There are at least three reasons for this particular diplomatic stance.[20] First, the United States was primarily concerned about preserving America's national security interests in South Korea, with its 40,000 troops facing down the Communist North Korean regime. The safety of American lives and the effective preservation of peace in the Korean peninsula necessitated having a stable, effective, pro-American South Korean government. Second, the Reagan administration was also concerned with preserving America's economic interest. By 1983, two-way trade between South Korean and the United States had reached US$12 billion, which made South Korea one of America's top 10 trading partners and fifth largest market for American agricultural products. Reagan's officials were therefore particularly interested in expanding American firms' access to sell products to Korean consumers, and to have greater investments in the country. Third and finally, Chun Doo Hwan had repeatedly committed himself both in private and in public to stepping down as South Korean president in 1988. There was little reason to doubt his word, save for the open question on how his successor would be chosen. From this perspective, it was unsurprising that President Reagan's overseas trip to South Korea in November 1983 emphasized security relations first, then economic relations, and then finally political liberalization.[21] This sequencing of priorities in the United States' relations with South Korea is reflected in Reagan's speech to the South Korean national assembly. The president first highlighted the two countries' mutual experience in the Korean War, their shared threats of Soviet and communist aggression, Korea's development into one of the fastest-growing economies in the world with American assistance and trade after the war, and America's deep commitment to engendering peaceful negotiations for reunification between the North and the South. The last topic his speech touched on was America's "warm support" for South Korea's "bold and necessary steps towards political development" because "the continuing development of democratic political institutions is the surest means by which to build the national consensus that is the foundation of true security."[22]

But after Marcos's fall in February 1986, "the success in the Philippines caused the Reagan administration to be more aggressive in South Korea" (Fowler 1999, 286). The Reagan administration abandoned its "quiet diplomacy" strategy to rely on *public statements* to put pressure on Chun Doo Hwan for political liberalization (Fowler 1999; Work 2019). These numerous public statements left no doubt in the minds of opposition elites that America was withdrawing its support for Chun and the military regime and was ready for South Korean democratization. The first salvo was launched on February 6, 1987, by Gaston Sigur, the US assistant secretary for East Asian and Pacific Affairs. He gave a landmark speech at the US-Korea Society in New York City signaling the United States' decisive withdrawal of its unconditional support for Chun's rule and its open endorsement of democratization and free and fair elections.[23] After noting South Korea's continued challenges in dealing with North Korea and its swift economic development over the past few decades, he said,

> At present, there appears to be a general consensus among South Koreans of various political persuasions that domestic political practices up to now—however well suited they may have been for a simpler, slower moving past—simply are inadequate to meet Korea's complex present and future needs. . . . It is essential for the future of the Republic of Korea, and for the future of our bilateral relations, that any new constitution, and the laws which support representative government, create a more open and legitimate political system. . . . Regardless of what specific governmental system emerges from the current debate, it surely must reflect elements of openness, fairness, and legitimacy. . . . History demonstrates that to be durable, constitutions must be carefully constructed. They emerge from

compromise and consensus among the major political players, not from violence, abuse of physical force, or obstinate confrontation. Lasting constitutions encompass broad principles, such as free and fair elections in an open atmosphere.

In order to support this new political system, Sigur noted that the United States would undertake three actions. First, it would work with South Korea's armed forces "to maintain and strengthen the military shield which protects the country." This explicitly suggests that the United States wanted the military to turn its focus away from domestic intervention into external protection. Second, it would continue to support open international trade with South Korea. Finally, it would "continue to urge accommodation, compromise, and consensus" among all the political actors to come to an agreement on the constitutional amendments. This speech would henceforth guide American policy for the next year until Chun's transfer of power to another person. It formed the central part of the discussion between Secretary of State Stephen Shultz and Chun when the two met in Seoul in March 1987,[24] and was the guiding policy document for National Security Council meetings headed by Frank Carlucci, the national security advisor at that time.[25]

While remarkable in and of itself, Sigur's speech summarizing American assessments and the purported actions America would take appears more familiar when read alongside the numerous speeches that Kim Dae Jung gave at churches and university campuses throughout America during his period of exile just four years earlier.[26] In these speeches, Kim would pontificate on the long history of Korean political development as well as its relationship with America, dwell on the role of Christianity and its relationship to human rights, and speculate on what it would take for further political liberalization. Near the end of these speeches, he would almost always ask for American support for South Korean democracy. On one occasion in a speech at Emory University on March 31, 1983, he concluded his speech by saying,

We are not asking the United States to fight in our stead or directly to interfere with the Chun Doo Hwan dictatorship. We only want the United States to provide us moral support as a democratic ally and to *encourage the Korean military to devote itself to national defense rather than to political maneuvers.* Above all, we want the United States to *recognize human rights and democracy as the essential building blocks of Korean stability and security.* We want our

American brothers and sisters in this room to impress upon their government that security without human rights and democracy is a political alchemy that has never worked. This will be your contribution to our struggle for human rights and democracy in Korea. We can do the rest. (Emphasis mine)

This ending was replicated in speeches at Princeton University, the University of Washington, the World Affairs Council in San Francisco, and the University of California, Berkeley. It appears that Sigur was inspired by a few talking points from Kim's speeches, which Kim himself would surely have recognized. As James Kelly, the resident Asia expert on the National Security Council, wrote in a memo to Frank Carlucci when attaching a copy of Sigur's speech, "We're in contact with *every element of government and opposition* in Korea. *Koreans know what our policies are.*"[27]

The United States' insistence that South Korea not mobilize the military to repress protestors but compromise with the opposition on democratic reforms is also revealed in America's diplomatic messages to Chun Doo Hwan during the mass street protests in June 1987 (Greene 1988). On June 19, 1987, newspapers reported that Ronald Reagan had sent a private letter to Chun warning him not to use repressive measures or declare martial law in response to the growing number of protests and demonstrations.[28] This letter was in response to intelligence assessments suggesting that Chun Doo Hwan was mobilizing the military to repress protestors (Adesnik and Kim 2008, 24–26). With protests escalating, Assistant Secretary of State Gaston Sigur was sent to South Korea to meet both government and opposition leaders and to deliver the letter to Chun. In his meeting with Chun, Sigur emphasized America's support for a "peaceful and orderly transition."[29] The same message of "no martial law" was delivered to the DJP's presumptive presidential candidate, Roh Tae Woo, in no uncertain terms.[30] Upon his return, he issued a press statement from the White House after a meeting with President Reagan, declaring unequivocally, "Military steps offer no solution."[31]

Once again, as in the Philippines, the entire series of events leading up to opposition coalition talks in the months prior to the December 1987 presidential election left little doubt in opposition elites' minds that Chun's autocratic regime was on its last legs (D. J. Kim 2019, 329–40). The United States had publicly signaled its support for democratization as well as free and fair elections. Ordinary citizens, from farmers to students, and from intellectuals to urban workers, were clearly in support of the opposition. South Korea's churches had lent symbolic legitimacy to the anti-regime protestors, just as nuns, pastors, priests, bishops, and cardinal had played pivotal symbolic and organizational roles in Marcos's downfall. The government's capitulation on June 29 was also a clear public signal of defeat. With the impending direct presidential election, promised as part of the overall package of concessions, the CIA concluded that "the *ruling party and the military face the real possibility of losing power* . . . the opposition has its *first chance* to gain the presidency in 16 years."[32] All there was left to do was for the opposition to unite behind a leader to compete against the military regime's candidate.

Lack of Mutual Dependency among Opposition Leaders

Because Roh Tae Woo agreed to grant longtime dissident Kim Dae Jung political amnesty as part of the overall package of concessions, June 29, 1987, would also mark the start of jostling between Kim Young Sam and Kim Dae Jung over who would be the opposition's candidate to contest against the military-backed Roh. In fact, some speculate that Roh granted Kim Dae Jung political amnesty to spur him to challenge Kim Young Sam for the mantle of opposition leader and split opposition votes (Heo and Roehrig 2010, 39–40). Regardless, almost immediately, newspapers began reporting that the two Kims were divided and coy over who would be the sole opposition candidate.[33] After breaking away from the NKDP, the formal opposition party in the legislature, earlier in April 1987, the two Kims were nominally joint leaders of the newly formed opposition RDP. Kim Young Sam was generally perceived to be the more moderate, traditional opposition politician who had led the talks with Roh, pressuring him for direct presidential elections. Kim Dae Jung, on the other hand, was generally perceived to be the more radical dissident, with formidable oratory skills, having once almost won against the military dictator Park Chung Hee in the 1971 presidential election.[34] Despite these differences in perceptions, however, an analysis of their ideologies with regards to democratization, foreign affairs, and socioeconomic issues revealed no clear variation in their positions (Cho 2000, 344–46).

At the outset, it was clear to the two leaders, their supporters, and the general public that cooperation to find one single candidate for the impending presidential election was important to enhancing their chances of victory. Political analysts noted that the two Kims "must reach agreement on policy and a presidential candidate if they want to win political power."[35] If they failed to agree, they would "condemn themselves to political limbo" because two opposition candidates on the ballot would "considerably increase" Roh's chances of victory. A September 23 poll by a leading Korean newspaper of 500 randomly selected Seoul residents also found that 69 percent of respondents "believed it was *necessary for the RDP to select one unified presidential candidate*," with 73 percent of respondents preferring an "early decision" (Cho 2000, 328). Corroborating this public sentiment were Kim Young Sam's own words when he explained that "the public expectation . . . for the nomination of one [opposition] candidate as soon as possible" was the reason why he had met Kim Dae Jung 10 times over six weeks to negotiate (Oberdorfer 2001, 214). Kim Dae Jung expressed similar sentiments, stating that "Kim Young Sam and I will cooperate in the face of military dictatorship. At the last minute, if it is needed to defeat the military dictatorship, we will make whatever sacrifice is necessary to make sure that the ruling party cannot win."[36] In his autobiography, Kim Dae Jung (2019, 340) also confirmed the necessity of joint nomination of a single opposition candidate, noting, "I thought the opposition party would have no problem coming up with a unified presidential candidate. I believed Mr. Kim Young Sam's frequent public promises that he would yield to be me as a presidential candidate once I was pardoned and reinstated." Finally, a CIA internal report confirmed that "both recognize that one opposition competitor would wage a far more effective campaign . . . a majority of Koreans disapprove of the Kims' dual candidacies."[37]

Yet, despite acknowledgments that opposition coordination was important, there were at least two further questions to consider. First, was coordinating on a single candidate so crucial that electoral victory was impossible without it? If either of the two Kims considered his chances of winning as already high without forming an alliance, then making a costly compromise by withdrawing as a presidential candidate might not be worth it. I answer this question in the next section on cross-party strategic voting for the two opposition leaders. Second, if coordination required one leader to step aside in favor of the other's candidacy, who should make that costly concession? In this section, I show that, unlike the Philippines in 1986, it was unclear what were the strengths and weaknesses of the two opposition party leaders and, ultimately, who was the leading coalition formateur.

The primary problem that caused uncertainty and disagreement over the contending candidacies of Kim Dae Jung and Kim Young Sam was the lack of clear public information about their relative electoral strengths and weaknesses. This severely undermined any notions of their mutual dependency. Unlike in the Philippines, where UNIDO was clearly a more organized opposition party and Corazon Aquino was clearly a more popular opposition leader, any publicly available information on the relative strengths of the two Kims in 1987 South Korea were vague, unreliable, and noncredible. At best, they revealed a stalemate between the two of them.

The first uncertainty they confronted was the absence of immediate past electoral results. After splitting from the NKDP in March 1987, the two Kims were the de facto coleaders of the RDP. Kim Young Sam formally headed the RDP, while Kim Dae Jung was nominally the party's adviser, as he was still under house arrest. As a newly created political party, the RDP was simply a faction of opposition elites with unclear linkages to the broader masses of anti-regime voters. The surprising gains of the newly formed NKDP in the February 1985 legislative elections had a hand in bolstering the two Kims' faith in their new political party. But whether this confidence and assumption were accurate or misplaced could not be reliably determined. No one knew whether the NKDP's mass support would simply switch to the RDP. Corroborating this lack of information about how voters would behave was a CIA intelligence assessment report in November 1987, just one month ahead of the elections.[38] It noted that "because open elections are the exception rather than the rule in Korea, *we lack an accurate record of the election behavior of well-established as well as new constituencies.*" Furthermore, the report mentioned that "against the backdrop of South Korea's changed electorate in 1987, both the government and *the opposition still appear to be a considerable distance from understanding where among the voters their strengths and weaknesses lie.* Their problems on this score are basic, in our view. Korean politicians generally have little experience in open election competition." This conclusion confirms that Kim Dae Jung and Kim Young Sam, alongside Roh Tae Woo himself, lacked reliable information about their relative electoral strengths and weaknesses.

Even if one could assess the relative popularity of the two Kims based on deeper historical evidence, there appeared to be a general stalemate between them. More than 15 years earlier, for the previous direct presidential elections held in 1971, an intraparty ballot was held to select the opposition party's candidate against the autocrat Park Chun Hee (H. Kim 2011, 16–17). Kim Yong Sam received 421 out of 885 total votes cast in the first round, just 22 votes shy of the number required for a simple majority to secure the nomination. Kim Dae Jung polled 382 votes. In the second round of polling, however, Kim Dae Jung surged ahead and secured the nomination, with 458 out of 884 votes cast, trumping Kim Young Sam's

410 votes. This event established their deep-rooted mutual animosity and entrenched general perceptions of an even split in their support among fellow elites. Additionally, US analyses of the opposition prior to opposition alliance negotiations also corroborated the leadership impasse. A Department of State Bureau of Intelligence and Research report in March 1986 highlighted that leadership problems were hobbling the opposition, "with Kim Dae Jung and Kim Yong Sam competing for predominant influence in the New Korea Democratic Party (NKDP) below the surface show of cooperation."[39] In April 1986, merely a year before the 1987 presidential elections, an American embassy telegram noted that "*the NKDP has been weakened by factional infighting* and the perception that Kim Dae Jung and Kim Young Sam were manipulating the party for their own interests . . . the NKDP was in some disarray and disrepute, *torn by conflicting orders from the two Kims, reversing itself repeatedly* over a number of issues."[40]

A second uncertainty further undermined coalition-building efforts—the lack of public opinion polling data. South Korean law in 1987 banned the publication of surveys soliciting the public's political preferences.[41] The two Kims, therefore, possessed very little clear and reliable information on who was more popular among which socioeconomic groups. Neither of them could accurately assess if his prospects for defeating Roh depended on coordination with the other. Consequently, each candidate sought to bolster his own identity as the superior opposition candidate through public rallies. As Cho (2000, 346–47) concluded, the two Kims had "strong incentives to organize larger mass rallies to *prove relative popular strength*, especially *because of the predicament of the high uncertainty that the public announcement of opinion poll results was legally prohibited.*" Saxer (2002, 71) corroborated this assessment, noting in his interview with a senior adviser to Kim Dae Jung that "the candidates and their followers *basically measured support by estimating the numbers of people at the rallies.*" If these public campaigns leaned decisively one way or another, with a clear leader as in the Philippines, negotiations could have been more productive. Unfortunately, the public posturing by both opposition leaders in the months between July 1987 and December 1987 revealed an even contest between them.

In September 1987, for example, Kim Dae Jung sought to assess and demonstrate his superior popularity by returning to his home province in South Jolla, touring Kwangju, Mokpo, and Hauido Island. In his own words (2019, 341), "There were many purposes for my visit, but *most of all, I wanted to gauge public opinion there.*" His return to Kwangju turned out to be "one of the largest street rallies ever held in South Korea," attended by "hundreds of thousands of people."[42] Visits with massive crowds in Daejeon, Incheon, Gyeonggi, and Cheongju bolstered his assessments of his popularity. Kim (2019, 342) concluded, "I could affirm the Korean people's constant support for me in those places and felt it was my duty not to ignore it." In the months thereafter, Kim also touted his superior candidacy following endorsements from university students and professors, religious groups, and a civil society group, the National Coalition for Democracy and Reconciliation (D. J. Kim 2019, 344). In a tit-for-tat response, Kim Young Sam returned to his hometown of Busan one month later, rallying "hundreds of thousands of supporters" in "one of the largest political gatherings" in the country's second largest city.[43] His intention to signal his superior candidacy and pressure Kim Dae Jung to concede was clear during the rally: "I've done my best to achieve a single candidacy, but I've not done it. *But now is the time and place to demonstrate the need for a single candidate.*"[44] Still, when the two opposition leaders organized rallies in Seoul, both candidates drew similarly large crowds of more than a million people (Cho 2000, 347).[45]

Spurred by the impasse, both candidates tried a different strategy. Each held public rallies in his rival's home base (Cho 2000, 352). Kim Dae Jung organized campaign events in Busan and nearby Taegu, while Kim Young Sam campaigned in Kwangju and nearby Yeosu. The objective was to turn out and demonstrate latent support in areas where they were thought to be weak. Yet these moves deepened the disagreement between the two leaders about their relative electability. Kim Dae Jung was pelted with stones and eggs in Taegu by Kim Young Sam's supporters.[46] Those supporters also smashed Kim Dae Jung's hotel windows and wounded his aides in Busan.[47] In turn, when Kim Young Sam tried to stage a rally in Kwangju, he was shouted down as "stones and eggs rained onto the stage."[48] Kim Young Sam's aides also had to use plastic shields to protect him from stones and objects thrown toward him as he traveled in a motorcade to Yeosu.[49]

As election day drew closer, ordinary citizens, hungry for unity, grew desperate. Civic society groups that had organized mass street protests in the spring and summer now issued statements urging the two Kims to coordinate behind one single leader (Cho 2000, 329–32). Two students immolated themselves in protest against the split between the two Kims.[50] Hundreds of students protested by occupying the campaign headquarters of the two candidates. As in the Philippines, South Korea's Catholic leader, Cardinal Kim Sou Hwan, was enlisted as a mediator. But his credibility was limited in that Catholics were a minority in Buddhist-majority South Korea, and smaller in number than Protestants (Cho 2000, 336–37). In a bizarre twist of fate, even the incumbent-backed Roh Tae Woo urged the two Kims to field a single opposition candidate against him, if only to reduce the violence within the opposition's ranks.[51] Yet both Kims remained belligerent. Each declared that he was the more viable candidate. At coordination talks to select a single candidate, Kim Young Sam "reportedly argued that he was the better choice because he is the party president."[52] Kim Dae Jung countered by saying that he was the elder and was "more popularly identified as leader of the anti-Government movement."

The public rivalry and posturing between the two Kims masked the intense private negotiations that were occurring behind closed doors, particularly in late September and early October 1987. Kim Dae Jung's autobiography provides some details of varying forms of selection procedures that the two leaders considered and the concessions they proposed to each other (D. J. Kim 2019, 340–49). At first, Kim Dae Jung appeared amenable to withdrawing his candidacy. He recognized that Kim Young Sam was a more moderate candidate whom the South Korean military would have less misgivings working with. Kim Dae Jung therefore proposed that in return for withdrawing he "be given the authority to appoint chief organizers for the 36 yet-to-be-founded district party chapters" for the RDP (D. J. Kim 2019, 342). He reasoned that control over the RDP was adequate compensation for giving up the presidency. But his proposal was rejected. Kim Dae Jung then proposed to open the nomination process to opposition supporters, either via an intraparty ballot or via televised debates and joint campaign tours. These selection procedures too were rejected by Kim Young Sam as being too risky for his own chances of nomination (Cho 2000, 333–34). A neutral arbitrator, Kim Byung-Kwan, chairman of the *Donga Ilbo* newspaper then proposed to allow Kim Young Sam to choose first between being the party president or being the presidential candidate. Although Kim Dae Jung agreed to this formula, Kim Young Sam rejected it, for reasons unknown. Another idea was floated to have one Kim be nominated for president first in 1987 and the other nominated in the next presidential election five years later (Cho 2000, 335–36). But uncertainty over who should be the candidate first and who second led to an impasse. When news broke that Kim Dae Jung was defecting from the RDP to form his own political party, Kim Young Sam, in a last act of desperation to keep him in the fold, finally agreed to Kim Dae Jung's original proposal that he have the power to appoint the leaders of the RDP's district party chapters. But it was too late.

Uncertainty and Disagreement over Cross-Party Strategic Vote Transfer

Beyond the uncertainties and disagreement over opposition leadership driven by the lack of information of their relative strengths and weaknesses, there were also strong reservations about the degree of vote transfers among their supporters even if one candidate withdrew and endorsed the other. This deepened the animosity between the two Kims and diluted any notions of mutual dependency. Kim Dae Jung defected from the RDP near the end of October 1987, just under two months before the mid-December elections, to create his own political party, the Party for Peace and Democracy. He reasoned that the compromises required to build a pre-electoral alliance were simply not worthwhile. Moreover, based on his own assessment, he had a path to electoral victory even in the absence of an opposition alliance.

The first factor that reduced confidence in the potential level of vote transfers in the case of an opposition alliance was the new electoral system—direct presidential elections among competing candidates with no joint ticket with vice-presidential candidates. This was part of the new constitution that was passed through a public referendum on October 27, 1987. Unlike in the Philippines, this one key institutional difference significantly reduced the prospects for strategic voting among opposition supporters, all else equal. If the opposition leaders formed an alliance with only one candidate on the ballot, they would be more uncertain about drawing the support from the followers of their rival, as compared to the Philippine case, where both opposition leaders were on the ballot. In other words, Kim Dae Jung would have had less confidence that he would be able to win the votes of Kim Young Sam's supporters and vice versa, as compared to Corazon Aquino's confidence that her joint ticket with Salvador Laurel would pool the support of both candidates.

Perhaps more importantly, the second factor that decreased confidence in the prospective degree of cross-party vote transfers was the different regional support bases of Kim Dae Jung and Kim Young Sam. As previously mentioned, Kim Dae Jung hails from South Jolla province, which is in the southwestern region of the Republic of Korea, whereas Kim Young Sam is from South Kyongsang province, within the southeastern region of the country. Theoretically, varying regional bases of support could complement each other if partisanship trumped regional identity. In other words, if voters placed stronger weight on their identities as opposition supporters than their identities as regional voters, then the votes of opposition supporters from different regions could potentially be pooled for a single opposition nominee. But in 1987 South Korea, *the two dueling opposition leaders perceived regional identity as an electoral cleavage more salient than their partisan identities.* CIA analysts noted that "both ruling and opposition politicians are weighing the question of regional loyalties heavily in their assessments of their candidates' chances."[53] The same report offered no reasons why the South Korean politicians were doing so. It did, however, note the puzzling fact that in a newspaper poll in mid-October voters themselves did not indicate regionalism was a major factor determining their vote choice. Nevertheless, the hostile environments Kim Dae Jung and Kim Young Sam encountered when they visited each other's "hometown" provinces led to doubt about vote transfers. When Kim Young Sam's aides had to use plastic shields to protect him as stones and eggs rained on his motorcade in Yeosu, all hopes of drawing the support of Kim Dae Jung's supporters were effectively dashed.

In fact, regional voting cleavages were perceived to be so strong approaching the 1987 presidential election that the two opposition leaders assess their chances of winning if they contested alone as very high. An opposition alliance would therefore make little difference in defeating Roh Tae Woo. "*Each Kim seemed to be convinced that he could and in fact would win the election* when both Kims ran against the governing party candidate, Roh Tae Woo," concluded HeeMin Kim (2011, 13). "The day before the election *both Kim Dae Jung and Kim Young Sam still predicted, against all odds, that they would win*," noted Saxer (2002, 74). The CIA agreed. A top-secret report on the eve of the election concluded that "*both Kim Young Sam and Kim Dae Jung remain convinced they can win the election*, and neither is responding to pressure for a last minute compromise on a single candidate."[54] This mutual belligerence was, in part, fostered by the overconfidence produced by the tremendous crowds at their mass rallies. As Cho (2000, 347) emphasized, "Both the opposition's [*sic*] overly strong emphasis on mass rallies and its apparent success turned out to mislead the candidates, facilitating their wishful thinking on the state of competition. Intense chanting and rallying by ardent followers of Kim Dae Jung and Kim Young Sam in their campaign rallies *made both Kims continue to be confident and reluctant to withdraw for the sake of candidate unification.*"

For his part, Kim Young Sam believed that being a moderate opposition candidate between the conservative Roh Tae Woo and radical Kim Dae Jung would secure him a majority of the voters near the ideological median. "*Kim Young Sam was sure, before the election, that he would win—*

and after the election, that he had actually won it" (H. Kim 2011, 13). Kim Dae Jung had similarly high hopes. "There was no attempt to assess the probability of either Kim Young-sam's or Roh Tae-woo's winning the election because *the Kim Dae Jung camp simply believed they would win*" (H. Kim 2011, 14). In fact, Kim Dae Jung had a particular label for his winning strategy called "Saja Pilseungron" (사자필승론 / 四者必勝論) (Cho 2000, 335; H. Kim 2011, 13–14).[55] To be more specific, Kim Dae Jung's logic was this—Roh Tae Woo and Kim Young San, who were both from Kyongsang province, would split the province's vote share of 7.5 million. Another minor conservative candidate called Kim Jong Pil would win his home province of Chungchong, with 2.6 million voters, and also draw some votes from Roh Tae Woo. Kim Dae Jung himself would sweep the 3.6 million votes of Jolla province while winning a plurality of the northern region's 11.6 million votes. In this manner, Kim Dae Jung believed he had a viable path to victory. His analysis relied on the idea that voting according to regional identities overshadowed all other determinants of voter behavior. He used this reasoning to beat back his own supporters who were asking him to withdraw his candidacy (Cho 2000, 338). Seen from this perspective, vote transfers from Kim Young Sam's supporters to a Kim Dae Jung candidacy were simply not needed. In other words, unlike the Philippines, building an opposition alliance was perceived as neither a necessary nor a sufficient condition for electoral victory.

Why regional identities exerted and continue to exert such a strong influence on voting behavior in South Korea is a question beyond the immediate scope of this book. But it is a question that has been asked and answered by numerous political scientists in recent years. For instance, many scholars attribute the political differences between Jolla and Kyongsang provinces to variation in socioeconomic development. Jolla province has historically been more agricultural than South Korea's other regions, whereas the more industrialized Kyongsang province has the advantage of having Busan as a major city of trade and commerce. As a result, farmers from Jolla province are likely to vote for a different candidate than manual workers and professionals in Kyongsang province. These differences in socioeconomic development can be traced back to regional differences over a thousand years ago, and persisted up to the 1980s due to social and family rivalries within the autocratic regime itself (Hong 2009, 204–5). But, as David Kang (2003) notes, despite their socioeconomic differences, pre-1987 voting differences between the provinces were fairly marginal. The two provinces provided very similar levels of support to the ruling DJP. Instead, regional antagonism and voting only emerged during 1987's presidential election and thereafter. Moreover, Woo Chang Kang (2016) argues that regional voting in South Korea actually reflects voters' "sophisticated" assessments of regional economic change rather than more "primordial" views of regional identity. In his view, regional voting is actually economic voting at work.

Even more, the legacy of repression of the Kwangju uprising in 1980 could be another plausible reason why regional cleavages appeared to trump the authoritarian-democratic cleavage. The large-scale suppression of the Kwangju protests that year led to almost 500 dead and close to 3,000 wounded, marking the incident one of the most horrific and contentious events in South Korea's political history and memory (Ch'oe 2006; Greitens 2016, 256; Katsiaficas and Na 2006). It has been called "Korea's Tiananmen nightmare in which students and young people were slaughtered on a scale the same as or greater than that in 'People's' China in June 1989" (Cumings 2005, 263). Most importantly, as Greitens highlights (2016, 255–58), most of the soldiers involved in the brutal suppression of the Kwangju protestors were from Kyongsang province. This led to a deep antipathy between South Koreans from Jolla province (of which Kwangju is the provincial capital) and their fellow citizens from Kyongsang province. Come 1987, with democratization "already won" given the regime's numerous concessions, perhaps voters sought partisan cues from their existing social networks and most recent historical memory, leading them to pledge loyalty to their rivalrous regional leaders—Kim Dae Jung for Jolla province and Kim Young Sam for Kyongsang province. What is also empirically true, moreover, is a lack of dense social network ties between Kim Dae Jung's and Kim Young Sam's closest elite supporters (Choi and Hong 2020). If ordinary voters sought cues about whom to vote for from these elite supporters, then the partisan division among the two Kims' elite supporters might have reproduced the same regional division among ordinary voters.

In any case, it is not entirely clear that the authoritarian-democratic cleavage was much less salient in the run-up to the December 1987 elections. Even though voters were perceived to be able to vote more freely than in the past, the conduct of elections were still very much biased toward the incumbent, who continued to hold all the levers of power. One indicator of this is V-Dem's Clean Election Index, which is an aggregate index measuring whether elections are free and fair. The index suggests that South Korea's December 1987 presidential elections were not much different from the February 1985 legislative elections (Lührmann et al. 2020). The score for the former was .44 on a 0 to 1 scale, statistically similar to the score for the latter, at .42. Arguably, South Korean voters were still voting in autocratic elections that favored the dominant incumbent, torn between voting for democracy or for their regional opposition leader.

Moreover, another indicator was in the mode of political campaigning via the mainstream media. Unlike the presence of alternative news media outlets such as Radio Veritas in the Philippines in 1986, South Korea in 1987 did not have a thriving alternative news media industry. Instead, the campaign for the presidency was marked by the prominence of television as the main medium of national communication. In this regard, the two major news broadcasters at that time—the Korean Broadcasting System and the Munwha Broadcasting Company—exerted unusually strong influence on the framing of the elections, as well as perceptions of the competing candidates (Cho 2000, 348–49; Woo 1996). Specifically, these two broadcasters framed the elections as a binary choice between "stability versus disorder." This perspective clearly favored the DJP and the military regime's endorsed candidate, Roh Tae Woo, symbols of incumbent "stability" (Woo 1996, 71). Coverage of his rallies highlighted the campaign's orderliness and support among diverse age groups (Kwak 2012, 27). In contrast, the dueling Kim Dae Jung and Kim Young Sam who motivated so many ordinary citizens to cause protest were the symbols of opposition "disorder." Images of the supporters of the two Kims hurling stones and eggs at their opponent saturated news coverage. Such violent disorder was presented as the opposite to stability. Even more, Roh's speeches were broadcast during prime time slots, and he had more time to answer debate questions than his opponents (Kwak 2012, 27–28).

Conclusion

As in the Philippines, opposition elites recognized that South Korea's autocratic regime was near its end. Recurring mass protests on the streets had forced the incumbent government to make significant concessions, including constitutional amendments. Religious organizations, farmers, middle-class workers, and professionals were firmly behind the opposition. America's gushing endorsement of Chun Doo Hwan's repressive military regime had slowed to a trickle in Ronald Reagan's second term. Direct presidential elections, instituted for the first time in 16 years, thus represented a golden opportunity to bring the military's influence in South Korean politics to a decisive end. But when it came to rallying behind one single opposition candidate to contest against Roh, opposition elites encountered very different electoral uncertainties than their compatriots in the Philippines. Abandoning the previously successful NKDP meant that both Kims were uncertain about their relative electoral strengths and weaknesses. The overwhelming salience of regional cleavages also suggested little prospect of cross-party strategic vote transfers for one candidate. In the face of rally crowds in the hundreds of thousands, both Kim Dae Jung and Kim Young Sam convinced themselves that a path to victory was possible even without an alliance. Coordinating behind one single candidate was too costly for either one of them to contemplate. The two Kims' intransigence allowed Roh Tae Woo to romp to victory, with a 36.6 percent vote share. Kim Young Sam polled 28 percent, while Kim Dae Jung garnered 27 percent of the votes. Their fears of intense regional cleavages affecting voting behavior materialized. Kim Dae Jung swept 88 percent of the votes in his native Jolla province, but only 7 percent of the votes in South Kyungsang province (Cho 2000, 370). Kim Young Sam won more than half of the votes in his native South Kyungsang province, but a mere 1 percent of the votes in Jolla province.

After the elections, the two Kims protested their loss. Both charged that Roh Tae Woo won only because of massive electoral fraud. Ballot boxes were stuffed amid widespread police harassment of opposition supporters, they alleged. Yet, despite some specific instances of electoral malpractice, there was no clear evidence of systemic fraud.[56] Roh Tae Woo's winning margin of close to two million votes was deemed too large to have been the result of ballot box stuffing. Most observers recognized that Roh's victory was due to the two Kims splitting the opposition vote share. When the two Kims found little domestic and international support for their claims of electoral fraud, however, they began to accept their own loss and their own role in failing to build a pre-electoral alliance.[57] In a front-page newspaper advertisement that he took out days after the elections, Kim Dae Jung addressed South Koreans and said, "I don't know what to say to console you for your disappointment, especially when I think that one of the reasons why I failed to change the regime is because I failed to achieve a single candidacy."[58]

Part III

Perceptions of Regime Vulnerability

6 | The Divergent Party Systems in Malaysia and Singapore

The Philippine and South Korean cases vividly demonstrate how opposition party leaders' similar perceptions of regime vulnerability but different perceptions of mutual dependency shape their efforts to construct alliances. But variation in these two variables do not only manifest as cross-national differences. In fact, both variables can fluctuate temporally. At certain times, surprising economic crises and intra-regime elite defections can puncture past perceptions of the regime's dominance (Reuter and Gandhi 2011; Reuter and Szakonyi 2019). At other times, responsive autocrats can implement a variety of innovative reforms to regain their precrisis dominance (Crouch 1996; Miller 2015; Slater 2019; Riedl et al. 2020). An economic depression can be quelled through monetary controls and fiscal stimulation, staving off mass grievances and protests (Pepinsky 2009a). Intra-regime elite defections can be brushed aside by co-opting new economic or social elites, buttressing and expanding mass support. New information can also emerge over time to boost inter-elite clarity of their relative strengths and weaknesses, or raise their expectations of their supporters' propensity to vote for an opposition alliance's jointly nominated candidates.

In chapters 7 and 8, by comparing the historical formation of opposition alliances in Malaysia and Singapore, I demonstrate how perceptions of regime vulnerability and mutual dependency can vary or stagnate temporally, leading to momentary bursts or persistently lack of effort to build pre-electoral opposition alliances. But before launching into those empirical chapters, it is crucial to have at least a foundational understanding of the very different party systems in these two most similar countries. This is particularly important given that the opposition landscape in both countries is fragmented among multiple parties and actors over the *longue durée*, unlike the Philippines and South Korean cases, where there were only two key opposition actors. Descriptively clarifying which opposition actors are major or minor characters and where they stand ideologically relative to the dominant party and to each other helps to guide readers through the empirical analyses that follow.

In short, although Malaysia and Singapore experienced similar histories as British colonies and adopted similar British political institutions after obtaining independence (such as the parliamentary system and its associated plurality electoral system), their party system development diverged significantly after their separation in 1965. In Malaysia, post–World War II ethnic-based mass mobilization resulted in ethnic-based political parties. The dominant ruling Barisan Nasional (BN) coalition competed with opposition parties based on which party would best be able to maintain and advance the Malay-Muslim majority's interests while minimally protecting the civil rights of the country's Chinese and Indian ethnic minorities. This emphasis on ethnoreligious cleavages in electoral competition is not unlike inter-ethnic and religious cleavages in electoral autocracies in the Middle East, North Africa, and some parts of sub-Saharan Africa (Albrecht 2010; Arriola 2013; Bleck and van de Walle 2019; Buttorff 2019; Kraetzschmar and Rivetti 2018; Lebas 2011; Shehata 2012). In sharp contrast, the lack of ethnic-based mass mobilization in Singapore resulted in a classic, centrist dominant ruling party, the People's Action Party (PAP). Through its pragmatic and successful management of the economy, which delivers widespread material benefits to the population alongside institutional control and manipulation, the PAP outcompetes and marginalizes weakly resourced and scarcely credible opposition parties (Chua 2017; Oliver and Ostwald 2018). In this sense, electoral competition in Singapore is primarily driven by nonpolicy, valence perceptions of political parties, a situation not unlike many electoral autocratic regimes in Latin America (Greene 2007; Hagopian and Mainwaring 2005; Levitsky et al. 2016; Magaloni 2006; Murillo and Calvo 2019).

The Party System in Malaysia

The Dominant Incumbent, BN

The Barisan Nasional was Malaysia's dominant ruling coalition from the country's independence in 1957 till its defeat in May 2018.[1] The major component parties in the BN are the United Malays National Organization (UMNO), the Malaysian Chinese Association (MCA), and the Malaysian Indian Congress (MIC).[2] All three are ethnic parties. Only ethnic Malay/Bumiputera are allowed to be party members of UMNO, ethnic Chinese members of MCA, and ethnic Indian members of MIC. Together, the three major parties of the BN ruling Malaysia for more than six decades reflect what Horowitz (1985, 396–410) terms a "permanent multiethnic alliance," or what Case (1991, 2001) calls a "consociational semi-democracy."

Ethnic-exclusive parties in the form of UMNO, MCA, and MIC grew from a rich soil of societal diversity with multiple cross-cutting cleavages and a protracted post–World War II decolonization process. Prior to World War II, Malaya was the leading tin and rubber producer of the world (Chai 1964; Huff 1992; L. K. Wong 1965; Yip 1969).[3] At the turn from the nineteenth to twentieth century, British Malaya produced about half the world's tin and one-third of the world exports of rubber. The expanding tin-mining and rubber industries fueled an insatiable demand for cheap labor met only by massive inward migration of peoples from southern China, the Middle East, British colonial India, and the surrounding Dutch East Indies archipelago. This produced a multiethnic immigrant society with significant intra-ethnic divisions along the timing of their immigration, the regions from which they emigrated, and linguistic and class cleavages. In the immediate post–World War II period, political elites used this fertile raw material to build, experiment with, and mold different types of mass social and political organizations. The latest official population estimates from the government indicate that Malaysia is 69.3 percent Malay/Bumiputera, 22.8 percent Chinese, 6.9 percent Indian, and 1 percent other.[4] The latest census data, from 2010, reveal that 61.3 percent of Malaysians are Muslims, 19.8 percent Buddhists, 9.2 percent Christians, and 6.3 percent Hindus, with the rest a mixture of Taoism, Chinese folk religion, or no religious affiliation at all.[5] Reflecting this ethnoreligious diversity where Malay-Muslims form the majority of the population, UMNO is the dominant component of the BN, always making up the majority of Malaysia's cabinet and overshadowing MCA and MIC.

The first ethnic-based political party to emerge in the aftermath of World War II was UMNO. After the Japanese withdrew from Malaya in 1945, the British colonial authorities introduced the Malayan Union plan to centralize administration and lay a path for prospective decolonization. Yet whatever the intentions of the British, they did not foresee the strident Malay-based opposition to the Malayan Union scheme when it was introduced publicly in January 1946. The Malayan Union's proposals to wrest sovereign power away from the Malay sultans and vest them in the British Crown, and also to extend equal citizenship to non-Malays, "hit the Malay population like political dynamite" and subsequently provoked a vociferous reaction from the Malays (Lau 1991, 130–35; Slater 2010, 77; Sopiee 1974, 21–22; Stockwell 1979, 60–86). "The vigour of the Malay opposition to the Malayan Union astounded all those convinced of Malay apathy," Stockwell (1979, 64) wrote. Sopiee (1974, 23) declared, "The Malays became a race awakened." Opposition to the Malayan Union rapidly gathered momentum behind Dato Onn Jaafar, leader of the Malay Peninsular Movement Johor, and his call for a Pan-Malayan Malay Congress. The Congress, a gathering of the leaders of numerous Malay associations throughout the country, was swiftly held on March 1, 1946. That day saw the establishment of the contemporary ethnic Malay-based UMNO, whose initial objective was to urge the British to repeal the Malayan Union plan, and to deter Chinese political power in any future governance arrangements through limiting the recognition of Chinese citizenship (Slater 2010, 77–79).

For the non-Malays in Peninsular Malaya such as the Chinese and the Indians, the general consensus was that "they cared not whether there was a Union" (Sopiee 1974, 35). Mass political organization among the Chinese only gained momentum with the formation of the MCA in February 1949. The MCA was initially formed as a social welfare organization whose work was primarily directed at the "New Villages" (Heng 1983, 303; Loh 1988, 208–36; Soh 1960, 46; Tregonning 1979, 62). These British-established Chinese settlements sought to resettle Chinese rural squatters during the outbreak of the Malayan Emergency, in which the Malayan Communist Party (MCP) battled the British colonial authorities for Malayan independence. The objective was to segregate the majority of the Chinese population away from the jungle-based MCP guerrillas, and deprive the MCP of food, water, shelter, and coethnic sympathy. About half a million Chinese were resettled into about 440 New Villages within two years (Slater 2010, 87). Initially no more than "prison camps," the lack of public service provision such as schools, roads, water, and sanitation "worsened rather than alleviated squatters' antagonism toward the state" (Slater 2010, 87–89). The MCA stepped into the public service vacuum by raising nearly four million Malayan dollars through regular sweepstakes lotteries, and spent it on building houses, Chinese schools, recreational community halls, pharmacies, and even piped water needed by the New Villagers (Heng 1983, 303; Stubbs 1979, 84, especially n. 37). The Chinese New Villagers thus began to recognize and build loyalty toward the MCA as an anticommunist welfare organization "concerned with the amelioration of social distress" (Heng 1983, 303). "New Villages became staunch bastions of the MCA," Tregonning (1979, 63) remarked.

The combination of UMNO and MCA in an electoral alliance occurred in 1952. As the first ever Kuala Lumpur municipal elections in February that year loomed, there was intense jostling among the political parties over the exact dimension of electoral competition (Fernando 1999, 128–35). Unbeknownst to the national leaders of the MCA and UMNO, the local MCA leader, H. S. Lee, and local UMNO leader, Datuk Yahya Abdul Razak, made an official announcement on January 8, 1952, to jointly contest the elections by coordinating their candidate selection and placement (Fernando 1999, 128–29; Heng 1983, 307, especially n. 32; Roff 1965, 43; Tregonning 1979, 67–68). They agreed to field a total of 12 candidates with only one UMNO-MCA alliance candidate contesting in each electoral district. Subsequently, the elections saw the UMNO-MCA alliance sweep nine out of the 12 seats. This winning formula was soon endorsed by the national leadership. The newly formed, ethnic-based UMNO-MCA alliance expanded rapidly throughout the country through grassroots liaison committees and local branches (Fernando 1999, 135–37). The final tally of all local elections in 1952 and 1953 saw the UMNO-MCA alliance sweeping 94 out of a total of 119 seats contested.

The UMNO-MCA alliance's joint success in electoral victories further induced the MIC to join the alliance in late 1954 (Ampalavanar 1981, 186–92). The result was an electoral coalition based on a mutually exclusive, ethnic-based, and Malay-dominant partnership formalized as the Alliance Party (known as the BN after 1969). In the first ever national-level General Election in 1955, the Alliance campaigned on a united platform of securing full independence from Britain. It tasted overwhelming success by sweeping 51 out of the 52 seats available (Carnell 1955; Tinker 1956). This near perfect sweep by the Alliance "thus established the pattern of communally-based politics in Malaya for many years to come" (Lau 1998, 5–6). Fernando (1999, 137) confirmed that "the results of these local elections established the Alliance as the leading political power and set a trend that the other parties . . . were unable to reverse."

While there are multiple reasons for the BN's prolonged rule from its initial success in 1955 till its demise in 2018, such as its ability to deliver economic growth and be responsive to demands from its citizenry, at least two key foundations of its rule deserve elaboration (Crouch 1996; Pepinsky 2009a, 61–77). First, in terms of ethnoreligious policies, the multiethnic BN coalition was decidedly conservative and relatively centrist (Horowitz 1985, 416–20). Like other dominant ruling parties elsewhere in the world, such as the Partido Revolucionario Institucional (PRI) in Mexico, the BN occupied the broad middle of a unidimensional policy spectrum. This involved, on the one hand, emphasizing the political dominance of Malay-Muslims in the country, with a majority of UMNO cabinet ministers. It also underscored the continuation of Malay-Muslim social dominance through a variety of public policies, such as reserved quotas for Malay-Muslims in the bureaucracy and university education system. Yet, on the other hand, the BN also shared significant powers with and made important policy concessions to non-Malay-Muslims. MCA and MIC leaders were allocated important cabinet positions, such as minister of health and minister of transport. Non-Malay-Muslims were also allowed to retain and manage their own places of religious worship and their own vernacular schools. Because the BN ultimately managed to strike a delicate balance between satisfying the demands of the Malay-Muslim majority and the not insignificant Chinese and Indian ethnic minorities, it found mass support at the ballot box over multiple electoral cycles.

Second, autocratic control over Malaysia's extensive and robust institutions means that they can be easily deployed in service of the BN's electoral interests. Through institutional packing, rigging, and circumvention, Malaysia's successive prime ministers, from Tun Dr. Mahathir Mohamad to Najib Razak, have managed to seize control of the country's judiciary, corporations, election commission, and media networks (Abbott and Givens 2015; Gomez et al. 2018; Slater 2003). In this manner, Malaysia's elections have frequently seen electoral districts being gerrymandered, electoral rules being applied with bias, and voters bought with extensive patronage and induced with partial views of government performance (Dettman and Gomez 2019; Gomez 2016; Ostwald 2013; Pepinsky 2013; Weiss 2013a, 2019). When faced with the BN's formidable grassroots machine, which penetrated deeply into society, at the household level lavishing gifts and encouraging snitching on voters' choices, Malaysia's voters think twice about defecting from the dominant ruling coalition they have grown up with and which has become synonymous with the state. It is hence no surprise that Malaysia's opposition parties have found every election to be a steep uphill battle fought with an asymmetry of resources amid an assortment of strenuous obstacles.

The Opposition Flanks, PAS and DAP

Because the BN appealed to Malaysia's median voter through its relatively centrist ethnoreligious policies, opposition parties grew from the "ethnic flanks" (Horowitz 1985, 410–16). On the conservative, Malay-Muslim right stood the Parti Islam Se-Malaysia (PAS). On the secularist, non-Malay-Muslim left was the Democratic Action Party (DAP).

The PAS is an Islamic party formed in November 1951 under the blessings of UMNO's original leader, Dato Onn, and head of its religious affairs bureau, Haji Ahmad Faud (Mohamed 1994; Noor 2004, 2014). PAS's subsequent leaders, Dr. Burhanuddin al-Helmy, Mohammad Asri Muda, Yusof Rawa, Fadzil Noor, and Abdul Hadi Awang, while each imbuing the party with his own interpretation of Islam, have all never wavered from PAS' stated objective of transforming Malaysia into an Islamic state governed by Islamic principles and law. For PAS, UMNO's moderate stance in sharing power with the MCA and MIC meant that it was not Islamic enough. Indeed, the party focused its campaign cavalry in the 1964 and 1969 general elections on two particular dimensions. First, the party argued that Malaysia's new constitution "was nothing but a sham since it did not specifically adopt 'Islamic principles of administration'" (Mohamed 1994, 91). Second, the party also focused its attacks on the new UMNO president and prime minister, Tunku Abdul Rahman, "whom [it] derided as a 'secular, Westernised' elite and aristocrat" (Noor 2014, 61). It warned Malay-Muslim voters that the real choice in the elections was either "God or the Tunku" (Drummond and Hawkins 1970, 324).

PAS party membership to this day remains closed to non-Muslims. Non-Muslims can only join the PAS Supporters Club—a PAS-affiliated organization with no official influence. Although PAS' leadership is technically headed by its 37-member central working committee, elected by its party members,[6] this committee is overshadowed by the Syura Council, an unelected group of 17 ulama, who directly oversee the committee's work and may overturn decisions made by the committee.[7] The Syura Council is headed by PAS's "spiritual leader," who at times wields as much or even more influence than the PAS president himself. Because of its exclusively Muslim membership and party hierarchy pursuing an extreme policy objective, PAS is an ideological niche party in a multireligious and multiethnic country. But, as we shall see in the next chapter on opposition alliance formation over three decades in Malaysia, PAS has found convenient ways to vary and reframe its emphasis on its stated objectives, depending on its intended audience, at different times.

The other important new opposition party that emerged after 1965 is the Democratic Action Party (DAP). Devan Nair became the leader of the DAP after Singapore's expulsion from the Federation of Malaysia in 1965. Lim Kit Siang, Nair's political secretary, took over as secretary-general of the DAP in 1969, and would remain as the DAP's leader for the next 30 years. Lim's son, Lim Guan Eng, took over as secretary-general in 2004. The DAP was founded on, and still adheres to, a niche ideology, that of a secular democratic socialist Malaysia primarily advocating for the interests of the non-Muslim ethnic minority Chinese and Indians. Its founding manifesto declares that the party is "irrevocably committed to the ideal of a free, democratic and socialist Malaysia, based on the principles of racial equality."[8] As a result, the DAP finds itself diametrically opposed to ethnic-based political parties such as the UMNO, MCA, MIC, and PAS. For DAP, no one race has superior claims of "ownership" of Malaysia, nor can any single religion claim to govern Malaysia based on its own principles.

Unsurprisingly, although membership in the DAP is nominally open to all ethnicities, the party's members and mass support base are overwhelmingly non-Malay-Muslim. Of the DAP's 42 members of parliament at the beginning of 2020, there were two Malays, seven Indians, 32 Chinese, and one ethnic Dayak.[9] Of its 109 elected representatives in state assemblies, there were eight Malays, 14 Indians, one ethnic Kadazan, and 86 Chinese.[10] An "ethnic count" of the combined national total reveals that the DAP's fully elected representatives consist of 78 percent Chinese, 14 percent Indians, and 6.5 percent Malays. This is a highly skewed proportion, considering that Malaysia is about 70 percent Malay/Bumiputera, and just less than one-quarter Chinese. The DAP's 30-strong central executive committee is also highly skewed, with 23 Chinese members.[11]

This situation of a PAS-DAP ideologically polarized opposition was not constant throughout the 1965 to 2018 period, however. PAS was, in fact, a component party of the BN between 1972 to 1977. At that time, the BN was reborn as the successor to the Alliance after inter-ethnic riots between the Malays and the Chinese erupted on May 13, 1969 (Mohamed 1994, 116–29; Noor 2014, 82–85). The objective was to have as large a consociational coalition government as possible in order to resolve inter-ethnic disputes within the government at the elite level, while preserving mass inter-ethnic peace. Regardless, PAS was expelled from the BN in late 1977 after an irreconcilable conflict between PAS and UMNO emerged over the leadership and management over the state of Kelantan (Mohamed 1994, 129–48; Noor 2014, 92–94). Henceforth, from the 1978 general elections onward, "The opposition was now effectively polarized between PAS on the Malay side and the DAP on the non-Malay side, each seeking totally incompatible ethnic demands" (Ramanathan and Mohamad Hamdan 1988, 17)

The Major Defector Parties, S46, PKR, PPBM, and Amanah

In addition to the opposition mainstays PAS and DAP, four other important opposition parties emerged beginning in the late 1980s. They were
Semangat 46 (S46), Parti Keadilan Rakyat (PKR), Parti Pribumi Bersatu
Malaysia (PPBM), and Parti Amanah Negara (Amanah). The first three of
these parties were defections from UMNO, the dominant component of
the BN ruling government. S46 was formed in 1989 after Tengku Razaleigh Hamzah, the minister for trade and industry, failed to oust Tun Dr.
Mahathir Mohamad as UMNO's leader in internal party elections in 1987
(James 1988; Mauzy 1988; Means 1990; Nathan 1990). Prime Minister
Mahathir then moved swiftly to remove Tengku Razaleigh's faction of fellow UMNO leaders completely from the cabinet, which resulted in their
subsequent defection to form S46. The party was named Semangat 46
because its leader, Tenku Razaleigh, wanted to signal to voters that his
newly formed party represented the "true" untarnished UMNO that had
emerged in 1946 fighting for Malay rights. In this manner, he sought to
compete directly with UMNO to vie for the support of centrist, moderate
Malay voters, which was widely viewed as the key to political victory.

The PKR was formed in 1999 under somewhat similar circumstances
(Slater 2003; Weiss 2006). Anwar Ibrahim, deputy prime minister and
Mahathir's heir apparent, was sacked by UMNO after he expressed disagreement with his mentor over his handling of the Asian financial crisis.
His subsequent arrest and abuse in jail on charges of adultery and sodomy
galvanized mass street protests supported by a broad range of civil society
organizations. These protests and the protesters were known as the "Reformasi Movement." Tear gas and water cannons were used against the protesters for the first time in the more than two and a half decades since the
May 1969 ethnic riots. The street protests of the Reformasi Movement
quickly morphed into an electoral movement when Wan Azizah Wan
Ismail, Anwar's wife, set up the PKR to institutionalize and transform
mass dissent into electoral seats. Unlike S46, PKR was, and still is, institutionalized as a multiethnic party, in order to draw support from the multiethnic mass activists of the Reformasi Movement. Despite this, a large
majority of its leaders and electoral candidates are Malay-Muslims, reflecting their centrist ideological position of maintaining Malay-Muslim dominance in a multiethnic society.

Finally, the PPBM was also born out of a UMNO defection in 2016.
This time, it was Mahathir's turn to defect from UMNO (Abdullah 2019b).
After being Malaysia's prime minister for 22 years, from 1981 to 2003,

Mahathir stepped down and passed the baton to Abdullah Badawi, who then passed on the prime ministership to Najib Razak in 2009. In July 2015, the *Wall Street Journal* broke a sensational story alleging that Prime Minister Najib was involved in a global money-laundering scandal involving the state sovereign wealth fund that he had set up, known as 1MDB, or 1Malaysia Development Berhad.[12] Billions of dollars worth of bonds were sold by Goldman Sachs, funneling unprecedented sums of money into Najib's personal bank accounts and his crony Jho Low. The money was allegedly used to finance a vast range of questionable activities, such as the BN's electoral campaign in the 2013 general elections, and luxury shopping sprees by his wife Rosmah. Jho Low, Najib's alleged coconspirator, used his ill-gotten gains to purchase more than US$1 billion in assets: a megayacht worth US$250 million, high-end real estate in Beverly Hills, New York City, and London, a Bombardier Global 500 plane, and artworks by Vincent Van Gough and Claude Monet. He bankrolled the production of the Hollywood movie *The Wolf of Wall Street*, starring Leonardo DiCaprio.[13] Najib's conduct was considered so egregious that Mahathir and Deputy Prime Minister Muhyiddin Yassin quit UMNO and formed PPBM.

The birth stories of Semangat 46, PKR, and PPBM thus different significantly from those of PAS and DAP. The three defector parties were all born from a split in UMNO, the dominant ruling party, in contrast to the organic growth of the latter two parties from polar ends of Malaysia's ethnoreligious cleavage. This explains why PAS and DAP advocate for polarized ideological positions at either flank of the BN, while the three defector parties straddle the ideological middle. In fact, all three parties campaigned on a relatively simple message—they were UMNO without its autocracy and corruption. In other words, Semangat 46, PKR, and PPBM believe in continuing the BN's form of Malay-Muslim-dominant politics alongside power-sharing with ethnic minority parties (the principal ideological cleavage in Malaysian society), but that they can do a better job of implementing economic reforms in the country in order to get rid of the autocratic corruption and cronyism that was stifling the country (Means 1990, 185; Weiss 2006, 130–42; Wan Saiful 2018a, 1).

The final defector party is Parti Amanah Negara (Amanah). The party was formed via a defection from PAS. In 2015, a faction of more progressive leaders in PAS lost the intraparty leadership race to a more conservative faction. Instead of staying within the party, these progressive leaders defected to form their own political party. As progressive Islamists, Amanah's party leadership and members are more accommodating toward

TABLE 6.1. Malaysia's Major Political Parties

Political Party	Acronym	Year Founded	Prominent Leaders	Role	General Ideological Orientation
United Malays National Organization	UMNO	1946	Tunku Abdul Rahman Mahathir Mohamed Najib Razak	Dominant component of BN ruling coalition	Malay dominance with consociational power-sharing with non-Malays
Malaysian Chinese Association	MCA	1949	Tan Siew Sin Liow Tiong Lai Wee Ka Siong	Secondary component of BN ruling coalition	Chinese interests
Malaysian Indian Congress	MIC	1946	Thirunyana-sambanthan Veerasamy Samy Vellu	Secondary component of BN ruling coalition	Indian interests
Parti Islam Se-Malaysia	PAS	1951	Abul Hadi Awang Nik Aziz Nik Mat Fadzil Noor	Opposition mainstay	Conservative Islamists
Democratic Action Party	DAP	1967	Lim Kit Siang Lim Guan Eng	Opposition mainstay	Secular ethnic minorities
Semangat 46	S46	1989	Tengku Razaleigh	Intra-regime defector opposition	UMNO without autocracy and corruption
Parti Keadilan Rakyat	PKR	1999	Anwar Ibrahim Wan Azizah	Intra-regime defector opposition	UMNO without autocracy and corruption
Parti Pribumi Bersatu Malaysia	PPBM	2016	Mahathir Mohamad Muhyiddin Yassin	Intra-regime defector opposition	UMNO without autocracy and corruption
Parti Amanah Negara	Amanah	2015	Mohamad Sabu Salahuddin Ayub Dzulkefly Ahmad	Intra-opposition split	Progressive Islamists

non-Muslims. Wan Saiful (2017, 5) writes that Amanah leaders "acknowledge that it is necessary to respect all views regardless of whether they come from Muslims or non-Muslims, and that all these ideas need to be negotiated within a liberal democratic framework." Why and how such a conservative-progressive fissure emerged within PAS is beyond the scope of this book (see Noor 2003; Case and Liew 2006; Hamayotsu 2010; Noor 2014). Suffice it to say that Amanah's formation in 2015 represented a further fracture of the Malay-Muslim voting block. In the May 2018 general elections, there were five political parties—UMNO, PAS, PKR, PPBM, and Amanah—competing for the support of Malay-Muslims.

Table 6.1 lists all the major political parties that I have discussed thus far. As can be readily discerned, the political parties align themselves on a unidimensional ideological policy spectrum of ethnoreligious politics. On the extreme left, parties like the DAP advocate for secular policies and ethnic minority interests. For the DAP, all ethnic and religious groups should be treated equally under the rule of law. On the extreme right, parties such as PAS advocate purely for Muslim interests. PAS's leaders and members want Malaysia to be an Islamic state with Islamic law. All other political parties fall within these ideological extremes. This party system and its associated ideological spectrum have been stable ever since the centrist, multiethnic, consociational alliance of the UMNO, MCA, and MIC won handsomely in the 1955 nationwide elections and won Malaysia's independence from the British in 1957 (Case 1996; Gomez 2016; Pepinsky 2009b, 2013).

The Plural Party System in Singapore

The Dominant Incumbent, PAP

The People's Action Party (PAP) has been the dominant party in Singapore ever since it won 43 out of 51 parliamentary seats in the first general elections, held while Singapore was still under British colonial rule in 1959. The party maintained its dominance even after Singapore obtained independence from Malaysia in August 1965. It swept all the parliamentary seats in the first four post-independence general elections from 1968 to 1980. Between 1980 and 2020, opposition parties occupied between one and 10 elected seats in the legislature. In other words, Singapore's opposition parties have never won more than 11 percent of all elected parliamentary seats at any point in Singapore's post-independence period.

The PAP's almost complete dominance of electoral politics in the country can be attributed to a number of proximate causes. First, while citizens are free to vote however they choose, elections are not entirely fair. The Elections Department (ELD), for starters, is housed under the Prime Minister's Office.[14] The ELD is staffed by professional bureaucrats, ensuring that all Singaporeans can vote freely in elections with no electoral fraud. But while all political parties are subject to the same electoral rules, the ELD's lack of independence and the absence of nonpartisan oversight implies that there are no guarantees that electoral rules are developed and implemented impartially. The clearest manifestation of this perception of partisanship is the role of the Electoral Boundaries Review Committee (EBRC). Supported by the ELD, the EBRC is responsible for demarcating the geographical boundaries of each single-member constituency (SMC) as well as multimember group representative constituencies (GRCs). Only the prime minister can appoint members of the EBRC.[15] They are typically professional government bureaucrats. Although the government claims that the EBRC determines electoral boundaries by "taking into account population shifts and new housing developments" and disregards past electoral results, there remains, at present, no nonpartisan, independent verification of this claim.[16] In a news article, the former head of the ELD, Lee Seng Lup, reiterated that reasons for electoral boundary changes include "population shifts," but still gave no transparent account of how such shifts were used to craft new electoral boundaries.[17]

In fact, a number of studies suggest that the non-independent status of both the ELD and the EBRC provides significant electoral advantages to the PAP. Tan's (2013, 2018) exhaustive research, for instance, suggests that the manner in which EBRC draws electoral boundaries has helped the PAP manufacture legislative supermajorities. She notes that traditional indices of disproportionality, that is, the gap between vote shares and seat shares, indicate that Singapore's electoral geography produces a disproportionality that is one of the highest, if not the highest, in the Asia Pacific region (N. Tan 2013, 638). This has been achieved through partisan gerrymandering whereby PAP's poorly performing SMCs have been combined into GRCs while new SMCs are created in PAP's strongholds. Evidently, expert coders with the Electoral Integrity Project corroborate Tan's findings.[18] In their latest report, Singapore received an overall score of 53 on a scale of 0–100 for the integrity of its elections (Norris and Grömping 2019). This placed the country 96th out of 167 countries worldwide. The middling score masks significant variation among the index's various components, moreover. While Singapore received very high scores of 75, 76, and 77 for the integrity of the election results, electoral procedures, and voter registration respectively, it received only a score of 14 for district boundaries, 27 for electoral laws, and 33 for media coverage. The low score of 14 for district boundaries rivals Malaysia's similar score of 12 and the United States' score of 16 for that same category, suggesting that Singapore's process for delineating electoral district boundaries is as biased as Malaysia's and the United States' infamously biased processes (Ostwald 2013).

The second factor explaining PAP's dominance of Singapore's electoral politics is its high degree of institutionalization (Kuhonta 2016). By party institutionalization, I refer to two crucial features of political institutions: (a) the extent to which the party has developed routinized rules and procedures through which to make and enforce decisions, (b) the degree to which the party has penetrated society to organize, mobilize, and even control the population (Mainwaring and Scully 1995; Kuhonta 2011, 23–34). On the first count of routinized rules and procedures, the party's cadre membership and its leadership succession systems explain how the party maintains such tight unity and discipline (Abdullah 2019a; N. Tan 2015). Since an intraparty rupture in 1957, the PAP has maintained a cadre membership arrangement. In this system, ordinary members of public can become PAP members, but not all PAP members can become PAP cadres. Only PAP cadres can choose the members of its central executive committee (CEC), the PAP's highest decision-making body. In turn, three panels of PAP cabinet ministers and members of parliament vet, interview, and select recommended PAP members to become PAP cadres. As Abdullah (2019a, 154) puts it succinctly, "Senior party leaders choose the cadres, and the cadres elect the CEC." It is a process not unlike how the pope chooses the cardinals and the cardinals choose the pope (N. Tan 2015, 64). In this manner, the ideological purity and discipline of the party is preserved.

Additionally, the PAP also has a somewhat institutionalized leadership succession procedure (N. Tan 2015, 66–67). In the PAP's nearly six decades of dominance, it has seen the party leadership and Singapore's prime ministership transit twice. The first time involved a transition from the venerable Lee Kuan Yew to Goh Chok Tong, and the second time from Goh Chok Tong to Lee Hsien Loong. In each transition process, a prospective candidate was initially nominated by the full PAP cabinet of ministers. This nominated candidate was then put forward to the PAP MPs for them to demonstrate their support. The PAP's CEC reserved the final authority to approve of the new successor. The consensus candidate to be Singapore's next Prime Minister appeared to be Heng Swee Keat. He had emerged as the PAP's first assistant secretary-general after CEC elections in November 2018, and was subsequently promoted to be deputy prime minister in May 2019.[19] Yet, in April 2021, he announced that he would step aside as the leader of the PAP's fourth-generation leadership team. At the time of writing, the frontrunners to be the next prime minister of Singapore include ministers Lawrence Wong, Ong Ye Kung, and Chan Chun Sing.

The PAP's cadres and leaders are supported by an extensive network of grassroots party members and supporters who penetrate deeply into society (Chan 1976; K. P. Tan 2003; Weiss 2017). These PAP party affiliates participate actively in the government's network of People's Association (PA) branches throughout Singapore, organizing community events such as block parties, reading and learning groups, sports groups, and local celebrations for significant public holidays. These branches include the Community Centre Management Committees (CCMCs) set up within each electoral constituency, Citizens' Consultative Committees that run parallel to the CCMCs, Residents' Committees established in small clusters of public housing blocks, and Neighborhood Committees established in small clusters of private housing estates. As they organize events throughout their communities, the PA's grassroots leaders actively help implement government policies, disseminate government messaging, and collect policy feedback for the government. What is more, parallel to the PA's self-proclaimed nonpartisan community networks are the PAP's overtly partisan Meet-the-People Sessions (E. Ong 2015). In these weekly meetings held in every electoral constituency throughout Singapore, PAP members of parliament and their team of party volunteers meet residents to listen to their concerns. In the process of setting up each week's meeting, processing residents' complaints, drafting appeal letters, and finally sending them off, PAP's party members and supporters socialize themselves into a world of active citizenry and solidarity. This particular social capital is the glue that holds the party together in the lull periods between elections and is the fuel that can be activated when electioneering kicks into high gear. During election campaigns, these party members and supporters are the ones responsible for designing posters, managing social media accounts, setting up rally stages, and organizing residents to attend election rallies. When one talks about the formidable PAP machine, these people are the very machine itself.

The PAP's near complete penetration and influence over state and society, however, does not mean that citizens vote under constant fear of repressive coercion. Instead, come election time, the majority of Singaporeans "sincerely" vote for the PAP. In making this vote choice, ordinary citizens indicate acceptance of the PAP's campaign rhetoric that the party represents stability, meritocracy, competency, incorruptibility, and multiculturalism. By contrast, all other opposition parties represent inexperience, chaos, infighting, and some form of ethnic chauvinism. In other words, unlike Malaysia, where ethnoreligious cleavages are a much more salient dimension of electoral conflict, voters assess political candidates and parties based on nonpolicy valence in Singapore (Oliver and Ostwald 2018, 2020). This ideological stranglehold of valence as the primary dimension of electoral competition is the third most crucial reason why the PAP dominates electoral politics.

By using the concept of valence, I refer to the idea that voters compare and vote for parties and politicians based perceived competency and credibility in delivering goods that are widely acknowledged to have positive value (Stokes 1992; Bleck and van de Walle 2011, 2013; Murillo and Calvo 2019). These goods can include national-level outcomes such as economic growth, rising wages, effective and efficient public services, societal peace and stability, and a robust foreign and security policy that can safeguard national interests (Duch and Stevenson 2008; Nadeau, Lewis-Beck, and Bélanger 2013; Palmer and Whitten 2000). The ability to deliver subnational-level pork, sometimes as a portion of the national budget or as some form of foreign direct investment, is also oftentimes favored by valence-focused voters (Jensen et al. 2014; Malesky 2008; Samford and Gómez 2014). In contrast, Singapore's opposition parties have little or no experience governing. Opposition parties and candidates therefore face tremendous obstacles in trying to exhibit their competency and to deliver these positive goods. They are thus naturally disadvantaged by such a valence-focused electoral environment.

The PAP's ideological hegemony of valence-focused pragmatic competency was not born overnight. The party has used its control over the state to reshape society and order preferences over multiple decades (Slater and Fenner 2011; Oliver and Ostwald 2018). In particular, various policy initiatives and institutional reforms, such as an ethnic quota housing policy, mandatory national service, and education system reforms have been implemented to wean citizens off notions of ethnoreligious conflict and ideological competition (Tremewan 1994; Rajah 2012; Chong 2010). Contests over ideology were deemed impractical and academic. Singaporeans should prize pragmatic competency instead (Barr and Skrbiš 2009; Chua 2017; Kausikan 1997; K. P. Tan 2008, 2012; B. Wong and Huang 2010). When campaigning during elections, therefore, the PAP brandishes its prolific track record since 1959 in transforming Singapore "from Third World to First,"[20] its achievements in upgrading the constituency's public environment during its elected term, as well as the stellar professional and educational background of its individual candidates in campaign paraphernalia. In particular, it almost always touts its fulfilled promise of upgrading of public housing estates, where 80 percent of Singaporeans live. Moreover, voters are also warned specifically that the state controls the funding and planning of such upgrading. If the opposition wins in any constituency, its voters should expect that constituency's upgrading plans to be shoved "to the back of the queue" (Mauzy and Milne 2002, 93–95 and 151). Through the restriction of such localized upgrading in the interim, voters will "pay a price, the hard way," and will have "five years to live and repent" for choosing the opposition.[21]

The Major Opposition Parties, WP, SDP, and PSP

Singapore's valence-focused electoral environment has significant impact on the origins and growth of its opposition parties. Because voters do not necessarily demand and vote for parties with coherent and substantive ideological orientations, unlike in Malaysia, Singapore's opposition parties are largely personality based. Charismatic leaders form their own parties with their small clique of followers. The media focuses on the education and professional qualifications of the opposition candidates, generally ignoring or neglecting the parties' policy proposals. Parties find electoral success by recruiting heavily credentialed candidates. Political accountability is generally determined by whether the elected MPs have delivered on their constituency services, and less on whether significant policy changes have been advocated in parliament or made during their tenure (B. Wong and Huang 2010; Kuhonta 2016).

The oldest opposition party, the Workers' Party (WP), was founded in 1957 by David Marshall, Singapore's first chief minister under limited self-government between 1956 and 1957. Lawyer J. B. Jeyaretnam took up the leadership mantle in 1971, and finally secured electoral victory 10 years later in 1981 in a by-election. His straight-talking manner earned him the ire of PAP leaders, and he soon found himself disqualified from parliament after he was found guilty of misreporting party accounts in 1986. The WP's third leader emerged in the 1991 general elections, when Low Thia Khiang, a Teochew-speaking former Chinese teacher, won in the Hougang SMC. After taking over the leadership of the WP in 2001, he was able to gradually expand the party's leadership team. In 2011, an "A" team comprising Low,

Sylvia Lim, a polytechnic lecturer, Pritam Singh, a budding lawyer, Muhamad Faisal bin Abdul Manap, a social worker, and Chen Show Mao, a world-renowned corporate lawyer, won the five-member Aljunied GRC in an unprecedented electoral victory. They prevailed over the PAP's five-member team, deposing George Yeo, the foreign minister, and Hwee Hua Tan, the second minister for finance and transport, among others.

In emphasizing the desirable qualities of their candidates, the WP mirrors the PAP's focus on valence credentials in their campaigning to voters. In a party-produced documentary promoting the sixtieth anniversary of the WP's founding released in late 2017, almost the entire 50 minutes was spent on promoting the personalities of the WP's numerous prominent party leaders.[22] No time was spent articulating its ideology. To be sure, the WP has begun articulating its economic or social agenda in recent years in lengthy print publications. Its manifestos for the 2015 and 2020 general elections support manpower, education, and social policies that are generally more progressive and liberal than the PAP's existing policies.[23] In recent years it has also produced two policy papers—one on managing population and immigration, and one on redundancy insurance—beyond its usual manifestos during the election period.[24] These papers reveal that the WP's economic ideologies are consistently to the left of center—advocating for a stronger social safety net, greater regulatory measures to allow families to have better work-life balance, and a national minimum wage. On social issues, however, the WP is more conservative, staying generally silent on divisive topics such as the role of race and religion in society, and on LGBTQ issues. In the final analysis, because of the generally small overall ideological distance between the PAP and the WP, analysts conclude that they "possess essentially similar core philosophies" (Abdullah 2017, 501).

After the WP, the next two most prominent parties are the Singapore Democratic Party (SDP) and the Progress Singapore Party (PSP). The SDP was founded by Chiam See Tong in 1980 (Loke 2014). He became only the second fully elected opposition member of parliament in post-independence Singapore after winning the Potong Pasir SMC in the 1984 general elections. Under Chiam's leadership, the SDP began to attract higher-caliber candidates to run in elections, most notably National University of Singapore lecturer Dr. Chee Soon Juan. Dr. Chee was fielded in the 1992 Marine Parade GRC by-election in a team of four SDP candidates against Prime Minister Goh Chok Tong's PAP team. Dr. Chee's candidature gained significant prominence before the elections because his education and professional credentials rivaled the PAP's highly educated candidates. After the election, he was sacked by the National University of Singapore for misusing research funds, which he protested by staging a five-day hunger strike (Loke 2019, chapter 11). The highly charged events surrounding Dr. Chee's hunger strike soon developed into an internal schism between Chiam and other members of the SDP. Chiam left the SDP in 1993 after falling out with the party's central executive committee, and joined the Singapore People's Party (SPP) in 1996.[25] The SDP's leadership mantle then passed to Dr. Chee.

The SDP has consistently articulated liberal and progressive socioeconomic policies, further to the left than the WP. It produced a slew of alternative policy programs in the run-up to the 2015 and 2020 general elections, most of which also indicated that it is progressive left on economic issues.[26] The party advocates for a minimum wage, for a single-payer universal health-care system, reinstating the estate tax, raising the income tax rate for the top 1 percent of income earners, and increasing social spending on education and welfare, among other policies. The party has also called for the repeal of existing Singapore legislation criminalizing homosexual acts, signaling its distinct progressive position on social issues as compared to other opposition parties (Abdullah 2017, 503).

At the time of writing, the most prominent new opposition party is the Progress Singapore Party (PSP). The party was formed and registered in March 2019 by Dr. Tan Cheng Bock, a former PAP member of parliament and CEC member. This was the first time ever that a PAP CEC member had defected from the ruling party to establish an opposition party on his own. For a young party, it has managed to attract a large number of supporters. Within a month of the party's official launch in early August 2019, it had enrolled more than 500 members, a sizable number for an opposition party in Singapore.[27] Its initial central executive committee included former election candidates from other opposition parties, such as the SDP and the NSP.[28] In the July 2020 general elections, the PSP surprised most observers when it emerged as the "best loser" among the opposition parties—winning two coveted non-constituency positions in the 104-seat parliament. Its unexpected performance can be attributed to the party's high credibility given that it was helmed by a former PAP insider (Oliver and Ostwald 2020).

The Minor Opposition Parties—SPP, SDA, NSP, PKMS, RP, and SF

After Chiam See Tong joined SPP in 1996, he undertook systematic effort to try to expand the SPP by forming the Singapore Democratic

Alliance (SDA) in 2001 (Loke 2019, chapter 15). The SDA was a coalition of parties that included the SPP, the National Solidarity Party (NSP), the Singapore Justice Party (SJP), and the Singapore Malay National Organization (PKMS). Of these parties, the NSP is the oldest, having been formed in March 1987. While the NSP has contested in every election since its formation, it has never won any electoral districts. Its best results came in the 2001 general elections, when it was part of the SDA coalition. The party's secretary-general at that time, Steve Chia, became a non-constituency MP by virtue of losing his contest in Choa Chu Kang SMC by the smallest margin against the PAP.[29] The SJP is effectively a shell party, free for any interested person to take over as an institutional vehicle to participate in elections. The PKMS was formed in 1961 originally as the Singapore branch of UMNO.[30] After Singapore's independence from Malaysia, the party rebranded itself as the PKMS, advocating for the rights of Malay-Muslims in Singapore. Over the decades, the party has struggled to attract members and stay relevant in Singapore's valence- and personality-focused electoral environment. In 2010, PKMS's party members were charged for rioting outside its headquarters in an intra-party struggle for leadership.[31] In 2011, its president was arrested, charged, and jailed for possessing and storing contraband cigarettes at its party headquarters.[32] As for the SPP, there is scant evidence that the party has developed any coherent party ideology or program. Instead, after Chiam suffered two debilitating strokes and a hip injury, the party passed the leadership baton to Jose Raymond in November 2019, who then quit the party in December 2020.

The other more recent minor opposition parties in Singapore are the Reform Party (RP) and the Singaporeans First Party (SF). Both were formed by opposition elites who had either joined other parties initially but fell out with the party leadership, or had gained some prominence on their own. Kenneth Jeyaretnam is the son of J. B. Jeyaretnam. The elder Jeyaretnam founded the RP in 2008 after he left the WP in 2001. His unfortunate passing just three months later saw his Cambridge-educated son, a hedge fund manager, take over the party's leadership in 2009. The SF was set up by Tan Jee Say, a former senior civil servant in 2014, after he left the SDP to contest in the 2011 presidential elections. As a former principal private secretary to former prime minister Goh Chok Tong, Tan's entry into opposition politics signaled a rare dissent and split from the country's hitherto monolithic bureaucratic establishment. But SF's anti-foreigner rhetoric found little traction in local politics. Tan Jee Say dissolved the party in June 2020 and rejoined the SDP.

TABLE 6.2. Singapore's Numerous Political Parties

Political Party	Acronym	Year Founded	Prominent Leader(s)	Best Electoral Performance	Ideology (If Any)
People's Action Party	PAP	1954	Lee Kuan Yew Goh Chok Kong Lee Hsien Loong	Sweeps first four general elections from 1968 to 1980. Has never lost more than 11 percent of all elected seats.	Competency Meritocracy Multiculturalism
Workers' Party	WP	1957	J. B. Jeyaretnam Low Thia Khiang Sylvia Lim	10 fully elected MPs	Economic: left of center Social: right of center
Singapore Democratic Party	SDP	1980	Chee Soon Juan Paul Tambyah	3 fully elected MPs	Economic: left Social: left
Progress Singapore Party	PSP	2019	Tan Cheng Bock	2 nonconstituency MPs	Unclear
Singapore People's Party	SPP	1994	Chiam See Tong Lina Chiam	1 nonconstituency MP	Unclear
Singapore Democratic Alliance	SDA	2001	Chiam See Tong Desmond Lim	1 fully elected MP, and 1 nonconstituency MP	Unclear
National Solidarity Party	NSP	1987	Sebastian Teo	Nil	Unclear
Singapore Malay National Organization	PKMS	1961	Abu Mohamed	Nil	Advocates for rights and privileges of Malay minorities
Reform Party	RP	2008	Kenneth Jeyaretnam	Nil	Unclear
Singaporeans First	SF	2014	Tan Jee Say	Nil	Reduced immigration rates

Beyond the WP and the SDP, it is generally unclear what the ideologies of the other opposition parties are. None have produced comprehensive manifestos to coherently articulate their ideologies on a range of issues. Even the SF, a party that proposes cutting down immigration rates as the central proposal of its platform, does not offer a clear articulation of additional policies. As Weiss, Loke, and Choa (2016, 869) concluded,

Arguably only the WP—the sole opposition party to win seats in 2011 or 2015—and the long-established but currently less successful SDP can claim to be meaningfully institutionalized. Other opposition parties are either heavily personality oriented (SPP, Reform Party), even if not new to the scene, or generally inchoate.

Consider the NSP, for instance. For the 2015 general elections, it fielded 12 candidates, the second largest number of opposition candidates, behind the WP's 28 candidates. Yet its manifesto, in stark contrast to the WP's 46-page tome, was a mere 6-page PowerPoint presentation. On the second slide, the manifesto claimed that "there is no need for a wordy manifesto as the critical issues facing the country and Singaporeans are clear." It went on to contend that, if elected, the party would (1) fight to protect Singaporeans jobs, (2) correct the PAP's population policy, (3) return Singaporeans' government-mandated retirement savings in the Central Provident Fund, and (4) reduce inequality by amending the government's current housing policy. There were no elaborations on these four points beyond their one-paragraph explanations. To conclude, table 6.2 summarizes the most important political parties in Singapore as I have discussed in this section. As mentioned, beyond the WP and the SDP, the ideological orientation of most of the other opposition parties is unclear.

Conclusion

This chapter has detailed the divergent party system development in Malaysia and Singapore, providing the empirical background in which to make sense of opposition alliance (non)formation among the many opposition parties in the two countries. In Malaysia, intense ethnoreligious cleavages resulted in the emergence and growth of the ideologically polarized DAP and PAS from the "ethnic flanks." Newly created opposition parties from intra-regime defections, such as S46, PKR, and PPBM, typically reproduced the ideas and policies of the BN, while claiming the be a "cleaner" version of them. As the next chapter demonstrates, creation of these intra-regime defector parties, when combined with other surprising regime-debilitating events within a short period of time, motivated the ideologically polarized opposition parties to construct opposition alliances. In Singapore, however, persistent PAP dominance and control resulted in an ideologically shallow and fragmented opposition landscape. Although there is some variation in the strength and size of opposition parties in recent years, with the WP, SDP, and the PSP being deemed more credible than the others, the vast majority of them pose little threat to PAP rule. The penultimate chapter of this book will demonstrate just how opposition interparty coordination can still occur in this alternative scenario.

7 | Constructing Opposition Alliances in Malaysia, 1965–2018

Malaysia's political development from 1965 to 2018 represents a classic case of opposition parties repeatedly building pre-electoral alliances on numerous occasions to gradually chip away at the overwhelming dominance of an electoral authoritarian regime. In the run-up to the 1990, 1999, 2013, and 2018 general elections, opposition parties built full-fledged alliances with both candidate allocation across electoral districts and joint campaigns against the autocratic incumbent. While the opposition failed to topple the incumbent in their first three attempts, the final effort by the Pakatan Harapan (PH) opposition alliance in 2018 was ultimately successful in seizing power from the hitherto dominant Barisan Nasional (BN) government. The remarkable fact about these pre-electoral alliances was that they were formed despite the intense ideological polarization between the secularist Democratic Action Party (DAP), representing ethnic Chinese and Indian minorities, and the Islamist Parti Islam Se-Malaysia (PAS), representing the ethnic Malay majority Muslims. The existing political science literature suggests that cooperation almost never emerges among such ideological adversaries. The task of this chapter is to illuminate why and how four such alliances were formed over some three decades.

Specifically, I illustrate how temporal variation in the perceptions of regime dominance alongside the growing recognition of mutual dependency among opposition parties can stimulate efforts to build pre-electoral alliances. This chapter triangulates data from several sources—newspaper archives, political party newsletter archives, the secondary literature, elite interviews, and field observation of the 2018 electoral campaign—to verify several hypotheses and observable implications from the theory. First, when the BN was overwhelmingly dominant and party system volatility was high between 1965 and 1986, opposition party leaders generally eschewed expending precious resources to build alliances. Absent any reliable information from a historical record of electoral participation, opposition parties struggled to identify and adopt the best electoral strategy to compete against the BN. Over time, however, as more information about the payoffs of different electoral strategies became available from iterated cycles of electoral participation, party leaders began to recognize that reducing the number of opposition candidates to avoid vote splitting was in their self-interest. By having the requisite information on relative popularities to decide which parties should have the "right of way" to contest in which electoral district, party leaders soon learned how best to coordinate allocating geographically segregated electoral districts in parliamentary elections.

Second, in the run-up to the 1990, 1999, 2013, and 2018 general elections, multiple regime-debilitating events occurred within a short period of time, such as economic crises, intra-regime defections, and mass street protests, leading opposition party leaders to perceive that the incumbent BN regime was newly vulnerable. The convergence of these events motivated opposition party leaders to upgrade their coordination from merely allocating electoral districts to pursue joint national election campaigns, thus constructing full-fledged pre-electoral alliances. In all four elections, all opposition parties recognized that only by coordinating to allocate electoral districts and campaigning together would they be able to take full advantage of the BN's surprising new vulnerability and maximize their chances of winning. Arguably, the accumulation of incremental experience in alliance building for more than two decades led to cohesive interparty cooperation in 2018 in the form of the PH opposition alliance.

Finally, this chapter also reveals how even as the members and supporters of ideologically polarized opposition parties generally resist any form of cooperation with their ideological rivals at the outset, their party leaders can still persuade them to reduce their hesitancy about alliance formation over time. In 1990 and 1999, DAP members and supporters were consistently reluctant to cooperate with PAS, and vice versa, even if both parties opposed the BN. Interparty coordination for joint election campaigns were therefore generally weak and ineffective in those years because opposition party leaders did not want to be seen as too close with their alliance counterparts. Yet, as the enticing prize of victory grew closer and more visible, opposition party leaders began to work harder to persuade their members and supporters to back their efforts to coordinate with their ideological rivals from 2010 onward. This involved opposition elites reminding their supporters about their mutual antipathy toward the

TABLE 7.1. Timeline of Key Events in Malaysian Politics from 1965 to 2018

Date	Event
August 1965	Singapore breaks away from the Federation of Malaysia as an independent state. The Alliance, comprising the United Malays National Organization (UMNO), the Malaysian Chinese Association, and the Malaysian Indian Congress, rules.
July 1967	The opposition Democratic Action Party (DAP) is formed.
May 1969	Inter-ethnic riots occur in the streets of Kuala Lumpur in the aftermath of the 1969 general elections. A state of emergency is declared, and parliament is suspended.
January 1972	The Parti Islam Se-Malaysia (PAS) joins the revamped Barisan Nasional (BN) ruling government coalition.
December 1977	PAS withdraws from BN to join the opposition.
June 1989	Tengku Razaleigh Hamzah forms a new centrist political party, Semangat 46, after defecting from UMNO.
October 1990	DAP forms opposition coalition called Gagasan Rakyat with Semangat 46 for the 1990 general elections. PAS forms separate opposition coalition called Angkatan Perpaduan Ummah also with Semangat 46 for the same elections.
September 1998	Deputy Prime Minister Anwar Ibrahim sacked from cabinet and expelled from UMNO. Anwar's followers form Parti Keadilan Rakyat (PKR).
November 1999	PKR joins with DAP and PAS to form Barisan Alternatif (BA) opposition alliance. BA only makes small dent in the BN's overall dominance.
May 2013	PKR joins with DAP and PAS again to form new Pakatan Rakyat (PR) opposition alliance. PR wins a majority of the vote share, but BN continues to win a majority of the seat share.
August 2015	A group of defectors quit PAS and form a new political party, Parti Amanah Negara (Amanah).
March 2016	Former prime minister Mahathir Mohamad quits UMNO and forms new political party, Parti Pribumi Bersatu Malaysia (PPBM).
May 2018	DAP, PKR, PPBM, and Amanah form the new Pakatan Harapan (PH) opposition alliance. PH wins a majority of the votes and seats, defeating the BN, which had ruled Malaysia since the country's independence in 1957.

regime, and the potential gains to be reaped if the alliance did indeed prevail against the BN. As a result, more and more supporters of Malaysia's ideologically polarized opposition parties were willing to "hold their noses" to vote for candidates from opposition parties professing ideologies contrary to their own, but who were still members of the same opposition alliance.

As with the previous chapters, a timeline of events is helpful to assist readers unfamiliar with the Malaysian case to have a clear knowledge of how particular sequences of events unfolded. The timeline in table 7.1 highlights the key political events in regime crises, opposition party formation, and opposition coordination for Malaysia since 1965.

Opposition Fracture during Overwhelming Regime Dominance from 1965 to 1986

The two decades from 1965 to 1986 were a sustained period of incumbent party dominance in Malaysia's history. Inter-ethnic riots, autocratic co-optation, and intraparty rebellion also engendered high volatility within and among opposition parties. Newly formed opposition parties struggled to learn how to best maximize their vote shares and seat shares when contesting against a dominant incumbent. Coordination on allocating electoral districts persistently failed as old and new opposition party leaders experimented with different electoral strategies. At times, they learned from their past successes and switched their electoral strategies. At other times, they remained belligerent about their past failures. Overall, inexperience with coalition building and deep concerns over intraparty dissent constrained the strategic options of opposition party leaders.

After Singapore broke off from Malaysia in August 1965, the incumbent UMNO-MCA-MIC coalition, formally known as the Alliance Party and later known as Barisan Nasional (BN), became the dominant ruling party of Malaysia. The first post-1965 electoral test against the Alliance Party was a by-election in Serdang electoral district in the state of Selangor in December 1968. At that time, the DAP and Gerakan were two newly formed, ideologically similar opposition parties (Vasil 1972, 16–20).[1] Both were multiethnic parties advocating for inter-ethnic accommodation and peace. But absent any historical electoral experience, there was a lack of reliable information about each other's relative popularity, electoral strengths, and chances of winning. Uncertainty about which party should give way to the other's candidate was high. Due to this initial uncertainty, neither party wanted to give way to the other. Candidates from both parties eventually contested against the Alliance candidate. As a result, the Alliance candidate won with only a slim majority of 607 votes. The second-best DAP candidate obtained 5,928 votes, while the Gerakan candidate secured 1,330 votes (Drummond and Hawkins 1970, 321).

The opposition's defeat due to a failure to run only one candidate against the Alliance became a harsh lesson for opposition party leaders. Having gained experience in the spectacular failure of noncoordination, the non-Malay opposition parties—the DAP, Gerakan, and the People's Progressive Party (PPP)—came to recognize the incentives of cooperating with each other for the 1969 general elections (Brown 2004, 97; Drummond and Hawkins 1970, 321–22; Saravanamuttu 2016, 98–99).[2] When a journalist asked about the motivations for cooperating with each other for the elections, Goh Hock Guan, then secretary-general of the DAP, referred to the 1968 Serdang by-election and declared, "The experience we have got from this election has been bitter enough, and I believe we will never again fight among ourselves and allow the Alliance to sit on our corpses."[3] In essence, Goh's words indicate how opposition party leaders learned about the consequences of not coordinating with each other, and subsequently updated their electoral strategy. Vasil (1972, 21) verified this theory of learning when he observed that a major motivation for coordinating on allocating electoral districts in the 1969 elections was the opposition party leaders' learning from their earlier defeat. As he wrote (Vasil 1972, 21–23),

> Past experience had shown that disunity among the opposition had been to the advantage of the Alliance. *A multiplicity of opposition candidates in the preceding elections had almost invariably led to Alliance success. Therefore, there was a strong wish to avoid a multiplicity of opposition candidates. . . . They feared that without such an arrangement the two parties could destroy each other and allow the Alliance to emerge with significant victories* in the multi-party contest. This fear, and the persistence and perseverance of the Gerakan leadership, eventually resulted in February in a three-way electoral arrangement among the DAP, the PPP, and the Gerakan. . . . They allocated both the Parliamentary and State constituencies to each of the three parties on the basis of its organization and an estimate of electoral support in the constituency.

This final 1969 agreement to coordinate district allocation among the three non-Malay political parties was a moderate success. While all component parties of the ruling Alliance lost seats, the MCA component was the hardest hit, having won only 13 seats in the 103-seat parliament, down from 27 seats in 1964 (Drummond and Hawkins 1970, 331; Ratnam and Milne 1970, 210; Vasil 1972, 43–45). In contrast with the DAP's 13 parliamentary seats, Gerakan's eight seats, and PPP's four seats, the MCA's results were dismal, suggesting that non-Malays were abandoning the Malay-dominant consociational arrangement between the UMNO, MCA, and MIC. The results were more stunning at the state level. Gerakan won control of the state assembly in Penang, together with half of the state seats in Selangor and Perak alongside the DAP and PPP. For its part, PAS captured the state government in Kelantan and also made significant gains in the state governments of Perlis, Terengganu, and Kedah. Although the UMNO itself retained 51 seats and was able to form a majority government in the 103-seat parliament with MCA (13 seats) and MIC (two seats) as its partners, the results were widely interpreted as a direct threat to the Malay dominance of political power (Saravanamuttu 2016, 91–105; Slater 2010, 116–24; Vasil 1972, 46–48).

The exact details of the inter-ethnic riots that occurred in the streets of Kuala Lumpur between the Malays and the Chinese on May 13, 1969, are beyond the scope of this book. Suffice to say, the incident remains a painful memory of inter-ethnic conflict among many Malaysians today—about 6,000 residents, 90 percent of whom were Chinese, had their houses torched and destroyed during the riots (Means 1991, 8). Close to 200 Malaysians lost their lives, although there still remain doubts as to the actual death toll. Immediately after the riots, a national emergency was declared, normal parliamentary process was suspended, and an all-powerful National Operations Council was promulgated. In the ensuing years, the Alliance ruling government transformed itself into the BN ruling coalition from 1972 onward by bringing Gerakan, PPP, and PAS into its fold (Means 1991, 27–32). Through such co-optation, the new prime minister, Tun Razak, had hoped to build a broader mass basis of support for implementing the government's new policy goal—the New Economic Policy (NEP) (Gomez and Saravanamuttu 2013; Means 1991, 23–27; Sundaram 1989). The NEP sought to reduce inter-ethnic social tensions by prioritizing economic growth while ensuring that Malays reaped a larger share of the benefits of such growth.

The DAP was the sole major opposition party not to be co-opted into the BN ruling government in 1972. There were other, smaller opposition parties such as Pekemas, Parti Sosialis Rakyat Malaya, and the United Independents, to be sure (Pillay 1974, 12–15). But none could match the ideological coherence and organization of the DAP. The twin opposition pincers of PAS and DAP only reemerged when PAS was expelled from the BN in late 1977, and then contested against the BN in the 1978 general elections. This was the first time when prospects of coordinating for candidate selection between the two ideologically polarized opposition parties might arise in the BN era. But in the absence of clear information about the payoffs to different electoral strategies approaching the general elections, interparty coordination was not pursued. Instead, it appeared that any secret "unholy alliance" between the DAP and PAS consisted of their *increasing* the number of opposition candidates by placing two opposition candidates in each electoral district (Mauzy 1979, 290; Ong 1980, 163–64).[4] The logic was this: in Malay-majority electoral districts, the DAP's entry would siphon away non-Malay support from the UMNO candidate. The PAS candidate could then potentially prevail if he secured the majority of the Malay votes. In electoral districts where non-Malays formed the majority, PAS's entry may help draw Malay votes away from the MCA or MIC candidate. The DAP candidate could win if he secured the overwhelming majority of non-Malay votes.

Regardless, this counterintuitive strategy of increasing the number of opposition candidates, if it was used at all, did not appear to help either party much in the 1978 general elections (Ong 1980, 164). While the DAP increased its number of parliamentary seats from 9 to 16 in the 154-seat parliament, it performed worse than expected in the state-level races (Mauzy 1979, 286). PAS's performance was even more underwhelming. Its number of parliamentary seats declined from 13 to 9, and its president lost his own parliamentary electoral contest in Kedah. PAS was also totally routed in Kelantan, its traditional home base, when it could only secure two parliamentary seats and two state seats for the entire state.

Despite the failed strategy of fielding two opposition candidates in multiple electoral districts in 1978, PAS and DAP leaders did not update their electoral strategy to seek coordination in the run-up to the 1982 general elections. They would go on to repeat the same strategy of fielding multiple candidates against the BN again (Mauzy 1983; Mukerjee 1982). Why the two opposition parties maintained their failed strategy is a puzzle that remains unexplained by the available secondary literature. Again, while there were rumors of DAP-PAS cooperating to repeat the strategy of fielding two opposition candidates in multiple electoral districts, there remains no available direct evidence to prove that the parties intentionally did so (Barraclough 1985, 42; Means 1991, 88). One can only surmise that the information that party leaders gleaned from the 1978 electoral results as not decisive enough to sway opposition leaders toward any other electoral strategy, or that opposition leaders discounted the previous election results on account of PAS's renewed status as an opposition party after its ouster from the BN in 1977. Ultimately, both parties contested against the BN in 30 out of 154 available parliamentary districts. This proportion was not insignificant to either party. For the DAP, it represented more than half of the 51 parliamentary seats that it contested in Peninsular Malaysia. For PAS, it was over one-third of the electoral districts it contested. The result was even worse than in 1978. The PAS maintained its 5 seats in the 154-seat parliament, while the DAP dwindled to only 6 seats.

Faced with repeated failure to expand their seat shares in the 1978 and 1982 general elections, PAS party members became disenchanted with their erstwhile leader, Asri Muda (Noor 2014, 105–25). A new group of young, conservative Islamic clerics took over the leadership of the party immediately after the 1982 elections. Although this new group, led by new party president Ustaz Yusof Rawa, and supported by Tuan Guru Nik Aziz Nik Mat, Ustaz Fadzil Noor, and Ustaz Abdul Hadi Awang, were stridently Islamic in their outlook, they were also political realists. They recognized that the party's experiment with multiple opposition candidates in each electoral district in the past two electoral cycles had not yielded increased seat shares for the party. A change in electoral strategy was needed. Hence, PAS attempted to coordinate with the DAP to allocate electoral districts for the first time ever approaching the 1986 general elections (Drummond 1987; Noor 2014, 135; Rachagan 1987; Ramanathan and Mohamad Hamdan 1988, 31).

As it was the PAS's new leaders' first attempt at building a coalition, the process was not smooth sailing. My review of newspaper clippings on alliance building kept at the Center for Malaysian Chinese Studies in Kuala Lumpur and the secondary literature on this period revealed that opposition parties faced at least three major challenges.[5] First, there was the question of the extent to which rank-and-file party members would accept the two ideologically polarized opposition parties working with each other. For the DAP this question revolved around the degree to which party members and supporters could accept PAS's public goal of transforming Malaysia into an Islamic state. Given that its members and supporters were overwhelmingly non-Malay-Muslims, the DAP was caught in a serious dilemma. Any hint of cooperation with PAS, even in the form of coordinating to allocate electoral districts, might send its party members and supporters fleeing. In a newspaper article published in *The Star* on July 14, 1986, Lee Lam Thye, a DAP leader, was reported to have the following position:

He said the "rank and file of the DAP" would not mind the party joining the Opposition front "so long as the party held firmly to its principles and objectives." "They would not mind if the party's conditions—which are against the setting up of an Islamic State and having a Muslim leadership—are accepted by the parties forming the front." Mr Lee said *the members would object if the DAP is to sacrifice its basic beliefs and objectives.*[6]

PAS's leaders also confronted the same internal party dissent. Barraclough (1985, 42) noted that "there were reports that PAS was deeply divided" and that "any substantial move by the PAS leadership towards cooperation with the DAP might well produce resentment among certain sections of the party and threaten its unity."

Second, even as interparty cooperation was considered, there was still the question of what form of cooperation was acceptable. Because of a lack of experience in coalition building, the two parties simply did not know where to start. If they wanted to coordinate to allocate the electoral districts to contest in, they would have to bargain with each other over the distribution of electoral districts. If a joint manifesto was to be launched, parties would have to coordinate on the language to be used in order to set aside or render vague PAS's commitment to an Islamic state. But where and how should the two parties begin negotiations?

Third and finally, there was scarcely any historical evidence that party leaders could rely on to suggest that a joint alliance would yield extra votes and seat shares in the face of BN dominance. Barraclough (1985, 42) noted that past attempts at coordination, if there were any among the minor opposition parties, had "produced few tangible benefits." Benefits from alliance formation were even more doubtful in the mid-1980s, when the BN was at the height of its power (Slater 2003). The UMNO leadership had been passed to Tun Dr. Mahathir Mohamad in 1981. His rule was notable for Malaysia's skyrocketing economic growth through rapid industrialization, and also its increasing authoritarianism, with strict controls on the media and on intra-UMNO dissent (Means 1991, chapters 4 and 5). Opposition parties confronting the dominant BN machine would have had scant hopes that a pre-electoral alliance would yield any positive outcomes.

Because of all these concerns, the DAP leadership eventually deemed it not worthwhile to cooperate with PAS for the 1986 general elections. It declared that it was open to coordinating with PAS on the condition that it abandon its goals of transforming Malaysia into an Islamic state (Means 1991, 184). PAS, of course, rejected that condition (Rachagan 1987, 228).

Other minor opposition parties and PAS managed to sign a vague joint declaration to coordinate with each other on allocating electoral districts.[7] Yet, when nomination day came around for the 1986 elections, there emerged 32 parliamentary constituencies and 13 state seats in which the opposition parties still found themselves facing each other alongside the BN candidate. The declaration was not made a reality.

The DAP's insistence on not associating with the newly rejuvenated but radicalized PAS proved to be a wise move for the 1986 general elections. Its number of electoral districts won increased from 6 to 24 in the 177-seat parliament, while its number of state seats more than tripled, from 12 to 37. This was its best-ever result (Drummond 1987; Rachagan 1987; Ramanathan and Mohamad Hamdan 1988, 50–56). For the PAS, however, it was a disaster. The party won only one parliamentary seat and saw its state assembly seats decline from 18 to 15. PAS's performance was "regarded as its worst general election performance over the last twenty-seven years of its existence" (Ramanathan and Mohamad Hamdan 1988, 60).

PAS's historically poor results were primarily attributed to party leaders' contradictory actions (Ramanathan and Mohamad Hamdan 1988, 59–67). On the one hand, the party attempted to form a united opposition front with other minor and non-Muslim opposition parties, particularly the DAP (although the attempt was unsuccessful). Party leaders even tried to reach out to non-Malay-Muslim supporters for the first time by establishing a nominal Chinese Consultative Committee. On the other hand, PAS campaigned on a platform of establishing an Islamic state. When pressed by the BN, PAS leaders explained that neither non-Muslims nor women would be allowed to vote under their vision of an Islamic state (Means 1991, 185). Such contradictory views confused potential voters despite the party leaders' best efforts to explain their political logic. A nationwide drive to "explain to PAS members and supporters the concept of the [opposition] front" and to avoid "misunderstanding" turned out to be futile.[8] From this perspective, PAS leaders' lack of consistency critically undermined their electoral results. The DAP's extra caution about alliance formation was deemed to be a correct assessment.

Opposition Coordination to Allocate Electoral Districts from 1990 to 2018

After more than two decades of opposition fracture between 1965 and 1986, the next three decades of elections between 1990 and 2018 saw much more consistent instances of interparty coordination. Table 7.2 summarizes a clear change in the dependent variable—opposition interparty coordination in allocating electoral districts—over time from 1974 to 1995. If opposition parties allocated electoral districts between them, then we should expect the average number of candidates per contested electoral district be two—one candidate from the dominant ruling party, and one candidate from an opposition party.

Table 7.2 demonstrates how the average number of candidates per electoral district declined toward two, as opposition parties in Malaysia became better at coordinating allocating electoral districts. As we can surmise, when the DAP was the sole major opposition party in 1974, small opposition parties attempted to fight against their irrelevance by forcing some multicornered contests. In 1978 and 1982, after PAS was expelled from the BN, both PAS and DAP reasoned counterintuitively that forcing electoral contests with three candidates in each electoral district—one each from DAP and PAS contesting against the BN candidate—might be advantageous to both parties. Hence, we observe the increase in the average number of candidates per contested constituency in the 1978 and 1982 general elections. Having realized their mistake, however, the two parties then began to try to coordinate with each other in 1986. There was a limited degree of improvement in coordination that year, nevertheless, due to the respective party leaders' fear of intraparty dissent over cooperating

TABLE 7.2. Average Number of Candidates per Constituency across Elections, 1974–95

General Election Year	Parliamentary Seats (N)	Candidates per Contested Parliamentary Seat (avg.)	State Seats (N)	Candidates per Contested State Seats (avg.)
1974	154	2.32	408	2.04
1978	154	2.32	276	2.56
1982	154	2.50	312	2.46
1986	177	2.18	351	2.26
1990	132*	2.01	351	2.01
1995	192	2.06	394	2.14

Source: State seats by author's calculation from Khong 1991b. For 1995, author's calculations from Gomez 1996, 15–16.

Note: I assume that all independents caused multicornered contests and excluded independent candidates. For 1974–1986, author's calculation from NSTP Research and Information Services (1990). For 1990, parliamentary seats by author's calculation from Business Times. 12 October 1990. "PAS-DAP ties show up in opposition front."

* Parliamentary seats for Peninsular Malaysia only.

with ideological rivals. Finally, a near perfect coordination was realized in 1990, when opposition party leaders abandoned their failed electoral strategies and finally coordinated with each other to allocate the vast majority of electoral districts. In fact, this pattern of interparty coordination would persist in the three decades from 1990 to 2018.

The 1990 general elections were most remarkable because they represented a second opportunity for opposition parties to forge an opposition coalition. This time around, the initial process to at least coordinate on electoral district allocation was somewhat smoother than in 1986. There were at least four reasons why this was so. First, historical experience from the failed 1978, 1982, and 1986 general elections meant that opposition parties now had a significant backlog of information and experience from which they could learn. They would now be able to better assess which party had a better chance of winning in a particular electoral district. Second, Tengku Razaleigh's defection from the UMNO and Semangat 46's (S46) emergence as a centrist political party meant that both the DAP and PAS could claim to their own supporters that they were coordinating with a moderate opposition party and not with their ideological rival. This reduced the costs of intraparty dissent insofar as party leaders could justifiably claim that they were not making ideological compromises. Third, and relatedly, S46 could act as a broker for the allocation of seats between opposition parties. DAP and PAS leaders need not negotiate with each other directly, but could simply negotiate with S46 instead. Fourth, there were minimal contests over ethnically heterogenous electoral districts, as they were mostly allocated to the centrist S46. Electoral districts with a majority of ethnic minorities would be allocated to the DAP, while those with a majority of Malay-Muslims would be allocated to PAS. As a result, the 1990 elections saw only one parliamentary district that had a three-cornered contest between the PAS, the DAP, and the BN.[9] In all other districts opposition parties managed to avoid contesting against each other.

Since 1990, Malaysia's opposition party leaders have coordinated to allocate electoral districts before every election. With multiple rounds of pre-electoral negotiations, opposition party leaders discovered an effective, informal rule that made more efficient the bargaining process between the DAP, PAS, and any other major opposition party. The rule is this: non-Malay/Bumiputera-majority electoral districts will be allocated to the Chinese-based DAP; districts with a high proportion of Malay/Bumiputera voters will be allocated to the Malay-Muslim-based PAS; and mixed districts will be allocated to any centrist and multiethnic party.[10] As framed, this informal rule has several important implications.

First, *the ethnic composition of each electoral district serves as a proxy measure for the district's expected relative levels of popularity for opposition parties*—the main independent variable that I contend influences opposition coordination for allocating geographically segregated electoral districts. In this manner, this proxy measure carved out particular geographical regions in which opposition parties expected their highest changes of winning. Since ethnic Chinese- and Indian-majority districts were expected to be more likely to support DAP candidates, the DAP would contest mostly in the western coast of Peninsular Malaysia, where most of them reside. Accordingly, since ethnic Malay-majority districts were expected to be more likely to support PAS candidates, PAS would contest mostly in the eastern coastal regions with a large proportion of ethnic Malays. Second, and perhaps most importantly, because using this informal rule significantly reduced uncertainty about opposition parties' relative popularity and winning chances in each electoral district, it allowed party leaders to save time and resources while bargaining with each other. This prior information established their baseline expectations about which party should contest in which electoral district even before interparty bargaining began. Subsequent negotiations, if any, centered around marginal districts that were not clearly DAP or PAS ethnic strongholds. Third and finally, the informal rule ensured that all parties maximized their own candidates' electoral viability against the BN when their respective ideologies matched the local demographics of the districts. This vote and seat share-maximizing incentive would be what made bargaining and allocating electoral districts a worthwhile coordination endeavor.

Available data from the 1999 and 2013 general elections illustrate this informal rule. Figure 7.1 shows the allocated electoral districts across all parliamentary seats in the entire country for the 1999 general elections. Each vertical bar represents an electoral district, and districts are arranged from having the lowest proportion of Malay voters to the highest proportion of Malay voters. We can infer that, for the most part, the DAP contested in electoral districts where Malays were not the majority. The PKR, the ideologically moderate defector party from UMNO in 1999, contested in ethnically heterogenous districts. Finally, PAS contested primarily in districts that were overwhelmingly Malay. Figure 7.2, illustrating the allocation of electoral districts in the 2013 general elections, repeats the same story. It focuses on parliamentary districts in Peninsular Malaysia only, and uses the proportion of Bumiputera voters as the scale in which to sort the vertical bars representing each electoral district. It demonstrates that the ethnic minority-based DAP contested almost exclusively in districts

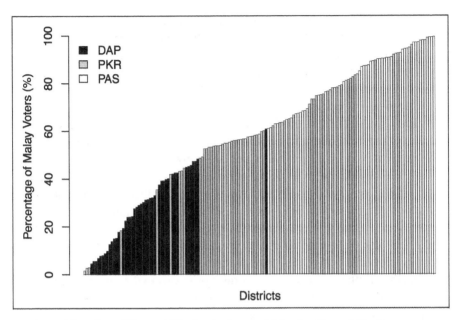

Fig 7.1. Allocation of Electoral Districts in the 1999 Malaysian General Elections

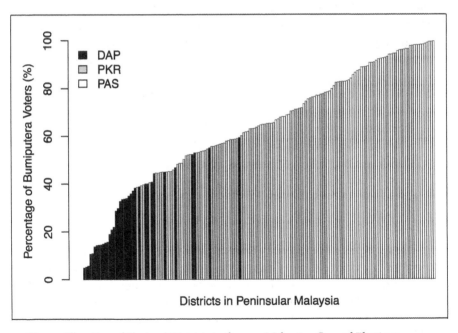

Fig 7.2. Allocation of Electoral Districts in the 2013 Malaysian General Elections

where there were less than 40% of Bumiputera voters, whereas PAS competed in most of the districts where the Bumiputera majority was very large. There was substantial variation in where the centrist PKR contested, however, because the multiethnic PKR could allocate its candidates to a large range of districts that were perceived to be ethnically heterogenous.

My field interviews with 15 opposition leaders in Malaysia between August 2016 and May 2017 also confirmed the application of the informal rule. An overwhelming majority of interviewees agreed that coordinating electoral district allocation was a beneficial exercise for all the opposition parties involved, and that the bargaining process was primarily based on the ethnic composition in that particular district. Essentially, the ethnic composition of each district served as a useful proxy indicator for each party's relative popularity and associated winning chances. Moreover, there was little dispute over district allocation between DAP and PAS because the districts that they were interested in contesting had little overlap with each other. Both parties sought to contest primarily in their own geographical strongholds. Instead, both parties had to spend the most time negotiating with the ideologically centrist and moderate PKR. These negotiations were difficult but surmountable, because there were so many electoral districts to trade with each other. Unlike presidential autocracies where party leaders had to battle each other to be the sole presidential candidate, opposition parties in parliamentary autocracies like Malaysia with multiple geographically segregated electoral districts have a relative easier time negotiating with each other for a share of the pie. For example, opposition leader K said the following in response to a question about how the parties coordinated in allocating their electoral districts in August 2016:

> Even though there are exceptions to the rule, the general guideline is where it is about 45–55 percent Malays, that's where Keadilan [PKR] will contest. . . . The ones from 45 below is DAP. And the ones 60 and above is PAS. That's the general idea. . . . There is no point putting PAS . . . where there is high [proportion of] non-Malay voter.[11]

The final piece of evidence about the strong self-interested benefits of coordinating electoral district allocation in an opposition alliance is from a coalition document itself. Figure 7.3 shows a screengrab from the PH opposition alliance agreement formed in Malaysia for the 2018 general elections. The document lists seven clauses in relation to the functioning of the opposition coalition in matters such as joint decision-making, how

TABLE 7.3. Interviews with Malaysian Opposition Party Leaders

Code	Opposition Party Leader	Gender	Race	Informal Rule?[a]	Benefit?[b]
MY009	W	M	Chinese	1	0
MY010	O	M	Chinese	1	1
MY011	K	M	Malay	1	1
MY012	Y	F	Chinese	0	1
MY013	D	M	Malay	1	1
MY014	T	M	Chinese	1	1
MY015	Q	F	Chinese	0	1
MY016	A	M	Chinese	1	1
MY017	H	M	Malay	1	1
MY018	L	M	Chinese	1	1
MY019	N	F	Malay	1	1
MY020	S	M	Malay	1	0
MY021	C	M	Chinese	1	1
MY022	M	M	Malay	1	0
MY023	R	M	Indian	0	0

Note: All 15 interviews were conducted in Kuala Lumpur between August 2016 and May 2017 for about one hour each. Interviewees were canvassed through snowball sampling. Due to the sensitive nature of the interviews, I agreed to conceal their identities, as per the rules of the Institutional Review Board. Before each interview, I explained the nature of my research project and obtained verbal consent to quote them.

Coding Rules:

a Did the interviewee say that coordinating over candidate selection utilized the informal rule of allocating districts based on the ethnic demographic of the electoral district? Coded 1 for yes, 0 otherwise.

b Did the interviewee say that there were large benefits of coordinating over candidate selection? Coded 1 for yes, 0 otherwise.

to solve disputes, as well as the common policies of the coalition.[12] Clause 5, in particular, describes how the parties should approach their participation in the general elections. Clause 5.2 explicitly mentions that the PH must field only one candidate per constituency, clearly highlighting that coordinating on allocating electoral districts to avoid multicornered contests is a critically important part of the opposition alliance and also in the self-interest of the various opposition parties. Furthermore, notice that Clause 5.3 specifies that the PH alliance should nominate a component party to contest in a particular electoral district by taking "into account the factor as to which party has the highest probability of an electoral victory in the said election." This particular quotation highlights and corroborates the crucial importance of my hypothesized independent variable influencing coordination over district allocation—*ex ante information about the relative popularities of the opposition parties.*

CLAUSE 5:
ELECTIONS

5.1   Clause 5 of the Pakatan Harapan Agreement outlines the binding principles in respect of decisions made by component parties of Pakatan Harapan with regards to elections conducted at all levels.

5.2   Pakatan Harapan shall jointly field one candidate per constituency seat to represent Pakatan Harapan in any election of any level. The said candidate shall be chosen by the parties and who shall enjoy the confidence of the Presidential Council to represent Pakatan Harapan in the said election.

5.3   In deciding which party shall represent Pakatan Harapan as set out in Clause 5.2, the Presidential Council shall take into account the factor as to which party has the highest probability of an electoral victory in the said election.

5.4   An Election Committee shall be responsible to conduct negotiations for seat allocations for any election within the Pakatan Harapan component parties in order to assist the Presidential Council to make an informed decision in accordance to Clause 5.3. The Election Committee shall consist of a Director of Elections from each party, and other representatives as appointed by each party subject to the approval of the Presidential Council.

5.5   The final decision of which party shall represent Pakatan Harapan in any election of any level shall be made by the Presidential Council and each party shall not announce its decision to contest in any seat at any level without the prior approval of the Presidential Council.

5.6   Any disagreements with regards to seat allocations at any level as described in Clause 5: Elections shall be brought for discussion and resolved by the Presidential Council.

5.7   Any component party of Pakatan Harapan shall not unilaterally negotiate with any non Pakatan Harapan component party regarding any matters whatsoever in connection with any election unless the Presidential Council has been informed in advance.

Fig. 7.3. Clause 5 of the Pakatan Harapan Alliance Agreement

To be sure, recognition of the incentives and informal rules needed to allocate electoral districts does not eliminate infighting among the opposition parties. They are only guardrails that prevent interparty negotiations from veering off course. Where and when there is high uncertainty about the relative popularity of opposition parties, or if there are incentives for misrepresenting relative popularity, opposition parties can still bicker over candidate allocation. Instances of coordination failure may still arise. For instance, consider the 2016 state elections in the eastern Malaysian state of Sarawak, where the DAP and PKR clashed over which party should contest in six electoral districts.[13] Because these electoral districts were newly created, both parties lacked prior information about which was more popular than the other. No one wanted to acquiesce to the other party, for that would mean losing the future right to contest in those particular districts. Eventually, both sets of party leaders agreed to commission an independent and reputable survey firm, Merdeka Center, to conduct polls in these districts to assess their parties' relative popularity. The results revealed that the DAP was more popular in five out of the six districts surveyed. It paved the way for the DAP's persistence belligerence in their subsequent negotiations with PKR. The PKR countered by noting that the survey questions only asked respondents about the parties' popularity and did not consider the qualities of their competing candidates. It claimed that its candidates were more popular than the DAP's candidates. Continued intransigence between the two parties meant that the six new electoral districts all witnessed at least three candidates on nomination day. The opposition infighting "had the obvious effect of diluting the vote in favor of the BN" even as bickering party leaders "portrayed themselves in a damning light before the Sarawakian public" (Mohamad Nawab and Rashaad 2017). This interparty squabbling, among other factors, led to the BN sweeping 72 out of 82 of Sarawak's state assembly seats (Weiss and Puyok 2017; Lian 2018).

Approaching the May 2018 general elections, the new PH alliance endeavored to avoid repeating earlier mistakes in Sarawak. In early January 2018 it announced that it had coordinated seat allocations for all electoral districts in Peninsular Malaysia.[14] Tun Dr. Mahathir's PPBM would be allocated 52 seats to contest in, Anwar Ibrahim's PKR 51 seats, the DAP 35 seats, and Amanah 27 seats. Unlike previous opposition alliances, where intracoalition coordination was completed at the eleventh hour, opposition party leaders learned from their previous attempts that intracoalition wrangling only hurt public perception of the coalition's unity. After setting aside the parliamentary districts already won, interparty negotiations pro-

ceeded relatively efficiently based on the earlier informal rule of using ethnic composition of the electoral district as a proxy for a party's expected
popularity in that district.

Building Full-Fledged Opposition Alliances with Joint Election Campaigns in the 1990, 1999, 2013, and 2018 General Elections

If Malaysia's ideologically polarized opposition parties could learn to
allocate electoral districts with better information obtained through
recurring electoral participation, then under what conditions would they
upgrade their cooperation to include joint electoral campaigns and hence
build full-fledged pre-electoral alliances? My theory suggests that two
other variables—perceptions about regime vulnerability and perceptions
of mutual dependency among opposition parties—motivate the shift in
strategic behavior. This section demonstrates that multiple regime-
debilitating events within a short period of time and increasing acknowledgment of their mutual dependency motivated party leaders to build
pre-electoral alliances with both types of coordination. At the same time,
moreover, PAS and DAP leaders were still aware of potential intraparty
resistance to mutual cooperation. So even as PAS and DAP leaders
decided it was worthwhile to forge joint campaigns and construct alliances, they frequently found themselves following a very narrow path
between the incentives for cooperation and the perils of resistance from
their own supporters.

To assess the causal impact of growing regime vulnerability and
mutual dependency on opposition alliance formation, I make two empirical inferences in my subsequent analytical narratives. We can first
observe that Malaysia's four instances of pre-electoral opposition alliances from 1990 to 2018 were all precipitated by multiple regime-
debilitating public episodes indicating new ruptures in the BN regime,
specifically within UMNO (see table 7.4). Almost all of these episodes
were historically unprecedented. A second empirical task is to assess if
opposition elites did indeed update their perceptions of regime vulnerability and if they perceived eventual victory against the BN to be conditional upon being mutually dependent. In the process tracing that I
undertake, I triangulate empirical evidence from the secondary literature
and newspaper reports, supplemented with elite interviews and field
observations in the run-up to the 2018 election campaign.

TABLE 7.4. Malaysia's Many Pre-electoral Opposition Alliances

General Election	Alliance Name	Component Opposition Parties	Regime-Debilitating Events
1990	Angkatan Perpaduan Ummah + Gagasan Rakyat	Semangat 46 DAP PAS	• 1987 UMNO internal party leadership challenge against Mahathir • 1988 Tengku Razaleigh defection from UMNO • 1988 deregistration of UMNO • 1989 Mahathir heart attack
1999	Barisan Alternatif	PKR DAP PAS	• 1997 Asian financial crisis • Anwar's sacking from UMNO in 1998 • Mass street protests in the Reformasi Movement
2013	Pakatan Rakyat	PKR DAP PAS	• 2008 Global financial crisis • 2008 "tsunami" general election • Bersih street protests
2018	Pakatan Harapan	PKR DAP PPBM Amanah	• 2015 *Wall Street Journal* 1MDB scandal • 2016 Mahathir defects from UMNO

The 1990 General Elections: The Angkatan Perpaduan Ummah and Gagasan Rakyat Opposition Alliances

In 1988, Tengku Razaleigh's defection from UMNO was the first time ever in Malaysian history that a cabinet-level minister defected from UMNO together with other elite party insiders. His defection came on the back of a bruising UMNO internal party election in April 1987 where he unsuccessfully challenged Tun Dr. Mahathir for UMNO's leadership (Means 1991, chapter 7). Despite the failed challenge, the alarming episode "represented not just an internecine power struggle, but a hegemonic crisis" (Hilley 2001, 87). No longer was Mahathir's personalism and corruption-fueled economic development going unchallenged within the party. Unwilling to admit to his loss, Tengku Razaleigh's subsequent legal challenge to pronounce the UMNO elections null and void resulted in a court declaring UMNO an "illegal society." UMNO's official deregistration sent shockwaves throughout Malaysia (Nathan 1989, 129–33). Tengku Razaleigh then seized the initiative to create a new political party in the form of S46, seeking to undermine the very legitimacy of UMNO itself as the main representative of Malay interests in the country. Finally, a massive heart attack in early 1989 further threatened Mahathir's aura of invincibility, suggesting that "Mahathir's political career hung in the balance" (Khoo 1995, 322).

The multiple historically unprecedented regime-debilitating events assailing Tun Dr. Mahathir and UMNO changed several political observers' and opposition elites' perceptions of the increasing vulnerability of the BN. S46 soon began negotiations with the DAP and PAS to try to form a unified opposition coalition to contest in the next general election. A potential united opposition front comprising the DAP, S46, and PAS was deemed potentially credible primarily because several pro-regime elites endorsed it (Khong 1991a, 161). They included state chief ministers, members of the Malay royal families, and even former prime minister Tunku Abdul Rahman. As Khong (1991a, 161) notes, "It was the first time since independence that a credible opposition which could actually form a government had emerged." Khong (1991b, 13) went on to summarize the sea change in perceived regime vulnerability of the BN:

The results of Malaysia's elections had always been dull in one respect: the ruling coalition was so well entrenched that in the past, no observer saw a possible change of government, nor even the remote chance that the opposition could break the government's two-third[s] majority in the national parliament. . . . However, in 1990, *the ruling Barisan Nasional coalition appeared vulnerable.* The opposition had galvanized around Tengku Razaleigh and organized two fronts to take on the ruling coalition. In this election, *the opposition was not only talking in terms of denying the Barisan Nasional of the two-third[s] majority, but of forming the next government* with the co-operation of some political parties in Sabah and Sarawak.

Additionally, in a separate analysis, Khong (1991a, 166) quotes a DAP leader to establish the updating of opposition elite expectations about possibly defeating the incumbent,

The opposition *saw this election as the best opportunity it would have in denying the ruling coalition the two-thirds majority or in wresting power from it.* In the words of a DAP leader, this was an *"unprecedented historic opportunity* to effect far-reaching meaningful changes to the political order in the country."

This quotation clearly indicates that the DAP leader had updated his views about the BN's weaknesses that an opposition alliance could profit from. Furthermore, the party leaders foresaw an optimistic scenario whereby if all three major opposition parties made significant gains, and combined them with favorable results from the eastern Malaysian states of Sabah and Sarawak, "Victory was not completely out of reach" (Crouch 1996, 125).

But even as DAP and PAS leaders became more motivated to cooperate with each other to take advantage of the BN's new vulnerability in the 1990 general elections, PAS and DAP supporters were still wary of jointly campaigning with each other. "The members and supporters of both parties are strongly against any such 'unholy alliance' but their leaders obviously feel that political expediency demands covert collaboration between the two," declared an op-ed in the *Business Times*.[15] Crouch (1996, 123) concurred, suggesting that "although Tengku Razaleigh seemed reasonably comfortable with both his major allies individually, they were not comfortable with each other." Specifically, for PAS, an op-ed in the *New Straits Times* noted that "some PAS leaders are eager to keep clear of the DAP because the issue is beginning to become a liability. Their stand on Islam is being questioned because of the relationship with the DAP via Semangat 46."[16] The same op-ed noted that a radical PAS group calling itself Al-Islah was recently formed because it "opposes cooperation with Semangat '46." The group even threatened to contest against PAS's own candidates should PAS forge a national-level coalition with the DAP. The DAP itself was not spared. In addition to internal pressure from its supporters, it was subject to consistent attacks from Gerakan (now firmly part of the BN) in Penang, which claimed that the DAP's association with S46 and with PAS meant that the DAP also supported the formation of an Islamic state.[17] As evidence, Gerakan pointed to posters produced by those parties urging voters to support the formation of an Islamic government in Malaysia.

Ultimately, DAP and PAS leaders found an uneasy compromise. They formed distinct opposition coalitions with S46 campaigning in different parts of the country. On the conservative right, S46 collaborated with PAS and other minor Islamic parties to form an opposition coalition called Angkatan Perpaduan Ummah (APU / United Islamic Front). The APU coalition campaigned together in the north and eastern coast of Peninsular Malaysia, such as in the states of Kelantan and Terengganu, where most of their candidates stood. Yet, beyond campaigning together under a common coalition name, there was no common coalition logo, and no common policy platform (Khong 1991b, 9). The only compromise that PAS made was to drop all references to forming an Islamic state from its own election manifesto (von der Mehden 1991, 166).[18] For the DAP, any direct relationship with PAS in the early 1990s was far too costly for its leaders to contemplate. Thus, the DAP eventually formed a coalition only with S46 called the Gagasan Rakyat (GR / People's Might). They then campaigned together primarily in the western coast of Peninsular Malaysia, where there more non-Malays residing in ethnically mixed electoral districts.

But regardless of the exact form of election campaigning that we observe, why did DAP and PAS leaders feel compelled to coordinate joint campaigns with S46 at the minimum even though there was significant internal party dissent? For sure, the UMNO's unprecedented fracture for the first time since 1965 and its perceived increasing vulnerability was a key reason. The other reason was that party leaders recognized that they depended on collaboration with other parties to maximize their vote shares and seat shares—my second hypothesized independent variable.

For PAS, its identity as an Islamist party was both its strength and its weakness. While it had the unflinching loyalty of its core supporters who were devout Muslims, it struggled to attract the votes of non-Muslims and those who were only moderately religious. Therefore, through campaigning with the more moderate S46, PAS leaders sought to "tone down its image of an extremist, fundamentalist party," and to "help to soften its image and make it more acceptable to people whose understanding of the 'true teachings' of Islam was not adequate" (Khong 1991b, 9). This could help PAS draw more votes from non-Malay-Muslim voters, a problem that the party had not solved in the 1986 general elections. Another observer of the cooperation between S46 and the PAS opined (Yahya 1989, 35),

> Both parties—PAS and S46—need each other to strengthen their base to effectively oppose Mahathir. . . . Each of them have their own strengths and weaknesses, which explains why they have to complement one another. . . . If PAS wants to be in power, it has to collaborate with S46 because Tengku Razaleigh can help to alleviate PAS' weaknesses. Similarly, S46's weaknesses can also be assisted by PAS.

Consequently, in the pursuit of interparty coordination to allocate electoral districts and campaign jointly with S46, PAS leaders took pains to persuade their reluctant supporters that such alliances were necessary. One way in which the party sought to persuade its own supporters was for the party's communication office to produce a booklet titled *At-Tafahum Al-Siasi* (Political Cooperation in the General Election) for distribution among its supporters. The document sought to explain to PAS supporters the numerous reasons why cooperating with S46 was important, necessary, and allowed under Islamic law. Thereafter, the party tasked its deputy president, Haji Abdul Hadi Awang, with using the book to persuade supporters who were still reluctant to cooperate with S46 (Ali 1998, 80–83). Specifically, the party maintained that such cooperation with "secular" parties was permissible because it brought "benefits" to the people while not affecting the party's fight for Islamic principles.

The logic of mutual dependency was similar for the DAP's leaders. As Khong (1991b, 11) describes, the precise purpose of the party's alliance with S46 was also to send a signal of opposition moderation and compromise in order to win extra Malay votes:

> *The alliance with a Malay party might also help the [DAP] party to secure more Malay votes* in the mixed constituencies. . . . the party hoped that its image as an extremist, chauvinistic Chinese party—due to its long campaign for equal rights for the Chinese and other minority communities—would be shed in the larger coalition led by a Malay party.

In pursuit of maximizing its seat and vote share by building an alliance with S46, moreover, the DAP also took numerous steps to reduce intraparty dissent and persuade its supporters to vote for DAP and S46 candidates. This was most evident in the numerous commentary and news articles featured in the party's newsletter, *The Rocket*, distributed to party members.[19] Throughout numerous issues of *The Rocket* published in 1989, the party published editorials and commentaries about whether and how the party should cooperate with S46 and PAS. For example, in the sixth issue of 1989, *The Rocket* devoted about 10 percent of its pages to publishing responses it had received after soliciting feedback on potential alliance building with other opposition parties. Titled "The Great Debate: Should We or Shouldn't We," the section vacillated between readers who said, "My family and all my neighbors do not support your party joining up with PAS and Semangat 46," and those who said, "I support the need for greater cooperation amongst the opposition parties and a united stand in the next general elections." Consequently, once the DAP's leaders decided to cooperate with S46 to campaign together, *The Rocket*'s tune changed to one of persuasion in late 1989 and early 1990. In the last issue of *The Rocket* in 1989, for instance, its front pages publicized Tengku Razaleigh's endorsement of DAP leader Lim Kit Siang for the post of Penang's chief minister if their joint forces were victorious in the state's local elections. The first issue of *The Rocket* in 1990 then carried a lengthy full-page commentary by the vice president of S46, Marina Yusoff, urging DAP supporters to "stand united against him [Prime Minister Mahathir] and his lapdogs." The front page of the second issue in 1990 carried a prominent photo of Tengku Razaleigh, publicizing the joint DAP-S46 speaking events in Penang, Ipoh, Kuala Lumpur, and Petaling Jaya, which had drawn "capacity crowds" that "sent seismic tremors into the camps of the Barisan Nasional parties."

Ultimately, with two coalitions—GR on the left and APU on the right—the opposition contested as a partially wedded whole (von der Mehden 1991, 166–67). The DAP performed reasonably, winning 20 seats in the 180-seat parliament. The PAS benefited most from the coalition, winning seven parliamentary seats, up from only one seat in 1986. Its alliance with S46 at the state level also saw the two parties win all the state seats in Kelantan, denying UMNO any seats in the state for the first time ever. Despite these moderate successes, however, the BN remained electorally invincible, having won more than two-thirds of the parliamentary seats.

The 1999 General Elections: The Barisan Alternatif (BA) Opposition Alliance

Almost a decade later, another series of unprecedented historical events signaling clear vulnerabilities in the BN's continued stranglehold on Malaysia occurred in rapid succession. They would pose a much stronger challenge undermining the BN's ruling legitimacy. First, the 1997 Asian financial crisis crippled the Malaysian economy (Pepinsky 2009a, chapter 5). The Malaysian currency, the ringgit, had half of its value wiped away. Bad loans spiked from about 4 percent to almost 20 percent (Meesook et al. 2001, 4). External and domestic demand collapsed. Quarterly real GDP growth plunged from more than 5 percent to minus 10 percent. Within a few months, the BN's much-touted governing legitimacy in producing spectacular economic growth was quashed. As Pepinsky (2009a, 195) noted, "Mahathir and his political allies within *the UMNO and the BN certainly viewed the economic crisis as a deep threat to the regime's hold on power*, even forbidding the Malaysian media from using the word 'crisis' until well after the crisis had passed." Second, behind-the-scenes dis-agreement about how to grapple with the economic crisis led to Deputy Prime Minister Anwar Ibrahim's dramatic sacking (Felker 1999; Abbott 2000; Pepinsky 2009a, 211–16). The protégé of Tun Dr. Mahathir was accused of sodomy, expelled from the UMNO supreme council, arrested, physically abused by the police while under arrest, and charged with and convicted of corruption. Some senior allies within UMNO were arrested without charges under the Internal Security Act, and then released after pledging loyalty to UMNO and to Mahathir. Other more junior UMNO allies were directly purged and expelled. Third, during and following Anwar's trial, thousands of ordinary citizens turned out into the streets of Kuala Lumpur, Malaysia's economic capital, protesting against the BN's cronyism and the sacking and torture of Anwar. These protestors, mobi-lized through a myriad of nongovernmental organizations within Malay-sian civil society, gradually congealed into a broad-based movement known as the Reformasi (Reform) Movement (Hilley 2001, 205–8; Weiss 2006). These massive anti-BN street protests were the first time ever that large numbers of ordinary Malaysians publicly displayed their antipathy toward the regime. They gave hope to opposition elites that the masses would be on the opposition's side if their voting power could be concen-trated against the BN. Wan Azizah Wan Ismail, Anwar's wife, thus formed the centrist multiethnic Party Keadilan Rakyat (PKR) as the first step toward electoral mobilization.

Several trends further supported perceptions of the BN's accelerating vulnerability. An important development was the shift in mass-media consumption. The BN government's control of mainstream media was slowly being undermined by the growing demand for and influence of alternative news sources (Abbott 2000; Hilley 2001, 209–13). The PAS's newsletter, *Harakah*, increased its circulation from 65,000 to 300,000 in a matter of months. This was more than the two leading English newspapers at that time, *The Star* (circulation 220,000), and the *New Straits Times* (cir-culation 156,000). Even *Aliran Monthly*, the liberal news magazine, saw its circulation more than double from 8,000 to just above 18,000. Further-more, the skyrocketing growth of the internet audience in Malaysia saw more than 50 pro-Anwar websites mushrooming, consistently criticizing the establishment's narrative of the Anwar saga. Galvanized by Malaysia's first ever mass-based anti-regime Reformasi social movement, PAS fur-ther claimed to have increased its membership almost 10-fold in the six months since Anwar's sacking (Hilley 2001, 211; Mutalib 2000, 67).

With this series of public challenges foreshadowing the BN's decline, opposition elites within the DAP and PAS increased their ambitions for toppling the BN in the 1999 general elections. Despite their failure in 1990, opposition elites were newly motivated because they thought that "the Anwar saga *clearly dealt a major blow* to the government's popular credibility" noted Felker (1999, 47). Case (2001, 35) concurred, noting that "*if ever the Barisan could be defeated in elections, now seemed the time.*" Finally, a key leader of the Reformasi Movement, in an interview concerning the opposition's changing expectations about the BN's vulnerability, recalled his participation in the movement in 1998 and 1999.

> *Clearly everyone could see massive momentum.* The split [in the BN] was unprecedented. Anwar's charisma at that time [was] unbeatable. We could see not only electorally there was a change of consciousness of the people. *It will clearly be a disadvantage for any [opposition] party to stay out of it, to stay aloof of that. . . . After a political crisis, therefore there is an opportunity for the opposition to strength[en] itself.* So that's what our warning to all the political parties is—you better get ready. I think being very pragmatist, they came along . . . *PAS [was] also very keen because they think that only through cooperation then they can defeat Barisan Nasional.*[20]

To be sure, both DAP and PAS leaders continued to be wary of dissent among their own supporters, even as they sought coordination on allocating electoral districts and joint nationwide campaigns. Hilley (2001, 214) noted that "while there appeared strong and growing support for a PAS-DAP coalition, both parties remained circumspect about its nature and timing." In particular, dissent within the DAP kept its leaders from overtly and actively seeking cooperation with PAS in the early stages of formulating electoral strategies (Hilley 2001, 215). When asked to assess the difficulties of alliance building in 1999, a key PKR leader said,

> The key leaders at that time, especially DAP, were reluctant. Because they think that the cooperation will again drag them into the polemic of Islamic state and all that thing, *which in the back of their mind their reading of it is their base voters will not ever accept it. That has always been their reluctance.*[21]

Yet, despite these misgivings over internal dissent, another crucial reason why opposition leaders took the risk to forge an alliance was the clear recognition of their mutual dependence on each other for potential victory. PAS and DAP leaders knew that they could not prevail over the BN if they contested alone. A key leader from the DAP remarked to me,

> In the case of the DAP, I think the top leaders are very clear where we should go. If you follow Kit Siang's writing, it is very clear that he understands the problem. The problem is that *we will never win alone*. Therefore, we need coalition partners. *We need strong coalition partners in order to win together.*[22]

Another DAP central executive member corroborated this logic, summarizing the DAP leader Lim Kit Siang's actions at that time:

> You brought up the issue of working with PAS. That was a very contentious issue in 1999. *But I think Kit Siang saw it was necessary. . . .* That was the risk. In politics you have to take risk[s]. That is what Kit Siang has been doing all his life. I think at this point in time, *most of us see that it was the necessary risk to take.*[23]

A key former leader in the PAS echoed a similar logic, saying that they could only win if they cooperated with their ideological rivals in a coalition:

> PAS must be reminded that it was *only when they are in coalition with others that they have a chance to increase their vote share. . . .* Well, you know very well that there is a lot of commonality and differences. And whether it is difficult or easy will really have to depend on leadership. *And leadership that is more focused on winning an election very close to the seat of power will really want to ensure their chances are not jeopardized by bickering and wrangling over policy matters.*[24]

Eventually, the DAP and PAS were once again brought together in the middle by the centrist and moderate PKR. The new opposition coalition would be called the Barisan Alternatif (BA). The BA saw a somewhat deeper form of cooperation between all parties. Not only did the top leaders of the DAP, PAS, and PKR campaigned together, they also launched a common manifesto which all parties signed onto. BA's anti-regime common policy platform downplayed PAS's goal of an Islamic state and DAP's aim of a noncommunalist Malaysia, but emphasized a generally liberal platform of human rights, social justice, rule of law, judicial independence, term limits for the prime minister, and other similar themes (Felker 2000, 52–53; Liow 2004, 367–68; Mutalib 2000, 68; Weiss 2006, 142). In particular, Case (2001, 44–46) noted certain peculiarities of the common policy platform that the BA put out:

> They [Barisan Alternative] also produced a common manifesto— "Toward a Just Malaysia"—which, while far more substantive than that of the BN, was most notable for what it left out. Specifically, there was no mention of the PAS's commitment to an Islamic state or the DAP's call for a Malaysian Malaysia. Instead, the PAS symbol of a full moon was coupled informally with the DAP's rocket, producing a popular refrain of "rocket to the moon."

This deliberate avoidance of key campaign terminologies that were dear to the ideological hearts of both the DAP and PAS thus signaled the quid pro quo ideological compromise that both parties sought to portray to voters. In exhibiting such compromise, their goal was to try to attract the votes of the supporters of their ideological rivals. Senior PAS leaders began courting urban non-Malay-Muslim voters by hosting meals at plush hotels "bedecked in coat and tie," a scene in stark contrast to their usual Islamic dress coats (Noor 2014, 157–58). For their part, DAP leaders too decided that it was worthwhile to take a risk to form the BA to take advantage of the BN's declining dominance to try to win more Malay-Muslim votes (Hilley 2001, 217–19).

Eventually, the 1999 elections resulted in uneven gains (Felker 2000; Mutalib 2000; Pepinsky 2009a, 220–22). The BN retained its two-thirds majority in parliament but with smaller votes and seat shares. PAS fared the best, almost quadrupling the number of its seats to 27 in the 193-seat parliament, tripling the number of state assembly seats that it held, and winning control over the state assemblies of Kelantan and Terengganu. The DAP, unfortunately, encountered electoral disaster. While it maintained its miserly 11 state assembly seats and increased its number of parliamentary seats from 7 to 11, all three of its top leaders—Lim Kit Siang, Karpal Singh, and Chen Man Hin—lost. Their strategy of consolidating support from their own non-Malay supporters while profiting from extra Malay votes did not bear fruit. With these disappointing results, the BA disbanded in two years as the BN reasserted its dominance, marginalizing and ignoring the demands of the three opposition parties (Gomez 2004).

The 2013 General Elections: The Pakatan Rakyat (PR)
Opposition Alliance

Fast-forward more than a decade later, the 2013 Pakatan Rakyat (PR) opposition alliance emerged as a result of prior extraordinary political developments. The story starts five years earlier in the 2008 electoral cycle, which occurred in the midst of the global financial crisis. During that time, opposition parties made unexpected, stunning gains even when they did not publicly coordinate their campaigns with each other (Chin and Wong 2009; Singh 2009). The BN lost its two-thirds majority in the 222-seat parliament for the first time. This meant that the PKR expanded its parliamentary presence from one seat in 2004 to 31 seats in 2008, the DAP's number of parliamentarians more than doubled from 12 to 28, with PAS almost quadrupling its presence from 6 to 23 parliamentarians. Altogether, the 82 seats from the three parties represented the best-ever results for Malaysia's opposition. At the state level, opposition parties gained control of five state governments—Kelantan, Kedah, Perak, Penang, and Selangor—where previously the BN had only ever lost two state governments at any one time. The BN's defeats in the last two states were particularly noteworthy because they were the most economically developed and richest states in Malaysia. Accordingly, these results were the BN's "worst election results since independence in 1957" (Singh 2009, 157). Consequently, the PKR, DAP, and PAS came together in the following months and years to form governing alliances for those five regional state governments. They called their governing alliance the Pakatan Rakyat (PR) coalition, which endured throughout the five-year term. For its part, leadership of the BN and UMNO passed in 2009 from Abdullah Badawi to Najib Razak, son of Tun Abdul Razak, Malaysia's prime minister from 1970 to 1976.

With five years of successfully governing five state governments under its belt, the PR alliance had several historically unprecedented advantages in undermining the BN's rule. First, it could finally signal to voters its ability to govern effectively. Voters would not have to fear the loss of their quality of life if an opposition alliance were to take over the government at the national level. In fact, PR candidates could campaign on a record of state-level policies that had benefited voters' everyday lives. Second, opposition parties leveraged their unprecedented numbers in state-level government and newfound mass popularity to enhance their party organizations. The PKR, for example, a mere three months after the 2008 election, shifted into a new RM$5 million multistory headquarters covering 20,000 square feet at the outskirts of Kuala Lumpur.[25] Part of the new space would serve as the new office of opposition party leader Anwar Ibrahim. The DAP followed suit, inaugurating a new RM$3.5 million headquarters at its party stronghold in the state of Penang in 2012.[26] It also recruited a larger group of journalists and graphic artists to produce *The Rocket*, the party's internal party newsletter. Their expanded organizations bolstered the parties' confidence about challenging the BN's feared party machinery. Third, recurring massive street protests by the nongovernmental organization Bersih signaled new mass discontent with the BN (Chan 2019; Khoo 2014, 2016). Advocating for extensive electoral reform to ensure free and fair elections, Bersih had already organized three street protests in 2007, 2011, and 2012 by the time of the 2013 general elections. The last of these was particularly important. It was the largest, involving some 300,000 participants, about six times that of the previous rally in 2011. It was also more contentious, with about three times the amount of tear gas used against the protestors alongside the deployment of water cannons.[27] These indicators portended an accelerating momentum in mass dissent against the BN.

Consequently, the PR was full of confidence approaching the 2013 elections. Most observers agreed that the BN's dominance would be undermined (Case 2014). Chin (2013, 499) submitted that "many were under the impression that, *for the first time, 50 years after the formation of Malaysia, the opposition alliance, Pakatan Rakyat (PR), had a real change of defeating the Barisan Nasional (BN).*" Ostwald (2013, 521) also noted that "the election was arguably the *first in Malaysia's history in which the outcome did not appear certain in the weeks preceding it.*" Ufen (2014, 9) went further, surmising that Prime Minister Najib Razak "was well aware that the Pakatan Rakyat would at least endanger BN's two-third[s] majority in Parliament and could even topple him." Case (2014, 57) concurred: "Many analysts expected that Pakatan would make still more gains, *perhaps even winning outright* and therein producing a 'dual transition' involving government turnover and democratization by election."

But despite everyone's optimism about the potential benefits of another new alliance approaching the 2013 elections, opposition leaders, particularly those from the DAP, were still wary about the devastating results under the BA alliance in 1999, whereby the DAP suffered historical defeats. A DAP central executive member commented,

> *The most important element for the DAP is there is still a massive phobia of PAS. We sort of learned our lesson, rightly or wrongly, from*

1999, when the association with PAS resulted in the backlash, particularly among the Chinese voters. And that being our core base, we have to be ultra careful. So we understand the electoral pact arrangement where one candidate versus one candidate benefits us. But at the same time, we were very wary to be seen . . . anywhere formally with PAS.[28]

So how did opposition party leaders, especially those from the DAP, reduce intraparty dissent and persuade their supporters to back the PR opposition alliance? Party leaders obviously recognized that they had to cooperate with their ideological rivals to win over new voters from new constituencies.[29] But they did not want to lose their core supporters in the process of doing so. A key strategy that DAP leaders adopted as part of the PR alliance between 2008 and 2013 (but not in 1999) was to redouble efforts to educate and persuade their own party members through the internal party newsletter, *The Rocket*.[30] If it is true that opposition parties face intraparty costs of dissent when forming alliances and strive hard to persuade their supporters to "hold their noses" to throw their support behind the alliance, then we should expect how *The Rocket* discussed the DAP's ideological rivals to vary over time depending on whether the party is in or out of an alliance. We can imagine that if the DAP is not part of a coalition, *The Rocket* should publish opposition-related articles that disparage parties other than the DAP itself ("negative image" articles) or provide reasons as to why it is impossible to work with these parties ("justify non-cooperation" articles). Alternatively, if the DAP is in a coalition with PAS and another centrist opposition party, then *The Rocket* should publish more articles that portray them in a positive light ("positive rival" article) or more articles that highlight the prospective gains to be made if they all cooperate with each other ("prospective gains" article).

Across 2001–2004 and 2010–2013, we can indeed observe *The Rocket* shift the way it discussed PAS and PKR. Figure 7.4 highlights my hand-coding of 196 opposition-related articles across 49 issues of *The Rocket* in the four years after the BA collapsed in 2001 and the four years of the PKR coalition leading up till the 2013 general elections.

In the four years between 2001 and 2004, about two-thirds of all the opposition-related articles published in *The Rocket* were either "negative image" articles or "justify non-cooperation" articles, with at least half of the articles being in either category in each year. An example of an opposition-related article that portrayed PAS negatively and justified the DAP's noncooperation with it is the article reproduced in figure 7.5, titled

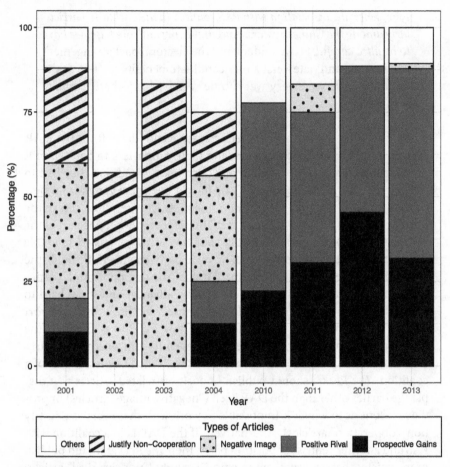

Fig. 7.4. Proportion of the Different Types of Articles Appearing in *The Rocket*

"PAS' Blueprint a Threat to the Federal Constitution." The article summarizes a statement put out by the DAP's national deputy chairman, Karpal Singh, criticizing PAS's "Islamic state" document released in November 2003. In that document, PAS clarified and reiterated its position that sharia and *hudud* laws are the essential foundations of an Islamic state, and that all other laws and democratic institutions were to be subsumed under them (Liow 2009, 89–91). In Singh's opinion, the PAS document "violates the 46-year 'social contract' of the major communities," "violates the 1999 Barisan Alternatif common manifesto," and "is an unadulterated threat to the continued existence of the Federal Constitution." He charged PAS with "trying to destroy the basic structure of the Constitution," and urged the PKR "to get out of the shadows of PAS and stick to their principles."

The Rocket Special Issue 2004 · Islamic State · 15

PAS' blueprint a threat to the Federal Constitution

The PAS' Islamic State blueprint, the Islamic State Document, is highly objectionable on four important grounds:

• It violates the 46-year "social contract" of the major communities entrenched in the 1957 Merdeka Constitution, the 1963 Malaysia Agreement and the 1970 Rukunegara that firstly, Malaysia is a democratic, secular and multi-religious nation with Islam as the official religion but not an Islamic state; and secondly, the Federal Constitution is the supreme law of Malaysia as provided in Article 4 and not the syariah law as intended by the PAS Islamic State blueprint;

• It violates the 1999 Barisan Alternatif common manifesto "Towards A Just Malaysia", to restore justice, freedom, democracy and good governance with clear commitment by all subscribing parties to uphold the fundamental principles of the Malaysian Constitution, binding PAS not to pursue the establishment of an Islamic State while in the Barisan Alternatif;

• It is incompatible with democracy in placing the PAS Islamic State concept beyond criticism by equating it with Allah's injunction; and

• It ratchets up the UMNO-PAS competition to out-Islamise each other and turn Malaysia into an Islamic state to new and unprecedented height and intensity.

As DAP National Deputy Chairman Karpal Singh has rightly warned, the PAS' blueprint for an Islamic State is an unadulterated threat to the continued existence of the Federal Constitution as envisaged by the framers of the solemn document which by Article 4 establishes it to be the supreme law of the land. An Islamic State, whether it be ala-PAS or ala-UMNO, is an affront to the Supreme Court which declared the country to be a secular state by a 5-man bench on 29 February, 1988.

"By the introduction of the blueprint, PAS is trying to destroy the basic structure of the Constitution. That this move is an election gimmick is apparent as PAS cannot obtain a 2/3 majority in Parliament to amend the Constitution to set up an Islamic State," says Karpal.

The Federal Constitution, as presently constituted, has entrenched provisions to safeguard the rights of both Muslims and non-Muslims in the country. Syariah law in the states provides for the perpetua-

tion of personal law of Muslims and the civil law provides for the protection of the rights of both Muslims and non-Muslims. It is mischievous for PAS, for the sake of gaining political mileage in the upcoming general election, to cause alarm and concern among the populace.

As for Keadilan and PRM, it is fruitless for them to wring their hands in hopelessness by rejecting the blueprint but stating it was PAS' right to issue the document. Keadilan and PRM should strive to get out of the shadow of PAS and stick to their principles if both parties have any credibility. They should place principle and the common good of all Malaysians above political expediency.

The controversial Islamic State document

Fig. 7.5. Example of "Negative Image" and "Justify Non-cooperation" Article in *The Rocket*

In contrast, between 2010 and 2013, only 3.5 out of 149 opposition-related articles were negative.[31] Over 80 percent of all opposition-related articles in this latter four-year period portrayed PAS or PKR or the PR coalition in a positive manner. For instance, Karpal Singh would make another statement in *The Rocket* marking a 180-degree turn from his position 10 years earlier (see fig. 7.6). The article, published in January 2013, summarized Karpal Singh's speech at the DAP's national congress held in December 2012. The report noted that Singh, now DAP chairperson, "stressed that PAS is an important friend in Pakatan Rakyat" and that despite their differences, PAS was "a solid party with ideology and principles." He justified his change in stance by suggesting that "if we do not change with the times, the times will change us." Evidently, the critical difference this time was that PAS was part of the broader PR alliance with the DAP and PKR. With the upcoming general elections in May 2013, Karpal thought it reasonable for him to reiterate to DAP members that it was crucial for them to view PAS in a positive manner, so that the coalition could win.

"Positive image" articles did not stop simply at DAP leaders' declarations of the good intentions of their fellow opposition "friends" and the

ᵀᴴᴱRocket

PAS is our friend

DAP national chairperson, Karpal Singh in his opening speech stressed that PAS is an important friend in Pakatan Rakyat. "We may have several differences, but it is a solid party with ideology and principles," he explained, followed by a thundering applause from the delegates and attending guests.

He said, what is important is Pakatan Rakyat (PR) should not be reckless as its enemies are always wanting to divide the understanding built between the parties in PR.

"Before this nobody would have expected that DAP can work with PAS, but now the Malaysian political scenario has changed. If we do not change with the times, the times will change us," he said confidently.

While referring to Penang as a good example, Karpal, who is also Member of Parliament for Gelugor puts a high optimism that PR can give an excellent service for the people. "Penang has achieved great success under PR. It is a good example to be followed. What has been achieved in Penang will be achieved in Putrajaya too."

Don't forget the veterans

Karpal also recounted many of the veterans contribution to the party. He called upon the delegates to appreciate the party veterans for their many sacrifices and having to endure many difficult times for the party struggle. "Without the veterans, DAP would not be what it is today," he said.

Moving on, Karpal rebutted the detractors for saying that DAP is no longer as principled as it was before when it was an opposition party checking on the government. He stressed that DAP will not give up on its principles. "In politics, there are no permanent friends or permanent enemies, there must only be permanent principles."

He also reemphasised DAP's stand in giving full support for Datuk Seri Anwar Ibrahim to become Prime Minister should Pakatan Rakyat be given the mandate to govern Malaysia.

In his serious and spirited speech, Karpal took a moment to share about his victory in his defamation suit against Utusan Malaysia, in which Karpal was awarded RM70,000.

"Looks like the number 70,000 is a lucky number for PR. PAS's vice presidents Mahfuz Omar and Salahuddin Ayub also won RM70,000 in their suits against Utusan Malaysia. Mahfuz suggested that I should sacrifice a goat to celebrate my victory. I said, 'not a goat, but let's put Barisan Nasional to the slaughter.'"

He also said that the media must practised fair and honest journalism, not propagate lies. "There must be responsible journalism on the part of the media. When PR comes to power, there will be responsible journalism."

Fig. 7.6. Example of "Positive Rival" Article in *The Rocket*

overall coalition. *The Rocket* between 2010 and 2013 oftentimes featured interviews with politicians from other opposition parties to highlight the commonalities between all of them, thus narrowing the perceived ideological differences between the parties.

For example, figure 7.7 shows the cover page of *The Rocket* in January 2012, featuring three prominent female politicians from the respective component parties of PR, titled "The Bold and the Beautiful." From left to right, they are Dr. Siti Mariah Mahmud, deputy chief of the women's wing of the PAS and member of parliament for Kota Raja; Teo Nie Ching, at that time the member of parliament for Serdang; and Nurul Izzah Anwar from the PKR, daughter of the formerly jailed deputy prime minister Anwar Ibrahim, at that time member of parliament for Lembah Pantai. A careful reading of the substantive content of their respective interviews reveals that *The Rocket* used women's issues as a foil to allow the respective members of parliament to highlight their similar commitment to pressurizing the incumbent government to reform existing public policies for women, and to publicize their policy priorities if they could govern as a coalition. In the interview with Nurul Izzah Anwar, she highlighted that she "pushed very hard for the amendment of 60 days maternity leave to 90 days" and that "the Women, Family, and Community Development Ministry is not doing enough to address the needs of the fairer sex." She proposed increasing the ministry's budget and implementing more effective

Fig. 7.7. Cover Page of *The Rocket* in January 2012

programs, such as the "MyKasih" program that provides points for poor households to purchase groceries. Dr. Siti Mariah Mahmud similarly emphasized enhancing initiatives such as building childcare centers "in areas where it is close to the commercial centers and factories for the convenience of the parents." Her pet priority, however, was strengthening the existing Malaysian sharia courts system insofar as there would be better enforcement of women-related Muslim marriage laws, such as alimony payments from divorce procedures.

While it is apparent that these different female politicians from different opposition parties emphasized varying policy priorities, their respective agendas were all linked together in a common theme and purpose—reforming existing bureaucracies, legislation, and public policies to empower women. That the DAP was willing to devote multiple pages showcasing politicians from other parties in the alliance in its party newsletter that is ostensibly circulated only to its own supporters reflects not just the strong relationships between the parties. It is also a somewhat risky strategy in positively portraying its allies by highlighting thematic commonalities across all opposition parties in the alliance. One can imagine that more than a few devoted Chinese or Indian supporters of the DAP were turned off by such interviews. For them, any talk of strengthening the sharia courts system would be sacrilegious to their secular worldview and commitment to a multireligious country. Yet the DAP's investment in this potentially costly strategy also reflects its own calculation that these devoted supporters could be persuaded to support the party regardless of such features, and that there are more benefits to be gained from appealing to all its supporters to engage in cross-party strategic voting.

Additionally, opposition-related articles in *The Rocket* also promoted the prospective gains that opposition supporters would enjoy if the PR coalition was victorious over the BN. In the run-up to the general elections, the coalition manifesto became the substantive focal point highlighting these prospective gains. On the cover page of the January 2013 edition of *The Rocket*, for example, the DAP made sure that it communicated these important prospective gains described in the manifesto if the PR coalition defeated the BN. The cover page publicized the recently launched PR election manifesto, highlighting key initiatives for Malaysians to enjoy cheaper consumer goods such as houses and cars, to feel safer through reduced crime and corruption, to be more economically secure with enhanced welfare and education, and to enjoy more liberal policies for women and the elderly.

For all the coalition's efforts, the results of the 2013 general election were an anticlimax. Although the PR opposition alliance managed to win a majority of the popular vote (51 percent), it failed to win a majority of the parliamentary seats due to pre-electoral malapportionment (Case 2014; Ostwald 2013; Saravanamuttu 2016, chapter 9; Weiss 2013a). While the DAP managed to boost its number of parliamentarians from 28 to 38, the PKR won only 30 seats (losing 1 seat), and the PAS won only 21 seats (losing 2 seats). The BN maintained its parliamentary dominance with a total of 133 seats, 88 of which were won by UMNO. The lopsided results showcased how effectively the BN-controlled election commission was able to gerrymander the boundaries of electoral districts to translate the BN's vote share of 47.4 percent to a seat share of nearly 60 percent.

The 2018 General Elections: The Pakatan Harapan (PH) Opposition Alliance

By June 2015, two years after the 2013 general elections, the Pakatan Rakyat opposition coalition was dead.[32] PAS's continued insistence on implementing Islamic law in the state of Kelantan and the rise of a newly conservative leadership strained its relations with the DAP to the breaking point. There was also evidence that the PAS was co-opted by the ruling BN (Gomez and Mohamed Nawab 2019, 1–15; Ostwald, Schuler, and Chong 2019, 41–43). Its leaders introduced a bill supported by UMNO leaders that would pave the way for implementing the Islamic sharia criminal code. PAS's leaders also publicly officiated at various events with UMNO leaders, and openly declared that they had received money from UMNO to finance their party's electoral expenses. But a new opportunity to form another opposition alliance contesting in the May 2018 general elections would arise with the emergence of the new opposition parties in the PPBM and Amanah. This opportunity would pose a new set of questions. To what extent would the four opposition parties—the DAP, PKR, PPBM, and Amanah—be able to coordinate their electoral campaign to maximize opposition turnout? Even more, having known that the past joint campaigns of APU and GR in 1990, BA in 1999, and PR in 2013 all fell short of the mark, what improvements could the new PH alliance make to push the ruling BN incumbent out of power? More precisely, how could these improvements more strongly induce cross-party vote transfers and also maximize the number of moderate voters that the opposition could peel away from the BN?

It is important to note that 2018's Pakatan Harapan (PH) alliance once again followed from two major, unprecedented events signaling the BN's growing weakness and the heightened probability of defeating it. The first major event was the 1MDB scandal, as exposed by the *Wall Street Journal*. As described in the previous chapter, the scale of the 1MDB scandal boggles the mind. It involved billions of US dollars' worth of bond sales arranged by Goldman Sachs and the rerouting of sales proceeds through secret accounts in the United States, Switzerland, the Middle East, and the Bahamas. The monies were allegedly used to fund a variety of expenses— the BN's electoral expenses in the 2013 general elections, shopping sprees by Prime Minister Najib Razak's wife, purchases of American real estate, Van Gogh and Monet artworks, and a US$250 million yacht, in addition to producing Hollywood movies such as *The Wolf of Wall Street*, starring Leonardo DiCaprio. Such opulence in the midst of stagnating wages and growing inflation from a new government-imposed goods and service (GST) tax dismayed a large number of Malaysians (Chin and Welsh 2019; Welsh 2019; Wong 2018; Wong and Ooi 2018).

This scandal prompted the second major event in the run-up to the 2018 general elections wherein the former prime minister, Tun Dr. Mahathir Mohamad and the deputy prime minister, Muhyiddin Yasin, both quit UMNO and set up PPBM. While an UMNO leader's defection was not unprecedented, Mahathir's stint as Malaysia's longest serving prime minister, and one who oversaw the country's meteoric economic development, gave extra symbolism to his defection. As the prime minister of Malaysia for 22 years, from 1981 to 2003, Mahathir represented the pinnacle of UMNO's political domination and symbolic power. During his administration, the country achieved stellar economic growth rates amid general inter-ethnic peace. Malaysia's GDP per capita grew 2.5 times, increasing from US$1,769 to US$4,461 during his tenure.[33] That Mahathir would switch sides to join the opposition and stand alongside his longtime political adversaries in the DAP, PKR, and Amanah left close observers of Malaysian politics astonished.[34] That these longtime opposition leaders would also openly accept Mahathir surprised many.

Regardless, these two unprecedented events increased opposition elites' confidence that they could topple the BN, even when polling data indicated it would be an uphill climb. Liew Chin Tong, the DAP's political strategist, openly discussed the forthcoming "Malay tsunami" (Liew 2018). By his reckoning, Mahathir's alignment with the opposition would be the critical factor that would induce Malay-Muslim voters to switch to the PH. Specially, Mahathir's leadership of the PH would increase Malay-Muslim voters' confidence that their rights would be protected even as a victorious opposition worked to restore economic growth (Abdullah

2019b).[35] Other opposition party leaders interviewed also boasted of their increased confidence. The PPBM's Che Zakaria Salleh, a prominent politician in Johor, bragged that "even in places considered as UMNO territories, people are behind us. *This is the time. They will be toppled*."[36]

A key question then remained—how could the PH alliance avoid the failures of the three earlier opposition alliances? It was clear to the opposition leaders that they needed to turn out their own supporters and also convince moderate BN supporters to defect from the BN and vote for the opposition. In this regard, two stylized facts about Malaysians' voting behavior were obvious to the PH's leaders. First, most voters were primarily concerned about economic issues, such as rising inflation stagnating wages. Pre-electoral focus groups conducted in the middle of 2017 by the Institute of Southeast Asian Studies in the key swing states of Kedah and Johor revealed that both urban and rural Malay voters were primarily concerned with pocketbook issues (Serina 2018; Wan Saiful 2018b). Respondents were particularly resentful of the GST that Prime Minister Najib Razak had introduced in 2015, and at the abolishing of petrol subsidies. A poll conducted in November 2017 just six months prior to the elections by the reputable survey firm Merdeka Center verified these concerns. The survey indicated that 72 percent of all voters had economic concerns at the top of their minds, over and above crime and social problems, concerns over race and religion, and issues of political governance and corruption.[37] Another survey conducted in April 2018, just a month prior to the elections, affirmed this finding. It indicated that 67 percent of all voters prioritized economic concerns in their vote choice for the upcoming elections.[38]

Second, there continued to be reservations about the PH's ability to attract enough Malay-Muslim support. Because previous electoral results from 2008 and 2013 had indicated Chinese and Indian support was firmly behind the opposition (especially the DAP), the key uncertainty in ethnic voting patterns rested with Malay-Muslim voters (Chin 2010, 2013; Khalid and Loh 2016; Gomez and Alagappar 2018; Kananatu 2018). Correspondingly, the PH's leadership was mindful that the key to toppling UMNO and the BN was to shift Malay support away from UMNO and PAS. Little had changed since James Scott (1985, 314) declared more than three decades earlier that political domination over the Malaysian state "requires the political support of the bulk of the Malay electorate." Yet, because of Mahathir's defection and the splintering within PAS, there were five political parties competing for the support of Malay-Muslim voters for the very first time in Malaysia's electoral history—PPBM, Amanah, PKR, PAS, and

UMNO. In particular, rural, agricultural Malay-Muslim regions in Peninsular Malaysia remained bastions of support for both UMNO and PAS. Whether the combination of PPBM, Amanah, and PKR within the PH opposition alliance could induce enough Malay-Muslim voters to swing away from UMNO and PAS depended very much on two interrelated factors. On the one hand, the PH had to craft an electoral message to reassure rural Malay-Muslim voters that the rights and privileges they had enjoyed under the BN's affirmative action policies would remain untouched. At the same time, the PH's leadership had to assure voters that the DAP would not exert outsized influence on the coalition's policies. After all, the idea that the DAP would become a dominant force in the PH, threatening the special position of Malays and Islam, was a narrative that had been advanced by UMNO and the BN for the longest time.[39]

Several pre-electoral studies confirmed the intuition that the PH faced an uphill task in maintaining and attracting Malay-Muslim support. First, my pre-electoral survey experiment revealed that when the PPBM's supporters were presented with a vignette reminding them that the DAP might win the most parliamentary seats and the DAP's leader might emerge as prime minister, about 30 percent of supporters declined to support the PH candidate contesting in their district, as compared to a control group (Gandhi and Ong 2019). These supporters were not willing to sacrifice the certainty of Malay-Muslim control of the government in pursuit of democratic change. Second, in the numerous surveys approaching the elections, voter uncertainty and an inability to account for social desirability bias led to a large proportion of respondents categorizing themselves as "undecided" on a whole range of issues, including, most importantly, their prospective vote choice. A failure to make sense of these "undecided" voters led most polling firms to lean conservative—assume that Malay-Muslim voters would continue to vote for the BN (Ibrahim 2018). Third, the polling data that were available, Merdeka Center's numerous polls, and the Institute of Southeast Asia's focus groups indicated that the outsized authority of the DAP was a particular concern to Malay voters. Wan Saiful (2018b, 26–27) noted that the focus groups participants saw the DAP as an "anti-Islam" "chauvinist Chinese party" exercising dominant influence in the PH alliance. My pre-electoral interview with a PPBM central executive committee member revealed clear recognition of these sentiments among the opposition coalition's leadership:

The strength of DAP is the Achilles' heel of Pakatan Harapan. It is ironic. The strength of the DAP becomes a weakness of the Pakatan

Harapan in the eyes of the Malays. This is why I think it is really one of the factors that really push[ed] me to decide to join PPBM now. I need to create this momentum so that people know that we [PPBM] are equally strong. PPBM is strong. But the public perception is that it is otherwise, because there is this narrative that UMNO is trying to stoke. And we need to counter that . . . . Malays in rural areas are buying into that narrative. It is hard work. I am trying my best to counter that. It is not working yet. It will take time. The reality is we are trying to counter 60 years of UMNO narrative within six weeks.[40]

My fieldwork in the weeks leading up to the May 2018 elections found that the PH alliance campaigned specifically to resolve Malaysian voters' two main concerns about the economy and the Malay-Muslim position in the country. Toward that end, the PH alliance coordinated on its campaign strategies and improved from previous iterations in at least five ways.

In the first instance, the PH developed a comprehensive election manifesto that was far more substantive than previous iterations. The PH 2018 manifesto contained 65 distinct promises and special commitments within 150 pages. This was far more than PR's 2013 manifesto with 38 recommendations within 35 pages, and BA's 1999 manifesto with 18 proposals in 44 pages. When the PH's manifesto was launched in early March 2018, two months before the elections, it represented the culmination of more than six months' worth of intraparty negotiations among the various parties' top leaders within a manifesto drafting committee.[41] In addition, extensive roundtable consultations were also conducted with civil society organizations such as the Institute for Democracy and Economic Affairs, G25, and the Bar Council. Some of their suggestions regarding institutional reforms of the bureaucracy and judiciary were incorporated into the manifesto. Proposals to abolish the GST and highway tolls were just some of the many eye-catching economic proposals. Also included in the manifesto were promises to "restore the dignity of the Malays and Malay institutions" (Promise 11) and "support the economic growth of Bumiputera and all citizens in the country" (Promise 30). When I attended the glitzy manifesto launch in early March 2018 at a massive auditorium on the outskirts of Kuala Lumpur, the host declared this manifesto was not simply an alternative program of the opposition. It was, more precisely, a "policy program of a government-in-waiting." Overall, by incorporating a diverse number of recommendations on economic, social, and political issues, this document was crafted to project the alliance's credibility and sensitivity in economic affairs and its intent to safeguard the positions of Malay-Muslims.

Of course, not all voters were sophisticated enough to gain access to and read the PH's 150-page election manifesto. As compared to previous iterations of opposition alliances that relied on a simplistic slogan or a lengthy manifesto, the PH attempted a new, simple, but still substantive campaign strategy. It vowed to implement 10 key promises in the manifesto within 100 days of defeating the BN.[42] These promises were the following:

1. Abolish the GST.
2. Stabilize petrol prices and introduce targeted petrol subsidies.
3. Abolish the debt of FELDA settlers.[43]
4. Mandate Employees Provident Fund pension contributions for housewives.
5. Increase the minimum wage to RM$1,500 over five years and equalize the minimum wage between East and West Malaysia.
6. Defer student loan repayment for low-wage university graduates.
7. Set up royal commissions of inquiry for the numerous corruption scandals across various government agencies.
8. Set up a special cabinet committee to enforce the Malaysia Agreement of 1963, which grants significant autonomy to the eastern Malaysian states of Sabah and Sarawak.
9. Introduce a health subsidy scheme for low-income citizens.
10. Initiate a comprehensive review of all large infrastructure projects awarded to foreign firms and investors.

Apart from the eighth promise about the Malaysia Agreement of 1963, the promises all focused on improving the immediate economic burden for ordinary citizens. The document demonstrates that the PH strategically appealed to economic voters in its general campaign messaging. These 10 promises were widely publicized through easy-to-distribute campaign leaflets. Even T-shirts were printed with the 10 promises to be implemented in 100 days. Figure 7.8 shows one such T-shirt hung up for sale at a Pakatan Harapan campaign event in Kuala Lumpur.

A comprehensive manifesto and its simplified sibling can easily appeal to the sophisticated and unsophisticated economic voters. But what about the PH's second problem of retaining and attracting Malay-Muslim voters who prioritized their ethnoreligious privileges over economic gain? In this regard, the PH once again improved on previous versions of Malay-

Fig. 7.8. T-shirt for Sale Printed with the Pakatan Harapan Manifesto

sian opposition alliances. In early January 2018, the PH coalition announced it had chosen Tun Dr. Mahathir as the coalition's candidate for prime minister, should it win power in the May 2018 elections.[44] Wan Azizah, wife of the still-incarcerated Anwar Ibrahim and the PKR's de facto leader, was to be the coalition's candidate for deputy prime minister. This unprecedented announcement was the first time that a Malaysian opposition alliance had declared who would occupy the top two cabinet positions prior to a general election. The alliance reckoned that because of Mahathir's long-standing reputation as a protector of Malay-Muslim rights in his earlier career as Malaysia's prime minister from 1981 to 2003, Malay-Muslim voters could be induced to switch allegiances from UMNO and PAS to the PH's component parties instead. His leadership of the alliance would also resolve doubts about the DAP's outsized influence on the coalition. Additionally, Wan Azizah's selection as the candidate for deputy prime minister could also attract the votes of a large number of Malay-Muslim women. Her position as the deputy prime minister would mark the highest level of political office a woman had ever occupied in the country's history.

Yet such an announcement did not come without its costs. To what degree would the longtime opposition supporters of the DAP, PKR, and Amanah be willing to maintain their support for the PH now that Mahathir and his PPBM were the leaders of the coalition? After all, Mahathir's tenure as prime minister from 1981 to 2003 was the country's most sustained period of increasing autocracy (Slater 2003). Many opposition party elites and supporters had organized themselves politically precisely because of their opposition to Mahathir's autocracy. Many of them had deep reservations about working with him because of historical legacies. The party leaders of the DAP and Amanah, for example, were once arrested and jailed by Mahathir's regime under the Internal Security Act in 1987. Similarly, the primary purpose for Anwar Ibrahim in setting up the PKR in 1999 was its direct opposition to Mahathir's regime. When Mahathir first publicly turned to cooperate with the opposition in March 2016, DAP member of parliament Charles Santiago decried Mahathir as "the root cause of the rot that is affecting every Malaysian today."[45] More than a year later, when Mahathir was announced as the PH's candidate for prime minister, a number of the PKR's party elites refused to endorse the decision. In the state of Selangor, where the PKR had been governing since 2008, the PKR Selangor state branch openly disagreed with the decision.[46] The PKR state deputy chief and the information director both told reporters that they opposed the decision, asserting that someone from the PKR should have been chosen instead. Referring back to the 1999 Reformasi Movement, where thousands of ordinary citizens turned out into the streets to oppose Mahathir's autocratic government, Selangor PKR information director Hizwan Ahmad claimed that "people will not forget, nor will the original reformists."[47]

My interviews with opposition party leaders indicated the opposite, however. They were fairly confident of their supporters pooling their votes behind the PH alliance, despite their misgivings about Mahathir's leadership of the coalition. Close to a decade of political cooperation between the DAP, PKR, and PAS within the earlier PR opposition alliance from 2008 onward, as well as political education from their respective parties, had sensitized opposition supporters to the parties' mutual dependencies. A DAP central committee member revealed to me in an interview two months before the elections that DAP supporters accepted that their party's victory over the BN depended on Mahathir:

I think, generally speaking, the non-Malay voters are quite practical. *If they support the opposition, they want to see a change in gov-*

Fig. 7.9. Tun Dr. Mahathir Mohamad Campaigning during the 2018 General Election in the Lembah Pantai Constituency

ernment. And if they see that Mahathir at this point in time is a strong advantage in terms of being able to win over the Malay vote, most of the non-Malays will accept that. It is only a very small number of, I think, mostly urban intellectuals or activists who would not vote for the opposition because of Mahathir. I don't think it is enough to shift the needle either way.[48]

A pre-electoral survey experiment also confirmed the optimism of the DAP leader interviewed (Gandhi and Ong 2019). When DAP supporters were presented with a vignette suggesting the PPBM's leader might become the future prime minister if the opposition won, there were no discernable differences in their support for the PH alliance as compared to a control group of opposition respondents. For them, the prospect of Mahathir as the next prime minister was a nonissue.

Other than the DAP, the PKR's leaders and supporters were likely to be most aggrieved about Mahathir's leadership of the coalition and his PPBM party. In addition to their party's beginnings in 1999 opposing Mahathir, their party and Anwar Ibrahim were the informal leaders of the opposition. Mahathir and the PPBM thus effectively displaced their front-runner position within the opposition. When interviewed, the PKR's leaders and members did express some initial reservations about Tun Dr. Mahathir's leadership of the PH alliance. But they quickly pivoted to argue that his leadership was necessary to help the alliance maximize the chances of victory. As a PKR central committee member commented on overcoming the party's internal resistance toward Mahathir,

> The resentment from PKR should be the highest because the party is formed from the victimization by Mahathir. We used to have this problem where people cannot accept Mahathir. So it took a good few months to calm things down for the party to work together. Anwar actually came up with statements to pacify and ask everyone to look at the bigger picture. *So the whole thing is about looking at the bigger picture.* We cannot continue to slide. . . . The biggest is Anwar, who can put down 20 years of victimization and really move forward. Then people say, "Hey if even Anwar can accept Mahathir, why not we?"[49]

Despite the confidence of various party leaders, however, the PH undertook another unprecedented electoral strategy to seal the deal on Mahathir's leadership for their own supporters and to appeal to moderate supporters of UMNO and PAS. By 2018, over two-thirds of all Malaysians were connected to the internet, and 9 out of 10 of them were using smartphones (Tapsell 2019, 13). The opposition leveraged this record internet penetration rate to disseminate articles and short video clips that went viral on WhatsApp, the social message application, and on social media platforms such as Facebook, Twitter, and Instagram (Tapsell 2019). One particular two-minute video clip featuring Mahathir's conversation with two young children went viral.[50] In that video, a teary and emotional Mahathir can be seen explaining to the two children that he needed to continue working at the age of 93 in order to rebuild the country. The present bad situation of the country was due to the existing corruption and the mistakes that he made in the past. In essence, the video sought to sell Mahathir's apology and obtain voters' sympathy and support for chance to correct his past mistakes. More than a year later, in 2019, the video has amassed close to half a million views on Twitter, receiving more than 22,000 retweets and just over 19,000 likes in the process.[51] A longer

10-minute version of the video depicting the backgrounds of the two children had more than a million views of YouTube, and close to 900,000 views on Mahathir's Facebook page.[52] The 10-minute video posted on Facebook received more than 43,000 reactions, 3,000 comments, and 25,000 shares. In the final analysis, Mahathir's leadership of the PH raised its overall credibility as an alliance that would "save" Malaysia from its malaise and restore the country to its glory days of meteoric economic growth amid inter-ethnic peace (Abdullah 2019b; Welsh 2019).

Lastly, one final new type of joint campaign coordination that the PH alliance forged was to campaign using common alliance logo.[53] The decision was made by early April 2018, a month in advance of the actual elections, for all of the PH's component parties to contest using only the PKR's logo. Again, this electoral strategy was unprecedented and extraordinary in a number of ways. First, previous iterations of Malaysian opposition coalitions had never coordinated behind one single coalition logo. All component parties contested using their own party logos. Second, the PKR's party logo was that of an eye formed by two crescent moons. This logo was adopted in 1999 in reference to Anwar Ibrahim's "black eye," obtained when he was punched while under police detention. For Mahathir and the PPBM to campaign using that logo is highly ironic. Third, since the DAP had the longest logo history, using its "rocket" logo since 1967, among all opposition parties, it had the most to lose if it abandoned its own logo. My informal conversations with the DAP's members and supporters revealed there were some concerns that the party might lose some non-Malay supporters, especially the elderly. These who were familiar with the rocket logo might inadvertently vote for other parties or spoil their ballots in the absence of the logo. Even Mahathir himself acknowledged that "DAP has used the 'Rocket' symbol for almost 60 years."[54]

Despite all these reservations, however, coordinating to contest in the elections using one single logo can be seen as a masterful stroke. On Malaysia's voting slip, voters must indicate who they are voting for by marking an X beside the candidate's name and his associated party logo. There is no space allocated for the party or alliance name. By contesting using only the PKR "black eye" logo, DAP candidates stood to benefit from the PKR's reputation as a multiethnic and moderate opposition party. They would be more likely gain the votes of Malay-Muslim voters who would otherwise have demurred from voting for them under the rocket logo. Correspondingly, unsophisticated opposition supporters would also vote for the PKR's "black eye" logo given that the PPBM and Amanah were relatively newer parties with limited publicity among the

Fig. 7.10. Candidates of Hulu Langat Constituency on Nomination Day for the 2018 Malaysian General Election

masses. By forcing all their candidates to contest using the most ideologically moderate and still relatively well-known opposition logo, the PH alliance maximized cross-party strategic voting.

Figure 7.10 shows the prominence of the PKR logo when PH candidates in the Hulu Langat constituency in Selangor gathered to file their nomination papers on nomination day. The three candidates standing in the middle are, respectively, Edry Faizal (DAP), contesting in the Dusun Tua state constituency; Hasanuddin Mohd Yunus (Amanah), contesting in the Hulu Langat federal constituency; and Bakhtiar Mohd Nor (PPBM), contesting in the Semenyih state constituency. None of the candidates were from the PKR. But all contested using the PKR logo. Throughout the day and at numerous campaign events I witnessed thereafter, there were scarcely any individual party logos from the DAP, Amanah, and PPBM displayed. If one was ignorant of the alliance's coordination efforts, one would have guessed that they were all from the same political party.

In the end, the new PH alliance finally toppled the BN in the May 2018 general elections, ending more than half a century of uninterrupted rule. With help from PH-affiliated political parties in eastern Malaysia, they won a majority of vote shares and also a majority of seat shares. The BN's co-optation of PAS to field candidates in a large number of electoral districts, thus forcing multiple three-cornered contests, failed spectacularly. Most anti-BN voters pooled their votes behind the PH candidates instead of splitting their loyalties between PH and PAS candidates (Ostwald, Schuler, and Chong 2019).

Conclusion

This chapter has detailed why and when Malaysia's opposition parties built pre-electoral alliances. Historically unprecedented events exposing the shaky foundations of the incumbent regime updated opposition party leaders' expectations about how vulnerable the incumbent regime was, motivating them to try to build alliances. Yet significant intraparty resistance to cooperating with their opposition counterparts led the leaders of ideologically polarized opposition parties adopt awkward and sometimes puzzling compromises at the beginning of their cooperative relationships. Through participating in recurring autocratic elections, opposition party leaders soon learned to educate and persuade their party's members and supporters about the necessity of cooperating with their ideological rivals. More and more supporters were persuaded that their mutual dependence, despite their ideological differences, was key to eventual victory. In this manner, Malaysia's opposition parties gradually increased cross-party strategic voting and maximized the amount of support they could peel away from the incumbent. Rome was not built in a day. Neither, it seems, is an opposition alliance required to topple a dominant autocrat.

8 | Failing to Build Opposition Alliances in Singapore, 1965–2020

The previous chapter, examining opposition alliance building in Malaysia, demonstrates that perceptions of regime vulnerability and mutual dependency can fluctuate over time, resulting in temporal waves of pre-electoral alliance building. By contrast, if an incumbent electoral autocrat is overwhelmingly dominant consistently, then we should expect opposition party leaders to remain unmotivated to build full-fledged pre-electoral alliances. Opposition party leaders will not want to engage in costly compromises to develop joint campaigns for little or no return. At the same time, however, opposition party leaders can still try to make the best out of a bad situation—coordinate with each other to allocate electoral districts to minimize vote splitting against the dominant incumbent.

Within the universe of possible cases to verify this counterfactual, Singapore represents the best "negative" case to examine (Mahoney and Goertz 2004). Its geographical proximity to Malaysia, their similar pre–World War II experience of British colonialism, similar ethnoreligious diversity, comparable dilemmas found in international relations, and similar postcolonial adoption of British parliamentary and first-past-the-post electoral institutions make the two countries resemble siblings (Slater 2012). In this chapter, I argue that Singapore's opposition parties strategically chose not to build opposition alliances even when they *could have* done so.

To be more specific, this chapter will first demonstrate that Singapore's opposition party leaders learned to recognize the benefits of coordinating electoral district allocation, just like their counterparts in Malaysia. By coordinating district allocation, they minimized the number of opposition candidates contesting against the People's Action Party's (PAP) in each electoral district, and maximized their vote share by avoiding the splitting of opposition votes, just as in Malaysia. Iterated electoral participation over time provided opposition parties crucial information about their relative popularity across the electoral map, which parties utilized for negotiations to allocate electoral districts. Moreover, an informal "first dibs" rule was also adopted to increase the negotiations' efficiency.

Yet, unlike their counterparts in Malaysia, those same Singaporean opposition leaders were never compelled or motivated to upgrade their coordination efforts to include joint election campaigns. The ruling PAP's persistent dominance meant that opposition leaders saw no explicit benefit to joint campaigns. There was no need to forge compromises with each other on their respective ideologies and controls over their own parties if there were no benefits to be reaped. Besides, even if some opposition elites foresaw at least some benefits in extra votes and seat shares by campaigning together using a common coalition logo and through a charismatic leader, they frequently disagreed with each other about whether those benefits were worth the costs of interparty compromise. As a result, when some opposition party leaders chose to campaign jointly with each other on rare occasions, such as in 1976 and in 2001, many other leaders resolved not to join them and to campaign on their own. Thus, these specific instances do not fulfill this book's criteria of building full-fledged opposition alliances among all possible members of the opposition.

As with previous chapters, I provide a timeline of key events in Singapore politics from 1965 through 2020. As keen observers will note, while Singapore's opposition parties made incremental electoral gains over time, none came on the back of joint campaign coordination in pre-electoral alliances.

Coordinating over Electoral District Allocation in Singapore

Within the electoral landscape of multiple small opposition parties contesting for a limited number of parliamentary seats, Singaporean opposition party leaders have gradually learned to coordinate their electoral district allocation, just like their Malaysian brethren. With the exception of the first fully contested general elections in 1972, opposition party leaders have almost always understood and appreciated coordinating to reduce the number of opposition candidates contesting in each electoral district against the dominant PAP (Ibrahim and Ong 2016, 71–72). Figure 8.1 shows the frequency of coordination failure—the proportion of contested districts with more than one opposition candidate in every election from

TABLE 8.1. Timeline of Key Events in Singapore Politics from 1965 to 2020

Date	Event
August 1965	Singapore breaks away from the Federation of Malaysia as an independent state. The People's Action Party (PAP) becomes the dominant ruling party in the country.
April 1968	All major opposition parties, except the Workers' Party (WP), boycott the first-ever general elections in Singapore. The PAP sweeps all parliamentary seats.
September 1972	All opposition parties return to contesting in the general elections that year. The PAP continues to win a clean sweep of all available parliamentary seats.
December 1976	Four opposition parties form the Joint Opposition Council to contest in the general elections. WP does not join. The PAP continues its clean sweep.
October 1981	WP's J. B. Jeyaretnam wins a by-election in the Anson electoral district, becoming the first opposition politician elected in post-independence Singapore.
December 1984	J. B. Jeyaretnam retains his Anson seat in the general elections. Singapore Democratic Party's Chiam See Tong wins in the Potong Pasir electoral district, becoming the second elected opposition politician in post-independence Singapore.
September 1988	Anson electoral district is wiped off the electoral map as J. B. Jeyaretnam is disqualified from being a member of parliament after being convicted of improper accounting of WP's funds. Only Chiam manages to retain his seat.
August 1991	The opposition makes unprecedented electoral gains, winning four single-member districts in the general elections. These are the first elections after Lee Kuan Yew stepped down as prime minister in November 1990.
June 2001	Singapore Democratic Alliance formed. It includes four major opposition parties, but excludes the WP.
May 2011	The WP wins the five-member Aljunied group representative constituency in addition to its Hougang single-member constituency. The six WP MPs mark the largest number of opposition MPs ever to be elected in the Singapore parliament at its time.
March 2019	Former PAP central executive committee member Tan Cheng Bock forms new opposition party called the Progress Singapore Party. Talks to form an opposition alliance led by Tan Cheng Bock persist into early 2020.
July 2020	The WP wins the four-member Sengkang group representative constituency, in addition to retaining its previously won districts of Aljunied and Hougang. The ten WP MPs mark the largest number of opposition MPs ever to be elected in the Singapore parliament.

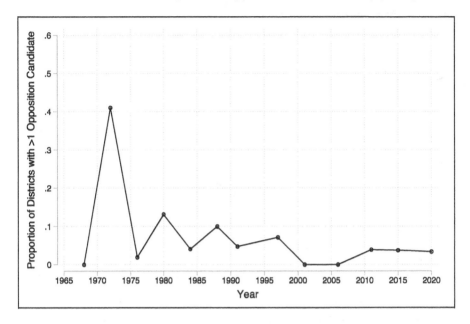

Fig. 8.1. Proportion of Electoral Districts with Coordination Failure in Singapore Elections, 1968–2020

1968 to 2020. The figure demonstrates that, except for general elections in 1972, opposition parties avoided competing against each other for the vast majority of districts that were contested.[1] Between 1976 and 2020, only an average of 7.2 percent of contested districts had more than one opposition candidate in an electoral cycle, disregarding independent candidates. This means that over four decades of autocratic elections, opposition parties in Singapore managed to coordinate the allocation of nearly 92.7 percent of all contested electoral districts, a remarkable achievement.

How and why did Singapore's opposition parties manage to achieve such a noteworthy outcome in the pre-electoral coordination of allocating electoral districts? An important part of the answer is that Singapore's generally weak opposition parties could hardly ever put up a decent fight against the PAP in the first place. Figure 8.2 shows the proportion of electoral districts with walkovers in each election between 1968 to 2020. With the exception of the 2011, 2015, and 2020 general elections, elections in Singapore have almost always seen a significant proportion of electoral districts go uncontested. With so many "excess" electoral districts to go around for opposition parties to contest, no wonder they had little prob-

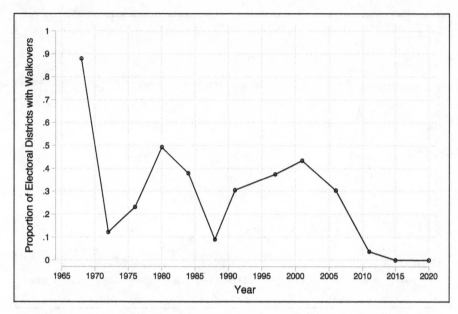

Fig. 8.2. Proportion of Electoral Districts with Walkover in Singapore Elections, 1968–2020

lem avoiding contesting in similar districts against each other and against the PAP.

But to attribute the opposition's entire coordination success to the general weakness of opposition parties is to claim too much. It does not explain why there was a spike in coordination failure in 1972 and continued low levels of coordination failure even after opposition parties grew much better able to contest against the PAP in almost all of the electoral districts in 2011, 2015, and 2020. Furthermore, to focus on the overt weakness of individual opposition parties is to completely ignore the intense interparty rivalry and negotiations that occur before every election cycle. A more complete understanding of the early historical anomalies and the more contemporary trajectories in opposition coordination requires closer attention to the learning process and perceived strategic logic of opposition party leaders.

The general elections in 1972 were exceptional, with a very high rate of opposition coordination failure because those elections were the first truly competitive elections in post-independence Singapore (Josey 1972). When Singapore separated from Malaysia in 1965, opposition parties objected to the separation and boycotted the first general elections in 1968 to delegitimize the PAP government. The PAP won a clean sweep of the parliamentary seats as it saw close to 90 percent of its candidates run uncontested. Only two Worker's Party (WP) candidates and five independent candidates braved the PAP onslaught. In approaching the 1972 elections, opposition parties reconsidered their boycott. With the PAP's complete dominance of political power in the country, they had been cast into the political wilderness. Eager to correct their earlier mistake and to use the opportunity to broadcast their message of democratic reform to the rest of the population, opposition parties jumped back into the electoral arena. Unfortunately, since no single opposition party had won any seats and the large majority of electoral districts went uncontested in 1968, there was no publicly available information about how strong each party was in 1972. Uncertainty about their relative popularity was high. Therefore, all had maximum incentives to misrepresent their weaknesses by making rhetorical claims to boost their perceived strengths to contest more electoral districts. Both the WP and the United National Front (UNF), for instance, announced that they were preparing to contest in all constituencies.[2] The People's Front (PF) declared that it would field candidates in about half of all the available constituencies.[3]

Close observers of domestic politics in 1972 were not convinced by such boastful claims. Declassified political reports from the American and British embassies suggest that these political parties were much weaker than they claimed to be. An American embassy airgram in late 1969 summarizing the notes of a meeting between an American diplomat and leaders of the UNF concluded that "the UNF has no significant popular support at present and has no prospect of gaining support under present conditions."[4] Another airgram analyzing the Barisan Socialis noted that active membership had declined from 5,000 in the early 1960s to only about 700.[5] The recantation of its previous leader, Lim Chin Siong, and the ineffective tenure of its new leader, Lee Siew Choh, had diminished what little influence it had among the Singaporean public. As for the Chinese-based PF, it was "the most active" among all opposition parties. But in truth, the influence of the party extended only to "yet another pressure group within Singapore agitating for closer ties with Mother China."[6] Summarizing these sentiments, a lengthy report analyzing all opposition parties described them as "lackluster," "desperate," "woefully lacking in political experience," with "small, weak shoe-string operations" that were "merely a phenomenon of an election year whose permanence is highly suspect; all of them could conceivably disappear following the next election."[7]

But despite their self-aggrandizement, opposition party leaders still undertook a significant effort to coordinate allocating electoral districts in the 1972 elections (Josey 1972, 60–99). The PF appealed to other opposition parties not to contest in its 20 "stronghold" districts, so as "to avoid splitting the anti-PAP votes."[8] The party explicitly stated, "What we want is a one by one straight fight with the PAP."[9] The PF even signed an agreement with the WP in an attempt to cement their coordination on allocating electoral districts between the two parties.[10] Yet the countervailing incentives to misrepresent their true strength in the first truly competitive general elections proved difficult to resist. This intransigence was reflected in the numerous rounds of negotiations, where the WP accused Dr. Lee Siew Choh's Barisan Socialis opposition party "of adopting a 'take it or leave it' attitude."[11] Similarly, PF leaders criticized the UNF leaders for being "a bunch of publicity seekers."[12] Ultimately, despite all the negotiations, 24 out of 57 contested districts, or about 40 percent, saw at least three candidates (two from opposition parties and one from the PAP). The public was not convinced by this display of opposition infighting, and the PAP won all the parliamentary seats.

Since the disastrous exhibition of intra-opposition conflict in 1972, Singaporean opposition leaders have learned to be cognizant of the negative consequences of not cooperating with each other. In the more recent general elections in 2015, bargaining over the allocation of 29 contested districts among eight opposition parties was resolved over two meetings in a little more than a month, with only one small district the subject of conflict. My interviews with the party leaders after those elections revealed several findings. At the outset, they all confirmed that the logic and benefit of coordinating over district allocation were clear. No one wanted to contest in electoral districts with multiple opposition candidates who would split the votes. Such a move by obstinate party leaders would serve up electoral victory to the PAP on a plate. Furthermore, opposition party leaders understood that time and resources spent in fruitless bargaining are time and resources wasted. In the narrow electoral campaign window, they could be better utilized to mount attacks against the ruling PAP.

To reduce the "transaction costs" spent negotiating over district allocation among so many parties, therefore, they have observed an informal rule over the multiple cycles of general elections since 1968, just like their counterparts in Malaysia. The informal rule is this: if party A contested in a district against the PAP in the previous election, it had first dibs on contesting in that district for the next election.[13] This rule applied for all parties unless a separate party B could create a justifiable reason why it should be allowed to contest instead. Debate then raged among opposing leaders about what was a justifiable reason. New parties staking their claims in districts previously contested by other parties oftentimes misrepresented their strength.[14] Dying parties seeking to protect their districts from expanding opposition parties would point to their longevity, the number and quality of potential candidates that they could field, or their long-standing grassroots activities in a district to bolster their claims of popular support. As opposition leader A confirmed,

> You start off first with having to look big and muscular, everybody huffing and puffing themselves up to look bigger than they actually are. Some will blink. Some won't. Then in the end, if we can agree, we agree. If not, three-cornered fight. *More often than not, you know someone will blink and then the game of chicken will come to an end.*[15]

Predictably, notwithstanding the informal rule and clear recognition of the benefits to coordination, opposition interparty disputes oftentimes arose due to incumbent meddling rather than intra-opposition intransigence. Gerrymandering by the Electoral Boundaries Review Committee (EBRC) creates conflicts between opposition parties over who should have the prerogative to contest in newly created electoral districts in two ways. First, because the boundaries of electoral districts change ahead of every election, opposition parties must wait until the exact boundaries of the new constituencies are released in the EBRC report. They cannot coordinate their district allocation prior to the report's release. Therefore, the informal rule of "first dibs" by the opposition party that contested previously in a district is oftentimes upended when parties realize that electoral districts that they have contested in previous election cycles have been wiped off the map. Second, even after the EBRC releases its report, newly created electoral districts again create uncertainty over each party's relative popularity in those new districts. While party leaders may rely on past electoral results of neighboring districts to boost their claims, the increased uncertainty in voting patterns hampers effective and efficient coordination.

For example, consider the dispute between the NSP and the WP over which party would contest in Marine Parade GRC and MacPherson SMC for the 2015 general elections (E. Ong 2016).[16] In the 2011 elections, the NSP had contested in the five-member Marine Parade GRC, while the WP had contested in the adjacent single-member Joo Chiat SMC. Approaching the 2015 elections, however, the EBRC absorbed Joo Chiat SMC into Marine Parade GRC, deleting it from the electoral map. At the same time, MacPherson SMC was carved out of Marine Parade to be a single-member district. By virtue of the fact that the WP had contested in Joo Chiat SMC in 2011, the party seized the opportunity to claim that it had legitimacy to contest in both Marine Parade GRC and MacPherson SMC in 2015. Incredulous at this "territorial grab," the NSP tried to negotiate a settlement in two rounds of all-party negotiations. Yet the WP rebuffed the NSP's approaches and did not attend the second meeting to negotiate terms.

At first, it appeared that the NSP recognized the futility of trying to get the WP to withdraw from Marine Parade and MacPherson. The NSP announced on August 10, 2015, almost a month before nomination day, that it would not contest in either constituency. After all, it was fairly obvious that the WP was by far the stronger opposition party from the publicly available information of its success in previous elections. It was the largest opposition party in parliament at that point, having seven fully elected members of parliament and two non-constituency members of parliament.[17] The NSP had no seats and, in fact, had had no parliamentary presence since its establishment in 1987, save for a single non-constituency member of parliament between 2001 and 2006. Yet nine days later the NSP reneged on its decision, declaring that it would contest in MacPherson SMC anyway "because the WP is too arrogant."[18] The NSP betrayed its status as an old and dying party when its candidate said,

> Everyone was surprised [by our decision to contest in MacPherson]. Even experts thought we wouldn't enter a three-corner fight. But this is life and death. *If we keep backing down, residents and the general population will think we are very weak.* An MP cannot be weak—how are you supposed to speak up for residents if you are weak?[19]

In justifying its decision, the acting secretary-general, Lim Tean, attempted to misrepresent his party's relative strength vis-à-vis the WP by emphasizing indicators of strength other than representation in parliament. He referred to his party's popularity from its previous electoral result, its internal discipline, and its leadership among the opposition:

> I believe to a very large extent we have avoided multi-cornered fights, but for MacPherson we had to do it. . . . We did very well in

the last GE (general election) and we have already made a huge concession to WP there. . . . That decision to contest in MacPherson was made a few weeks ago, and we've never departed form that decision. NSP has been the most active party promoting opposition unity. We initiated talks to avoid three-cornered fights.[20]

In the end, the results in MacPherson SMC verified the relative strengths of the two opposition parties. While the PAP romped to victory with 65.6 percent of the votes, the WP's candidate earned a credible 33.6 percent vote share, and the NSP candidate polled less than 1 percent. The NSP wasted precious time and resources contesting in MacPherson SMC, including the candidate's US$10,000 election deposit. A member of the central committee of the NSP at that time confirmed that influential party members who did not want to back down in the fight against the WP pushed the party's leadership to renege on its pre-electoral promise.[21] The overwhelming loss by the NSP's candidate in MacPherson SMC was not anticipated by these dissenting members.

To summarize the discussion so far: I have triangulated empirical evidence demonstrating that Singapore's opposition elites typically focus their energies on bargaining and coordinating with each other to reduce the number of opposition candidates in each electoral district in order to maximize their vote shares within those districts. Bargaining between opposition parties is generally successful, as shown by the nearly 93 percent success rate over four decades of elections, aided by the "first dibs" informal rule that opposition parties developed. Infrequent instances of bargaining failures occurred when information about the relative strengths of opposition parties was missing, such as during the first competitive elections in 1972, or when incumbent gerrymandering impaired the bargaining process.

Nonexistent Joint Campaigns and Full-Fledged Opposition Alliances in Singapore

Given that Singapore's opposition parties have been so successful at electoral district coordination, one might think that coordinating joint campaigns against the PAP would be an easier endeavor. Afterall, unlike Malaysia's ideologically divided opposition parties, which must coordinate their campaigning across a large geographical territory (Malaysia is about three-quarters the size of the state of California) and make signifi-

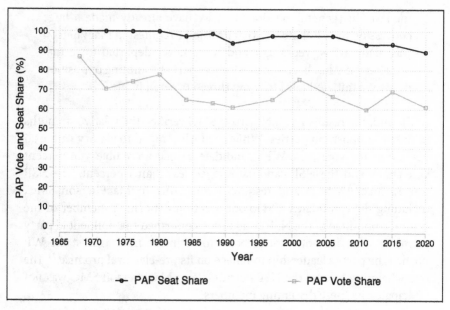

Fig. 8.3. PAP's Performance in Singapore Elections, 1968–2020

cant compromises on important ideological positions, Singapore's ideo-logically similar opposition parties campaign at the national level in a geo-graphical area approximately half the size of Los Angeles. Yet several indicators confirm this book's hypothesis that the persistent, overwhelm-ing dominance of an autocratic incumbent deters Singaporean opposition party leaders from building opposition alliances with joint campaigns.

Consider, in the first instance, the PAP's domineering performance over the multiple election cycles between 1968 to 2020, as shown in figure 8.3. It reveals that even as the PAP's vote share has fluctuated between 60 percent and 80 percent for the past five decades, its stranglehold on the vast majority of seats in parliament has been unrelenting. It was only in the most recent general elections in 2020 that opposition parties won just over 10 percent of parliamentary seats. If Singapore's opposition parties' experience over more than five decades has been repeated failure to win a substantial number of seats from the PAP, how could they ever contemplate campaigning together to overthrow the PAP and form a new government?

Consider also the fact that Singapore's PAP has never experienced regime-debilitating events like those in the Philippines, South Korea, and Malaysia, as described in the preceding chapters. Transitions from the first prime minister, Lee Kuan Yew, to the second prime minister, Goh Chok Tong, and to the third prime minister, Lee Hsien Loong, were all very smooth. There have been no mass protests on the streets (particularly violent protests), even as dissent on specific topics has spiked from time to time. The economy has weathered multiple financial crises, bouncing back even stronger through the government's robust fiscal and monetary interventions to prevent job losses. The PAP is so disciplined that one rarely hears rumors of internal dissent, much less witness defections from the party's top leadership. Internationally, the small country wields significant influence within the region as a founding member of the Association of Southeast Asian Nations, and has cultivated durable and productive ties with major powers like the United States and China. Most importantly, it has almost never experienced any form of pressure from the United States for democratization. The military has always been professional, disciplined, and subordinate to civilian leadership, with no hint of intramilitary fracture. Lastly, the political leadership has almost always been corruption free—Singapore's very high ranking in the Corruption Perceptions Index alongside other developed nations in Europe has always been the envy of its East and Southeast Asian counterparts.[22] In fact, its anticorruption practices have been exported as a model for other developing countries around the world (Ortmann and Thompson 2014; Quah 2001).

Third and finally, my field interviews with opposition party leaders revealed that they foresaw no explicit benefit if they campaigned jointly (see table 8.2). They reiterated that there was no need for any pre-electoral coalition between the opposition parties because "there was no use for it." They consistently expressed the opinion that joint alliance campaigns would be futile—campaigning jointly would not actually increase their vote share or their chances of winning extra constituencies. All assumed that they would be able to maximize their vote share so long as they did not split the opposition votes by fielding multiple opposition candidates in each electoral district. The idea of campaigning jointly to induce PAP supporters to switch their votes to the opposition did not cross their mind. Opposition party leader C declared to me about the uncertain electoral benefit of building pre-electoral alliances, "I can tell you this. If I can make the guarantee that if we come together in an alliance we will win, then everyone will come. *I cannot. The pull factor is not strong enough.*"[23]

In addition to clear recognition of weak "pull factors," opposition party leaders were also crystal clear that the numerous obstacles hindering the coordination of joint campaigns were strong. Throughout my interviews, opposition leaders referred to the personal costs of coalition formation—

TABLE 8.2. Interviews with Singapore Opposition Party Leaders

Code	Opposition Party Leader	Gender	Age	Race	Informal Rule?[a]	Mis-represent?[b]	Ideologically Similar?[c]	No Benefit?[d]
SG004	A	M	55	Chinese	1	1	1	1
SG005	D	F	54	Chinese	1	1	1	1
SG006	E	M		Indian	0	1	0	1
SG007	F	M	67	Malay	1	1	1	1
SG008	G	M	61	Chinese	1	1	1	1
SG009	C	M	47	Chinese	0	1	1	1
SG010	H	M	63	Chinese	1	1	1	1
SG011	B	M	52	Chinese	1	1	1	1
SG012	I	M	49	Chinese	1	1	1	1
SG013	J	M	32	Chinese	1	1	1	1
SG014	K	M	40	Chinese	1	1	0	1

Note: All 11 interviews were conducted in Singapore between July 2016 and July 2017 for about 1 hour each. Interviewees were canvassed through snowball sampling. Due to the sensitive nature of the interviews, I agreed to conceal their identities, as per the rules of the Institutional Review Board. Before each interview, I explained the nature of my research project and obtained verbal consent to quote them.

Coding Rules:

a Did the interviewee articulate the informal rule for bargaining between opposition parties over the allocation of different electoral districts for opposition parties to contest (i.e., the "first dibs" informal rule)? Coded 1 for yes, 0 otherwise.

b Did the interviewee agree that opposition parties oftentimes attempted to misrepresent their relative strengths? Coded 1 for yes, 0 otherwise.

c Did the interviewee say that opposition parties in Singapore were ideologically similar to each other? Coded 1 for yes, 0 otherwise.

d Did the interviewee say that there was little or no benefit to forming a pre-electoral coalition with joint campaigns, such as a common policy platform? Coded 1 for yes, 0 otherwise.

the reduced autonomy to make decisions when they need to work with other opposition leaders whom they have personality differences with.[24] For instance, as mentioned in chapter 6, a rift occurred between Chee Soon Juan and Chiam See Tong, who were both in the Singapore Democratic Party (SDP) in 1993. Chiam left the SDP and established the Singapore People's Party (SPP). Since then, the parties have refused to work with each other, with both sides citing "past political baggage" for their irreconcilable differences. Opposition leader A claimed, for all opposition parties in general,

> Going into the next general election, I do not think you are going to see any substantive significant change in terms of the opposition forming up. . . . They got their own constituencies. . . . But then the big difference is in terms of how XXX and YYY[25] can get along. . . .

You still got to talk to that guy. You have to work with him. Is that worth all the trouble? Worth all the effort? That kind of situation. And when you think about it, it does not really matter.[26]

Of course, all this is not to say that opposition leaders have not experimented with weaker signals of opposition unity to try to improve their electoral odds over the decades. But these experiments with developing some form of joint campaigns yielded very few electoral returns, and have hence deterred future efforts at building fully fledged alliances. In 1976, for example, the Barisan Socialis, the United Front, the Singapore Malay National Organization (PKMS), and the Justice Party came together to form the Joint Opposition Council (JOC) alliance. This was the first time in Singapore's electoral history that opposition interparty coordination in both electoral district allocation and joint electoral campaigning occurred. Opposition party leaders were much more motivated to coordinate allocating electoral districts and campaigning together at that time, due to their disastrous electoral results four years earlier, when no opposition candidate won a seat in parliament. The alliance produced a common manifesto.[27] In it, the JOC called for numerous policy changes, such as the reduction of various taxes, the release of political detainees, and the revocation of the Internal Security Act. Yet beyond the mere release of this manifesto, the component parties did not develop or coordinate other joint anti-PAP campaigns (Donough 1977, chapters 3 and 4). The parties campaigned using their respective party logos. They also campaigned separately in the districts where they contested. Moreover, the JOC did not include the largest opposition party at that time, the WP. Evidently, the WP did not want to associate with smaller opposition parties within the JOC. Consequently, the common manifesto lacked credibility as a united anti-regime signal, undermining its effect in mobilizing opposition voters and in persuading moderate PAP supporters to defect to the opposition. In general elections that year, the PAP won a clean sweep of all available parliamentary seats.

Two and a half decades later, approaching the 2001 general elections, opposition party leaders would once again attempt to form an opposition alliance to improve their electoral fortunes. Recall that by the end of the 1990s, Chiam See Tong had become leader of the SPP after his acrimonious split with the SDP in 1993. Eager to improve his new party's standing after another set disastrous electoral results for the opposition in the 1997 general elections, Chiam created the Singapore Democratic Alliance (SDA) together with the NSP, the PKMS, and the Singapore Justice Party.

The key objective was to gather the strongest leaders from each component party in order to contest in and win a multimember GRC (Loke 2019, 312–13). By pooling the charisma of the top leaders from each component party, the coalition hoped to convince moderate PAP supporters to vote for more opposition candidates. More opposition members of parliament would mean more opportunities to gain experience debating in parliament and in delivering constituency service. On the surface, the SDA appeared to be Singapore's second pre-electoral coalition: the component parties campaigned using the common name and logo of the SDA, produced a common manifesto, and ran only one or a team of opposition candidates in each electoral district they contested in. Key decision-making authority was centralized under Chiam as chairman, who had the power to appoint the top officials of the alliance (Loke 2019, 313–14). For the 2001 general elections, it fielded 13 candidates, the most of all the opposition parties—more than the SDP's 11 and the WP's two candidates.

Yet at least two reasons undermined the SDA's credentials as a comprehensive pre-electoral opposition alliance, as I define it in this book. First, and most important, the SDA included neither the WP nor the SDP—the other two most prominent opposition parties. While Chiam apparently invited the two parties to join the alliance, they both declined. The WP, under Low Thia Khiang's leadership, refused to join even though Low was under "immense pressure" to do so (Loke 2019, 315). Ultimately, the WP's central executive committee concluded that it was not worth it for the party to join the alliance. By their calculations, the party would have a better chance of winning votes and electoral districts through building its own brand and contesting on its own outside of the alliance. Unsurprisingly, the SDP did not join due to continued animosity between the SDP's leader, Chee Soon Juan, and the SDA's leader, Chiam See Tong, over the latter's exit from the SDP in 1993 (Loke 2019, 315). With few electoral benefits to be expected from Chiam's new SDA experiment, the costly compromises required to work with one's rival were deemed not worthwhile.

Second, the SDA's joint campaigns among ideologically similar opposition parties signaled little substantive difference from their previous identities as distinct individual entities.[28] The alliance campaigned on a platform of having more opposition parliamentarians being good for the country—an issue that was recycled from previous election campaigns (Mauzy and Milne 2002, 152). Furthermore, the component parties also adopted stances on the economic recession and foreign immigration similar to those of the WP and the SDP, both of which were outside of the alliance. Everyone "tried to shift the blame for the recession from global circumstances to the PAP," while "all the opposition parties complained about jobs going to foreigners while Singaporeans were being laid off" (Mauzy and Milne 2002, 152). Thus, even when the SDA campaigned collectively against the PAP, it did not appear to matter to voters, as there was little substantive difference from the opposition's past political messaging.

Ultimately, without the inclusion of the WP and the SDP, the opposition and the SDA underperformed in the 2001 general elections (Loke 2019, 316–20; Mauzy and Milne 2002, 152–53). The parliamentary status quo was maintained—the PAP again lost only two seats in parliament, to the WP's Low Thia Khiang and the SDA's Chiam See Tong. Even more surprisingly, the PAP increased its vote share to just above 75 percent, its highest share since 1980. The SDA ceased being a major player in the opposition ranks after the NSP withdrew from the alliance in 2007 and when Chiam pulled the SPP out in 2011. Although the SDA still competes in more recent elections, it is a shadow of its former self. It contested only in one electoral district in the 2015 and 2020 elections.

Lastly, beyond the JOC in 1972 and the SDA in 2001, the 2015 general elections also saw a fairly weak experiment of joint campaigning against the PAP. Five out of the eight opposition parties contesting the elections— the Democratic Progressive Party, SDA, PPP, SF, and RP—came together to campaign using a badge with the phrase "Vote for Change."[29] By recalling Barack Obama's 2008 presidential campaign slogan, "Change We Can Believe In," the parties sought to display "a sign of unity among the opposition parties." Yet nothing more was forthcoming beyond some opposition candidates wearing the badge. The parties did not follow up by campaigning with the slogan. Everyone continued contesting in the elections in their own districts using their own party logo. There were no further substantive and comprehensive policy proposals. The badge and slogan generated no attention beyond mention of its existence at a press conference. As expected, it did little to galvanize support, and the PAP won the 2015 elections with nearly 70 percent of the votes, its best share since 2001 (Lee and Tan 2016; Weiss, Loke, and Choa 2016; Welsh 2016).

Approaching the 2020 General Elections

Singapore's latest general elections were held on July 10, 2020, amid the Covid-19 global pandemic outbreak. Singapore was not unaffected—on the day of the elections, there were already 45,590 recorded cases of Covid-

19 in the country.[30] But because the government implemented a strict "circuit breaker" period from April 7 to June 1, Covid-19 cases were largely restricted to foreign worker dormitories, and community spread was low. Of the total cases at that time, 609 were imported, 2,004 were cases in the community, while 42,977 cases were in the foreign worker dormitories. The seven-day moving average of community cases on that day was only 14.28 cases per day. In order to stem the spread of Covid-19 during the campaign period and on election day itself, a wide variety of mitigation measures were undertaken. Large public rallies were banned, although politicians were still allowed to conduct face-to-face outreach to voters in public spaces such as wet markets and coffee shops. Social distancing ambassadors made sure that campaigning politicians followed social distancing regulations. In line with existing requirements, everyone in public wore a mask. On election day, socially distanced voters were provided with hand sanitizers before and after they voted. Voters of different age groups were also allocated different two-hour time bands to vote, so as to minimize possible intergenerational transmissions.

But despite the unprecedented nature of the elections, opposition parties did nothing to change their time-tested strategies of only coordinating to allocate electoral districts among themselves. On nomination day, when the candidates of all the contesting parties were confirmed, there was only coordination failure in one among the 31 electoral districts—Pasir Ris Punggol GRC saw a three-cornered contest between the PAP, the Singapore Democratic Alliance, and People's Voice. In all other districts, there was coordination success—only the incumbent PAP's candidate(s) and one opposition party contested.[31] Despite talks since July 2018 among the opposition parties to upgrade their cooperation to form a pre-electoral alliance with joint campaigns, the previous status quo of only coordinating to allocate electoral districts was ultimately maintained.[32] Why was this the outcome?

As the elections approached, there were indeed a handful of indications of growing anti-PAP dissent. These can be generally divided into economic and social dissent among the citizenry on the one hand, and the uncertainty of leadership transition on the other. In the economic and social realm, there are primarily growing concerns among Singaporeans about growing income and wealth inequality in the country (Wah 2012; Weiss 2014a). The country's Gini coefficient among resident employed households per household member increased from .442 in 2000, to a peak of .482 in 2007, stayed fairly stable for the next five years, before decreasing till .452 in 2019 on the back of a slew of government redistributive programs.[33] While greatly welcomed, these redistributive programs, such as the government's massive S$8 billion Pioneer Generation Package[34] and S$6.1 billion Merdeka Generation Package,[35] did little to undermine the structural forces of high wage inequality in Singapore's highly liberalized labor market (Low and Vadaketh 2014; Rahim and Yeoh 2019). In 2020, there continued to be no minimum wage and no comprehensive unemployment insurance policy, even as the workforce aged. Reflecting this mass concern about inequality is the stellar sales of *This is What Inequality Looks Like*, an acclaimed book authored by Singapore sociologist Teo You Yenn (2018). Through provocative narratives of how the poor in Singapore navigate their everyday lives, the book was a resounding success, selling more than 20,000 copies in its first print run in 2018, and is now into its third print edition. The impact of the book got Teo nominated to be a contender of the Straits Times Singaporean of the Year 2018 award.[36] Societal discourse on income inequality obtained so much traction that several PAP ministers from various ministries were compelled to make statements addressing how their respective departments would address the issue in the March 2019 budget debates.[37]

But Singaporeans' frustrations over stubbornly high inequality did not quite spill out into the open as much as their resentment over its perceived primary cause—the PAP's liberal foreign immigration policies in recent decades. In 1990, Singapore's foreign workforce comprised only 16.1 percent (or 248,000 people) of its total workforce (Y. Ong 2014, 445). Within 10 years, the proportion of workforce that is foreign almost doubled to 29.2 percent (or 612,200 people). In 2008, the proportion was nearly 34 percent of the total workforce. By 2019, Singapore's 1.4-million-strong foreign workforce made up 37.5 percent of the total workforce.[38] Because of their rapid increase, foreign workers were blamed for a panoply of issues at the workplace and in broader society—depressing the wages of low-income Singaporean workers, displacing Singaporean workers from their existing jobs as employers preferred hard-working foreigners, workplace discrimination against locals by foreign bosses, foreign worker enclaves in certain parts of the island, and their inability to speak English, among other problems. Existing survey research also disclosed that the majority of Singaporeans were resolutely against the PAP's liberal immigration policies (Welsh and Chang 2019). The PAP did not help matters by publishing a parliamentary white paper in January 2013, projecting a population of 6.9 million people by the year 2030.[39] The document sparked such a furious resistance from ordinary Singaporeans that unprecedented protests were organized in early February 2013 and in May 2013 at Hong Lim Park, a government-sanctioned public space for protest.[40] About three thousand protestors turned up in what was noted to be Singapore's largest protest since independence.[41]

Predictably, opposition elites have seized on the mass dissent to organize against the PAP in the last decade. In the 2015 general elections, Singaporeans First, a new opposition party led by Tan Jee Say, an ex senior civil servant, was formed, advocating for more restrictive immigration policies and specific workplace policies to ensure that Singaporeans were not discriminated against. More recently, at the official launch of the new Progress Singapore Party (PSP) held in August 2019, the party's leaders spoke on a number of issues they would campaign on against the PAP. They spoke out, in particular, against Singapore's free trade agreement with India, otherwise known as the India-Singapore Comprehensive Economic Cooperation Agreement (CECA).[42] They alleged that CECA, under its chapter on the movement of natural persons, allowed too many Indian professionals to undertake work in Singapore, thus depressing wages and depriving Singaporeans of those jobs. The PAP government was subsequently forced to issue a significant number of statements clarifying that CECA did not, in fact, allow Indian professionals to work in Singapore with any special immigration privileges.[43] That the PSP, the newest opposition party, led by Dr. Tan Cheng Bock, a PAP defector, would also seize on mass discontent with the government's immigration policies speaks volumes about the importance of the topic and how the new party was trying to make itself relevant to the public.

The final source of dissent against the PAP was the growing uncertainty about the party's impending leadership transition. After having successfully transferred the baton of prime minister from the venerable Lee Kuan Yew to the popular Goh Chok Tong in 1990, and then to Lee Hsien Loong in 2004, the PAP was in the midst of its third transfer of leadership. At the time of the elections in July 2020, the de facto prime-minister-in-waiting was Heng Swee Keat, the finance minister, and the de facto deputy-prime-minister-in-waiting was Chan Chun Sing, the minister for trade and industry. They ascended to second and third in command at the annual PAP party convention held in November 2018.[44] But questions remain over the mass popularity of the new PAP leadership team. In the first instance, survey data showed that Singaporeans' first choice as prime minister was neither of the two. Instead, their overwhelming first choice was Tharman Shanmugaratnam, the country's previous finance minister.[45] Behind Tharman was Teo Chee Hean, Singapore's previous deputy prime minister. Heng and Chan came in third and fourth, respectively. Shanmugaratnam was not chosen ostensibly because he was deemed too old for the position, and because older Singaporeans were "not ready" for a non-Chinese prime minister.[46] Shanmugaratnam is ethnic Indian. Moreover, both Heng and Chan were seen as flawed politicians who would not be able to command parliamentary respect and mass popularity. A series of stumbles in parliament by Heng were viewed as indicative of his inability to think on his feet (Barr 2019), while a leaked audio recording of Chan labeling some Singaporeans "idiots" while speaking to industry leaders at a closed-door session revealed his crass elitism (Vadaketh 2020).

Yet ultimately, in the run-up to the 2020 general elections, it was quite clear that opposition elite perceptions of the PAP's overwhelming dominance did not waver much. Indeed, despite increasing frustrations with growing inequality, the government's liberal immigration policies, and increased political uncertainty over the PAP's leadership transition, there was nothing equivalent to the multiple regime-debilitating events occurring within a short period of time, as in the Philippines, South Korea, or Malaysia. Recall that in these countries, there were severe economic depression necessitated drastic policy actions, recurring mass protests publicly condemning the regime while disrupting everyday lives, publicly exposed grand corruption amounting to billions of dollars, mass defections from within the core of the ruling party, a health crisis of the ruling autocrat, and public withdrawals of support for the ruling regime from international patrons. In Singapore, however, none of these incidences have come to pass. In the economic realm, incomes were still rising—between 2014 to 2019, real median income for Singapore residents increased 3.8 percent annually.[47] During the entire year of 2020, moreover, the government announced four separate budgets aimed at stimulating the Covid-19-depressed economy by sending direct checks to households and by directly subsidizing the cost of wages to prevent job losses. Politically, while there were some protests over the decade, participation at those events had dwindled, and none have caused any particular disruption that state security forces could not manage. And even though Heng Swee Keat suffered a stroke during a cabinet meeting in May 2016, while Prime Minister Lee Hsien Loong himself fainted on stage while delivering the National Day Rally in August 2016, there has been no public health scares for any major leader since then. In the face of continued PAP dominance, no wonder opposition elites had little appetite to make costly efforts to construct an alliance when there are few prospective benefits for it. When interviewed, a PSP central executive committee member stated,

My opinion is that for our situation, *I don't see much benefit to a coalition* because we are not yet at the stage where we are trying to form the government. I mean you go into a coalition to be strong enough to form a government. That is where you need the numbers. But if you are not aiming to do that yet, then the reason to do it doesn't really exist. You actually bring coordination problems. *There are more minuses than there are pluses.*[48]

All this is not to say that there was no attempt to try to change the status quo. Indeed, since July 2018, there were various efforts by opposition parties primarily to enlist Dr. Tan Cheng Bock as the leader of a pre-electoral alliance.[49] Many in the opposition saw Dr. Tan's decision to overtly contest in the 2011 presidential elections against the PAP's preferred candidate, and narrowly lose by a margin of 0.3 percent vote share, as an indicator of the PAP's increasing weakness and intraparty fracture.[50] Even more compelling was his decision to create the PSP in early 2019 to challenge the PAP in parliamentary elections. In addition, opposition elites were inspired by the watershed elections in Malaysia in May 2018, when the Mahathir-led Pakatan Harapan alliance toppled the long-ruling BN. Some had hoped that Dr. Tan would be Singapore's Mahathir. By allying themselves with Dr. Tan, some opposition elites hoped to improve their electoral fortunes by borrowing his stellar reputation. Confirming this logic, the leader of the People's Power Party, Mr. Goh Meng Seng, proclaimed,

We're at rock bottom. When we come to that stage, nothing can be worse [than] to try . . . a new approach to get a different result. If we don't change, the results won't change. . . . All the leaders have their differences in their ideologies, policy-wise and how things should be done, but I do not think they are so egoistic as to say they can do it all by themselves. *We understand that we cannot do it alone and we need to unite and depend on each other for our future success.*[51]

But despite all their overtures, Dr. Tan remained unmoved. His new party was intent on cutting the PAP down to size, but not out to replace the incumbent regime.[52] The PAP was still dominant, and the PSP had no need to rely on the help of the other opposition parties to achieve its own circumscribed objectives.

Even as most opposition elites recognized the futility of forming a full-fledged alliance with joint campaigns, interparty negotiations to allocate electoral districts were still at the top of the minds of opposition party leaders and proceeded at a brisk pace. My interviews with three PSP leaders confirm that the party still sought to coordinate with other existing parties to avoid multiple opposition candidates in electoral districts.[53] In their view, stubborn belligerence—contesting in districts with multiple opposition candidates—was "not rational" and would only result in electoral disaster for everyone involved.[54] Evidently, other opposition parties frequently felt the same way and were jostling with each other to take steps to call first dibs on which electoral districts to contest in. Private negotiations via text messaging and face-to-face meetings proceeded based on the "first dibs rule" and using the previous electoral map, even as a new EBRC was formed in August 2019 to redraw the electoral boundaries for the impending general elections. The SDP publicly staked its claim the earliest, holding a press conference in September 2019 to declare its intention to contest in five electoral districts for the next general election—all districts that it had previously contested in during the 2015 elections.[55] Another central executive committee member of an opposition party whom I interviewed in October 2019 revealed that the leaders of other opposition parties had already sent him text messages declaring where they intended to contest more than eight months before elections were called.[56] Eventually, even as there were well-publicized disputes between some opposition parties over the specific districts each party had agreed to contest, almost all conflicts were resolved on nomination day.[57]

Conclusion

This chapter has revealed the implications for constructing opposition alliances when an autocratic regime is consistently dominant. Opposition parties in a parliamentary electoral autocracy can coordinate by allocating geographically segregated electoral districts through adopting informal rules and as uncertainty over their relative popularity decreases over time. In so doing, they minimize the number of opposition candidates contesting against the autocratic incumbent in each district, thus maximizing their own individual votes shares and probability of winning. Yet these same opposition party leaders almost always eschew upgrading their coordination to full-fledged opposition alliances with joint electoral campaigns. No amount of cajoling and references to foreign experiences of successful opposition alliance formation can jolt them out of their noncoordination equilibrium when everyone perceives the costs of alliance building to exceed its meager benefits.

9 | Conclusion

Electoral authoritarian regimes are harsh environments for opposition parties to survive in, let alone thrive. Dominant autocrats and their ruling parties strategically deploy and manipulate state institutions to constantly shift the goalposts for making electoral gains, rendering prospective victory for the opposition appear like an unattainable, blurry mirage. Demoralized and resource-starved opposition parties must scavenge for public sympathy and financial support during normal times while launching sporadic guerrilla strikes at the dominant incumbent. Approaching election time, opposition parties rally their supporters to full-scale attacks on the regime even as they dodge its swinging cudgel of repression. Yet intra-opposition divisions further dull its already-blunt attacks. Ideological differences, mutual distrust, and uncertainty with the rules of the game undermine pre-electoral interparty cooperation at precisely the moment where it is most needed in challenging the dominant incumbent. Clarifying the conditions under which opposition pre-electoral alliances are built in the face of these tremendous obstacles brings us closer to understanding when electoral autocrats will encounter their sternest contests.

This book has argued that opposition party leaders are highly sensitive to the costs and benefits of building opposition alliances, and only construct alliances when they perceive that it is worth doing so. Risk-averse opposition elites loathe to waste what little resources they have in terms of time, personal energy, and organizational manpower in protracted negotiations without reasonable certainty about the benefits constructing alliances may bring. This logic is most discernable when opposition elites observe that an incumbent autocrat is consistently dominant and invulnerable. Under such circumstances, when the probability of victory is very low, opposition elites will be very unlikely to build full-scale alliances, with both candidate coordination and joint campaigns. Costly compromises such as sacrificing personal control over the party's strategy or staying silent on the party's long-cherished policy proposals are not considered worthwhile investments. Of course, as the Singaporean case reveals, compromises in terms of allocating geographically segregated electoral districts may still occur in order to maximize each party's own chance of winning in its own specific districts. Candidate coordination at this level is most likely to be successful when parties possess ex ante information about their relative popularity and associated winning chances in particular districts, which informs and lubricates interparty negotiations.

By contrast, when opposition parties assess electoral autocratic regimes to be vulnerable approaching election time, they are much more likely to build full-scale opposition alliances. An acceleration of regime-debilitating events such as economic crises, intra-regime defections, withdrawal of international support, and recurring mass street protests all occurring within a short period of time increase opposition elites' expectations about their chances of victory in forthcoming elections. The enticing smells of prospective victory motivate opposition elites to find the necessary information and agree on creative solutions to forge compromises and overcome their coordination problems. Beyond elites, opposition supporters themselves may also be more open to persuasion to "hold their noses" to vote for candidates from ideologically distant opposition parties, where previously they may not have been able to do so. As the Malaysian case demonstrates, the country's opposition elites worked hard over the years to persuade their mass supporters of their joint destiny in defeating the autocratic incumbent, particularly after their surprising electoral gains in 2008. Heightened, but still cautious, expectations of cross-party strategic voting among their opposition supporters undoubtedly helped grease the construction of the Pakatan Rakyat alliance in 2013, and the Pakatan Harapan alliance in 2018.

Yet, as this book has also argued, a second variable affecting the likelihood of alliance formation is perceptions of interparty dependency. With clear ex ante knowledge of their parties' relative strengths and weaknesses, opposition party leaders find it easier to recognize that their prospective chances of victory are highly dependent on their parties working with each other. The Philippines case clearly illustrates how one opposition leader's weakness in mass party organization can be mitigated by combining with another opposition leader's superior party machinery. Another party leader's weakness in charismatic popularity can be alleviated by another party leader's greater mass popularity. By contrast, as in the South Korean case, where there was a lack of clear ex ante information about relative strengths and weaknesses, opposition party leaders were more likely to be belligerent about their own chances of winning. No opposition party leader who believes in his or her own chances of winning will want to step aside for another leader to claim the role of opposition flagbearer and potential victory.

In sum, opposition elites' perceptions of regime vulnerability and mutual dependency work as twin forces galvanizing alliance construction. Opposition party leaders will be most likely to assess pre-electoral alliance building as a worthwhile endeavor when they believe they have a reasonable chance of winning, and when they believe victory is dependent on interparty support. These beliefs motivate opposition elites to exhibit flexibility on their most cherished policy objectives and accept costly concessions, even as they devise innovative joint campaigns to mobilize mass support against the incumbent autocrat. Malaysia's recurring opposition alliances with new forms of joint campaign in each iteration suggest that there are a variety of ways in which a majority of voters can be persuaded and convinced to defect from the dominant incumbent.

Implications for Social Science Research

Temporality

This book's arguments generate a variety of theoretical, methodological, and empirical implications for the study of comparative democratization of electoral autocracies. At the minimum, they suggest scholars must take the role of temporality much more seriously (Büthe 2002; Pierson 2004; Thelen 2000). Specifically, the timing, momentum, and sequencing of events occurring within a specified duration are crucial lenses through which to analyze particular causal mechanisms and processes of democratization (Grzymala-Busse 2011).

With regards to the *timing* of regime-debilitating events, the existing literature on comparative democratization frequently examines the consequences of one specific regime-debilitating event on particular regime liberalization processes and overall democratization. Economic crises can cripple autocratic stability (Shih 2020; Treisman 2020). Mass protests occurring in one country can encourage coups (Casper and Tyson 2014), increase the chances of democratic reforms (Beaulieu 2014; Hollyer, Rosendorff, and Vreeland 2015), or spill over to other countries in the region, resulting in a cascade of democratic revolution (Bunce and Wolchik 2011; Hale 2013). Other scholarly work, however, suggest that regime-debilitating events are not isolated, independent events. They are oftentimes frequently found occurring together. Economic crises and depression, for instance, encourage regime defection (Reuter and Gandhi 2011; Reuter and Szakonyi 2019). The masses may act collectively against the incumbent autocrat by observing cues from defecting elites, who in turn act strategically by observing the behavior of the dissenting masses (Little 2017; Little, Tucker, and LaGatta 2015; Schedler 2002).

If and when regime-debilitating events occur closely together, disaggregating and isolating their causal effects on regime stability and democratization is a perilous task (Pepinsky 2014). Not only is it theoretically and methodologically challenging for scholars to parse out the independent causal effects of interrelated episodes, but our theoretical models may also be mis-specified if we ignore their complex relationships with each other. Already, in the cognate research field of political economy, there have been some benefits in a few scholars utilizing the tools of complexity and systems theory to model complex political and economic outcomes (Ang 2016). Arguably, by embracing the full empirical complexity of a regime's democratization process, one can obtain a better picture of how the entire elephant moves and behaves.

The concurrence of regime-debilitating events also underlines the necessity of further clarifying the *momentum* of democratization. As this book has argued, multiple regime-debilitating events within a short period of time generate a subjective perception of accelerating regime vulnerability, motivating elites to update their assessments of the probability of defeating the regime at the ballot box. Such instances were observed in the Philippines, in South Korea, and in particular periods in Malaysia. Yet acceleration is by no means the only means through which regime-debilitating events can occur. Such events can occur at a slow, steady pace over a long period of time, or even at a decelerating pace after an initial burst. Taiwan's process of democratization, for example, was arguably slower and much more evenly paced. Its democracy emerged and matured only after a gradual, liberalizing reforms were initiated by a dominant party bent on preserving its staying power (Cheng and Haggard 1992; Rigger 1999; Wong 2001). In these alternative worlds, opposition elites are much less likely to be motivated to undertake quick short-term action to resolve their immediate coordination problems surrounding elections. Instead, opposition party leaders may take time to build broader alliances with civil society actors who lend support through their mass networks, or with the international diaspora, who engage the international community to exert external pressure on the regime (Koinova 2009; Quinsaat 2019).

Rather than the immediate goal of regime defeat, these broader opposition networks build gradual pressure on electoral autocracies to gradually concede different degrees of democratic reforms in different institutional arenas (Eisenstadt 2004; Lehoucq and Molina Jiménez 2002; Ong 2018).

Finally, the *sequencing* of events in an electoral autocracy can profoundly alter its fate by revealing information about the state of the regime and the opposition. Opposition parties' experience with and results from prior electoral contests reveal information about their relative strengths and weaknesses (Miller 2015; Pop-Eleches and Robertson 2015). Similarly, prior experience with mass protests reveals information to opposition party leaders about whether the masses are ready to defect from the incumbent. Initial intra-regime defection divulges information about the cohesion of the autocrat's ruling coalition. Absent these initial events that publicly reveal information about the true state of the regime, the motors of regime decline might not be set into motion. That is why autocrats keen on masking their true health invest so heavily in repertoires and institutions of censorship and self-censorship (King, Pan, and Roberts 2013; Lee 1998; Lorentzen 2014; Ong 2021; Sinpeng 2013; Stockmann and Gallagher 2011).

This notion of paying theoretical attention to the sequencing of events is closely related to the idea of learning. Learning denotes a process of an actor taking in new information from a source or a variety of sources, and then using the new knowledge to achieve a particular objective. States can learn about their relative strengths and resolve to reach new bargains even as they fight against each other (Powell 2004; Spaniel and Bils 2018). Autocratic regimes can learn new ways to repress from other autocratic regimes and thus entrench their dominance (Heydemann and Leenders 2011; Ortmann and Thompson 2014). Citizens can learn to coordinate against a regime when they learn new information about the regime's vulnerability (Angeletos, Hellwig, and Pavan 2007; Little 2017; Shurchkov 2013). Conservative Islamists can learn to be Muslim democrats (Grewal 2020). In a similar manner, this book has explicitly demonstrated that opposition elites changing their actions after learning new, or reevaluating old, information is a key causal mechanism in realizing pre-electoral alliance formation. Furthermore, the Malaysian case has also demonstrated that opposition elites can learn from the past failures of previous alliances to render more effective their joint election campaigns. Where previously opposition votes were splintered by the use of different party logos and unimpressive manifestos in 1999 and 2013, the 2018 Pakatan Harapan (PH) opposition alliance undertook more compromises to use one party logo and campaigned much more vigorously on its manifesto to mobilize opposition support and subsequent victory.

Of course, scholars should take care not to overestimate the frequency of learning. Empirical reality is replete with numerous examples of political actors staying stubborn in the face of a rapidly changing empirical context. Whether it is because of strong partisan identity, ideological purity, or principled convictions, political actors can frequently fail to update their priors and adopt their strategies to changed environments. Again, as the Malaysian case demonstrates, opposition elites from the DAP and PAS failed to adapt to coordinate allocating electoral districts within three election cycles, in 1978, 1982, and 1986. It was only with the emergence of S46 in the late 1980s that opposition parties finally managed to coordinate allocating electoral districts in the 1990 general elections. From this perspective, then, opposition elites' learning was conditional upon a third actor emerging to mediate interparty negotiations. Moving forward, the primary challenge for researchers is to investigate the particular conditions under which learning occurs, and what outcomes for comparative democratization emerge if the opposition and the incumbent learn and respond to each other at the same time over the long term.

After Victory

Now, suppose that constructing an opposition alliance does indeed lead to opposition victory. Can the ideologically diverse opposition alliance survive to consolidate democracy after having slayed the demons of autocracy? It is on this question that Malaysia's recent experience is the most instructive. After the PH opposition alliance won the 2018 general elections, the new government sought to implement reforms that expanded franchise, enhanced civil liberties, and further protected civil rights. These reforms include a reduction of the voting age from 21 to 18, which added approximately 7.8 million new voters, a 50 percent increase, for the next elections, due by 2023. New heads of the judiciary, the election commission, and the anticorruption commission and a new attorney general were promoted to replace politically biased bureaucrats. The election commission was pulled from the prime minister's office to be placed under parliamentary oversight, while an anti-fake news law was repealed.

Yet, despite these changes, the new government was thwarted at every step by the new opposition, the previous autocratic incumbent UMNO, alongside its erstwhile partner PAS (Dettman 2020). They deployed their supporters in the streets to protest against the new government's intention to ratify the International Convention on the Elimination of All Forms of Racial Discrimination, arguing that the special privileges of the majority of the Malay-Muslims would be eroded. They also used extremist language, decrying the outsized influence of the DAP on the new government's policies while vehemently criticizing the policies of government ministries with DAP ministers. Moreover, PH ministers, having seen stiff resistance from the civil service to their reformist policies, blamed Malaysia's "deep state" for their uneven progress. Therefore, on an initial evaluation of PH's nearly two-year performance at the beginning of February 2020, Malaysia's overall trajectory toward deepening democratization appears to have decelerated significantly but not stalled.

At the end of February 2020, however, PH's reform agenda appeared to have finally exhausted itself. An attempt by Anwar Ibrahim, PKR's leader, to force Tun Dr. Mahathir Mohamad to anoint him as the next prime minister sparked a furious reshuffling of political allegiances both within and outside of PH. After a week's worth of surprising intrigue involving Tun Dr. Mahathir Mohamad's resignation, a fracturing of both the PPBM and PKR, and the Malaysian sultan's unexpected move to appoint Home Minister Tan Sri Muhyiddin Yassin as prime minister, the PH alliance suddenly found itself short of numbers to command a majority of the parliament. In the middle of March 2020, a new Perikatan Nasional government was formed, primarily comprising defectors from PPBM and PKR, UMNO, PAS, and their allies from the eastern Malaysian states of Sabah and Sarawak. Through subtle backroom maneuvers, the authoritarian parties that lost the May 2018 general election found their way back into power in less than two years. In this sense, then, Malaysia's democratization appears to have been dramatically reversed.

The PH opposition alliance's precarious victory in Malaysia therefore raises new questions and research agendas about the conditions under which democratization's momentum can be sustained even after opposition victory. Democratic consolidation requires those in power to be subject to vertical and horizontal constraints on their power. In so doing, power has to be decentralized, rather than be consolidated in a single office or around a narrow circle of elites. But which newly victorious government would willingly give up exercise of power, having now acquired it? It is hard to imagine democratic consolidation being one of the main policy priorities of a newly elected opposition alliance when there are so many other pressing issues to resolve. Even more, when faced with a hostile bureaucracy and an ex-incumbent party that has fallen from grace, to what extent can the new government remain resolute? There is no guarantee that the previously autocratic incumbent will play by the new rules of the game. For institutional innovations consolidating democracy to endure, they must be accepted by all the key political actors (Fearon 2011; Mittal and Weingast 2013; Przeworski 2006; Weingast 1997). Understanding how power decentralization unfolds or how new institutions are built over the long term will demand more longitudinal theoretical frameworks than we currently possess.

Resisting Democratic Erosion

Beyond opposition parties fighting for democracy in electoral autocracies, this book also has important lessons for opposition parties fighting against populists with autocratic tendencies in existing democracies. In such existing democracies undergoing democratic erosion, popularly elected executives test the limits of constraints on their power, frequently breaking hitherto accepted democratic shackles (Bermeo 2016; Dresden and Howard 2016; Levitsky and Ziblatt 2018; Lührmann and Lindberg 2019; Waldner and Lust 2018). They appoint partisan loyalists to control key formal institutions such as the judiciary and the election commission. They use their legislative majorities and allies to minimize or exclude the opposition from previously bipartisan governance institutions. They undermine the press through their intimidating rhetoric and selective repression. Ultimately, whether it is through overt enablers or crafty rhetoric, autocratic executives use the tools handed to them by democracy to break democracy itself (Gandhi 2018).

Insofar as this book has proposed that opposition elites may disagree with each other about an incumbent regime's vulnerability and only update their expectations under exceptional circumstances, opposition elites in democracies too may disagree with each other about what exactly constitutes democratic erosion. An autocratic executive's individual transgressions are not likely to trigger alarm bells. Rather, because reasonable people can disagree about what specific executive action constitutes an erosion of democracy, autocratic executives in democracies can frequently get away with their transgressions. Among opposition elites, for instance, the enactment of new legislation to curtail democratic institutions or the media under the rhetorical guise of national security can generate intraopposition disputes about whether national security trumps democratic accountability. By the time multiple particularly egregious transgressions occur, causing everyone to reassess the state of democratic erosion, democracy may have already been broken. Hence, more scholarly attention is warranted on the conditions under which the masses and opposition elites converge on a consensus that democratic erosion is occurring.

Moreover, even while opposition elites in democracies may agree on the alarming decline of democracy in their country, they may yet disagree about how to best fight to preserve it (Gamboa 2017). Shut out of legislative influence, some opposition elites and parties may prefer to mobilize their supporters in the streets, utilizing popular pressure to force incumbent executives to back away from their transgressive actions. Others may rely on cultivating domestic allies such as the press, or foreign allies such as the diaspora, to campaign against the incumbent autocratic executive. More desperate opposition elites and parties may even be forced to appeal to major foreign powers such as European countries or the United States to intervene on their behalf. Which strategy each opposition party prefers is likely to be conditional on its pre-existing capabilities and resources, such as the availability of funds, the party's rootedness in society, and its organizational capacity (Lebas 2011).

Finally, it will be crucial to clarify the conditions under which opposition elites in backsliding democracies can learn to collectively defend democracy in time. Toward that end, more comprehensive, detailed, longitudinal, empirical data will need to be collected on the key political actors, the particular institutional context in which they operate in, their relative strengths and weaknesses, their relationships with each other, their strategies, alongside the processes and outcomes of interparty negotiations (Gandhi 2015). For instance, consider the case of contemporary Turkey. As Erdoğan dramatically expanded his powers over one and a half decades, Turkey's opposition were ridden by intraparty conflicts and interparty ideological divisions between Islamists, secularists, and pro- and anti-Kurdish parties (Esen and Gumuscu 2016; Öniş 2013). It was only in the 2019 subnational local elections that some opposition parties managed to coordinate with each other and experience moderate electoral success (Esen and Gumuscu 2019, 325–27). While this alliance excluded the pro-Kurdish and Islamist opposition parties, the limited coordination brought substantial gains for the opposition. Most symbolically, the opposition secured unprecedented victories in major cities like Ankara and Istanbul. Precisely how and why opposition parties got from one noncooperative equilibrium to a semi-cooperative equilibrium over the long term remains unexplained.

Implications for Policy Practitioners in Democracy Promotion

Other than generating new agendas for future research, this book also has some implications for policy practitioners engaged in promoting democracy. Given the importance of opposition elites and parties learning from past experience in enhancing their capabilities and cooperative relationships over time, policy practitioners can potentially do more to help facilitate learning. After each electoral cycle, opportunities to learn from past failures can be facilitated to help the opposition parties find new ways to engage that are specific to their country and regional context. If opposition elites and parties can innovate new strategies of mobilization and organization, new ways of campaigning, and new rhetoric, their political standing might improve significantly among the electorate in the future.

Once again, Malaysia's recent experience is exemplary. After the BN's dominant victory in the 2004 general elections, opposition parties were demoralized. They won only 20 out of 219 parliamentary seats, giving BN its best electoral victory since 1974. Stung by defeat, the opposition convened a workshop together with civil society organizations entitled the "Advocacy and the Role of the Opposition," funded by the National Democratic Institute (Khoo 2016, 422). At that workshop, the opposition parties reached a consensus to jointly focus their attention on advocating for electoral reform—a new common objective that could mobilize more voters in the future. Their efforts soon snowballed into the Bersih movement, which turned out mass protestors in the streets campaigning for electoral reform and against the BN government in 2007, 2011, 2012, 2015, and 2016. Eventually, activists involved in these recurring street protests formed the organizational backbone of the opposition in the 2013 and 2018 general elections, and also raised voter awareness of the electoral malfeasance committed by the BN government (Chan 2019; Khoo 2014). On hindsight, a collective opportunity to learn from their past mistakes to organize and mobilize voters based on new social cleavages helped push Malaysian democratization into a positive trajectory over the long term.

The degree to which opposition elites and parties are willing to try new strategies for attracting new voters is dependent on their assessments of how such voters may react to the new strategies. If the opposition lacks information about how voters will react, it is likely to be more skeptical about attempting new mobilization strategies. It might prefer more traditional methods of appealing to erstwhile core supporters. From this perspective, policy practitioners can help fund public opinion surveys that will be critical in helping the opposition assess voter preferences, how voters form those preferences, and what factors inform those preferences. Even more, survey experiments embedded within public opinion surveys can be especially useful tools for test-bedding new opposition rhetoric or campaign strategies. My own survey experiment conducted in Malaysia suggests that a joint manifesto is likely to substantially improve voter support for the opposition, contrary to common misperceptions of its marginal utility (E. Ong 2019).

The saturation of positive news from regime-controlled media, self-censorship, and preference falsification means that public opinion surveys in electoral autocracies are frequently biased. Opposition supporters, or even moderate, independent voters, may prefer to mask their true preferences. Researchers and policy practitioners will need to rely on new survey techniques to try to elicit responses to sensitive political questions in electoral autocracies. These techniques include the list experiment, the endorsement experiment, and the randomized response technique. By taking social desirability bias into account, researchers and policy practitioners can provide better estimates of voters' opinions and preferences, lending greater confidence to the surveys' reliability.

Conclusion

Opposition actors within electoral autocracies have to maneuver within restricted political environments. If they are careless enough to breach those restrictions, they are likely to find themselves at the sharp end of the autocrat's repressive tool. Their influence will be further curtailed, fostering the demise of the opposition's cause. In short, they have to take their political environment as it is, not as what they hope it will be.

But agency among the opposition is ever present and is at its most active when the shifting winds of political change motivate opposition elites to enlist their supporters to mount a counterattack against the autocratic incumbent. The degree to which opposition elites can agree on a coordinated plan of counterattack has been the subject of this book. That question this book has answered by suggesting that the opposition's joint perceptions of the incumbent's vulnerability and their mutual dependency are the two most important variables affecting coordination outcomes. Even as they desire to coordinate, differing perceptions of these two variables lead to divergent consequences.

Over the long term, democratizing electoral autocracies will require the opposition not just to swallow harsh compromises. It will also necessitate learning from past mistakes and innovating to improve campaign rhetoric and methods in future electoral cycles. The end objective is to convince a majority of the population that regime change is plausible and good not only in and of itself, but also because it will deliver a better material future for voters and their loved ones. It is on this fundamental vision, which is both normative in its meaning and substantive in its practicality, that the opposition in electoral autocracies will have to ground its agenda.

Notes

CHAPTER 1

1. Seth Mydans, "Philippine Opposition Works Out Agreement for a Unified Ticket." *New York Times.* December 12, 1985.

2. Clyde Haberman, "2 Suicides Protest South Korea Opposition Disunity." *New York Times.* December 11, 1987.

3. Throughout this book, I use the terms "coalition" and "alliance" interchangeably.

4. Throughout this book, "opposition party" refers to any political party that is not the dominant ruling party and not created by or affiliated with the dominant ruling party. Any reference to "party elites" or "party leaders" specifically refers to their positions within "opposition parties," unless otherwise noted.

5. In this book, I use the concept "ideology" to refer very broadly to interparty differences in orientations toward class, economic strategies, ethnicity, and religion.

6. "Opposition Politics in Tanzania and Why the Country Will Benefit from a Strong Unified Opposition." *Africa at LSE Blog.* June 29, 2015. https://blogs.lse.ac.uk/africaatlse/2015/06/29/opposition-politics-in-tanzania-and-why-the-country-will-benefit-from-a-strong-unified-opposition/

7. "Manifestos for Change? 12 Observations on the CCM and Chadema Documents." *Africa Research Institute.* September 30, 2015. https://www.africaresearchinstitute.org/newsite/blog/manifestos-for-change/

8. "Ugandan Popstar and Opposition Politician Bibi Wine Jailed." *CNN.* April 29, 2019. https://www.cnn.com/2019/04/29/africa/ugandan-bobi-wine-arrested-intl/index.html

9. "Will Thailand's Future Forward Party Survive a Prayuth Government?" *South China Morning Post.* December 11, 2019. https://www.scmp.com/week-asia/politics/article/3041476/will-thailands-future-forward-party-survive-prayuth-government

CHAPTER 2

1. "Manifestoes for Change? 12 Observations on the CCM and Chadema Documents." *Africa Research Institute.* September 30, 2015. https://www.africaresearchinstitute.org/newsite/blog/manifestos-for-change/

2. "Mahathir Mohamad Named Opposition Candidate for Malaysian PM." *The Straits Times*. January 7, 2018. http://www.straitstimes.com/asia/se-asia/mahathir-nam ed-opposition-candidate-for-pm

3. "Rare Mass Rally over Singapore Immigration Plans." *BBC*. February 16, 2013. https://www.bbc.com/news/world-asia-21485729

4. "Thousands Rally for Marcos in Manila." *New York Times*. April 14, 1986. https:// www.nytimes.com/1986/04/14/world/thousands-rally-for-marcos-in-manila.html

5. "Turkey's Opposition Wins Rerun of Istanbul Mayoral Vote." *Al-Jazeera*. June 23, 2019. https://www.aljazeera.com/news/2019/06/erdogan-candidate-concedes-defe at-istanbul-vote-190623162700306.html

6. "Turkey's Opposition Wins Rerun of Istanbul Mayoral Vote."

CHAPTER 3

1. The Digital National Security Archives are managed by the George Washington University. They can be accessed at https://nsarchive.gwu.edu/digital-national-security -archive or at the Proquest-managed database at https://proquest.libguides.com/dnsa

2. All the documents can be searched for and accessed at https://www.cia.gov/libr ary/readingroom/

3. To see what the archives at the Ronald Reagan Presidential Library contain, see https://www.reaganlibrary.gov/

4. National Security Decision Directive Number 163. "United States Policy towards the Philippines (S)." February 20, 1985. Ronald Reagan Presidential Library and Museum, Simi Valley, California. https://www.reaganlibrary.gov/digital-library/nsdds

5. 100th Congress, House of Representatives, Committee on Foreign Affairs. "Update on Political Developments in Korea, June 1987." *Hearing before the Subcommittee on Asian and Pacific Affairs*. June 30, 1987. https://hdl.handle.net/2027/pst.0000136 02956

6. See World Bank Indicators https://data.worldbank.org/indicator/NY.GDP.PC AP.KD and https://data.worldbank.org/indicator/NY.GDP.MKTP.KD (last accessed September 20, 2021).

7. Salvador Laurel Diary Entry. June 14, 1985. The Philippine Diary Project. https://philippinediaryproject.com/1985/06/14/june-14-1985/

8. Salvador Laurel Diary Entry. September 17, 1985. The Philippine Diary Project. https://philippinediaryproject.wordpress.com/1985/09/17/september-17-1985/

9. American Embassy Cable. "The Philippine Election Campaign—the Financial Dimension." May 5, 1984. Digital National Security Archive (DNSA): The Philippines: U.S. Policy during the Marcos Years, 1965–1986.

10. American Embassy Cable. "The Opposition: Uniting or Fragmenting?" Telegram 85MANILA05814. Digital National Security Archive (DNSA): The Philippines: U.S. Policy during the Marcos Years, 1965–1986.

11. "Bumiputera" refers to the indigenous people of Malaysia. Malays are recognized as indigenous to Malaysia. Source: "Population Distribution and Basic Democratic Characteristics Report 2010." Department of Statistics Malaysia. https://www.do sm.gov.my/v1/index.php?r=column/ctheme&menu_id=L0pheU43NWJwRWVSZklW dzQ4TlhUUT09&bul_id=MDMxdHZjWTk1SjFzTzNkRXYzcVZjdz09 (last accessed June 18, 2019).

12. "Population Trends 2018." Department of Statistics Singapore. https://www.sing stat.gov.sg/-/media/files/publications/population/population2018.pdf (last accessed June 18, 2019).

13. "GDP Per Capita in Constant 2010 US$." World Bank Development Indicators. https://data.worldbank.org/indicator/NY.GDP.PCAP.KD (last accessed September 20, 2021).

CHAPTER 4

1. American Embassy Manila. "National Assembly Elections—Initial Impressions." Telegram 83MANILA12825. Digital National Security Archive (DNSA): The Philippines: U.S. Policy during the Marcos Years, 1965–1986.

2. "Twilight of the Marcos Era." New York Times. January 6, 1986. https://www.nyt imes.com/1985/01/06/magazine/twilight-of-the-marcos-era.html

3. Director of Central Intelligence Special Intelligence Estimate: "Near-Term Prospects for Stability in the Philippines." In Executive Secretariat, National Security Council: Country File. RAC Box 10. Folder: "Philippines—22 November 1983 to 23 February 1984." Ronald Reagan Presidential Library and Museum, Simi Valley, California.

4. American Embassy Cable. "Pre-election Assessment." May 9, 1984. Digital National Security Archive (DNSA): The Philippines: U.S. Policy During the Marcos Years, 1965–1986.

5. Executive Secretariat, National Security Council: Country File. RAC Box 10. Folder: "Philippines—21 April 1984 to 6 February 1985." Ronald Reagan Presidential Library and Museum, Simi Valley, California.

6. American Embassy Manila. "Post Election Developments—Opposition Views." Telegram 84MANILA15167. Digital National Security Archives (DNSA): The Philippines: U.S. Policy during the Marcos Years, 1965–1986.

7. American Embassy Manila. "National Assembly Elections—Initial Impressions." Telegram 83MANILA12825. Digital National Security Archive (DNSA): The Philippines: U.S. Policy during the Marcos Years, 1965–1986.

8. "Twilight of the Marcos Era." New York Times. January 6, 1986. https://www.nyt imes.com/1985/01/06/magazine/twilight-of-the-marcos-era.html

9. "Aide Confirms Illness of Marcos." New York Times. December 4, 1984. https://www.nytimes.com/1984/12/04/world/aide-confirms-illness-of-marcos.html

10. Association for Diplomatic Studies and Training. "Stephen Bosworth, Ambassador, Philippines (1984–1987)." Philippines Country Reader. https://adst.org/wp-conte nt/uploads/2018/04/Philippines.pdf (last accessed July 15, 2019).

11. See videos of Marcos's grandiose state visit to the United States uploaded on YouTube by the Reagan Library: (1) https://youtu.be/t8AxvM1JVDM, (2) https://youtu .be/NdNWzAV-a60, (3) https://youtu.be/m0KGfR4rZJE, and (4) https://youtu.be/bRE WN6eCB4A. See also C-SPAN video of Marcos's speech at the National Press Club: https://www.c-span.org/video/?88357-1/philippine-issues (all last accessed July 9, 2019).

12. CIA Intelligence Memorandum. "The State Visit: President Marcos' Objectives." In Executive Secretariat, National Security Council: Country File. RAC Box 10. Folder: "Philippines—24 August 1982 to 18 January 1983." Ronald Reagan Presidential Library and Museum, Simi Valley, California.

13. "After the Marcos Visit: The Future of a Special Relationship." *Christian Science Monitor.* September 20, 1982. https://www.csmonitor.com/1982/0920/092044.html

14. "Shultz, in Manila, Affirms Support of U.S. for Marcos." *New York Times.* June 26, 1983. https://www.nytimes.com/1983/06/26/world/shultz-in-manila-affirms-suppo rt-of-us-for-marcos.html

15. See Marcos personal letters to Reagan in Executive Secretariat, NSC: Head of State Files. Box 27. Ronald Reagan Presidential Library and Museum, Simi Valley, California.

16. Memo from David D. Gries, National Intelligence Officer for East Asia, to Judge Clark, Director of Central Intelligence. "After Marcos—a Contingency the US Could Face." In Executive Secretariat, National Security Council: Country File. RAC Box 10. Folder: "Philippines—25 August 1983 to 5 October 1983." Ronald Reagan Presidential Library and Museum, Simi Valley, California.

17. American Embassy Manila. "Meeting with President Marcos." Telegram MANILA4904. In Executive Secretariat, National Security Council: Country File. RAC Box 10. Folder: "Philippines—25 August 1983 to 5 October 1983." Ronald Reagan Presidential Library and Museum, Simi Valley, California.

18. Director of Central Intelligence Special Intelligence Estimate: "Near-Term Prospects for Stability in the Philippines." In Executive Secretariat, National Security Council: Country File. RAC Box 10. Folder: "Philippines—22 November 1983 to 23 February 1984." Ronald Reagan Presidential Library and Museum, Simi Valley, California.

19. National Security Decision Directive Number 163. "United States Policy towards the Philippines." February 20, 1985. Ronald Reagan Presidential Library and Museum, Simi Valley, California. https://www.reaganlibrary.gov/digital-library/nsdds

20. Childress, Richard T. RAC Box 11. Ronald Reagan Presidential Library and Museum, Simi Valley, California.

21. "Interview with Congressman Stephen Solarz." The Association for Diplomatic Studies and Training Foreign Affairs Oral History Project. https://www.adst.org/OH %20TOCs/Solarz,%20Stephen.toc.pdf (last accessed July 7, 2019).

22. "Foreign Assistance Legislation for Fiscal Year 1985 (Part 5)," Hearings and Markup before the Subcommittee on Asia and Pacific Affairs of the Committee on Foreign Affairs, 98th Congress, Second Session. February 6, 7, 22, 23, and 28, 1984.

23. "Foreign Assistance Legislation for Fiscal Years 1986–1987 (Part 5)." Hearings and Markup before the Subcommittee on Asia and Pacific Affairs of the Committee on Foreign Affairs, 98th Congress, Second Session. February 20, 27, 28, March 5, 6, 12, and 20, 1985.

24. "Investigation of Marcos by Solarz Is Issue in U.S. as well as Manila." *New York Times.* February 7, 1986. https://www.nytimes.com/1986/02/07/world/investigation-of -marcos-by-solarz-is-issue-in-us-as-well-as-manila.html

25. "Interview with Congressman Stephen Solarz." The Association for Diplomatic Studies and Training Foreign Affairs Oral History Project. https://www.adst.org/OH %20TOCs/Solarz,%20Stephen.toc.pdf (last accessed July 7, 2019).

26. American Embassy Manila. "Ambassador's Conversation with Opposition Leader Salvador Laurel." Telegram 83MANILA023798. Digital National Security Archive (DNSA): The Philippines: U.S. Policy during the Marcos Years, 1965–1986.

27. Memorandum "Subject: Visit by Philippine Opposition Leader Salvador Laurel on the Vice President." In Executive Secretariat, National Security Council: Country

File. RAC Box 10. Folder: "Philippines—22 November 1983 to 23 February 1984." Ronald Reagan Presidential Library and Museum, Simi Valley, California.

28. Salvador Laurel Diary Entry. June 12, 1985. The Philippine Diary Project. https://philippinediaryproject.wordpress.com/1985/06/12/june-12-1985/

29. Salvador Laurel Diary Entry. October 18, 1985. The Philippine Diary Project. https://philippinediaryproject.wordpress.com/1985/10/18/october-18-1985/

30. Mydans, Seth. "Marcos' Surprise Move: Philippine Leader's Call for Early Elections Puts His Scrambling Opponents on the Spot." *New York Times*. November 6, 1985.

31. American Embassy Manila. "Marcos Announces Snap Elections." Telegram 85MANILA034138. Digital National Security Archive (DNSA): The Philippines: U.S. Policy during the Marcos Years, 1965–1986.

32. Mydans, Seth. "Foes of Marcos Debate Who'll Run against Him." *New York Times*. November 14, 1985.

33. Mydans, Seth. "Aquino's Widow a New Focus of Opposition Hope." *New York Times*. November 10, 1985.

34. American Embassy Manila. "EXCISED on opposition activities." Telegram 85MANILA034905. Digital National Security Archive (DNSA): The Philippines: U.S. Policy during the Marcos Years, 1965–1986.

35. American Embassy Manila. "Snap Presidential Election." Telegram 85MANILA034352. Digital National Security Archive (DNSA): The Philippines: U.S. Policy during the Marcos Years, 1965–1986.

36. "Widow of Aquino Hints Election Bid." *New York Times*. December 2, 1985.

37. Mydans, Seth. "Aquino's Widow a New Focus of Opposition Hope." *New York Times*. November 10, 1985. See also note 7.

38. Mydans, Seth. "Marcos Foes Are Hindered by New Rifts." *New York Times*. November 26, 1985.

39. US Department of State Bureau of Intelligence and Research. "Implications of the Presidential Elections in the Philippines." Briefing Paper. November 9, 1985. Digital National Security Archive (DNSA): The Philippines: U.S. Policy during the Marcos Years, 1965–1986.

40. American Embassy Manila. "The Political Opposition in the Aftermath of the Aquino Assassination." Telegram 83MANILA023450. Digital National Security Archive (DNSA): The Philippines: U.S. Policy during the Marcos Years, 1965–1986.

41. American Embassy Manila. "Election Campaign Finance and the Economy." Telegram 85MANILA039289. Digital National Security Archive (DNSA): The Philippines: U.S. Policy during the Marcos Years, 1965–1986.

42. American Embassy Manila. "The Opposition: Uniting or Fragmenting?" Telegram 85MANILA05814. Digital National Security Archive (DNSA): The Philippines: U.S. Policy during the Marcos Years, 1965–1986.

43. "The Current Situation in the Philippines." A Staff Report Prepared for the Committee on Foreign Relations, US Senate. September 1984. Digital National Security Archive (DNSA): The Philippines: U.S. Policy during the Marcos Years, 1965–1986.

44. Association for Diplomatic Studies and Training. "Stephen Bosworth, Ambassador, Philippines (1984–1987)." Philippines Country Reader. https://adst.org/wp-content/uploads/2018/04/Philippines.pdf (last accessed July 15, 2019).

45. Mydans, Seth. "Marcos Foes Try to Resolve Rift before Deadline: Anti-Marcos Forces Struggle to Reunite after Last-Minute Breakup." *New York Times*. December 9, 1985.

46. Salvador Laurel Diary Entry. December 7, 1985. The Philippine Diary Project. https://philippinediaryproject.com/1985/12/07/december-7-1985/

47. Salvador Laurel Diary Entry. December 11, 1985. The Philippine Diary Project. https://philippinediaryproject.wordpress.com/1985/12/11/december-11-1985/

48. Mydans, Seth. "Manila Opposition to Marcos Splits: Alliance Talks Fail Just before Slate Is to Be Announced." *New York Times.* December 8, 1985.

49. "Special Interagency Philippine Analytic Group Meeting." CIARDP87S00734R000100020045-4. CIA Freedom of Information Act Electronic Reading Room.

50. "HPSCI Briefing—19 November 1985." CIA-RDP91B00874R00040001-7. CIA Freedom of Information Act Electronic Reading Room.

51. "The Philippines: President Marcos' Snap Election Strategy." CIA-RDP04T00447R000302320001-4. CIA Freedom of Information Act Electronic Reading Room.

52. US Department of State Bureau of Intelligence and Research. "Implications of the Presidential Elections in the Philippines." Briefing Paper. November 9, 1985. Digital National Security Archive (DNSA): The Philippines: U.S. Policy during the Marcos Years, 1965–1986.

53. "Ex-Senator Registers to Run." *New York Times.* December 10, 1985.

54. Quinn-Judge, Paul. "Opposition Unites at 11th Hour to Challenge Marcos." *Christian Science Monitor.* December 12, 1985.

55. American Embassy Manila. "Opposition Unity Threatened Anew." Telegram 85MANILA038237. Digital National Security Archive (DNSA): The Philippines: U.S. Policy during the Marcos Years, 1965–1986.

56. Association for Diplomatic Studies and Training. "Philip S. Kaplan, Deputy Chief of Mission, Manila (1985–1987)." Philippines Country Reader. https://adst.org/wp-content/uploads/2018/04/Philippines.pdf (last accessed July 15, 2019).

57. Myans, Seth. "The Battle, Aquino Finds, Recasts Her as the Leader." *New York Times.* December 10, 1985.

58. Mydans, Seth. "Marcos Foes Try to Resolve Rift before Deadline: Anti-Marcos Forces Struggle to Reunite after Last-Minute Breakup." *New York Times.* December 9, 1985.

59. Salvador Laurel Diary Entry. December 11, 1985. The Philippine Diary Project. https://philippinediaryproject.com/1985/12/11/december-11-1985/

60. American Embassy Manila. "Doy Laurel Hangs Tough." Telegram 85MANILA038382. Digital National Security Archive (DNSA): The Philippines: U.S. Policy during the Marcos Years, 1965–1986.

61. "Big Stakes in the Philippines." *New York Times.* December 13, 1985.

62. "The Philippine Moderate Opposition: Can It Make a Difference?" CIA-RDP90T01298R000200220001-8. CIA Freedom of Information Act Electronic Reading Room.

63. "Aquino in Assurance on Bases." *New York Times.* December 27, 1985. https://www.nytimes.com/1985/12/27/world/aquino-in-assurance-on-bases.html

64. American Embassy Manila. "Meeting with President Marcos." Telegram MANILA4904. In Executive Secretariat, National Security Council: Country File. RAC Box 10. Folder: "Philippines—25 August 1983 to 5 October 1983." Ronald Reagan Presidential Library and Museum, Simi Valley, California.

65. "The Philippines: Implications of Marcos' Moves against the Opposition." CIA-RDP84S00553R000100120002-4. CIA Freedom of Information Act Electronic Reading Room.

66. "Memcon: President's Meeting with Cardinal Jaime Sin." In Executive Secretariat, National Security Council: Country File. RAC Box 10. Folder: "Philippines—21 April 1984 to 6 February 1985." Ronald Reagan Presidential Library and Museum, Simi Valley, California.

67. Memorandum. "Thinking the Unthinkable in the Philippines: Is Sudden Change Possible?" CIA-RDP85T01058R000201850001–0. CIA Freedom of Information Act Electronic Reading Room.

CHAPTER 5

1. "Korea and the Philippines: November 1972." A Staff Report prepared for the use of the Committee on Foreign Relations, United States Senate. February 18, 1973.

2. "South Korea Chief Orders Martial Law." *New York Times*. October 18, 1972. https://www.nytimes.com/1972/10/18/archives/south-korea-chief-orders-martial-law-assembly-dissolved-and-all.html

3. "South Korea: Reenacting the Philippine Drama?" CIA-RDP86T01017R000605920001–8. CIA Freedom of Information Act Electronic Reading Room.

4. "South Korea: Warning Signs of Political Change." CIA-RDP86T00590R000400620002–2. CIA Freedom of Information Act Electronic Reading Room.

5. "A Korean Exile's Long Journey Home." *New York Times*. December 23, 1984. https://www.nytimes.com/1984/12/23/magazine/a-korean-exile-s-long-journey-home.html

6. "Leading South Korea Dissident Discloses Plan to End Exile: Kim Dae Jung Gets Support of Senator Cranston." *Los Angeles Times*. January 19, 1985. https://www.latimes.com/archives/la-xpm-1985-01-19-me-8112-story.html

7. "South Korea: The Rise in Anti-US Incidents." CIA-RDP04T00447R000200840001–0. CIA Freedom of Information Act Electronic Reading Room.

8. "South Korea: The Rise in Anti-US Incidents."

9. See note 4.

10. "Seoul Eases Stand against Dissidents." *New York Times*. February 25, 1986. https://www.nytimes.com/1986/02/25/world/seoul-eases-stand-against-dissidents.html

11. "Seoul Eases Stand against Dissidents."

12. "Korean Cardinal Backs Opposition." *New York Times*. March 10, 1986. https://www.nytimes.com/1986/03/10/world/korean-cardinal-backs-opposition.html

13. "Seoul Student's Torture Death Changes Political Landscape." *New York Times*. January 31, 1987. https://www.nytimes.com/1987/01/31/world/seoul-student-s-torture-death-changes-political-landscape.html

14. "Main Seoul Opposition Figures Form a New Party." *New York Times*. April 8, 1987.

15. "Death of Student Triggers Renewed Clashes in Seoul." *Washington Post*. July 6,

1987. https://www.washingtonpost.com/archive/politics/1987/07/06/death-of-student-triggers-renewed-clashes-in-seoul/511f991f-0eb7-491c-97c4-704563e3c73f/?utm_term=.e207b9014931

16. "Fury and Turmoil: Days That Shook Korea." *New York Times*. July 16, 2019. https://www.nytimes.com/1987/07/06/world/fury-and-turmoil-days-that-shook-korea.html

17. 100th Congress, House of Representatives, Committee on Foreign Affairs. "Update on Political Developments in Korea, June 1987." *Hearing before the Subcommittee on Asian and Pacific Affairs*. June 30, 1987. https://hdl.handle.net/2027/pst.000013602956

18. Haberman, Clyde. "Bombshell in Seoul; 'People Power', Korean Style, Forces Party Chief into Bold Political Gamble." *New York Times*. June 30, 1987.

19. "National Security Planning Group Meeting 156. 4 July 1987." Ronald Reagan Presidential Library and Museum, Simi Valley, California.

20. US Department of State Briefing Paper. "Background and Supplementary Talking Points: Your Presentation on the Objectives and Strategy for the Korea Trip." November 2, 1983. Digital National Security Archive (DNSA): The United States and the Two Koreas (1969–2000).

21. Memo from George P. Shultz to the President. "Your Asia Trip." In Sigur, Gaston RAC Box 15. Ronald Reagan Presidential Library and Museum, Simi Valley, California.

22. "Presidential Address: National Assembly, Seoul, Korea, Saturday, November 12, 1983." In Sigur, Gaston RAC Box 15. Ronald Reagan Presidential Library and Museum, Simi Valley, California.

23. The subsequent quotations in this paragraph are drawn from his speech, which was compiled into a booklet and widely circulated thereafter. "Korean Politics in Transition." Current Policy Number 917. US Department of State Bureau of Public Affairs. In WHORM Country Files Korea C0082-02 Box 117. Folder "494000 to 512499." Ronald Reagan Presidential Library and Museum, Simi Valley, California.

24. "The Secretary's Meeting with President Chun Doo Hwan." Telegram SEOUL02624 070811Z. March 7, 1987. Digital National Security Archive (DNSA): The United States and the Two Koreas (1969–2000).

25. See memos by James Kelly to Frank Carlucci. WHORM Country Files Korea C0082-02 Box 117. Folder "494000 to 512499." Ronald Reagan Presidential Library and Museum, Simi Valley, California.

26. See the special issue of the *Korea Scope* magazine, March 1983, for a collection of Kim's speeches, "Special Issue on: Kim Dae Jung in America." In Sigur, Gaston. RAC Box 10. Folder "1 Jan 1983 to 2 March 1983." Ronald Reagan Presidential Library and Museum, Simi Valley, California.

27. Memo by James Kelly to Frank Carlucci. "Korea Policy." June 17, 1987. WHORM Country files Korea C0082-02 Box 117. Folder "494000 to 512499." Ronald Reagan Presidential Library and Museum, Simi Valley, California.

28. "Reagan Cautions Korean President on Unrest." *New York Times*. June 19, 1987. https://www.nytimes.com/1987/06/19/world/reagan-cautions-korean-president-on-unrest.html

29. "Assistant Secretary Sigur's Meeting with President Chun Doo Hwan." Telegram SEOUL 07478. June 24, 1987. Digital National Security Archive (DNSA): The United States and the Two Koreas (1969–2000).

30. "Assistant Secretary Sigur's Meeting with DJP Chairman Roh Tae Woo." Telegram SEOUL 07472. June 24, 1987. Digital National Security Archive (DNSA): The United States and the Two Koreas (1969–2000).

31. "Statement by A/S Sigur at White House, 6/27/87." Telegram 262315Z. In Kelly, James. Box 3. Folder "Korea (19 June 1987)." Ronald Reagan Presidential Library and Museum, Simi Valley, California.

32. CIA Intelligence Assessment. "South Korea's Presidential Election: A Difficult Road to Transition." C05828916. This document, alongside many others, was obtained and released by the *South China Morning Post* via a Freedom of Information Act request. https://www.scmp.com/news/asia/east-asia/article/3019614/south-korea-no-2-former -president-roh-dismisses-dirty-tricks (last accessed July 30, 2019).

33. "Two Kims Differ over Presidency." *Japan Economic Newswire Kyodo.* July 3, 1987; Ford, Maggie. "Seoul Opposition Leaders Struggle to Agree Stance." *Financial Times.* July 4, 1987; Kristof, Nicholas D. "Sour Mood in Seoul: Opposition Factions at Knives Drawn as South Koreans Talk of Democracy." *New York Times.* July 22, 1987.

34. Haberman, Clyde. "The 2 Kims: Can They Keep a United Front?" *New York Times.* July 2, 1987.

35. Lee, Su-wan. "Seoul Opposition Must Unite or Face Possible Defeat." *Reuters.* July 3, 1987.

36. Habermans, Clyde. "2d Seoul Opposition Leader Set to Run." *New York Times.* October 12, 1987.

37. See note 32.

38. CIA Intelligence Assessment. "South Korea's Move toward Democracy: A New Look at the Electorate." C05845743. Part of the *South China Morning Post* source. See note 32.

39. US Department of State Bureau of Intelligence and Research. "South Korea: Domestic Political Outlook in 1986." March 10, 1986. Digital National Security Archive (DNSA): The United States and the Two Koreas (1969–2000).

40. American Embassy Seoul. "Assessment of Korean Internal Political Scene on the Eve of Secretary Shultz' Visit." Telegram 250228Z. April 25, 1986. Digital National Security Archive (DNSA): The United States and the Two Koreas (1969–2000).

41. Chira, Susan. "Koreans View Their Election with Hope—and Cynicism." *New York Times.* November 8, 1987.

42. Haberman, Clyde. "Cheers for Korean Opposition Leader." *The New York Times.* September 9, 1987.

43. Chira, Susan. "Rally May Widen South Korea Split." *New York Times.* October 18, 1987.

44. Chira, "Rally May Widen Korea Split."

45. Habermans, Clyde. "Koreans Vie for the 'Undecided' Vote." *New York Times.* December 6, 1987.

46. Haberman, Clyde. "South Korea's Rivalries Are Provincial as well as Political." *New York Times.* November 22, 1987.

47. Chira, Susan. "Korean Takes Campaign to Rival's Door." *New York Times.* November 2, 1987.

48. "A Korean Candidate Is Forced to Leave Rally for Campaign." *New York Times.* November 14, 1987.

49. Haberman, Clyde. "Ballot Fever Grips Koreans on Farms Too." *New York Times.* December 8, 1987.

50. Haberman, Clyde. "2 Suicides Protest South Korea Opposition Disunity." *New York Times*. December 11, 1987.

51. Haberman, Clyde. "Fears of Violence Dominate Korea Campaign's Last Days." *New York Times*. December 12, 1987.

52. Habermans, Clyde. "2 Koreans at Impasse on President Race." *New York Times*. September 30, 1987.

53. See note 38.

54. CIA. "National Intelligence Daily—Tuesday 15 December 1987." CO06799612. Part of the *South China Morning Post* source. See note 32.

55. See also the Korean-language article at http://www.mediaus.co.kr/news/articleV iew.html?idxno=28784. October 5, 2012.

56. Habermans, Clyde. "Korean Opposition, Declaring Extensive Fraud, Pledges to Keep Fighting." *New York Times*. December 18, 1987.

57. CIA National Intelligence Daily. "The Day After." December 18, 1987. Co6799614. Part of the *South China Morning Post* source. See note 32.

58. Chira, Susan. "Seoul Opposition Candidate Apologizes." *New York Times*. December 22, 1987.

CHAPTER 6

1. The ruling coalition was only known as the BN from 1972 onward. Its precursor, the Alliance, consisted of the same constellation of major parties, UMNO, MCA, and MIC, from 1957 to 1969. For simplicity, I treat the duration of their rule as continuous.

2. In the rest of this chapter and the rest of the book, I refer to the party system and political parties of Peninsular Malaysia whenever I mention Malaysia. The eastern states of Sabah and Sarawak are components of the Federation of Malaysia. But their electoral politics are so distinct as to warrant separate treatments altogether. For more on these two states, see, at least, Chin 2019; Mersat 2018; Hazis 2012; and Weiss and Puyok 2017.

3. Malaya refers to Peninsular Malaysia and the Straits Settlements of Penang, Malacca, and Singapore.

4. Department of Statistics Malaysia Official Portal. "Current Population Estimates, Malaysia, 2019." https://www.dosm.gov.my/v1/index.php?r=column/cthemeBy Cat&cat=155&bul_id=aWJZRkJ4UEdKcUZpT2tVT090Snpydz09&menu_id=L0pheU 43NWJwRWVSZklWdzQ4TlhUUT09 (last accessed February 15, 2020). The term "Bumiputera" is a local term directly translated as "sons of the soil," which refers to the indigenous people of the country. The vast majority of Bumiputeras are Malays, but there are substantial minorities both in Peninsular Malaysia and the eastern states of Sabah and Sarakwak.

5. Department of Statistics Malaysia Official Portal. "Population Distribution and Basic Demographic Characteristic Report 2010." https://www.dosm.gov.my/v1/index .php?r=column/ctheme&menu_id=L0pheU43NWJwRWVSZklWdzQ4TlhUUT09&b ul_id=MDMxdHZjWTk1SjFzTzNkRXYzcVZjdz09 (last accessed February 15, 2020).

6. See List of PAS Central Working Committee Members 2019–2021. https://pas .org.my/senarai-pimpinan-pas-pusat-sesi-2019-2021/ (last accessed February 15, 2020).

7. The term "ulema" refers to a learned Muslim teacher of Islam who has received his education directly from a line of teachers traced back to Prophet Muhammad him-

self. See List of PAS Syura Council Members 2015–2020. https://pas.org.my/senarai-ma jlis-syura-ulamak-sesi-2015-2020/ (last accessed February 15, 2020).

8. Source: Democratic Action Party. 1969. *Who Lives If Malaysia Dies? A Selection from the Speeches and Writings of DAP Leaders—C.V. Devan Nair, Lim Kit Siang, Nor Jetty, Goh Hock Guan, Chen Man Hin and Others.* Selangor, Malaysia: Rajiv Printers.

9. See the DAP's list of members of parliament at https://dapmalaysia.org/en/about -us/elected-representatives/parliament/ (last accessed December 29, 2017).

10. My count of the DAP's listed State Assembly representatives at https://dapmalay sia.org/en/about-us/elected-representatives/state-assemblies/ (last accessed December 29, 2017).

11. See "DAP Finalizes CEC Lineup." *The Star Online.* November 12, 2017. https:// www.thestar.com.my/news/nation/2017/11/12/dap-finalises-cec-lineup/

12. For a complete review of the multi-billion-dollar 1MDB scandal, see the *Wall Street Journal*, which broke the story in July 2015 at "Malaysia's 1MDB Decoded." http:// graphics.wsj.com/1mdb-decoded/ (last accessed February 15, 2020).

13. "US DOJ Reaches Settlement with Kho Low in 1MDB Forfeiture Case." *Financial Times.* October 30, 2019. https://www.ft.com/content/d0e1ed4e-fb3e-11e9-a354-36 acbbb0d9b6

14. For more on the ELD, see https://www.eld.gov.sg/ (last accessed September 27, 2019).

15. "Explainer: Who's on the Electoral Boundaries Review Committee and How It Draws Up the GE Battle Lines." *Today.* September 5, 2019. https://www.todayonline .com/singapore/whos-electoral-boundaries-review-committee-and-how-it-draws-ge -battle-lines

16. "What Is the Role of the Electoral Boundaries Review Committee (EBRC)?" *Factually.* https://www.gov.sg/factually/content/what-is-the-role-of-the-electoral-boun daries-review-committee (last accessed September 27, 2019).

17. "ELD Marks 70 Years of Ensuring Fair Elections." *The Straits Times.* December 25, 2017. http://www.straitstimes.com/singapore/eld-marks-70-years-of-ensuring-fair -elections. For a more explicit but still unsatisfactory account of "population shifts," see "How the Electoral Boundaries Review Committee Arrived at Its Report." *The Straits Times.* July 24, 2015. http://www.straitstimes.com/politics/how-the-electoral-boundari es-review-committee-arrived-at-its-report

18. For more on the Electoral Integrity Project, see https://www.electoralintegritypr oject.com/ (last accessed September 27, 2019).

19. "Heng Swee Keat Promoted to Deputy Prime Minister." *Today.* April 24, 2019. https://www.todayonline.com/singapore/heng-swee-keat-promoted-deputy-prime-mi nister

20. This phrase was made popular when it emerged as the title of one of Lee Kuan Yew's memoirs published in 2000. See Lee (2000).

21. "Aljunied Voters Will Regret Choosing WP: MM Lee" *Yahoo! Newsroom.* April 30, 2011. https://sg.news.yahoo.com/aljunied-voters-will-regret-choosing-wp--mm-lee .html

22. See "Walking with Singapore: Road to 2011." https://youtu.be/78K6A9pnaek (last accessed December 6, 2017).

23. See the WP's 2015 manifesto "Empower Your Future." http://wpge2015.s3-ap-so utheast-1.amazonaws.com/wp-content/uploads/2015/08/29111924/Manifesto-2015-Of

ficial-online-version.pdf (last accessed December 6, 2017). See also the WP's 2020 manifesto "Make Your Vote Count." https://d3bnzwrhehvhbjiwmja.s3-ap-southeast-1.amaz onaws.com/The+Workers+Party+Manifesto+2020.pdf (last accessed February 8, 2021).

24. See "A Dynamic Population for a Sustainable Singapore" and "Redundancy Insurance: The Workers' Party Proposal for a Resilient 21st Century Workforce" at http://wpge2015.s3-ap-southeast-1.amazonaws.com/wp-content/uploads/2016/05/180 05439/wp-population-policy-paper-feb-2013.pdf and http://wpge2015.s3-ap-southeast -1.amazonaws.com/wp-content/uploads/2016/12/11203623/WP-Redundancy-Insuran ce-FINAL-30112016.pdf, respectively (last accessed December 6, 2017).

25. For Dr. Chee Soon Juan's version of events of Chiam See Tong's exit, see Chee 2012, chapter 9. For a third-party retelling and analysis of the events, see Loke 2019, chapters 10–13.

26. See the various policies on healthcare, housing, etc., at http://yoursdp.org/publ /sdp_39_s_alternatives/23 (last accessed December 6, 2017).

27. "Tan Cheng Bock's Progress Singapore Party Has over 500 Members in Less Than a Month." *Mothership*. August 27, 2019. https://mothership.sg/2019/08/tan-cheng -bock-psp-members-500/

28. "PSP's Younger Members Given room to 'Manage the Ground,' Says Leader Tan Cheng Bock after Party's First Islandwide Walkabout." *Yahoo! Newsroom*. September 29, 2019. https://sg.news.yahoo.com/ps-ps-younger-members-given-room-to-manage-the -ground-says-leader-tan-cheng-bock-after-partys-islandwide-walkabout-102807165 .html

29. The "non-constituency member of parliament" is an electoral innovation introduced by the PAP in 1984. See "Non-constituency Member of Parliament (NCMP) Scheme." *Singapore Infopedia*. http://eresources.nlb.gov.sg/infopedia/articles/SIP_1743 _2010-12-24.html (last accessed September 28, 2019).

30. For more details on the party's history, see https://www.pkms.org.sg/about -pkms/ (last accessed October 1, 2019).

31. "12 Charged over PKMS Brawl." Asiaone. March 19, 2010. https://www.asiaone .com/News/the%2BStraits%2BTimes/Story/A1Story20100319-205462.html

32. "Ex-PKMS Chief Jailed for Contraband Cigarettes Offences." *Asiaone*. October 7, 2011.

CHAPTER 7

1. Gerakan, also known as Parti Gerakan Rakyat Malaysia, was formed in 1968 from the remnants of the United Democratic Party. The party began as an opposition party, but later joined the BN governing alliance after the 1969 racial riots.

2. The People's Progressive Party was a minor non-Malay opposition party during this period.

3. "DAP and GRM Announce Pact to Contest the General Election." *The Straits Times*. February 22, 1969.

4. The viability of such an electoral strategy was raised twice during seminars at the Institute of Southeast Asian Studies in late 2017. Yet ISEAS researchers that I spoke to all dismissed such a strategy. See also "Port Klang By-Election." Diplomatic Report by the British High Commission. December 5, 1979. National Archives of Singapore, NAB 2045, FCO 15/2496, Blip 00002–00005. Original Source: British National Archives.

5. A listing of the newspaper clippings kept at the Center for Malaysian Chinese Studies can be found at http://www.malaysian-chinese.net/library/clipping/ (last accessed January 4, 2018). I spent about two weeks in October 2016 primarily reviewing the files P39.10, P39.10.1, and P39.10.2, which were concerned with opposition coalition formation in the 1980s.

6. Emphasis mine. "DAP Likely to Stay Out of the front." *The Star*. July 14, 1986.

7. "Reduced to Polls Pact." *The Star*. July 15, 1986. Center for Malaysian Chinese Studies, Newspaper clippings collection, P39.10.

8. See "PAS Drive to Explain Role in Opposition Front." *The Star*. July 18, 1986. Center for Malaysian Chinese Studies, Newspaper clippings collection, P39.10.

9. For more regarding the bargaining process over the noncompetition agreement, see "PAS and DAP Set to Fight Despite Pact." *New Straits Times*. October 10, 1990. "Opposition Still Undecided over Seat Allocation." *New Straits Times*. October 9, 1990. "Semangat and Pas Yet to Agree on Seat Allocation." *The Star*. October 8, 1990. All from Center for Malaysian Chinese Studies, Newspaper clippings collection, P39.10.

10. "Bumiputera" is a Malay term directedly translated as "sons of the soil." They include ethnic Malays as well as the indigenous minorities of Malaysia.

11. MY011 Interview.

12. Coalition Agreement Pakatan Harapan 2016. http://pakatanharapan.my/EN .pdf (last accessed January 5, 2017).

13. "PKR Veep Says DAP Not Giving Full Facts of Sarawak Seat Survey." April 28, 2016. *Malay Mail*. https://www.malaymail.com/news/malaysia/2016/04/28/pkr-veep-sa ys-dap-not-giving-full-facts-of-sarawak-seat-survey/1108987

14. "Pakatan's Seat Allocation Makes Sense, but Is It Enough to Hurt BN?" *Today*. January 13, 2018. https://www.todayonline.com/commentary/pakatans-seat-allocatio ns-make-sense-it-enough-hurt-bn

15. "PAS-DAP Ties Show Up in Opposition Front." *Business Times*. October 12, 1990. Center for Malaysian Chinese Studies, Newspaper clippings collection, P39.10.

16. "Strange Bedfellows Trying to Stay Together." *New Straits Times*. April 15, 1990. Center for Malaysian Chinese Studies, Newspaper clippings collection, P39.10.

17. "Zhen Ming Fan Dui Dang Zhen Xian Mu Di Jian Hui Jiao Zhen Fu" *Guang Hua*. August 8, 1990. Center for Malaysian Chinese Studies, Newspaper clippings collection, P39.10.

18. "Opposition under Razaleigh's Spell." *New Straits Times*. October 9, 1990. Center for Malaysian Chinese Studies, Newspaper clippings collection, P39.10.

19. Nearly comprehensive archives of both the English and Mandarin Chinese editions of *The Rocket* from 1980 to 2015 were made available to me from the archives at the DAP headquarters in Kuala Lumpur. These were reviewed and cataloged over several visits from August 2016 to January 2017. Yet these archives were incomplete, as the DAP did not always retain copies of its own party newsletters. After supplementing those copies with copies stored at the Institute of Southeast Asian Studies in Singapore in January and February 2018, I was able to compile a complete listing of all the issues of both the English and Mandarin Chinese *Rocket* in both periods, in which I could then read systematically from cover to cover.

20. Emphasis mine. Interview MY021.

21. Interview MY021.

22. Emphasis mine. Interview MY018.

23. Emphasis mine. Interview MY010.

24. Emphasis mine. Interview MY013.

25. "PKR Moves into New Home on Sunday." *Malaysiakini*. June 4, 2008.

26. "Penang DAP to Launch New HQ in May 5." *The Star*. April 2, 2012.

27. "Hisham: Three Times More Tear Gas Used at Bersih 3.0 Than Last Year." *The Edge*. June 12, 2012.

28. MY014 Interview.

29. MY018 and MY013 Interviews.

30. *The Rocket* is sold and distributed only to party members and supporters. It began circulation as early as 1966. The national publicity secretary is the key party member who has overall political responsibility for the content of *The Rocket*, and is also a member of the DAP's central executive committee, the party's top decision-making body.

31. Articles are coded 0.5 if their main subject was not about other opposition parties, but included related side commentary.

32. "Breakup of Malaysia's Opposition Bloc Pakatan Rakyat: What Happened and What's Next?" *The Straits Times*. June 18, 2015. https://www.straitstimes.com/asia/se-as ia/break-up-of-malaysias-opposition-bloc-pakatan-rakyat-what-happened-and-whats -next

33. World Development Indicators. "GDP Per Capita (current US$)." https://data .worldbank.org/indicator/NY.GDP.PCAP.CD (last accessed September 15, 2019).

34. "Malaysia's Mahathir and Opposition Sign Declaration to Oust Najib." *The Straits Times*. March 4, 2016. https://www.straitstimes.com/asia/se-asia/mahathir-and -opposition-sign-declaration-to-oust-najib

35. "Shifting Political Alliances Point to 'Malay Tsunami' in Malaysia's Next GE" *Today*. November 30, 2017. https://www.todayonline.com/world/shifting-political-allia nces-point-malay-tsunami-ge14.

36. "Malay Tsunami Unlikely to happen; Johor to Remain UMNO Stronghold: Analysts." *ChannelNewsAsia*. May 5, 2018. https://www.channelnewsasia.com/news/asia/ malay-tsunami-unlikely-to-happen-johor-to-remain-umno-stronghold-10203900

37. "National Public Opinion Survey on Economic Hardship Indicators." Merdeka Center. http://merdeka.org/v4/index.php/downloads/category/2-researches?download =181:nov-2017-economic-hardship-indicators (last accessed September 22, 2019).

38. "Malaysia General Elections XIV Outlook: Prospects and Outcome, 26 April 2018." Merdeka Center. http://merdeka.org/v4/index.php/downloads/category/2-resear ches?download=183:ge14-26042018-survey-findings-release-27042018 (last accessed September 22, 2019).

39. "DAP Made Bogeyman to Rally Malay Support, Divert Attention, Say Analysts." *Malaysian Insider*. December 14, 2015. https://www.theedgemarkets.com/article/dap -made-bogeyman-rally-malay-support-divert-attention-say-analysts

40. PPBM leader interview. Kuala Lumpur. March 13, 2018.

41. DAP Leader Interview. Kuala Lumpur. March 12, 2018. PPBM Leader Interview. Kuala Lumpur. March 13, 2018. PKR Leader Interview. Kuala Lumpur. March 15, 2018.

42. For a live tracker of PH's implementation of those 10 promises, see "10 Promises in 100 Days: Monitoring Pakatan Harapan's Manifesto Pledges." *Malaysiakini*. https://pa ges.malaysiakini.com/100days/en/ (last accessed September 24, 2019).

43. FELDA settlers Malaysians who have been re-settled into rural agricultural plantations under the auspices of the Federal Land Development Authority (FELDA) between 1958 and 1990.

44. "Dr Mahathir Unanimously Chosen as Pakatan Harapan PM Candidate." *The Star*. January 7, 2018. https://www.thestar.com.my/news/nation/2018/01/07/mahathir -unanimously-chosen-as-pakatan-harapan-pm-candidate

45. "Dr M Root Cause of Rot, Says DAP MP on 'Save Malaysia' Declaration." *The Star*. March 6, 2016. https://www.thestar.com.my/news/nation/2016/03/06/charles-sant iago-dap-mahathir-pact/

46. "Pakatan Harapan Will Deal Privately with Dissent over PM Pick, Says Dr Mahathir." *Today*. January 16, 2018. https://www.todayonline.com/world/pakatan-hara pan-will-deal-privately-dissent-over-pm-pick-says-dr-mahathir

47. "Not All Thrilled by Idea of Mahathir As PM." *The Straits Times*. January 9, 2018. https://www.straitstimes.com/asia/se-asia/not-all-thrilled-by-idea-of-mahathir-as-pm

48. Emphasis mine. DAP Leader Interview. Kuala Lumpur. March 12, 2018.

49. Emphasis mine. PKR Leader Interview. Kuala Lumpur. March 15, 2018.

50. "Tun M Tears Up and Vows to Make Amends for His Past Mistakes." *Says*. April 30, 2018. https://says.com/my/news/dr-m-tears-up-and-says-he-wants-to-make-amen ds-for-past-mistakes

51. The two-minute video can be found on Twitter at https://twitter.com/chedetoffi cial/status/990025361952944128?ref_src=twsrc%5Etfw (last accessed September 24, 2019).

52. The ten-minute video can be found on YouTube at https://youtu.be/YWmCAW hBM3I and on Facebook at https://www.facebook.com/TunDrMahathir/videos/101555 60382108652/ (last accessed September 24, 2019).

53. "Pakatan to Use PKR Logo in GE14." *New Straits Times*. April 6, 2018. https:// www.nst.com.my/news/politics/2018/04/354079/pakatan-use-pkr-logo-ge14

54. "Dr M: All Pakatan Harapan Parties to Use PKR Logo for GE14." *Today*. April 7, 2018. https://www.todayonline.com/dr-m-all-pakatan-harapan-parties-use-pkr-logo-ge14

CHAPTER 8

1. Note that these are figures based on the total number of districts that opposition parties contested in. Oftentimes, districts were not contested. For instance, in 1980 and 2001, nearly half of all districts available were not contested. For GRCs, I counted each team of candidates as a single candidate because victory continued to rely on the first-past-the-post plurality rule for the entire team.

2. "Workers' Party to Contest All 58 seats." *The Straits Times*. September 23, 1971. And "UNF to Contest All the 65 Seats: Vetrivelu." *The Straits Times*. October 25, 1971. Unless otherwise indicated, all newspaper articles referred to in this chapter are publicly available online at "NewspaperSG," which is the National Library Board's online archive of Singapore's newspapers.

3. "People's Front Hits at UNF leaders." *New Nation*. June 15, 1972.

4. "The United National Front." A-217. Airgram from the American Embassy in Singapore to the Department of State. Source: National Archives of Singapore, NA3230, Blip 199. Original source: U.S. National Archives and Records Administration.

5. "The Extreme Left Wing in Singapore." A-57 Airgram from the American Embassy in Singapore to the Department of State. Source: National Archives of Singa- pore, NAB1100, Blip 159. Original Source: US National Archives and Record Administration.

6. "13/109: The People's Front Party." Report from the British High Commission. Source: National Archives of Singapore (NAB 1423, FCO 24/1463). Original Source: UK National Archives.

7. "Parliamentary Elections Approaching in Singapore." A136 Airgram from the American Embassy in Singapore to the Department of State. Source: National Archives of Singapore, NAB1100, Blip 166. Original Source: US National Archives and Record Administration.

8. "It Won't Work, Say the Other Opposition Parties." *The Straits Times*. February 11, 1971.

9. "Lay Off Our 20 Wards Plea by the Front." *The Straits Times*. February 10, 1972.

10. "Opposition Move to Avoid Splitting of Votes: People's Front and Worker's Party Sign Electoral Pact." *The Straits Times*. August 6, 1972.

11. "Parties Fail to Form a Common Front: Outlook Dim and Dr Lee Is Blamed." *The Straits Times*. June 13, 1972.

12. "People's Front Hits at UNF leaders." *New Nation*. June 15, 1972.

13. SG004, SG005, SG007, SG008, SG010, SG011, SG012, SG013, SG014 Interviews. All locations: Singapore.

14. SG004, SG005, SG006, SG007, SG008, SG009, SG010, SG011, SG012, SG013, SG014 Interviews.

15. SG004 Interview.

16. For the exact boundaries, see "The Report of the Electoral Boundaries Review Committee, 2015." http://www.eld.gov.sg/pdf/White%20Paper%20on%20the%20Repo rt%20of%20the%20Electoral%20Boundaries%20Review%20Committee%202015.pdf (last accessed December 26, 2017).

17. "Nonconstituency" members of parliament are opposition MPs who have a seat in parliament by virtue of the fact that they were the "best loser" in the election. This scheme was introduced in 1984, and was instituted to induct some opposition members into parliament to give the PAP some opposition to spar with. For more details, see "Non-constituency Member of Parliament Scheme." *Singapore Infopedia*. https://eresou rces.nlb.gov.sg/infopedia/articles/SIP_1743_2010-12-24.html (last accessed February 21, 2021).

18. "Tin Pei Ling's New Status as a Mum Is a weakness: Cheo." *Today*. September 4, 2015.

19. "Tin Pei Ling's New Status as a Mum Is a weakness: Cheo."

20. "We Had to Enter a 3-Cornered Fight in MacPherson, Say NSP Leaders." *ChannelNewsAsia*. September 1, 2015. http://www.channelnewsasia.com/news/singapore/we -had-to-enter-a-3-cornered-fight-in-macpherson-say-nsp-leaders-8252754

21. SG Interview. October 3, 2019.

22. "Singapore." *Transparency International*. https://www.transparency.org/en/coun tries/singapore (last accessed February 21, 2021).

23. SG009 Interview.

24. SG004, SG005, SG006, SG007, SG008, SG009, SG010, SG011, SG012, SG013, SG014 Interviews.

25. The identities of specific politicians have been anonymized as agreed with the interviewee.

26. SG004 Interview.

27. See the appendix in Donough, Gerardine. 1977. "The 1976 Singapore General

Elections." History BA Thesis Submitted to the National University of Singapore. Located at the Institute of Southeast Asian Studies Library.

28. SG008, SG009 Interviews.

29. "Opposition Parties Launch Campaign Badge." *The Straits Times*. August 27, 2015. https://www.straitstimes.com/singapore/7-opposition-parties-launch-campaign -badge

30. Data from Covid-19 Situation Report, Singapore Ministry of Health. https://cov idsitrep.moh.gov.sg/ (last accessed February 20, 2021).

31. This excludes the unknown independent candidate contesting in Pioneer SMC, which also forced a three-cornered contest there.

32. "The Big Read: Opposition Parties Banding Together—a Grand Plan or a Last Throw of the Dice?" *Today*. August 4, 2018. https://www.todayonline.com/big-read/big -read-opposition-parties-banding-together-grand-plan-or-last-throw-dice

33. "Key Household Income Trends." Department of Statistics. https://www.singstat .gov.sg/find-data/search-by-theme/households/household-income/visualising-data /key-household-income-trends (last accessed February 23, 2020).

34. "Full \$8b for Pioneer Generation Package to Be Set Aside in Budget." *Today*. https://www.todayonline.com/singapore/full-s8b-pioneer-generation-package-be-set -aside-budget (last accessed February 23, 2020).

35. "Singapore Budget 2019: \$6.1b for Merdeka Generation Package Includes Medisave Top-Ups, Higher Chas Subsidies." *The Straits Times*. February 18, 2019. https://www.straitstimes.com/singapore/singapore-budget-2019-61-billion-for-merde ka-generation-package-includes-medisave-top-ups

36. "Teo You Yenn: Bringing Inequality to Forefront of Discussions." *The Straits Times*. December 18, 2018. https://www.straitstimes.com/singapore/bringing-inequali ty-to-forefront-of-discussions

37. "Parliament: Inequality Has Many Causes and Needs to Be Tackled Practically, Not Ideologically, Says Desmond Lee." *The Straits Times*. March 5, 2019. https://www.st raitstimes.com/politics/parliament-inequality-has-many-causes-and-needs-to-be-tackl ed-practically-not-ideologically

38. See "Foreign Workforce Numbers." https://www.mom.gov.sg/documents-and -publications/foreign-workforce-numbers and "Summary Table: Labor Force." Ministry of Manpower. https://stats.mom.gov.sg/Pages/Labour-Force-Summary-Table.aspx (both last accessed February 23, 2020).

39. "Amended Motion on White Paper Adopted; 6.9 Million Is Not a Target." *The Straits Times*. February 9, 2013. https://www.straitstimes.com/singapore/amended-mot ion-on-white-paper-adopted-69-million-is-not-a-target (last accessed February 23, 2020).

40. "Protest, Voter Anger Put Political Risk in Singapore's Future." *Reuters*. https:// www.reuters.com/article/us-singapore-politics/protest-voter-anger-put-political-risk -in-singapores-future-idUSBRE91E07520130215 (last accessed February 23, 2020).

41. "Singapore Protest Biggest since Independence." *South China Morning Post*. February 17, 2013. https://www.scmp.com/news/asia/article/1152046/singapore-protest -population-policy-biggest-independence (last accessed February 23, 2020).

42. "India-Singapore Comprehensive Economic Cooperation Agreement (CECA)." *Enterprise Singapore*. https://www.enterprisesg.gov.sg/non-financial-assistance/for-sing apore-companies/free-trade-agreements/ftas/singapore-ftas/ceca (last accessed February 23, 2020).

43. "Govt Takes 'Very Serious View' of Falsehoods on CECA That Try to Divide Singapore: Chan Chun Sing." *Today*. November 10, 2019. https://www.todayonline.com /singapore/govt-takes-very-serious-view-falsehoods-ceca-try-divide-singapore-chan -chun-sing

44. "Heng Swee Keat and Chan Chun Sing 'Make a Strong Pairing': PM Lee." *ChannelNewsAsia*. November 23, 2018. https://www.channelnewsasia.com/news/singapore/ pap-pm-lee-heng-swee-keat-chan-chun-sing-asg-10962310

45. "Most Singaporeans Would Choose Tharman as the next Prime Minister: Survey." *Yahoo News*. September 25, 2016. https://sg.news.yahoo.com/most-singaporeans -would-choose-tharman-1523976433713206.html

46. "Older Generation of Singaporeans Not Ready for Non-Chinese Prime Minister: Heng Swee Keat." *Today*. December 25, 2019. https://www.todayonline.com/singap ore/older-generation-singaporeans-not-ready-non-chinese-pm-heng-swee-keat

47. "Income Growth Slows in Singapore; Median Salary Now above S\$4,500: MOM Report." *ChannelNewsAsia*. November 29, 2019. https://www.channelnewsasia.com/ne ws/singapore/singapore-income-wages-labour-market-report-mom-12133236

48. Emphasis mine. SG Interview. October 3, 2019.

49. "7 Opposition Parties Discuss Forming a New Coalition, Invite Former PAP MP Dr Tan Cheng Bock to Be Leader." *The Straits Times*. July 28, 2018.

50. Singapore's elected presidency has some important constitutional roles, but primarily plays a symbolic role in everyday governance. For more, see Tan 2014 and Mutalib 2002.

51. Emphasis mine. "The Big Read: Opposition Parties Banding Together—a Grand Plan or a Last Throw of the Dice?" *Today*. August 4, 2018. https://www.todayonline.com /big-read/big-read-opposition-parties-banding-together-grand-plan-or-last-throw -dice

52. "GE2020: PSP's Credible Maiden Showing a 'Head Start' for the Future, Says Tan Cheng Bock." *Today*. July 11, 2020. https://www.todayonline.com/singapore/ge2020 -psp-average-40-score-head-start-future-says-tan-cheng-bock

53. SG Interviews. October 3, October 8, October 16, 2019.

54. SG Interview. October 3, 2019.

55. "SDP to Contest Five constituencies at Next General Election." *Channel News Asia*. September 5, 2019. https://www.channelnewsasia.com/news/singapore/sdp-conte st-five-constituencies-next-general-election-11778416

56. SG Interview. October 8, 2019.

57. "Singapore GE2020: Reform Party and PSP in Dispute over 'Deal' on Yio Chu Kang." *The Straits Times*. June 26, 2020.

Bibliography

Abbott, Jason. 2000. "Bittersweet Victory: The 1999 Malaysian General Election and the Anwar Ibrahim Affair." *Round Table* 89 (354): 245.

Abbott, Jason, and John Wagner Givens. 2015. "Strategic Censorship in a Hybrid Authoritarian Regime? Differential Bias in Malaysia's Online and Print Media." *Journal of East Asian Studies* 15 (3): 455–78, 497.

Abdullah, Walid Jumblatt. 2017. "Bringing Ideology In: Differing Oppositional Challenges to Hegemony in Singapore and Malaysia." *Government and Opposition* 52 (3): 483–510.

Abdullah, Walid Jumblatt. 2019a. "Intra-party Dynamics in the People's Action Party: Party Structure, Continuity and Hegemony." In *The Limits of Authoritarian Governance in Singapore's Developmental State*, ed. Lily Zubaidah Rahim and Michael D. Barr, 151–71. Singapore: Springer Singapore.

Abdullah, Walid Jumblatt. 2019b. "The Mahathir Effect in Malaysia's 2018 Election: The Role of Credible Personalities in Regime Transitions." *Democratization* 26 (3): 521–36.

Adesnik, David, and Sunhyuk Kim. 2008. "If at First You Don't Succeed: The Puzzle of South Korea's Democratic Transition." Stanford, CA. CDDRL Working Papers.

Albrecht, Holger, ed. 2010. *Contentious Politics in the Middle East: Political Opposition under Authoritarianism*. Gainesville: University Press of Florida.

Albrecht, Holger. 2013. *Raging against the Machine: Political Opposition under Authoritarianism in Egypt*. Syracuse: Syracuse University Press.

Albrecht, Holger, and Dorothy Ohl. 2016. "Exit, Resistance, Loyalty: Military Behavior during Unrest in Authoritarian Regimes." *Perspectives on Politics* 14 (1): 38–52.

Aldrich, John. 1995. *Why Parties? The Origin and Transformation of Political Parties in America*. Chicago: University of Chicago Press.

Ali, Mazlan. 1998. "Hubungan Semangat 46 Dan PAS 1988–1996: Satu Tinjauan Terhadap Politik Malaysia." University of Malaya. http://studentsrepo.um.edu.my/2394/

Alizada, Nazifa, et al., eds. 2021. *Autocratization Turns Viral*, September 7. Varieties of Democracy Institute. https://www.v-dem.net/media/filer_public/74/8c/748c68ad-f224-4cd7-87f9-8794add5c60f/dr_2021_updated.pdf

Ampalavanar, Rajeswary. 1981. *The Indian Minority and Political Change in Malaya, 1945–1957*. Kuala Lumpur: Oxford University Press.

Ang, Yuen Yuen. 2016. *How China Escaped the Poverty Trap*. Ithaca: Cornell University Press.

Angeletos, George-Marios, Christian Hellwig, and Alessandro Pavan. 2007. "Dynamic Global Games of Regime Change: Learning, Multiplicity, and the Timing of Attacks." *Econometrica* 75 (3): 711–56.

Arriola, Leonardo R. 2013. *Multi-ethnic Coalitions in Africa: Business Financing of Opposition Election Campaigns*. New York: Cambridge University Press.

Bak, Daehee, and Chungshik Moon. 2016. "Foreign Direct Investment and Authoritarian Stability." *Comparative Political Studies* 49 (14): 1998–2037.

Bargsted, Matias A., and Orit Kedar. 2009. "Coalition-Targeted Duvergerian Voting: How Expectations Affect Voter Choice under Proportional Representation." *American Journal of Political Science* 53 (2): 307–23.

Barr, Michael. 2019. "Heng Swee Keat's Awkward Start to Succession." *East Asia Forum*. December 19. https://www.eastasiaforum.org/2019/12/19/heng-swee-keats-awkward-start-to-succession/

Barr, Michael, and Zlatko Skrbiš. 2009. *Constructing Singapore: Elitism, Ethnicity and the Nation-Building Project*. Copenhagen: NIAS Press.

Barraclough, Simon. 1985. "Barisan Nasional Dominance and Opposition Fragmentation: The Failure of Attempts to Create Opposition Co-operation in the Malaysian Party System." *Asian Profile* 13 (1): 33–44.

Batto, Nathan F., and Henry A. Kim. 2012. "Coordinative Advantages of State Resources under SNTV: The Case of Taiwan." *Japanese Journal of Political Science* 13 (3): 355–77.

Bautista, Felix B. 1987. *Cardinal Sin and the Miracle of Asia: A Biography*. Manila: Vera-Reyes.

Beach, Derek, and Rasmus Brun Pedersen. 2013. *Process-Tracing Methods: Foundations and Guidelines*. Ann Arbor: University of Michigan Press.

Beardsworth, Nicole. 2016. "Challenging Dominance: The Opposition, the Coalition and the 2016 Election in Uganda." *Journal of Eastern African Studies* 10 (4): 749–68.

Beaulieu, Emily. 2014. *Electoral Protest and Democracy in the Developing World*. New York: Cambridge University Press.

Beaulieu, Emily, and Susan D. Hyde. 2009. "In the Shadow of Democracy Promotion: Strategic Manipulation, International Observers, and Election Boycotts." *Comparative Political Studies* 42 (3): 392–415.

Bellin, Eva. 2000. "Contingent Democrats: Industrialists, Labor, and Democratization in Late-Developing Countries." *World Politics* 52 (2): 175–205.

Bello, Walden. 1984. "Benigno Aquino: Between Dictatorship and Revolution in the Philippines." *Third World Quarterly* 6 (2): 283–309.

Bennett, Andrew. 2010. "Process Tracing and Causal Inference." In *Rethinking Social Inquiry: Diverse Tools, Shared Standards*, ed. Henry Brady and David Collier, 207–20. Lanham, MD: Rowman & Littlefield.

Bermeo, Nancy. 2016. "On Democratic Backsliding." *Journal of Democracy* 27 (1): 5–19.

Bermeo, Nancy, and Deborah J. Yashar, eds. 2016. *Parties, Movements and Democracy in the Developing World*. New York: Cambridge University Press.

Bhasin, Tavishi, and Jennifer Gandhi. 2013. "Timing and Targeting of State Repression in Authoritarian Elections." *Electoral Studies* 32 (4): 620–31.

Birch, Sarah. 2010. "Perceptions of Electoral Fairness and Voter Turnout." *Comparative Political Studies* 43 (12): 1601–22.

Birch, Sarah. 2011. *Electoral Malpractice*. Oxford: Oxford University Press.

Bischof, Daniel. 2017. "Towards a Renewal of the Niche Party Concept: Parties, Market Shares and Condensed Offers." *Party Politics* 23 (3): 220–35.

Blaydes, Lisa. 2011. *Elections and Distributive Politics in Mubarak's Egypt.* New York: Cambridge University Press.

Bleck, Jaimie, and Nicolas van de Walle. 2011. "Parties and Issues in Francophone West Africa: Towards a Theory of Non-mobilization." *Democratization* 18 (5): 1125–45.

Bleck, Jaimie, and Nicolas van de Walle. 2013. "Valence Issues in African Elections: Navigating Uncertainty and the Weight of the Past." *Comparative Political Studies* 46 (11): 1394–1421.

Bleck, Jaimie, and Nicolas van de Walle. 2019. *Electoral Politics in Africa since 1990: Continuity in Change.* New York: Cambridge University Press.

Bonner, Raymond. 1987. *Waltzing with a Dictator: The Marcoses and the Making of American Policy.* New York: Times Books.

Browers, Michaelle. 2007. "Origins and Architects of Yemen's Joint Meeting Parties." *International Journal of Middle East Studies* 39 (4): 565–86.

Brown, Graham. 2004. "The Enemy of My Enemy? Opposition Parties during the Mahathir Years." In *Reflections: The Mahathir Years*, ed. Bridget Welsh, 96–109. Baltimore: Johns Hopkins University Press.

Brownlee, Jason. 2007. *Authoritarianism in an Age of Democratization.* New York: Cambridge University Press.

Bunce, Valerie, and Sharon L. Wolchik. 2009. "Defeating Dictators: Electoral Change and Stability in Competitive Authoritarian Regimes." *World Politics* 62 (1): 43–86.

Bunce, Valerie, and Sharon L. Wolchik. 2011. *Defeating Authoritarian Leaders in Postcommunist Countries.* New York: Cambridge University Press.

Büthe, Tim. 2002. "Taking Temporality Seriously: Modeling History and the Use of Narratives as Evidence." *American Political Science Review* 96 (3): 481–93.

Buttorff, Gail. 2015. "Coordination Failure and the Politics of Tribes: Jordanian Elections under SNTV." *Electoral Studies* 40: 45–55.

Buttorff, Gail. 2019. *Authoritarian Elections and Opposition Groups in the Arab World.* Cham, Switzerland: Springer International.

Buttorff, Gail, and Douglas Dion. 2017. "Participation and Boycott in Authoritarian Elections." *Journal of Theoretical Politics* 29 (1): 97–123.

Cameron, Maxwell A. 1992. "Rational Resignations: Coalition Building in Peru and the Philippines." *Comparative Political Studies* 25 (2): 229–50.

Carkoğlu, Ali, and Kerem Yildirim. 2018. "Change and Continuity in Turkey's June 2018 Elections." *Insight Turkey: Ankara* 20 (4): 153–82.

Carnell, Francis G. 1955. "The Malayan Elections." *Pacific Affairs* 28 (4): 315.

Carreras, Miguel, and Yasemin İrepoğlu. 2013. "Trust in Elections, Vote Buying, and Turnout in Latin America." *Electoral Studies* 32 (4): 609–19.

Case, William. 1991. "Revisiting a Consociational Democracy: Elite Relations and Regime Form in Malaysia." PhD dissertation, University of Texas at Austin. http://se arch.proquest.com/docview/303938858/abstract/E079290A717A40BEPQ/1 (September 11, 2019).

Case, William. 1996. "UMNO Paramountcy: A Report on Single-Party Dominance in Malaysia." *Party Politics* 2 (1): 115–27.

Case, William. 2001. "Malaysia's General Elections in 1999: A Consolidated and High-Quality Semi-democracy." *Asian Studies Review* 25 (1): 35–55.

Case, William. 2014. "Malaysia in 2013: A Benighted Election Day (and Other Events)." *Asian Survey* 54 (1): 56–63.

Case, William, and Chin Tong Liew. 2006. "How Committed Is PAS to Democracy and How Do We Know It?" *Contemporary Southeast Asia* 28 (3): 385–406.

Casper, Brett Allen, and Scott A. Tyson. 2014. "Popular Protest and Elite Coordination in a Coup d'état." *Journal of Politics* 76 (2): 548–64.

Chai, Hon Chan. 1964. *The Development of British Malaya, 1896–1909*. Kuala Lumpur: Oxford University Press.

Chan, Heng Chee. 1976. *The Dynamics of One Party Dominance: The PAP at the Grass-roots*. Singapore: Singapore University Press.

Chan, Tsu Chong. 2019. "Democratic Breakthrough in Malaysia: Political Opportunities and the Role of Bersih." *Journal of Current Southeast Asian Affairs* 37 (3): 109–37.

Chang, Paul. 2015. *Protest Dialectics: State Repression and South Korea's Democracy Movement, 1970–1979*. Palo Alto, CA: Stanford University Press.

Chassang, Sylvain. 2010. "Fear of Miscoordination and the Robustness of Cooperation in Dynamic Global Games with Exit." *Econometrica* 78 (3): 973–1006.

Chee, Soon Juan. 2012. *Democratically Speaking*. Singapore: Chee Soon Juan.

Cheng, Tun-jen. 1990. "Is the Dog Barking? The Middle Class and Democratic Movements in the East Asian NICs." *International Studies Notes* 15 (1): 10–40.

Cheng, Tun-jen, and Deborah A. Brown. 2006. *Religious Organizations and Democratization: Case Studies from Contemporary Asia*. Florence: Taylor and Francis.

Cheng, Tun-jen, and Lawrence B. Krause. 1991. "Democracy and Development: With Special Attention to Korea." *Journal of Northeast Asian Studies* 10 (2): 3–25.

Cheng, Tun-jen, and Stephan Haggard, eds. 1992. *Political Change in Taiwan*. Boulder: Lynne Rienner.

Chernykh, Svitlana, and Milan W. Svolik. 2015. "Third-Party Actors and the Success of Democracy: How Electoral Commissions, Courts, and Observers Shape Incentives for Electoral Manipulation and Post-election Protests." *Journal of Politics* 77 (2): 407–20.

Chin, James. 2010. "Malaysian Chinese Association Politics a Year Later: Crisis of Political Legitimacy." *Round Table* 99 (407): 153–62.

Chin, James. 2013. "Editorial: Chinese Tsunami or Urban Revolt? It Is Both Actually." *Round Table* 102 (6): 499–501.

Chin, James. 2019. "Sabah and Sarawak in the 14th General Election 2018 (GE14): Local Factors and State Nationalism." *Journal of Current Southeast Asian Affairs* 37 (3): 173–92.

Chin, James, and Bridget Welsh. 2019. "Special Issue Introduction: The 2018 Malaysian General Election: The Return of Mahathir and the Exit of UMNO." *Journal of Current Southeast Asian Affairs* 37 (3): 3–8.

Chin, James, and Chin Huat Wong. 2009. "Malaysia's Electoral Upheaval." *Journal of Democracy* 20 (3): 71–85.

Cho, Jung-Kwan. 2000. "From Authoritarianism to Consolidated Democracy in South Korea." PhD dissertation, Yale University. http://search.proquest.com/dnsa/docview/304643294/abstract/5ABB794397084D8CPQ/2 (July 27, 2019).

Ch'oe, Chŏng-un. 2006. *The Gwangju Uprising: The Pivotal Democratic Movement That Changed the History of Modern Korea*. Paramus, NJ: Homa & Sekey Books.

Choe, Hyun, and Jiyoung Kim. 2012. "South Korea's Democratization Movements,

1980–1987: Political Structure, Political Opportunity, and Framing." *Inter-Asia Cultural Studies* 13 (1): 55–68.

Choi, Joon Nak, and Ji Yeon Hong. 2020. "Social Networks as a Political Resource: Revisiting the Korean Democratic Transition." *Journal of East Asian Studies* 20 (1): 75–98.

Chong, Terence. 2010. *Management of Success: Singapore Revisited*. Singapore: ISEAS–Yusof Ishak Institute.

Chua, Beng Huat. 2017. *Liberalism Disavowed: Communitarianism and State Capitalism in Singapore*. Singapore: NUS Press.

Chwe, Michael. 2003. *Rational Ritual: Culture, Coordination, and Common Knowledge*. Princeton: Princeton University Press.

Cox, Gary W. 1997. *Making Votes Count: Strategic Coordination in the World's Electoral Systems*. Cambridge: Cambridge University Press.

Collier, David. 2011. "Understanding Process Tracing." *PS: Political Science & Politics* 44 (4): 823–30.

Corsino, MacArthur. 1981. "The Philippines in 1980: At the Crossroads." In *Southeast Asian Affairs 1981*, 235–57. Singapore: Institute of Southeast Asian Studies.

Croissant, Aurel. 2004. "From Transition to Defective Democracy: Mapping Asian Democratization." *Democratization* 11 (5): 156–78.

Croissant, Aurel. 2016. *Electoral Politics in Cambodia: Historical Trajectories and Current Challenges*. Singapore: ISEAS Publishing.

Crouch, Harold. 1996. *Government and Society in Malaysia*. Ithaca: Cornell University Press.

Cumings, Bruce. 2005. *Korea's Place in the Sun: A Modern History*. New York: Norton.

Curtice, Travis B., and Brandon Behlendorf. 2021. "Street-Level Repression: Protest, Policing, and Dissent in Uganda." *Journal of Conflict Resolution* 65 (1): 166–94.

Dettman, Sebastian. 2020. "Authoritarian Innovations and Democratic Reform in the 'New Malaysia.'" *Democratization* 27 (6): 1037–52.

Dettman, Sebastian, and Edmund Terence Gomez. 2019. "Political Financing Reform: Politics, Policies and Patronage in Malaysia." *Journal of Contemporary Asia* 50 (1): 36–55.

Diermeier, D., and K. Krehbiel. 2003. "Institutionalism as a Methodology." *Journal of Theoretical Politics* 15 (2): 123–44.

Diamond, Larry Jay. 2002. "Thinking about Hybrid Regimes." *Journal of Democracy* 13 (2): 21–35.

Diaz-Cayeros, Alberto, Beatriz Magaloni, and Barry R. Weingast. 2003. "Tragic Brilliance: Equilibrium Party Hegemony in Mexico." Rochester, NY. SSRN Scholarly Paper. https://papers.ssrn.com/abstract=1153510 (June 21, 2017).

Dimitrov, Martin K. 2017. "The Political Logic of Media Control in China." *Problems of Post-communism* 64 (3–4): 121–27.

Doner, Richard F., Bryan K. Ritchie, and Dan Slater. 2005. "Systemic Vulnerability and the Origins of Developmental States: Northeast and Southeast Asia in Comparative Perspective." *International Organization* 59 (2): 327–61.

Donno, Daniela. 2013. "Elections and Democratization in Authoritarian Regimes." *American Journal of Political Science* 57 (3): 703–16.

Donough, Gerardine. 1977. "The 1976 Singapore General Election." BA thesis, National University of Singapore.

Dresden, Jennifer Raymond, and Marc Morjé Howard. 2016. "Authoritarian Backsliding and the Concentration of Political Power." *Democratization* 23 (7): 1122–43.

Drummond, Stuart. 1987. "The Malaysian Elections." *Round Table* 76 (301): 93–109.

Drummond, Stuart, and David Hawkins. 1970. "The Malaysian Elections of 1969: An Analysis of the Campaign and the Results." *Asian Survey* 10 (4): 320–35.

Duch, Raymond M., and Randolph T. Stevenson. 2008. *The Economic Vote: How Political and Economic Institutions Condition Election Results*. New York: Cambridge University Press.

Duong, Mai. 2017. "Blogging Three Ways in Vietnam's Political Blogosphere." *Contemporary Southeast Asia* 39 (2): 373–92.

Duverger, Maurice. 1954. *Political Parties, Their Organization and Activity in the Modern State*. New York: Wiley.

Edgell, Amanda B., et al. 2018. "When and Where Do Elections Matter? A Global Test of the Democratization by Elections Hypothesis, 1900–2010." *Democratization* 25 (3): 422–44.

Eisenstadt, Todd A. 2004. *Courting Democracy in Mexico: Party Strategies and Electoral Institutions*. New York: Cambridge University Press.

Escribà-Folch, Abel. 2013. "Repression, Political Threats, and Survival under Autocracy." *International Political Science Review* 34 (5): 543–60.

Esen, Berk, and Sebnem Gumuscu. 2016. "Rising Competitive Authoritarianism in Turkey." *Third World Quarterly* 37 (9): 1581–1606.

Esen, Berk, and Sebnem Gumuscu. 2019. "Killing Competitive Authoritarianism Softly: The 2019 Local Elections in Turkey." *South European Society and Politics* 24 (3): 317–42.

Falleti, Tulia G., and Julia F. Lynch. 2009. "Context and Causal Mechanisms in Political Analysis." *Comparative Political Studies* 42 (9): 1143–66.

Farrell, Joseph. 1987. "Cheap Talk, Coordination, and Entry." *Rand Journal of Economics* 18 (1): 34–39.

Farrell, Joseph, and Matthew Rabin. 1996. "Cheap Talk." *Journal of Economic Perspectives* 10 (3): 103–18.

Fearon, James D. 1991. "Counterfactuals and Hypothesis Testing in Political Science." *World Politics* 43 (2): 169–95.

Fearon, James D. 1994. "Signaling versus the Balance of Power and Interests: An Empirical Test of a Crisis Bargaining Model." *Journal of Conflict Resolution* 38 (2): 236–69.

Fearon, James D. 1995. "Rationalist Explanations for War." *International Organization* 49 (3): 379–414.

Fearon, James D. 1997. "Signaling Foreign Policy Interests: Tying Hands versus Sinking Costs." *Journal of Conflict Resolution* 41 (1): 68–90.

Fearon, James D. 2011. "Self-Enforcing Democracy." *Quarterly Journal of Economics* 126 (4): 1661–1708.

Felker, Greg. 1999. "Malaysia in 1998: A Cornered Tiger Bares Its Claws." *Asian Survey* 39 (1): 43–54.

Felker, Greg. 2000. "Malaysia in 1999: Mahathir's Pyrrhic Deliverance." *Asian Survey* 40 (1): 49–60.

Fernando, Joseph M. 1999. "Revisiting the Origins of the Alliance." *Sejarah* 7: 121–43.

Fibiger, Mattias. 2019. "The Pivot: Neoconservatives, the Philippines, and the Democracy Agenda." In *The Reagan Administration, the Cold War, and the Transition to*

Democracy Promotion, ed. Robert Pee and William Michael Schmidli, 209–30. New York: Palgrave Macmillan.

Fjelde, Hanne, and Kristine Höglund. 2016. "Electoral Institutions and Electoral Violence in Sub-Saharan Africa." *British Journal of Political Science* 46 (2): 297–320.

Forest, Jim, and Nancy Forest. 1988. *Four Days in February: The Story of the Nonviolent Overthrow of the Marcos Regime*. Basingstoke, Hants, UK: Marshall Pickering.

Fowler, James. 1999. "The United States and South Korean Democratization." *Political Science Quarterly* 114 (2): 265–88.

Freedom House. 2021. *Freedom in the World 2021: Democracy Under Siege*. https://freed omhouse.org/sites/default/files/2021-02/FIW2021_World_02252021_FINAL-web -upload.pdf

Frye, Timothy, Ora John Reuter, and David Szakonyi. 2018. "Hitting Them with Carrots: Voter Intimidation and Vote Buying in Russia." *British Journal of Political Science* 49 (3): 857–81.

Fudenberg, Drew, and David K. Levine. 2009. "Learning and Equilibrium." *Annual Review of Economics* 1 (1): 385–420.

Fudenberg, Drew, and David K. Levine. 2014. "Recency, Consistent Learning, and Nash Equilibrium." *Proceedings of the National Academy of Sciences* 111 (Supplement 3): 10826–29.

Fudenberg, Drew, and David K. Levine. 2016. "Whither Game Theory? Towards a Theory of Learning in Games." *Journal of Economic Perspectives* 30 (4): 151–70.

Gainous, Jason, Kevin M. Wagner, and Charles E. Ziegler. 2018. "Digital Media and Political Opposition in Authoritarian Systems: Russia's 2011 and 2016 Duma Elections." *Democratization* 25 (2): 209–26.

Gamboa, Laura. 2017. "Opposition at the Margins: Strategies against the Erosion of Democracy in Colombia and Venezuela." *Comparative Politics* 49 (4): 457–77.

Gandhi, Jennifer. 2008. *Political Institutions under Dictatorship*. New York: Cambridge University Press.

Gandhi, Jennifer. 2014. "The Role of Presidential Power in Authoritarian Elections." In *Constitutions in Authoritarian Regimes*, ed. Tom Ginsburg and Alberto Simpser, 199–217. New York: Cambridge University Press.

Gandhi, Jennifer. 2015. "Elections and Political Regimes." *Government and Opposition* 50 (3): 446–68.

Gandhi, Jennifer. 2018. "The Institutional Roots of Democratic Backsliding." *Journal of Politics* 81 (1): e11–16.

Gandhi, Jennifer, and Ellen Lust-Okar. 2009. "Elections under Authoritarianism." *Annual Review of Political Science* 12 (1): 403–22.

Gandhi, Jennifer, and Elvin Ong. 2019. "Committed or Conditional Democrats? Opposition Dynamics in Electoral Autocracies." *American Journal of Political Science* 63 (4): 948–63.

Gandhi, Jennifer, and Adam Przeworski. 2006. "Cooperation, Cooptation, and Rebellion Under Dictatorships." *Economics & Politics* 18 (1): 1–26.

Gandhi, Jennifer, and Adam Przeworski. 2007. "Authoritarian Institutions and the Survival of Autocrats." *Comparative Political Studies* 40 (11): 1279–1301.

Gandhi, Jennifer, and Ora John Reuter. 2013. "The Incentives for Pre-electoral Coalitions in Non-democratic Elections." *Democratization* 20 (1): 137–59.

Geddes, Barbara. 1999. "What Do We Know about Democratization after Twenty Years?" *Annual Review of Political Science* 2 (1): 115–44.

Gehlbach, Scott, and Alberto Simpser. 2015. "Electoral Manipulation as Bureaucratic Control." *American Journal of Political Science* 59 (1): 212–24.

Gehlbach, Scott, Konstantin Sonin, and Milan W. Svolik. 2016. "Formal Models of Non-democratic Politics." *Annual Review of Political Science* 19 (1): 565–84.

George, Cherian. 2007. "Consolidating Authoritarian Rule: Calibrated Coercion in Singapore." *Pacific Review* 20 (2): 127–45.

George, Cherian. 2012. *Freedom from the Press: Journalism and State Power in Singapore.* Singapore: NUS Press.

Gerring, John. 2012. "Mere Description." *British Journal of Political Science* 42 (4): 721–46.

Gerschewski, Johannes. 2018. "Legitimacy in Autocracies: Oxymoron or Essential Feature?" *Perspectives on Politics* 16 (3): 652–65.

Goertz, Gary. 2017. *Multimethod Research, Causal Mechanisms, and Case Studies: An Integrated Approach.* Princeton: Princeton University Press.

Golder, Sona Nadenichek. 2006. *The Logic of Pre-electoral Coalition Formation.* Columbus: Ohio State University Press.

Goldring, Edward, and Sheena Chestnut Greitens. 2020. "Rethinking Democratic Diffusion: Bringing Regime Type Back In." *Comparative Political Studies* 53 (2): 319–53.

Gomez, Edmund Terence. 1996. *The 1995 Malaysian General Elections: A Report and Commentary.* Singapore: Institute of Southeast Asian Studies.

Gomez, Edmund Terence. 2004. *The State of Malaysia: Ethnicity, Equity, and Reform.* London: Routledge.

Gomez, Edmund Terence. 2016. "Resisting the Fall: The Single Dominant Party, Policies and Elections in Malaysia." *Journal of Contemporary Asia* 46 (4): 570–90.

Gomez, Edmund Terence. 2018. *Minister of Finance Incorporated: Ownership and Control of Corporate Malaysia.* Singapore: Palgrave Macmillan.

Gomez, Edmund Terence, and Ponmalar N. Alagappar. 2018. "Failed Broker State: Malaysia's Indian Poor and the Fall of UMNO." *Round Table* 107 (6): 793–94.

Gomez, Edmund Terence, and Mohamed Osman Mohamed Nawab, eds. 2019. *Malaysia's 14th General Election and UMNO's Fall: Intra-elite Feuding in the Pursuit of Power.* New York: Routledge.

Gomez, Edmund Terence, and Johan Saravanamuttu, eds. 2013. *The New Economic Policy in Malaysia: Affirmative Action, Ethnic Inequalities, and Social Justice.* Singapore: SIRD, NUS Press, and ISEAS Publishing.

Gonzalez, Hernando. 1988. "Mass Media and the Spiral of Silence: The Philippines from Marcos to Aquino." *Journal of Communication* 38 (4): 33–48.

Goodno, James B. 1991. *The Philippines: Land of Broken Promises.* Atlantic Highlands, NJ: Zed Books.

Greene, Fred. 1988. "The United States and Asia in 1987: Progress Brings Problems." *Asian Survey* 28 (1): 10–22.

Greene, Kenneth. 2002. "Opposition Party Strategy and Spatial Competition in Dominant Party Regimes: A Theory and the Case of Mexico." *Comparative Political Studies* 35 (7): 755–83.

Greene, Kenneth. 2007. *Why Dominant Parties Lose: Mexico's Democratization in Comparative Perspective.* Oxford: Oxford University Press.

Greitens, Sheena Chestnut. 2016. *Dictators and Their Secret Police: Coercive Institutions and State Violence*. Cambridge: Cambridge University Press.

Grewal, Sharan. 2020. "From Islamists to Muslim Democrats: The Case of Tunisia's Ennahda." *American Political Science Review*: 1–17.

Grzymala-Busse, Anna. 2011. "Time Will Tell? Temporality and the Analysis of Causal Mechanisms and Processes." *Comparative Political Studies* 44 (9): 1267–97.

Hafner-Burton, Emilie M., Susan D. Hyde, and Ryan S. Jablonski. 2018. "Surviving Elections: Election Violence, Incumbent Victory and Post-election Repercussions." *British Journal of Political Science* 48 (2): 459–88.

Haggard, Stephan, and Robert R. Kaufman. 2016. *Dictators and Democrats: Masses, Elites, and Regime Change*. Princeton: Princeton University Press.

Hagopian, Frances, and Scott P. Mainwaring, eds. 2005. *The Third Wave of Democratization in Latin America: Advances and Setbacks*. Cambridge: Cambridge University Press.

Hale, Henry E. 2013. "Regime Change Cascades: What We Have Learned from the 1848 Revolutions to the 2011 Arab Uprisings." *Annual Review of Political Science* 16 (1): 331–53.

Hamayotsu, Kikue. 2010. "Crises of Identity in PAS and Beyond: Islam and Politics in Post 8 March Malaysia." *Round Table* 99 (407): 163–75.

Han, Sung-Joo. 1988. "South Korea in 1987: The Politics of Democratization." *Asian Survey* 28 (1): 52–61.

Handlin, Samuel. 2016. "Mass Organization and the Durability of Competitive Authoritarian Regimes: Evidence from Venezuela." *Comparative Political Studies* 49 (9): 1238–69.

Hao, Shinan, and Qiqi Gao. 2016. "East Asian Pathways toward Democracy: A Qualitative Comparative Analysis of 'the Third Wave.'" *Journal of East Asian Studies* 16 (2): 239–60.

Hasan, Abdul Rahman, and Prema Letha Nair. 2014. "Urbanisation and Growth of Metropolitan Centres in Malaysia." *Malaysian Journal of Economic Studies* 51 (1): 87–101.

Hassner, Ron E. 2009. *War on Sacred Grounds*. Ithaca: Cornell University Press.

Haugbølle, Rikke Hostrup, and Francesco Cavatorta. 2011. "Will the Real Tunisian Opposition Please Stand Up? Opposition Coordination Failures under Authoritarian Constraints." *British Journal of Middle Eastern Studies* 38 (3): 323–41.

Hawes, Gary. 1986. "United States Support for the Marcos Administration and the Pressures That Made for Change." *Contemporary Southeast Asia* 8 (1): 18–36.

Hazis, Faisal S. 2012. *Domination and Contestation: Muslim Bumiputera Politics in Sarawak*. Singapore: Institute of Southeast Asian Studies.

Hellmann, Olli. 2018. "High Capacity, Low Resilience: The 'Developmental' State and Military-Bureaucratic Authoritarianism in South Korea." *International Political Science Review* 39 (1): 67–82.

Heng, Pek Koon. 1983. "The Social and Ideological Origins of the Malayan Chinese Association." *Journal of Southeast Asian Studies* 14 (2): 290–311.

Heo, Uk, and Terence Roehrig. 2010. *South Korea since 1980*. New York: Cambridge University Press.

Heydemann, Steven, and Reinoud Leenders. 2011. "Authoritarian Learning and Authoritarian Resilience: Regime Responses to the 'Arab Awakening.'" *Globalizations* 8 (5): 647–53.

Hill, Hal. 1986. "The Philippine Economy in 1985: The Decline Continues." *Southeast Asian Affairs* (1986): 239–57.

Hilley, John. 2001. *Malaysia: Mahathirism, Hegemony, and the New Opposition*. New York: Zed Books.

Hollyer, James R., B. Peter Rosendorff, and James Raymond Vreeland. 2015. "Transparency, Protest, and Autocratic Instability." *American Political Science Review* 109 (4): 764–84.

Hong, Joshua Young-gi. 2009. "Evangelicals and the Democratization of South Korea since 1987." In *Evangelical Christianity and Democracy in Asia: Evangelical Christianity and Democracy in the Global South*, ed. David Halloran Lumsdaine. New York: Oxford University Press.

Horowitz, Donald L. 1985. *Ethnic Groups in Conflict*. Berkeley: University of California Press.

Horowitz, Donald L. 2013. *Constitutional Change and Democracy in Indonesia*. New York: Cambridge University Press.

Howard, Marc Morjé, and Philip G. Roessler. 2006. "Liberalizing Electoral Outcomes in Competitive Authoritarian Regimes." *American Journal of Political Science* 50 (2): 365–81.

Howard, Philip N., and Muzammil M. Hussain. 2013. *Democracy's Fourth Wave? Digital Media and the Arab Spring*. New York: Oxford University Press.

Huff, W. G. 1992. "Sharecroppers, Risk, Management, and Chinese Estate Rubber Development in Interwar British Malaya." *Economic Development and Cultural Change* 40 (4): 743–73.

Huntington, Samuel P. 1993. *The Third Wave: Democratization in the Late Twentieth Century*. Norman: University of Oklahoma Press.

Hyde, Susan D., and Nikolay Marinov. 2014. "Information and Self-Enforcing Democracy: The Role of International Election Observation." *International Organization* 68 (2): 329–59.

Hyug, Baeg Im. 2006. "Christian Churches and Democratization in South Korea." In *Religious Organizations and Democratization: Case Studies from Contemporary Asia*, ed. Tun-jen Cheng and Deborah A. Brown, 136–56. Armonk, NY: M.E. Sharpe.

Ibenskas, Raimondas. 2016. "Understanding Pre-electoral Coalitions in Central and Eastern Europe." *British Journal of Political Science; Cambridge* 46 (4): 743–61.

Ibrahim, Zuraidah, and Andrea Ong. 2016. *Opposition*. Singapore: Institute of Policy Studies and Straits Times Press.

Izama, Angelo, and Michael Wilkerson. 2011. "Uganda: Museveni's Triumph and Weakness." *Journal of Democracy* 22 (3): 64–78.

James, Kenneth. 1988. "Malaysia in 1987: Challenges to the System." *Southeast Asian Affairs* (1988): 153–69.

Javate-de Dios, Aurora, Petronilo Daroy, and Lorna Kalaw-Tirol, eds. 1988. *Dictatorship and Revolution: Roots of People's Power*. Manila: Conspectus Foundation.

Jensen, Nathan M., Edmund Malesky, Mariana Medina, and Ugur Ozdemir. 2014. "Pass the Bucks: Credit, Blame, and the Global Competition for Investment." *International Studies Quarterly* 58 (3): 433–47.

Josey, Alex. 1972. *The Singapore General Elections 1972*. Kuala Lumpur: Eastern Universities Press.

Kadima, Denis, and Felix Owuor. 2006. "The National Rainbow Coalition." In *The Politics of Party Coalitions in Africa, 179–221. South Africa: Konrad Adenauer Foundation. http://www.content.eisa.org.za/pdf/kadima2006coalitions6.pdf (November 13, 2015).

Kadivar, Mohammad Ali. 2013. "Alliances and Perception Profiles in the Iranian Reform Movement, 1997 to 2005." American Sociological Review 78 (6): 1063–86.

Kam, Christopher J. 2011. Party Discipline and Parliamentary Politics. Cambridge: Cambridge University Press.

Kananatu, Thaatchaayini. 2018. "The Politico-Legal Mobilisation of Ethnic Indians before Malaysia's 2018 Election." Round Table 107 (6): 703–16.

Kang, David C. 2003. "Regional Politics and Democratic Consolidation in Korea." In Korea's Democratization, ed. Samuel S. Kim, 161–80. Cambridge: Cambridge University Press.

Kang, Woo Chang. 2016. "Local Economic Voting and Residence-Based Regionalism in South Korea: Evidence from the 2007 Presidential Election." Journal of East Asian Studies 16 (3): 349–69.

Kann, Peter R. 1974. "The Philippines without Democracy." Foreign Affairs 52 (3): 612–32.

Katsiaficas, George N., and Kan-ch'ae Na, eds. 2006. South Korean Democracy: Legacy of the Gwangju Uprising. New York: Routledge.

Kausikan, Bilahari. 1997. "Governance That Works." Journal of Democracy 8 (2): 24–34.

Kessler, Richard J. 1984. "Politics Philippine Style, Circa 1984." Asian Survey 24 (12): 1209–28.

Kessler, Richard J. 1986. "Marcos and the Americans." Foreign Policy (63): 40–57.

Khalid, Khadijah, and Jason Loh. 2016. "Contemporary Electoral Trends among Malaysian Chinese Voters: Changing Political Socialisation and Orientation in the Post 2008 General Election." European Journal of East Asian Studies 15 (2): 174–208.

Khong, Kim Hoong. 1991a. "Malaysia 1990: The Election Show-Down." Southeast Asian Affairs (1991): 161–79.

Khong, Kim Hoong. 1991b. Malaysia's General Election 1990: Continuity, Change, and Ethnic Politics. Singapore: Institute of Southeast Asian Studies.

Khoo, Boo Teik. 1995. Paradoxes of Mahathirism: An Intellectual Biography of Mahathir Mohamad. New York: Oxford University Press.

Khoo, Boo Teik. 2000. "The Malaysian General Election of 29 November 1999." Australian Journal of Political Science 35 (2): 305–11.

Khoo, Ying Hooi. 2014. "Mobilization Potential and Democratization Processes of the Coalition for Clean and Fair Elections (Bersih) in Malaysia: An Interview with Hishamuddin Rais." ASEAS: Austrian Journal of South-East Asian Studies 7 (1): 111–20.

Khoo, Ying Hooi. 2016. "Malaysia's 13th General Elections and the Rise of Electoral Reform Movement." Asian Politics & Policy 8 (3): 418–35.

Kim, Dae Jung. 2019. Conscience in Action: The Autobiography of Kim Dae-Jung. New York: Palgrave Macmillan.

Kim, Eugene. 1985. "The Meaning of Korea's 12th National Assembly Election." Korea Observer 16 (4): 363–79.

Kim, Eugene. 1986. "South Korea in 1985: An Eventful Year amidst Uncertainty." Asian Survey 26 (1): 66–77.

Kim, Eugene. 1987. "South Korea in 1986: Preparing for a Power Transition." Asian Survey 27 (1): 64–74.

Kim, HeeMin. 2011. *Korean Democracy in Transition*. Lexington: University Press of Kentucky.

Kim, Insoo. 2013. "Intra-military Divisions and Democratization in South Korea." *Armed Forces & Society* 39 (4): 695–710.

Kimura, Masataka. 1991. "Martial Law and the Realignment of Political Parties in the Philippines (September 1972–February 1986): With a Case in the Province of Batangas." *Southeast Asian Studies* 29 (2): 205–26.

King, Gary, Jennifer Pan, and Margaret E. Roberts. 2017. "How the Chinese Government Fabricates Social Media Posts for Strategic Distraction, Not Engaged Argument." *American Political Science Review* 111 (3): 484–501.

Kleiboer, Marieke. 1996. "Understanding Success and Failure of International Mediation." *Journal of Conflict Resolution* 40 (2): 360–89.

Knutsen, Carl Henrik, Håvard Mokleiv Nygård, and Tore Wig. 2017. "Autocratic Elections: Stabilizing Tool or Force for Change?" *World Politics* 69 (1): 98–143.

Knight, Jack. 1992. *Institutions and Social Conflict*. New York: Cambridge University Press.

Koh, B. C. 1985. "The 1985 Parliamentary Election in South Korea." *Asian Survey* 25 (9): 883–97.

Koinova, Maria. 2009. "Diasporas and Democratization in the Post-communist World." *Communist and Post-communist Studies* 42 (1): 41–64.

Komisar, Lucy. 1987. *Corazon Aquino: The Story of a Revolution*. New York: G. Braziller.

Kraetzschmar, Hendrik. 2010. "Opposition Alliances under Electoral Authoritarianism: The United Front for Change in Egypt's 2005 Parliamentary Elections." In *Contentious Politics in the Middle East: Political Opposition under Authoritarianism*, ed. Holger Albrecht, 94–114. Gainesville: University Press of Florida.

Kraetzschmar, Hendrik. 2011. "Mapping Opposition Cooperation in the Arab World: From Single-Issue Coalitions to Transnational Networks." *British Journal of Middle Eastern Studies* 38 (3): 287–302.

Kraetzschmar, Hendrik, ed. 2013. *The Dynamics of Opposition Coalitions in the Arab World: Contentious Politics in Times of Change*. London: Routledge.

Kraetzschmar, Hendrik, and Paola Rivetti, eds. 2018. *Islamists and the Politics of the Arab Uprisings: Governance, Pluralisation and Contention*. Edinburgh: Edinburgh University Press.

Kuhonta, Erik. 2011. *The Institutional Imperative: The Politics of Equitable Development in Southeast Asia*. Stanford: Stanford University Press.

Kuhonta, Erik. 2016. "Social Cleavages, Political Parties, and the Building of Performance Legitimacy in Southeast Asia." In *Parties, Movements, and Democracy in the Developing World*, ed. Nancy Bermeo and Deborah J. Yashar, 61–92. Cambridge: Cambridge University Press.

Kuran, Timur. 1991. "Now Out of Never: The Element of Surprise in the East European Revolution of 1989." *World Politics* 44 (1): 7–48.

Kwak, Ki-Sung. 2012. *Media and Democratic Transition in South Korea*. New York: Routledge.

Kydd, Andrew. 2003. "Which Side Are You On? Bias, Credibility, and Mediation." *American Journal of Political Science* 47 (4): 597–611.

Landé, Carl H. 1981. "Philippine Prospects after Martial Law." *Foreign Affairs* 59 (5): 1147–68.

Lau, Albert. 1991. *The Malayan Union Controversy, 1942–1948*. New York: Oxford University Press.

Lau, Albert. 1998. *A Moment of Anguish: Singapore in Malaysia and the Politics of Disengagement*. Singapore: Times Academic Press.

Lebas, Adrienne. 2011. *From Protest to Parties: Party-Building and Democratization in Africa*. Oxford: Oxford University Press.

Lee, Chin-Chuan. 1998. "Press Self-Censorship and Political Transition in Hong Kong." *Harvard International Journal of Press/Politics* 3 (2): 55–73.

Lee, Junhan. 2000. "Political Protest and Democratization in South Korea." *Democratization* 7 (3): 181–202.

Lee, Junhan. 2002. "Primary Causes of Asian Democratization: Dispelling Conventional Myths." *Asian Survey* 42 (6): 821–37.

Lee, Kuan Yew. 2000. *From Third World to First: The Singapore Story, 1965–2000*. New York: HarperCollins.

Lee, Namhee. 2007. *Making of Minjung: Democracy and the Politics of Representation in South Korea*. Ithaca: Cornell University Press.

Lee, Terence. 2015. *Defect or Defend: Military Responses to Popular Protests in Authoritarian Asia*. Baltimore: Johns Hopkins University Press.

Lee, Terence, and Kevin Tan, eds. 2016. *Change in Voting*. Singapore: Ethos Books.

Lees, Lynn Hollen. 2017. *Planting Empire, Cultivating Subjects: British Malaya, 1786–1941*. Cambridge: Cambridge University Press.

Lehoucq, Fabrice Edouard, and Iván Molina Jiménez. 2002. *Stuffing the Ballot Box: Fraud, Electoral Reform, and Democratization in Costa Rica*. New York: Cambridge University Press.

Letsa, Natalie Wenzell. 2019a. "Expressive Voting in Autocracies: A Theory of Noneconomic Participation with Evidence from Cameroon." *Perspectives on Politics* 18 (2): 439–53.

Letsa, Natalie Wenzell. 2019b. "The Political Geography of Electoral Autocracies: The Influence of Party Strongholds on Political Beliefs in Africa." *Electoral Studies* 60: 102047.

Levitsky, Steven, James Loxton, Brandon Van Dyck, and Jorge I. Dominguez, eds. 2016. *Challenges of Party-Building in Latin America*. New York: Cambridge University Press.

Levitsky, Steven, and Lucan A. Way. 2010. *Competitive Authoritarianism: Hybrid Regimes after the Cold War*. New York: Cambridge University Press.

Levitsky, Steven, and Daniel Ziblatt. 2018. *How Democracies Die*. New York: Crown.

Lian, Hah Foong. 2018. "'Us' versus 'Them': An Ideological Battle for Electorates on Political YouTube Videos in the 2016 Sarawak State Election." *Contemporary Southeast Asia* 40 (1): 27–49.

Liddle, R. William. 2000. "Indonesia in 1999: Democracy Restored." *Asian Survey* 40 (1): 32–42.

Liew, Chin Tong. 2018. "How I Could See the Malay Tsunami Coming." *Round Table* 107 (6): 787–88.

Lijphart, Arend. 1969. "Consociational Democracy." *World Politics* 21 (2): 207–25.

Lindberg, Staffan I. 2009. *Democratization by Elections: A New Mode of Transition*. Baltimore: Johns Hopkins University Press.

Liow, Joseph. 2004. "Exigency or Expediency? Contextualising Political Islam and the PAS Challenge in Malaysian Politics." *Third World Quarterly* 25 (2): 359–72.

Liow, Joseph. 2009. *Piety and Politics: Islamism in Contemporary Malaysia*. New York: Oxford University Press.

Lipset, Seymour Martin. 1959. "Some Social Requisites of Democracy: Economic Development and Political Legitimacy." *American Political Science Review* 53 (1): 69–105.

Lipset, Seymour Martin, and Stein Rokkan. 1967. *Party Systems and Voter Alignments: Cross-National Perspectives*. Toronto: Free Press.

Little, Andrew T. 2017. "Coordination, Learning, and Coups." *Journal of Conflict Resolution* 61 (1): 204–34.

Little, Andrew T., Joshua A. Tucker, and Tom LaGatta. 2015. "Elections, Protest, and Alternation of Power." *Journal of Politics* 77 (4): 1142–56.

Liu, Amy H. 2015. *Standardizing Diversity: The Political Economy of Language Regimes*. Philadelphia: University of Pennsylvania Press.

Loh, Francis Kok-Wah. 1988. *Beyond the Tin Mines: Coolies, Squatters, and New Villagers in the Kinta Valley, Malaysia, c. 1880–1980*. New York: Oxford University Press.

Loke, Hoe Yeong. 2014. *Let the People Have Him: Chiam See Tong. The Early Years*. Singapore: Epigram Books.

Loke, Hoe Yeong. 2019. *The First Wave: JBJ, Chiam & the Opposition in Singapore*. Singapore: Epigram Books.

Lorentzen, Peter. 2014. "China's Strategic Censorship." *American Journal of Political Science* 58 (2): 402–14.

Low, Donald, and Sudhir Thomas Vadaketh. 2014. *Hard Choices: Challenging the Singapore Consensus*. Singapore: NUS Press.

Lucardi, Adrián. 2016. "Building Support from Below? Subnational Elections, Diffusion Effects, and the Growth of the Opposition in Mexico, 1984–2000." *Comparative Political Studies* 49 (14): 1855–95.

Lührmann, Anna, and Staffan I. Lindberg. 2019. "A Third Wave of Autocratization Is Here: What Is New about It?" *Democratization* 26 (7): 1095–1113.

Lührmann, Anna, et al., eds. 2020. *Autocratization Surges—Resistance Grows. Democracy Report 2020*. Varieties of Democracy Institute. https://www.v-dem.net/media/fi ler_public/51/43/51434648-2383-4569-84d0-e02fbd834b3e/v-dem_democracyrep ort2020_20-03-18_final_lowres.pdf (March 25, 2020).

Lust, Ellen. 2004. "Divided They Rule: The Management and Manipulation of Political Opposition." *Comparative Politics* 36 (2): 159–79.

Lust, Ellen. 2005. *Structuring Conflict in the Arab World: Incumbents, Opponents, and Institutions*. New York: Cambridge University Press.

Lust, Ellen. 2006. "Elections under Authoritarianism: Preliminary Lessons from Jordan." *Democratization* 13 (3): 456–71.

Lust-Okar, Ellent, and Amaney A. Jamal. 2002. "Rulers and Rules: Reassessing the Influence of Regime Type on Electoral Law Formation." *Comparative Political Studies* 35 (3): 337–66.

Lustick, Ian S. 1996. "History, Historiography, and Political Science: Multiple Historical Records and the Problem of Selection Bias." *American Political Science Review* 90 (3): 605–18.

Magaloni, Beatriz. 2006. *Voting for Autocracy: Hegemonic Party Survival and Its Demise in Mexico*. New York: Cambridge University Press.

Magaloni, Beatriz, and Ruth Kricheli. 2010. "Political Order and One-Party Rule." *Annual Review of Political Science* 13 (1): 123–43.

Mahoney, James. 2000. "Strategies of Causal Inference in Small-N Analysis." *Sociological Methods & Research* 28 (4): 387–424.

Mahoney, James. 2012. "The Logic of Process Tracing Tests in the Social Sciences." *Sociological Methods & Research* 41 (4): 570–97.

Mahoney, James, and Gary Goertz. 2004. "The Possibility Principle: Choosing Negative Cases in Comparative Research." *American Political Science Review* 98 (4): 653–69.

Mainwaring, Scott, and Timothy Scully, eds. 1995. *Building Democratic Institutions: Party Systems in Latin America*. Stanford, CA: Stanford University Press.

Malesky, Edmund J. 2008. "Straight Ahead on Red: How Foreign Direct Investment Empowers Subnational Leaders." *Journal of Politics* 70 (1): 97–119.

Malin, Herbert S. 1985. "The Philippines in 1984: Grappling with Crisis." *Asian Survey* 25 (2): 198–205.

Mauzy, Diane K. 1979. "A Vote for Continuity: The 1978 General Elections in Malaysia." *Asian Survey* 19 (3): 281–96.

Mauzy, Diane K. 1983. "The 1982 General Elections in Malaysia: A Mandate for Change?" *Asian Survey* 23 (4): 497–517.

Mauzy, Diane K. 1988. "Malaysia in 1987: Decline of 'the Malay Way.'" *Asian Survey* 28 (2): 213–22.

Mauzy, Diane K., and R. S. Milne. 2002. *Singapore Politics under the People's Action Party*. New York: Routledge.

McClendon, Gwyneth H., and Rachel Beatty Riedl. 2019. *From Pews to Politics: Religious Sermons and Political Participation in Africa*. New York: Cambridge University Press.

McLellan, Rachael. 2019. "The Politics of Local Control in Electoral Autocracies." PhD dissertation, Princeton University.

Means, Gordon P. 1990. "Malaysia in 1989: Forging a Plan for the Future." *Southeast Asian Affairs* (1990): 183–203.

Means, Gordon P. 1991. *Malaysian Politics: The Second Generation*. New York: Oxford University Press.

Mechkova, Valeriya, Anna Lührmann, and Staffan I. Lindberg. 2017. "How Much Democratic Backsliding?" *Journal of Democracy* 28 (4): 162–69.

Meesook, Kanitta et al. 2001. *Malaysia: From Crisis to Recovery*. Washington, DC: International Monetary Fund. http://elibrary.imf.org/view/IMF084/04463-9781589060604 70/04463-9781589060470/04463-9781589060470.xml (September 14, 2019).

Mersat, Neilson Ilan. 2018. "The Sarawak Dayaks' Shift in Malaysia's 2018 Election." *Round Table* 107 (6): 729–37.

Miller, Michael K. 2015. "Elections, Information, and Policy Responsiveness in Autocratic Regimes." *Comparative Political Studies* 48 (6): 691–727.

Mills, L. A. 1966. *British Malaya, 1824–67*. Kuala Lumpur: Oxford University Press.

Mittal, S., and B. R. Weingast. 2013. "Self-Enforcing Constitutions: With an Application to Democratic Stability in America's First Century." *Journal of Law, Economics, and Organization* 29 (2): 278–302.

Mohamad Nawab, Osman, and Ali Rashaad. 2017. "Sarawak State Elections 2016: Revisiting Federalism in Malaysia." *Journal of Current Southeast Asian Affairs* 36 (1): 29–50.

Mohamed, Alias. 1994. *PAS' Platform: Development and Change, 1951–1986*. Selangor, Malaysia: Gateway Publishing House.

Moore, Barrington. 1966. *Social Origins of Dictatorship and Democracy: Lord and Peasant in the Making of the Modern World.* Boston: Beacon Press.

Morales, Maryhen. 2018. "Challenging the Autocrat: Opposition Responses to Regime Repression in Venezuela." Conference paper presented for the American Political Science Association Conference in Boston, MA.

Morgenbesser, Lee, and Thomas B. Pepinsky. 2019. "Elections as Causes of Democratization: Southeast Asia in Comparative Perspective." *Comparative Political Studies* 52 (1): 3–35.

Morse, Yonatan L. 2012. "The Era of Electoral Authoritarianism." *World Politics* 64 (1): 161–98.

Mount, Frank. 1980. "The Philippines, 1980." *Asian Affairs: An American Review* 8 (2): 113–23.

Mukerjee, Dilip. 1982. "Malaysia's 1982 General Election: The Tricky Triangulars." *Contemporary Southeast Asia* 4 (3): 301–15.

Munro, Ross H. 1984. "Dateline Manila: Moscow's Next Win?" *Foreign Policy* (56): 173.

Murillo, Maria Victoria, and Ernesto Calvo. 2019. *Non-Policy Politics: Richer Voters, Poorer Voters, and the Diversification of Electoral Strategies.* Cambridge: Cambridge University Press.

Mutalib, Hussin. 2000. "Malaysia's 1999 General Election: Signposts to Future Politics." *Asian Journal of Political Science* 8 (1): 65.

Mutalib, Hussin. 2002. "Constitutional-Electoral Reforms and Politics in Singapore." *Legislative Studies Quarterly* 27 (4): 659–72.

Nadeau, Richard, Michael S. Lewis-Beck, and Éric Bélanger. 2013. "Economics and Elections Revisited." *Comparative Political Studies* 46 (5): 551–73.

Nathan, K. S. 1989. "Malaysia in 1988: The Politics of Survival." *Asian Survey* 29 (2): 129–39.

Nathan, K. S. 1990. "Malaysia in 1989: Communists End Armed Struggle." *Asian Survey* 30 (2): 210–20.

Ndegwa, Stephen N. 2003. "Kenya: Third Time Lucky?" *Journal of Democracy* 14 (3): 145–58.

Nix, Crystal. 1988. "South Korea: United States Policy and the 1987 Presidential Elections." *Harvard Human Rights Yearbook* 1: 248–59.

Noor, Farish A. 2003. "Blood, Sweat and Jihad: The Radicalization of the Political Discourse of the Pan-Malaysian Islamic Party (PAS) from 1982 Onwards." *Contemporary Southeast Asia* 25 (2): 200–232.

Noor, Farish A. 2004. *Islam Embedded: The Historical Development of the Pan-Malaysian Islamic Party PAS (1951–2003).* Kuala Lumpur: Malaysian Sociological Research Institute.

Noor, Farish A. 2014. *The Malaysian Islamic Party PAS, 1951—2013: Islamism in a Mottled Nation.* Amsterdam: Amsterdam University Press.

Norris, Pippa, and Max Grömping. 2019. *Electoral Integrity Worldwide*, May. University of Sydney, Sydney, Australia. http://www.electoralintegrityproject.com

NSTP Research and Information Services, ed. 1990. *Elections in Malaysia: A Handbook of Facts and Figures on the Elections, 1955–1986.* Kuala Lumpur: Balai Berita.

Oates, Sarah. 2013. *Revolution Stalled: The Political Limits of the Internet in the Post-Soviet Sphere.* New York: Oxford University Press.

Oberdorfer, Don. 2001. *The Two Koreas: A Contemporary History.* New York: Basic Books.

Oliver, Steven, and Kai Ostwald. 2018. "Explaining Elections in Singapore: Dominant Party Resilience and Valence Politics." *Journal of East Asian Studies* 18 (2): 129–56.

Oliver, Steven, and Kai Ostwald. 2020. "Singapore's Pandemic Election: Opposition Parties and Valence Politics in GE2020." *Pacific Affairs* 93 (4): 759–80.

Olson, Mancur. 1965. *The Logic of Collective Action: Public Goods and the Theory of Groups*. Cambridge, MA: Harvard University Press.

Ong, Elvin. 2015. "Complementary Institutions in Authoritarian Regimes: The Everyday Politics of Constituency Service in Singapore." *Journal of East Asian Studies* 15 (3): 361–90.

Ong, Elvin. 2016. "Opposition Coordination in Singapore's 2015 General Elections." *Round Table* 105 (2): 185–94.

Ong, Elvin. 2018. "Electoral Manipulation, Opposition Power, and Institutional Change: Contesting for Electoral Reform in Singapore, Malaysia, and Cambodia." *Electoral Studies* 54: 159–71.

Ong, Elvin. 2019. "What Are We Voting For? Opposition Alliance Joint Campaigns in Electoral Autocracies." Conference paper presented for the APSA conference, San Francisco.

Ong, Elvin. 2021. "Online Repression and Self-Censorship: Evidence from Southeast Asia." *Government and Opposition* 56 (1): 141–62.

Ong, Elvin, and Mou Hui Tim. 2014. "Singapore's 2011 General Elections and Beyond: Beating the PAP at Its Own Game." *Asian Survey* 54 (4): 749–72.

Ong, Kian Ming. 2015. "Malaysian Political Parties and Coalitions." In *Routledge Handbook of Contemporary Malaysia*, ed. Meredith L. Weiss, 22–35. London: Routledge / Taylor & Francis.

Ong, Michael. 1980. "The Democratic Action Party and the 1978 General Election." In *Malaysian Politics and the 1978 Election*, ed. Harold Crouch, Kam Hing Lee, and Michael Ong, 137–75. Kuala Lumpur: Oxford University Press.

Ong, Yanchun. 2014. "Singapore's Phantom Workers." *Journal of Contemporary Asia* 44 (3): 443–63.

Öniş, Ziya. 2013. "Sharing Power: Turkey's Democratization Challenge in the Age of the AKP Hegemony." *Insight Turkey* 15 (2): 103–22.

Open Singapore Centre. 2000. *Elections in Singapore: Are They Free and Fair?* Singapore: Open Singapore Centre.

O'Rourke, Lindsey A. 2018. *Covert Regime Change: America's Secret Cold War*. Ithaca: Cornell University Press.

Ortmann, Stephan, and Mark R. Thompson. 2014. "China's Obsession with Singapore: Learning Authoritarian Modernity." *Pacific Review* 27 (3): 433–55.

Ostwald, Kai. 2013. "How to Win a Lost Election: Malapportionment and Malaysia's 2013 General Election." *Round Table* 102 (6): 521–32.

Ostwald, Kai, Paul Schuler, and Jie Ming Chong. 2019. "Triple Duel: The Impact of Coalition Fragmentation and Three-Corner Fights on the 2018 Malaysian Election." *Journal of Current Southeast Asian Affairs* 37 (3): 31–55.

Owen, John M., and Michael Poznansky. 2014. "When Does America Drop Dictators?" *European Journal of International Relations* 20 (4): 1072–99.

Palmer, Harvey D., and Guy D. Whitten. 2000. "Government Competence, Economic Performance and Endogenous Election Dates." *Electoral Studies* 19 (2): 413–26.

Parmer, J. Norman. 1960. *Colonial Labor Policy and Administration: A History of Labor in the Rubber Plantation Industry in Malaya, c. 1910–1941.* Locust Valley, NY: Association for Asian Studies.

Pascual, Dette. 1990. "Organizing 'People Power' in the Philippines." *Journal of Democracy* 1 (1): 102–9.

Pee, Robert, and William Michael Schmidli. 2019. *The Reagan Administration, the Cold War, and the Transition to Democracy Promotion.* New York: Palgrave Macmillan.

Pepinsky, Thomas. 2007. "Autocracy, Elections, and Fiscal Policy: Evidence from Malaysia." *Studies in Comparative International Development* 42 (1–2): 136–63.

Pepinsky, Thomas. 2009a. *Economic Crises and the Breakdown of Authoritarian Regimes: Indonesia and Malaysia in Comparative Perspective.* New York: Cambridge University Press.

Pepinsky, Thomas. 2009b. "The 2008 Malaysian Elections: An End to Ethnic Politics?" *Journal of East Asian Studies* 9 (1): 87–120.

Pepinsky, Thomas. 2013. "The New Media and Malaysian Politics in Historical Perspective." *Contemporary Southeast Asia: A Journal of International and Strategic Affairs* 35 (1): 83–103.

Pepinsky, Thomas. 2014. "The Institutional Turn in Comparative Authoritarianism." *British Journal of Political Science* 44 (3): 631–53.

Pepinsky, Thomas. 2015. "Interpreting Ethnicity and Urbanization in Malaysia's 2013 General Election." *Journal of East Asian Studies* 15 (2): 199–226.

Pierson, Paul. 2000. "Not Just What, but When: Timing and Sequence in Political Processes." *Studies in American Political Development* 14 (1): 72–92.

Pierson, Paul. 2004. *Politics in Time: History, Institutions, and Social Analysis.* Princeton: Princeton University Press.

Pillay, Chandrasekaran. 1974. *The 1974 General Elections in Malaysia: A Post-mortem.* Singapore: Institute of Southeast Asian Studies.

Pop-Eleches, Grigore, and Graeme B. Robertson. 2015. "Information, Elections, and Political Change." *Comparative Politics* 47 (4): 459–95.

Posusney, Marsha Pripstein. 2002. "Multi-party Elections in the Arab World: Institutional Engineering and Oppositional Strategies." *Studies in Comparative International Development* 36 (4): 34–62.

Powell, Robert. 2002. "Bargaining Theory and International Conflict." *Annual Review of Political Science* 5 (1): 1–30.

Powell, Robert. 2004. "Bargaining and Learning While Fighting." *American Journal of Political Science* 48 (2): 344–61.

Przeworski, Adam. 1991. *Democracy and the Market: Political and Economic Reforms in Eastern Europe and Latin America.* New York: Cambridge University Press.

Przeworski, Adam. 2006. "Self-Enforcing Democracy." In *Handbook of Political Economy*, ed. Barry R. Weingast and Donald A. Wittman, 312–29. Oxford: Oxford University Press.

Quah, Jon S. T. 2001. "Combating Corruption in Singapore: What Can Be Learned?" *Journal of Contingencies and Crisis Management* 9 (1): 29–35.

Quinsaat, Sharon Madriaga. 2019. "Linkages and Strategies in Filipino Diaspora Mobilization for Regime Change." *Mobilization: An International Quarterly* 24 (2): 221–39.

Rachagan, S. Sothi. 1987. "The 1986 Parliamentary Elections in Peninsular Malaysia." *Southeast Asian Affairs*: 217–35.

Rahim, Lily Zubaidah, and Lam Keong Yeoh. 2019. "Social Policy Reform and Rigidity in Singapore's Authoritarian Developmental State." In *The Limits of Authoritarian Governance in Singapore's Developmental State*, ed. Lily Zubaidah Rahim and Michael Barr, 95–130. Singapore: Springer Singapore.

Rahman, Serina. 2018. "Malaysia's General Elections 2018: Understanding the Rural Vote." *Trends in Southeast Asia* 9 (e-journal).

Rajah, Jothie. 2012. *Authoritarian Rule of Law: Legislation, Discourse and Legitimacy in Singapore*. New York: Cambridge University Press.

Rakner, Lise, and Nicolas van de Walle. 2009. "Opposition Weakness in Africa." *Journal of Democracy* 20 (3): 108–21.

Ramanathan, Sankaran, and Adnan Mohamad Hamdan. 1988. *Malaysia's 1986 General Election: The Urban-Rural Dichotomy*. Singapore: Institute of Southeast Asian Studies.

Ramsay, Kristopher W. 2017. "Information, Uncertainty, and War." *Annual Review of Political Science* 20: 505–27.

Ratnam, K. J., and R. S. Milne. 1970. "The 1969 Parliamentary Election in West Malaysia." *Pacific Affairs* 43 (2): 203–26.

Reiter, Dan. 2003. "Exploring the Bargaining Model of War." *Perspective on Politics* 1 (1): 27–43.

Reiter, Dan. 2009. *How Wars End*. Princeton: Princeton University Press.

Resnick, Danielle. 2011. "In the Shadow of the City: Africa's Urban Poor in Opposition Strongholds." *Journal of Modern African Studies* 49 (1): 141–66.

Resnick, Danielle. 2014. *Urban Poverty and Party Populism in African Democracies*. New York: Cambridge University Press.

Reuter, Ora John. 2017. *The Origins of Dominant Parties: Building Authoritarian Institutions in Post-Soviet Russia*. New York: Cambridge University Press.

Reuter, Ora John, and Jennifer Gandhi. 2011. "Economic Performance and Elite Defection from Hegemonic Parties." *British Journal of Political Science* 41 (1): 83–110.

Reuter, Ora John, and Graeme B. Robertson. 2015. "Legislatures, Cooptation, and Social Protest in Contemporary Authoritarian Regimes." *Journal of Politics* 77 (1): 235–48.

Reuter, Ora John, and David Szakonyi. 2015. "Online Social Media and Political Awareness in Authoritarian Regimes." *British Journal of Political Science* 45 (1): 29–51.

Reuter, Ora John, and David Szakonyi. 2019. "Elite Defection under Autocracy: Evidence from Russia." *American Political Science Review* 113 (2): 552–68.

Ricks, Jacob I., and Amy H. Liu. 2018. "Process-Tracing Research Designs: A Practical Guide." *PS: Political Science & Politics* 51 (4): 842–46.

Riedl, Rachel Beatty, Dan Slater, Joseph Wong, and Daniel Ziblatt. 2020. "Authoritarian-Led Democratization." *Annual Review of Political Science* 23 (1): https://doi.org/10.1146/annurev-polisci-052318-025732

Rigger, Shelley. 1999. *Politics in Taiwan: Voting for Democracy*. New York: Routledge.

Rigos, Cirilo A. 1975. "The Posture of the Church in the Philippines under Martial Law." *Southeast Asian Affairs* (1975): 127–32.

Riker, William H. 1976. "The Number of Political Parties: A Reexamination of Duverger's Law." *Comparative Politics* 9 (1): 93.

Rivera, Temario C. 2001. "The Middle Classes and Democratization in the Philippines: From the Asian Crisis to the Ouster of Estrada." In *Southeast Asian Middle Classes: Prospects for Social Change and Democratisation*, ed. Embong Abdul Rahman, 230–61. Bangi: Penerbit Universiti Kebangsaan Malaysia.

Roff, Margaret. 1965. "The Malayan Chinese Association, 1948–65." *Journal of Southeast Asian History* 6 (2): 40–53.

Roop, Sterling, and Keith Weghorst. 2016. "The 2015 National Elections in Tanzania." *Electoral Studies* 43: 190–94.

Rosario-Braid, Florangel, and Ramon R. Tuazon. 1999. "Communication Media in the Philippines: 1521–1986." *Philippine Studies* 47 (3): 291–318.

Samford, Steven, and Priscila Ortega Gómez. 2014. "Subnational Politics and Foreign Direct Investment in Mexico." *Review of International Political Economy* 21 (2): 467–96.

Saravanamuttu, Johan. 2016. *Power Sharing in a Divided Nation: Mediated Communalism and New Politics in Six Decades of Malaysia's Elections.* Singapore: ISEAS Yusof Ishak Institute.

Sartori, Giovanni. 1970. "Concept Misformation in Comparative Politics." *American Political Science Review* 64 (4): 1033.

Sato, Yuko, and Michael Wahman. 2019. "Elite Coordination and Popular Protest: The Joint Effect on Democratic Change." *Democratization* 26 (8): 1419–38.

Saxer, Carl. 2002. *From Transition to Power Alternation: Democracy in South Korea, 1987–1997.* New York: Routledge.

Schedler, Andreas. 2002a. "The Menu of Manipulation." *Journal of Democracy* 13 (2): 36–50.

Schedler, Andreas. 2002b. "The Nested Game of Democratization by Elections." *International Political Science Review* 23 (1): 103–22.

Schedler, Andreas, ed. 2006. *Electoral Authoritarianism: The Dynamics of Unfree Competition.* Boulder: Lynne Rienner.

Schedler, Andreas. 2013. *The Politics of Uncertainty: Sustaining and Subverting Electoral Authoritarianism.* Oxford: Oxford University Press.

Schuler, Paul, and Edmund J. Malesky. 2014. "Authoritarian Legislatures." In *The Oxford Handbook of Legislative Studies*, ed. Shane Martin, Thomas Saalfeld, and Kaare W. Strøm, 676–95. Oxford University Press.

Scott, James C. 1985. *Weapons of the Weak: Everyday Forms of Peasant Resistance.* New Haven: Yale University Press.

Selçuk, Orçun, and Dilara Hekimci. 2020. "The Rise of the Democracy: Authoritarianism Cleavage and Opposition Coordination in Turkey (2014–2019)." *Democratization* 27 (8): 1496–1514.

Shadmehr, Mehdi, and Dan Bernhardt. 2011. "Collective Action with Uncertain Payoffs: Coordination, Public Signals, and Punishment Dilemmas." *American Political Science Review* 105 (4): 829–51.

Shehata, Dina. 2010. *Islamists and Secularists in Egypt: Opposition, Conflict, and Cooperation.* New York: Routledge.

Shehata, Samer S., ed. 2012. *Islamist Politics in the Middle East: Movements and Change.* New York: Routledge.

Shen-Bayh, Fiona. 2018. "Strategies of Repression: Judicial and Extrajudicial Methods of Autocratic Survival." *World Politics* 70 (3): 321–57.

Shih, Victor C., ed. 2020. *Economic Shocks and Authoritarian Stability: Duration, Financial Control, and Institutions.* Ann Arbor: University of Michigan Press.

Shorrock, Tim. 1986. "The Struggle for Democracy in South Korea in the 1980s and the Rise of Anti-Americanism." *Third World Quarterly* 8 (4): 1195–1218.

Shorrock, Tim. 1988. "South Korea: Chun, the Kims and the Constitutional Struggle." *Third World Quarterly* 10 (1): 95–110.

Shurchkov, Olga. 2013. "Coordination and Learning in Dynamic Global Games: Experimental Evidence." *Experimental Economics* 16 (3): 313–34.

Shurchkov, Olga. 2016. "Public Announcements and Coordination in Dynamic Global Games: Experimental Evidence." *Journal of Behavioral and Experimental Economics* 61: 20–30.

Simpser, Alberto. 2012. "Does Electoral Manipulation Discourage Voter Turnout? Evidence from Mexico." *Journal of Politics* 74 (3): 782–95.

Simpser, Alberto. 2014. *Why Governments and Parties Manipulate Elections: Theory, Practice, and Implications*. New York: Cambridge University Press.

Singh, Bilveer. 2009. "Malaysia in 2008: The Elections That Broke the Tiger's Back." *Asian Survey* 49 (1): 156–65.

Sinpeng, Aim. 2013. "State Repression in Cyberspace: The Case of Thailand." *Asian Politics & Policy* 5 (3): 421–40.

Siriyuvasak, Ubonrat. 2005. "People's Media and Communication Rights in Indonesia and the Philippines." *Inter-Asia Cultural Studies* 6 (2): 245–63.

Slater, Dan. 2003. "Iron Cage in an Iron Fist: Authoritarian Institutions and the Personalization of Power in Malaysia." *Comparative Politics* 36 (1): 81–101.

Slater, Dan. 2010. *Ordering Power: Contentious Politics and Authoritarian Leviathans in Southeast Asia*. Cambridge: Cambridge University Press.

Slater, Dan. 2012. "Strong-State Democratization in Malaysia and Singapore." *Journal of Democracy* 23 (2): 19–33.

Slater, Dan. 2013. "Democratic Careening." *World Politics* 65 (4): 729–63.

Slater, Dan. 2019. "Conclusion: Democratising Singapore's Developmental State?" In *The Limits of Authoritarian Governance in Singapore's Developmental State*, ed. Lily Zubaidah Rahim and Michael Barr, 305–19. Singapore: Springer Singapore.

Slater, Dan, and Sofia Fenner. 2011. "State Power and Staying Power: Infrastructural Mechanisms and Authoritarian Durability." *Journal of International Affairs* 65 (1): 15–29.

Slater, Dan, and Joseph Wong. 2013. "The Strength to Concede: Ruling Parties and Democratization in Developmental Asia." *Perspectives on Politics* 11 (3): 717–33.

Slater, Dan, and Daniel Ziblatt. 2013. "The Enduring Indispensability of the Controlled Comparison." *Comparative Political Studies* 46 (10): 1301–27.

Smith, Ian O. 2014. "Election Boycotts and Hybrid Regime Survival." *Comparative Political Studies* 47 (5): 743–65.

Soh, Eng Lim. 1960. "Tan Cheng Lock: His Leadership of the Malayan Chinese." *Journal of Southeast Asian History* 1 (1): 29–55.

Sopiee, Mohamed Noordin. 1974. *From Malayan Union to Singapore Separation: Political Unification in the Malaysia Region, 1945–65*. Kuala Lumpur: University Malaya Press.

Spaniel, William, and Peter Bils. 2018. "Slow to Learn: Bargaining, Uncertainty, and the Calculus of Conquest." *Journal of Conflict Resolution* 62 (4): 774–96.

Staton, Jeffrey K., and Will H. Moore. 2011. "Judicial Power in Domestic and International Politics." *International Organization* 65 (3): 553–87.

Stepan, Alfred. 2016. "Multiple but Complementary, Not Conflictual, Leaderships: The Tunisian Democratic Transition in Comparative Perspective." *Daedalus* 145 (3): 95–108.

Stepan, Alfred. 2018. *Democratic Transitions in the Muslim World: A Global Perspective.* New York: Columbia University Press.

Stephenson, Laura Beth, John H. Aldrich, and André Blais, eds. 2018. *The Many Faces of Strategic Voting: Tactical Behavior in Electoral Systems around the World.* Ann Arbor: University of Michigan Press.

Stier, Sebastian. 2015. "Democracy, Autocracy and the News: The Impact of Regime Type on Media Freedom." *Democratization* 22 (7): 1273–95.

Stockmann, Daniela, and Mary E. Gallagher. 2011. "Remote Control: How the Media Sustain Authoritarian Rule in China." *Comparative Political Studies* 44 (4): 436–67.

Stockwell, A. J. 1979. *British Policy and Malay Politics during the Malayan Union Experiment, 1942–1948.* Kuala Lumpur: Malaysian Branch of the Royal Asiatic Society.

Stokes, Donald. 1992. "Valence Politics." In *Electoral Politics,* ed. Dennis Kavanagh, 141–64. Oxford: Clarendon Press.

Strangio, Sebastian. 2014. *Hun Sen's Cambodia.* New Haven: Yale University Press.

Stubbs, Richard. 1979. "The United Malays National Organization, the Malayan Chinese Association, and the Early Years of the Malayan Emergency, 1948–1955." *Journal of Southeast Asian Studies* 10 (1): 77–88.

Sullivan, William H. 1983. "Living without Marcos." *Foreign Policy* (53): 150.

Sundaram, Jomo Kwame. 1989. "Malaysia's New Economic Policy and National Unity." *Third World Quarterly* 11 (4): 36–53.

Svolik, Milan W. 2012. *The Politics of Authoritarian Rule.* Cambridge: Cambridge University Press.

Svolik, Milan W. 2013. "Contracting on Violence: The Moral Hazard in Authoritarian Repression and Military Intervention in Politics." *Journal of Conflict Resolution* 57 (5): 765–94.

Svolik, Milan W. 2019. "Polarization versus Democracy." *Journal of Democracy* 30 (3): 20–32.

Tan, Kenneth Paul. 2003. "Democracy and the Grassroots Sector in Singapore." *Space & Polity* 7 (1): 3–20.

Tan, Kenneth Paul. 2008. "Meritocracy and Elitism in a Global City: Ideological Shifts in Singapore." *International Political Science Review* 29 (1): 7–27.

Tan, Kenneth Paul. 2012. "The Ideology of Pragmatism: Neo-liberal Globalisation and Political Authoritarianism in Singapore." *Journal of Contemporary Asia* 42 (1): 67–92.

Tan, Netina. 2013. "Manipulating Electoral Laws in Singapore." *Electoral Studies* 32 (4): 632–43.

Tan, Netina. 2014. "The 2011 General and Presidential Elections in Singapore." *Electoral Studies* 35: 374–78.

Tan, Netina. 2015. "Institutionalized Succession and Hegemonic Party Cohesion in Singapore." In *Party System Institutionalization in Asia: Democracies, Autocracies, and the Shadows of the Past,* ed. Allen Hicken and Erik Kuhonta, 49–73. New York: Cambridge University Press.

Tan, Netina, and Bernard Grofman. 2018. "Electoral Rules and Manufacturing Legislative Supermajority: Evidence from Singapore." *Commonwealth & Comparative Politics* 56 (3): 273–97.

Tapsell, Ross. 2019. "The Smartphone as the 'Weapon of the Weak': Assessing the Role of

Communication Technologies in Malaysia's Regime Change." *Journal of Current Southeast Asian Affairs* 37 (3): 9–29.

Tarrow, Sidney. 2010. "The Strategy of Paired Comparison: Toward a Theory of Practice." *Comparative Political Studies* 43 (2): 230–59.

Teo, Youyenn. 2018. *This Is What Inequality Looks Like*. Singapore: Ethos Books.

Teorell, Jan, and Michael Wahman. 2018. "Institutional Stepping Stones for Democracy: How and Why Multipartyism Enhances Democratic Change." *Democratization* 25 (1): 78–97.

Thelen, Kathleen. 2000. "Timing and Temporality in the Analysis of Institutional Evolution and Change." *Studies in American Political Development* 14 (1): 101–8.

Thompson, Mark R. 1995. *The Anti-Marcos Struggle: Personalistic Rule and Democratic Transition in the Philippines*. New Haven: Yale University Press.

Tinker, Irene. 1956. "Malayan Elections: Electoral Pattern for Plural Societies?" *The Western Political Quarterly* 9 (2): 258.

Timberman, David G. 1991. *A Changeless Land: Continuity and Change in Philippine Politics*. Armonk, NY: M.E. Sharpe.

Tregonning, K. G. 1979. "Tan Cheng Lock: A Malayan Nationalist." *Journal of Southeast Asian Studies* 10 (1): 25–76.

Tremewan, Chris. 1994. *The Political Economy of Social Control in Singapore*. New York: St. Martin's Press.

Treisman, Daniel. 2020. "Economic Development and Democracy: Predispositions and Triggers." *Annual Review of Political Science* 23 (1): 241–257.

Tucker, Joshua A. 2007. "Enough! Electoral Fraud, Collective Action Problems, and Post-communist Colored Revolutions." *Perspectives on Politics* 5 (3): 535–51.

Tudor, Maya, and Adam Ziegfeld. 2019. "Social Cleavages, Party Organization, and the End of Single-Party Dominance: Insights from India." *Comparative Politics* 52 (1): 149–88.

Turnbull, C. M. 1972. *The Straits Settlements, 1826–67: Indian Presidency to Crown Colony*. London: Athlone Press.

Ufen, Andreas. 2014. "Introduction: The 2013 Malaysian Elections: Business as Usual or Part of a Protracted Transition?" *Journal of Current Southeast Asian Affairs* 32 (2): 3–17.

Vadaketh, Sudhir Thomas. 2020. "Chan Chun Sing, Our Beng?" *Musings from Singapore*. https://sudhirtv.com/2020/02/23/chan-chun-sing-our-beng/ (February 25, 2020).

van de Walle, Nicolas. 2006. "Tipping Games: When Do Opposition Parties Coalesce?" In *Electoral Authoritarianism: The Dynamics of Unfree Competition*, ed. Andreas Schedler, 77–92. Boulder: Lynne Rienner.

Vasil, Raj. 1972. *The Malaysian General Election of 1969*. Singapore: Oxford University Press.

Villegas, Bernardo M. 1986. "The Philippines in 1985: Rolling with the Political Punches." *Asian Survey* 26 (2): 127–40.

von der Mehden, Fred R. 1991. "Malaysia in 1990: Another Electoral Victory." *Asian Survey* 31 (2): 164–71.

Wah, Tan Meng. 2012. "Singapore's Rising Income Inequality and a Strategy to Address It." *ASEAN Economic Bulletin* 29 (2): 128.

Wahman, Michael. 2011. "Offices and Policies: Why Do Oppositional Parties Form Pre-electoral Coalitions in Competitive Authoritarian Regimes?" *Electoral Studies* 30 (4): 642–57.

Wahman, Michael. 2013. "Opposition Coalitions and Democratization by Election." *Government and Opposition* 48 (1): 3–32.

Wahman, Michael. 2014. "Electoral Coordination in Anglophone Africa." *Commonwealth & Comparative Politics* 52 (2): 187–211.

Wahman, Michael. 2016. "Opposition Coordination in Africa." *APSA-Comparative Democratization Newsletter* 14 (1). http://www.compdem.org/wp-content/uploads/2016/01/APSA-CD-Jan-2016.pdf (April 22, 2016).

Wahman, Michael. 2017. "Nationalized Incumbents and Regional Challengers: Opposition- and Incumbent-Party Nationalization in Africa." *Party Politics* 23 (3): 309–22.

Waldner, David, and Ellen Lust. 2018. "Unwelcome Change: Coming to Terms with Democratic Backsliding." *Annual Review of Political Science* 21 (1): 93–113.

Walter, Barbara F. 2009. "Bargaining Failures and Civil War." *Annual Review of Political Science* 12 (1): 243–61.

Wan Saiful, Wan Jan. 2017. "Parti Amanah Negara in Johor: Birth, Challenges and Prospects." *Trends in Southeast Asia* 9 (e-journal).

Wan Saiful, Wan Jan. 2018a. "Parti Pribumi Bersatu Malaysia in Johor: New Party, Big Responsibility." *Trends in Southeast Asia* 2 (e-journal).

Wan Saiful, Wan Jan. 2018b. "GE14: Will Urban Malays Support Pakatan Harapan?" *Trends in Southeast Asia* 10 (e-journal).

Webster, Anthony. 2011. "The Development of British Commercial and Political Networks in the Straits Settlements 1800 to 1868: The Rise of a Colonial and Regional Economic Identity?" *Modern Asian Studies* 45 (4): 899–929.

Wegner, Eva. 2011. *Islamist Opposition in Authoritarian Regimes: The Party of Justice and Development in Morocco.* Syracuse: Syracuse University Press.

Wegner, Eva, and Miquel Pellicer. 2011. "Left-Islamist Opposition Cooperation in Morocco." *British Journal of Middle Eastern Studies* 38 (3): 303–22.

Weingast, Barry R. 1997. "The Political Foundations of Democracy and the Rule of Law." *American Political Science Review* 91 (2): 245–63.

Weiss, Meredith L. 2006. *Protest and Possibilities: Civil Society and Coalitions for Political Change in Malaysia.* Stanford: Stanford University Press.

Weiss, Meredith L. 2013a. "Malaysia's 13th General Elections: Same Result, Different Outcome." *Asian Survey* 53 (6): 1135–58.

Weiss, Meredith L. 2013b. "Parsing the Power of 'New Media' in Malaysia." *Journal of Contemporary Asia* 43 (4): 591–612.

Weiss, Meredith L. 2014a. "Of Inequality and Irritation: New Agendas and Activism in Malaysia and Singapore." *Democratization* 21 (5): 867–87.

Weiss, Meredith L., ed. 2014b. *Electoral Dynamics in Malaysia: Findings from the Grassroots.* Petaling Jaya, Selangor, Malaysia: Strategic Information and Research Development Centre, Malaysia and Institute of Southeast Asian Studies.

Weiss, Meredith L. 2017. "Going to the Ground (or AstroTurf): A Grassroots View of Regime Resilience." *Democratization* 24 (2): 265–82.

Weiss, Meredith L. 2019. "Duelling Networks: Relational Clientelism in Electoral-Authoritarian Malaysia." *Democratization* 27 (1): 100–118.

Weiss, Meredith L. 2020. *The Roots of Resilience: Party Machines and Grassroots Politics in Southeast Asia*. Ithaca: Cornell University Press.

Weiss, Meredith L., Hoe-Yeong Loke, and Luenne Angela Choa. 2016. "The 2015 General Election and Singapore's Political Forecast." *Asian Survey* 56 (5): 859–78.

Weiss, Meredith L., and Arnold Puyok, eds. 2017. *Electoral Dynamics in Sarawak: Contesting Developmentalism and Rights*. Singapore: Institute of Southeast Asian Studies.

Welsh, Bridget. 2016. "Clientelism and Control: PAP's Fight for Safety in GE2015." *Round Table* 105 (2): 119–28.

Welsh, Bridget. 2019. "'Saviour' Politics and Malaysia's 2018 Electoral Democratic Breakthrough: Rethinking Explanatory Narratives and Implications." *Journal of Current Southeast Asian Affairs* 37 (3): 85–108.

Welsh, Bridget, and Alex Chang. 2019. "PAP Vulnerability and the Singapore Government Model: Findings from the Asian Barometer Survey." In *The Limits of Authoritarian Governance in Singapore's Developmental State*, ed. Lily Zubaidah Rahim and Michael Barr, 195–216. Singapore: Springer Singapore.

White, Mel. 1989. *Aquino*. Dallas: Word Pub.

Wickham, Carrie Rosefsky. 2002. *Mobilizing Islam: Religion, Activism, and Political Change in Egypt*. New York: Columbia University Press.

Wickham, Carrie Rosefsky. 2015. *The Muslim Brotherhood: Evolution of an Islamist Movement*. Princeton: Princeton University Press.

Wong, Benjamin, and Xunming Huang. 2010. "Political Legitimacy in Singapore." *Politics & Policy* 38 (3): 523–43.

Wong, Chin Huat. 2018. "The Rise, Resilience and Demise of Malaysia's Dominant Coalition." *Round Table* 107 (6): 755–69.

Wong, Chin Huat, James Chin, and Norani Othman. 2010. "Malaysia: Towards a Topology of an Electoral One-Party State." *Democratization* 17 (5): 920–49.

Wong, Chin Huat, and Kee Beng Ooi. 2018. "Introduction: How Did Malaysia End UMNO's 61 Years of One-Party Rule? What's Next?" *Round Table* 107 (6): 661–67.

Wong, Joseph. 2001. "Dynamic Democratization in Taiwan." *Journal of Contemporary China* 10 (27): 339–62.

Wong, Lin Ken. 1965. *The Malayan Tin Industry to 1914*. Tucson: Association for Asian Studies.

Woo, Jisuk. 1996. "Television News Discourse in Political Transition: Framing the 1987 and 1992 Korean Presidential Elections." *Political Communication* 13 (1): 63–80.

Work, Clint. 2019. "Stable Imperatives, Shifting Strategies: Reagan and Democracy Promotion in the Republic of Korea." In *The Reagan Administration, the Cold War, and the Transition to Democracy Promotion*, ed. Robert Pee and William Michael Schmidli, 231–51. New York: Palgrave Macmillan.

Wright, Joseph, and Abel Escribà-Folch. 2012. "Authoritarian Institutions and Regime Survival: Transitions to Democracy and Subsequent Autocracy." *British Journal of Political Science* 42 (2): 283–309.

Wurfel, David. 1977. "Martial Law in the Philippines: The Methods of Regime Survival." *Pacific Affairs* 50 (1): 5.

Wurfel, David. 1985. "The Aquino Legacy and the Emerging Succession Struggle in the Philippines, 1984." *Southeast Asian Affairs* (1985): 261–78.

Wurfel, David. 1988. *Filipino Politics: Development and Decay*. Ithaca: Cornell University Press.

Yahya, Ismail. 1989. *Perpaduan Ummah Semangat 46 PAS*. Kuala Lumpur: Dinamika Kreatif.

Yardımcı-Geyikçi, Şebnem, and Hakan Yavuzyilmaz. 2020. "Party (de)Institutionalization in Times of Political Uncertainty: The Case of the Justice and Development Party in Turkey." *Party Politics*. https://journals.sagepub.com/doi/abs/10.1177/1354068820960010

Yeoh, Seng Guan. 2015. "Urbanisation and Urbanism in Malaysia." In *Routledge Handbook of Contemporary Malaysia*, ed. Meredith L. Weiss, 249–60. London: Routledge.

Yip, Yat Hoong. 1969. *The Development of the Tin Mining Industry of Malaya*. Kuala Lumpur: University of Malaya Press.

Youngblood, Robert L. 1984. "Church and State in the New Republic of the Philippines." *Contemporary Southeast Asia* 6 (3): 205–20.

Youngblood, Robert L. 1986. "The Philippines in 1985: A Continuing Crisis of Confidence." *Southeast Asian Affairs* (1986): 225–38.

Youngblood, Robert L. 1990. *Marcos against the Church: Economic Development and Political Repression in the Philippines*. Ithaca: Cornell University Press.

Ziblatt, Daniel. 2017. *Conservative Parties and the Birth of Democracy*. Cambridge: Cambridge University Press.

Ziegfeld, Adam, and Maya Tudor. 2017. "How Opposition Parties Sustain Single-Party Dominance: Lessons from India." *Party Politics* 23 (3): 262–73.

Index

Abdul Hadi Awang, 139, 163
Abdullah Badawi, 141–42
Abdul Rahman, 139
Abdul Razak, 137, 161
Ahmad Faud, 139
Alberto, Teopisto V., 99
Al-Islah (Malaysia), 177
Alliance Party (Malaysia), 137, 158–61. *See also* Barisan Nasional (BN) [Malaysia]
Amanah. *See* Parti Amanah Negara (Amanah)
Angkatan Perpaduan Ummah alliance (APU), 158, 175–78, 180
Anwar Ibrahim: and Mahathir, 200, 201, 234; ouster from UMNO, 46, 141, 158, 175, 181, 182; and PKR, 141, 186, 200, 203
April 6 Liberation Movement (Philippines), 77
APU. *See* Angkatan Perpaduan Ummah alliance (APU)
Aquino, Agapito "Butz," 81, 82, 88
Aquino, Benigno: assassination of, 74, 75, 78–80, 84–85, 86, 96–97, 100–101; colors of, 3; and PDP-Laban, 91
Aquino, Corazon: campaign coordination, 3, 75, 102–3; and Convenor's Group, 88; filing for joint candidacy, 3, 94; and mutual dependency, 53, 57, 58–64, 74–75, 88–95, 103, 229; negotiations, 74–75, 88–96; and 1984 campaign, 81
Armacost, Michael, 84, 87, 96
Armitage, Richard, 85
Asian financial crisis (1997), 46, 175, 180–81

Asri Muda, 163
August Twenty-One Movement (Philippines), 97
authoritarian regimes. *See* electoral authoritarian regimes

Barisan Alternatif (Malaysia), 10, 158, 175, 180–84, 197
Barisan Nasional (BN) [Malaysia]: co-optation of parties, 161, 193, 205; creation of, 161; dominance of, 67, 134–38, 143, 159, 237; election manipulation by, 138; election results (1982), 163; election results (1999), 10, 184; election results (2004), 237; election results (2008), 185; election results (2013), 193; election results (2016), 173; election results (2018), 156, 158, 205; 1MDB scandal, 142, 175, 194; PAS expulsion, 140, 158, 162. *See also* Malaysian Chinese Association (MCA); Malaysian Indian Congress (MIC); United Malays National Organization (UMNO)
Barisan Socialis (Singapore), 211, 212, 219
Ben Ali, Zine El Abidine, 5
Bersih street protests, 175, 186, 237
Besigye, Kizza, 50
BN. *See* Barisan Nasional (BN) [Malaysia]
Bobi Wine (Kyagulanyi, Robert), 16
Bosworth, Stephen, 83, 92
boycotts, election: in Philippines, 77, 81, 82; reasons for, 55; in Singapore, 208, 210–11
boycotts, media, 101

Bumiputera-Malay ethnicity: Bumiputera term, 242n11, 250n4; and candidate coordination, 167–70; and dominance of BN, 134–38; and inter-ethnic riots, 140, 158, 161; parties courting, 144, 195–96; privileges, 67, 68, 142, 196–97, 234

Burhanuddin al-Helmy, 139

Bush, George H. W., 83, 87

Cameroon, lack of coordination in, 17

campaign coordination: with common logos, names, etc., 3, 41, 178, 184, 198, 199, 203–4, 220, 221, 233; with common manifestos, 41–42, 238; and communication with voters, 40–41, 179–80, 187–92, 198, 202–3, 205; declaring positions and appointees early, 41, 42, 199; and democracy-authoritarian cleavage, 21, 41, 42; described, 38–44; and level of election, 43; overview of, 20–24; in Philippines, 3, 75, 102–3; strategies, 21, 40–44; task overview, 6; and type of electoral system, 39–40, 43, 65

campaign coordination in Malaysia: overview, 156–59; failures, 162–63, 166, 233; 1990 general election, 177–80; 2013 general election, 185–93, 229; 2018 general election, 193–205, 229, 233

campaign coordination in Singapore, 147, 207, 221; failures, 207, 215–21

candidate coordination: bargaining considerations, 32–38; defined, 20; described, 32–38; under dominant regimes, 25, 26, 53–55, 58, 69–70, 228–29; by ethnicity, 167–70; "first dibs" rule, 207, 212–13, 227; and information on party strength/weakness, 22, 37, 52, 54–55; and level of election, 20, 32–38, 43, 54; overview of, 20–24; reasons for avoiding, 34–36; task overview, 5–6; and type of electoral system, 11, 20, 34, 65

candidate coordination in Malaysia: overview of, 156–59; 1965 to 1986, 159–65; 1990 to 2018, overview, 165–74; 1990 general election, 175–80; 1999 general election, 180–84; 2013 general election,

185–93, 229; 2018 general election, 193–205, 229, 233; failures, 162–63, 166, 173, 233

candidate coordination in Philippines: and cross-party vote transfer, 74–75, 95–102, 103, 124; filing of joint candidacy, 3, 94; and mutual dependency, 53, 57, 58–64, 74–75, 88–95, 103, 229; negotiations in, 74–75, 88–95; overview of, 3, 57, 73–76; role of third-parties in, 53, 62, 74, 76, 85, 93–94, 98, 99–102

candidate coordination in Singapore, 206–15, 226–27, 229; failures, 207–9, 210–11, 214–15

candidate coordination in South Korea: and cross-party voting uncertainty, 59, 105, 124–28; as failure, 3–4, 34, 57–58, 59, 104–5; and mutual dependency, 58–64, 104, 105, 118–23, 128–29, 229–30

Carlucci, Frank C., 114, 117

Catholic Bishops' Conference of the Philippines, 99–100, 102

Catholic Church: role in Philippines, 53, 62, 74, 76, 85, 93–94, 98, 99–102; role in South Korea, 62, 105, 111, 112, 122–23

censorship and self-censorship, 18, 44, 53

Chan Chun Sing, 147, 224–25

Chee Soon Juan, 150–51, 218, 220

Chen Man Hin, 184

Chen Show Mao, 150

Che Zakaria Salleh, 195

Chia, Steve, 152

Chiam See Tong, 150, 151, 152, 208, 218, 219, 220, 221

Chiang Ching Kuo, 57

Childress, Richard, 81

Chinese Consultative Committee (Malaysia), 165

Chinese minority in Malaysia: and candidate coordination, 167–70; and DAP, 140, 156; demographics, 66, 67, 135; and inter-ethnic riots, 140, 158, 161; and Malayan Emergency, 136; and Malaysian parties, 134, 135, 136–37, 138, 140, 143; and "New Villages," 136–37. *See also* Malaysian Chinese Association (MCA)

Chinese minority in Singapore, 67
Christianity: role in Philippines, 53, 62, 74, 76, 85, 93–94, 98, 99–102; role in South Korea, 62, 105, 110, 111–12, 113, 116, 117–18, 122–23
Chun Doo Hwan: concessions by, 3–4, 105, 106, 111; election manipulation by, 56; rise of, 104, 106; and US relations, 61, 114–17
Church-Military Liaison Committee (Philippines), 99–100
Citizens' Consultative Committees (Singapore), 147
civil society: and boycotts of elections, 55; in Malaysia, 141, 181, 197, 237; in Philippines, 97; in South Korea, 110, 122
Clean Election Index, 127–28
coalition formateurs: and commitment to power sharing, 13–14; defined, 13; and uncertainty about party strength/weakness, 49–50
colonialism: and Malaysia, 65–66, 135–36; and Philippines, 60–61, 73; and Singapore, 65–66, 206; and South Korea, 60
colors, coordinating, 3, 41
communication, party: and assessing party strength, 49; and campaign coordination, 40–41, 179–80, 187–92, 198, 202–3, 205
communism: and Malaysia, 136; and Philippines, 84, 85–86, 95, 100
Communist Party of the Philippines, 85, 95
Community Centre Management Committees (Singapore), 147
Convenor's Group (Philippines), 88
co-optation of opposition: as challenge, 14–15, 56; in Malaysia, 161, 193, 205
corruption, 45, 142, 175, 194, 217
Cory Aquino for President Movement, 88
Covid-19, 221–22, 225
credible commitment, as challenge, 13–14
Croatia, coordination in, 4

DAP. See Democratic Action Party (DAP) [Malaysia]
defections: in Malaysia, 141–44, 157, 158,

167, 175–76, 194, 234; military, 3, 47, 73, 75, 98, 102; in Philippines, 3, 73, 74, 75, 76–77, 87, 98, 102; as regime vulnerability event, 21, 22, 45, 46–47, 48, 232; in Singapore, 151, 152, 154; in South Korea, 106, 110, 112–13, 124
democracy-authoritarian cleavage: and campaign coordination, 21, 41, 42; in Philippines, 96–102; role in formation of alliances, 17–18
Democratic Action Party (DAP) [Malaysia]: background on, 139–40, 143, 154, 158, 159, 160; Barisan Alternatif alliance (1999), 158, 175, 180–84; candidate coordination 1990 to 2018, 165–74; candidate coordination failures, 157, 166, 173, 233; election results (1978), 162; election results (1982), 162–63; election results (1986), 165; election results (1999), 10, 158, 184; election results (2008), 185; election results (2013), 193; as ethnically neutral, 68, 140, 143; founding of, 158; Gagasan Rakyat alliance (1990), 158, 175, 178–80; as main opposition party, 161–62; 1986 alliance, 163–65; 1969 alliance, 160–61; organizational growth, 186; Pakatan Harapan alliance (2018), 158, 173–74, 175, 193–205; Pakatan Rakyat alliance (2013), 158, 175, 185–93; The Rocket, 179–80, 186, 187–92; strength/weakness of information, 159–60; use of PKR logo, 203
democratic erosion, 5, 235–36
Democratic Justice Party (DJP) [South Korea]: dominance of, 63; election results (1984), 63, 107; election results (1985), 109
democratization: alliances' role in, 5, 7; and democratic erosion, 5, 235–36; democratic opposition implications, 70; policy promotion implications, 237–38; scholarship on, 26–27; strength of ruling party as factor in, 63; sustaining momentum of, 234; temporality implications, 230–33
Diokno, Jose S., 88

DJP. *See* Democratic Justice Party (DJP) [South Korea]

economic crises: Asian financial crisis (1997), 46, 175, 180–81; global financial crisis (2008), 175, 185; and Malaysia, 157, 175, 180–81, 185; as regime vulnerability event, 21, 22, 46; and uncertainty about governance experience, 40

economics: inequality as factor in alliances, 100, 222–23; and Malaysian economic growth and policy, 161, 164; and Malaysian opposition policies, 142, 197, 198; and Malaysian regime vulnerability, 157, 180–81, 185, 194, 195; and patronage, 8, 97; and Philippines regime vulnerability, 62–64, 74, 75, 80–81, 85, 87, 97, 100; role in formation of alliances, 17; and Singapore opposition policies, 150, 151, 219; and Singapore regime vulnerability, 222–23, 225; and social justice, 100; and South Koream geographic voting, 126–27; and South Korean regime vulnerability, 62–64; and South Korea-US relations, 114, 115; uncertainty about governance experience in, 40; and validity of Malaysia and Singapore comparison, 66–67

Edry Faizal, 204

Egypt, coordination in, 12–13, 43

election manipulation: and assessing regime vulnerability, 44, 56; Clean Election Index, 127–28; in Malaysia, 138, 237; and military defections, 47, 73, 75, 98, 102; overview of, 7–8, 12, 15; in Philippines, 3, 73, 75, 77, 78, 81, 98, 102; in Singapore, 15, 145–46, 213, 214; in South Korea, 56, 107, 108, 127–28, 129; and voting behavior, 47

election observers: in Philippines, 75, 81, 92, 98–99, 101, 102; role in alliances, 17

elections: boycotts of, 55, 77, 81, 82, 208, 210–11; level of and coordination, 20, 32–38, 43, 54; past elections as information source, 51–52; violence in, 47, 98. *See also* campaign coordination; candidate coordination

Elections Department (Singapore), 145–46

electoral authoritarian regimes: candidate coordination in dominant regimes, 25, 26, 53–55, 58, 69–70, 228–29; challenges for alliances in, 7–16; as common, 7; co-optation of opposition by, 14–15, 56; and democracy-authoritarian cleavage, 17–18, 21, 41, 42, 96–102; described, 7; elections as stabilizing to, 27; interference in alliances, 14–15; role of alliances in, 5, 7. *See also* campaign coordination; candidate coordination

Electoral Boundaries Review Committee (Singapore), 145–46, 213, 214

electoral systems: challenges of, 11–13; changes to, 12, 124, 128; implications for, 69–70; similarities between South Korea and Philippines, 61–62; single, nontransferable vote (SNTV) system, 11–12, 69; strategic entry problem, 11, 33; type of and coordination, 11, 20, 34, 39–40, 43, 65

Enrile, Juan Ponce, 83, 100

Erdoğan, Recep Tayyip, 5, 17–18, 236

ethnicity and Malaysia: and Bumiputera-Malay privilege, 67, 68, 142, 196–97, 234; and candidate coordination, 167–70; demographics, 66, 135; ethnoreligious voting, 67, 68, 134–44, 167–70, 196–97; riots, 140, 158, 161

ethnicity and Singapore: demographics, 66, 206; lack of ethnic parties in, 134; policies on, 148

ethnoreligious voting: and assessing party strength/weakness, 52; and candidate coordination under dominant regimes, 55; in Malaysia, 67, 68, 134–44, 167–70, 196–97; and viability of alliances, 26

executive health crises: in Malaysia, 175, 176; in Philippines, 45, 62, 74, 75, 82–83, 87; as regime vulnerability event, 45, 62

executive level elections: and campaign coordination challenges, 43; changes to in South Korea, 124, 128; and intensity of bargaining, 36; and post-election policy uncertainty, 39; and strategic entry problem, 11, 33

Fadzil Noor, 139, 163
Fru Ndi, John, 17

Gagasan Rakyat alliance (Malaysia), 158, 175, 178–80
GDP: Malaysia, 66, 180, 194; Philippines, 63, 80; Singapore, 66; South Korea, 63
geographic voting: and assessing party strength/weakness, 52, 168–70; and candidate coordination, 54; in Malaysia, 168–70; in Singapore, 145–46; in South Korea, 109, 124–27
Gerakan (Malaysia), 159–60, 177
global financial crisis (2008), 175, 185
GNP, Philippines, 80
Goh Chok Tong, 146, 217
Goh Hock Guan, 160
Goh Meng Seng, 226
governance ability, uncertainty about: as challenge, 40; in Malaysia, 185, 197–98
Guingona, Teofisto, 88

health crises. See executive health crises
Heng Swee Keat, 146–47, 224–25

ideology: as challenge in alliances, 9–10, 38–40; coherence of as proxy for strength/weakness, 49; and post-victory implications, 233–35; regime's control of center, 8, 9, 137–38; as term, 241n5; in Turkey, 17–18; and validity of Malaysia and Singapore comparison, 67–68; as viable approach, 21, 26, 38–40, 42–43, 65. See also campaign coordination in Malaysia; candidate coordination in Malaysia
İmamoğlu, Ekrem, 52
immigration as issue in Singapore, 150, 153, 200, 223–24
Indian minority in Malaysia: and candidate coordination, 167–70; and DAP, 156; demographics, 66, 67, 135; and Malaysian parties, 134, 135, 138, 143, 156.

See also Malaysian Indian Congress (MIC)
Indian minority in Singapore, 67
India-Singapore Comprehensive Economic Cooperation Agreement, 224
Indonesia, democratization in, 57
inequality as factor in alliances, 100, 222–23
information: on cross-party voting behavior, 22, 49; learning implications, 232–33; and mutual dependency, 49–53; on party strength/weakness, 22, 23, 49–53, 54–55, 229; on party strength/weakness in Malaysia, 157, 159–60, 162–63, 164, 167, 171, 173; on party strength/weakness in Singapore, 211; on party strength/weakness in South Korea, 105, 119–22, 129; policy practioners' implications, 237–38; resources on, 51–53
Islamic opposition parties: and campaign coordination issues, 38, 39, 43; as ideologically focused, 9; in Middle East and North Africa, 9, 10, 43. See also Parti Amanah Negara (Amanah); Parti Islam Se-Malaysia (PAS)

Japan, funding of NAMFREL, 98
Jeyaretnam, J. B., 149, 152, 208
Jeyaretnam, Kenneth, 152
Joint Opposition Council (Singapore), 208, 219
Juangroongruangkit, Thanathorn, 16
Justice for Aquino-Justice for All, 97

Kalaw, Eva Estrada, 88, 90, 91
Kaplan, Philip S., 94
Kelly, James, 117
Kenya, coordination in, 4–5, 16–17, 19–20, 52
Kenyatta, Uhuru, 4, 19–20
Kerry, John, 87
Kibaki, Mwai, 4, 16–17, 19–20
Kilusang Bagong Lipunan (Philippines): strength of, 63, 75. See also Marcos, Ferdinand
Kim Byung-Kwan, 123

Kim Dae Jung: defection from RDP, 124; election results, 4, 105, 129; exile and return of, 106, 108, 118; formation of RDF, 106, 112–13; lack of coordination with Kim Young Sam, 3–4, 34, 57–58, 105, 118–29; on party resources, 64; and Philippines parallels, 107, 108, 111; protest of loss, 129; rallies by, 121–22, 125, 128; restoration of rights, 113; and US involvement, 116–17
Kim Jae Kyu, 104
Kim Jong Pil, 4
Kim Sou Hwan, 111, 112, 122–23
Kim Young Sam: election results, 4, 105, 129; endorsement of by Catholic Church, 111; formation of RDP, 106, 112–13; lack of coordination with Kim Dae Jung, 4, 34, 57–58, 105, 118–29; and Philippines regime change, 107; protest of loss, 129; rallies by, 122, 125, 128
Korea Council of Churches, 111
Kwangju uprising, 62, 110, 112, 127

Laurel, Jose, Jr., 76–77
Laurel, Salvador: campaign coordination, 3, 75, 102–3; defection from ruling party, 76–77; filing for joint candidacy, 3, 94; and mutual dependency, 53, 57, 58–64, 74–75, 88–95, 103, 229; and National Unification Committee, 88–90, 92; negotiations, 74–75, 88–96; 1984 election, 77; on party resources, 64; US interactions, 87
Laxalt, Paul, 86, 87
learning: implications, 232–33, 237; in Malaysia, 157, 167, 230, 232–33, 237; and policy practioners, 237
Lee, H. S., 137
Lee Chul, 109
Lee Han Yol, 106
Lee Hsien Loong, 146, 217, 225
Lee Kuan Yew, 146, 217
Lee Lam Thye, 163–64
Lee Min Woo, 113
Lee Seng Lup, 145
Lee Siew Choh, 211, 212
Lee Tae Sup, 109

Lee Teng Hui, 57
LGBTQ issues in Singapore, 150, 151
Liberal Party (Philippines), 88, 91
Liew Chin Tong, 194
Light-A-Fire Movement (Philippines), 77
Lim Chin Siong, 211
Lim Guan Eng, 140
Lim Kit Siang, 10, 139–40, 180, 183, 184
Lim Sylvia, 150
Lim Tean, 214–15
list-proportional representation, 69
logos and symbols, common: in Malaysia, 178, 184, 198, 199, 203–4, 233; in Singapore, 219, 220, 221; as strategy, 41
Low, Jho, 142
Low Thia Khiang, 149–50, 220, 221

Mahathir Mohamad: conflict with Anwar Ibrahim, 234; economic growth under, 164; health of, 175, 176; and PH alliance, 173, 199–203; PPBM formation, 141–42, 158, 175, 194; S46 formation, 141, 175–76
Malayan Communist Party (MCP), 136
Malayan Emergency, 136
Malayan Union plan, 135–36
Malay-Muslims. See Bumiputera-Malay ethnicity
Malaysia: average number of candidates table, 166; background on opposition parties, 138–44; break away of Singapore, 158, 208, 210; corruption scandal, 45, 142, 175, 194; defections in, 141–43, 157, 158, 167, 175–76, 194, 234; effect of 2018 election on Singapore, 226; election manipulation in, 138, 237; ethnicity demographics, 66, 135; GDP, 66, 180, 194; learning by opposition alliances in, 157, 167, 230, 232–33, 237; mutual dependency in, 59, 65, 156, 174, 177–80, 183–84, 186–92, 195–205; nonconstituency MPs, 252n29, 256n17; overview of alliances in, 156–58; party strength/weakness in, 59, 157, 159–60, 162–63, 164, 167–71, 173; party system in, 133–43, 153–55; party table, 143; post-2018 victory, 233–35; protests in, 46, 141, 157, 175, 181, 186, 233–34, 237; regime vul-

nerability in, 45, 46, 59, 65, 156–57, 174–77, 180–82, 185–86, 193–95; table of alliances, 175; timeline, 158; validity of comparison with Singapore, 58, 64–68

Malaysia, campaign coordination in: overview, 156–59; failures, 162–63, 166, 233; 1990 general election, 177–80; 2013 general election, 185–93, 229; 2018 general election, 193–205, 229, 233

Malaysia, candidate coordination in: overview of, 156–59; failures, 162–63, 166, 173, 233; 1965 to 1986, 159–65; 1990 to 2018, overview, 165–74; 1990 general election, 175–80; 1999 general election, 180–84; 2013 general election, 185–93, 229; 2018 general election, 193–205, 229, 233

Malaysia, election results: elections table, 59; 1968 election, 160; 1969 election, 160, 161; 1978 election, 162; 1982 election, 162–63; 1986 election, 165; 1999 election, 10, 158, 184; 2008 election, 175, 185; 2013 election, 158, 192–93; 2016 election, 173; 2018 election, 156, 158, 205

Malaysia Agreement of 1963, 198

Malaysian Chinese Association (MCA): development of, 136–37; election results (1969), 161; first alliances, 137, 145, 159; role in BN, 67, 135, 136–37, 138. See also Barisan Nasional (BN) [Malaysia]

Malaysian Indian Congress (MIC): election results (1969), 161; first alliances, 158; role in BN, 67, 135, 137, 138, 143. See also Barisan Nasional (BN) [Malaysia]

Manglapus, Raul, 88

manifestos: in Malaysia, 183, 184, 192, 197–98; in Singapore, 150, 154, 219, 220; using common, 41–42, 238

Marcos, Ferdinand: call for snap election, 75, 89–90; and economic patronage, 97; flight of, 3, 74, 75, 102; health of, 45, 62, 74, 75, 82–83, 87; martial law declaration, 75, 76–77, 99; and US relations, 61, 83–87, 90

Marcos, Imelda, 83

Marina Yusoff, 180

Marshall, David, 149

martial law: in Philippines, 75, 76–77, 99; in South Korea, 104, 106

Mbabazi, John Patrick Amama, 50

MCA. See Malaysian Chinese Association (MCA)

MCP (Malayan Communist Party), 136

media: alternative, 45, 101, 128, 181; boycotts of, 101; control of by regime, 7–8, 53, 238; in Malaysia, 179–81, 186; party media as proxy for strength/weakness, 49; and perceptions of regime vulnerability, 18, 44–45; in Philippines, 101; and policy practioners, 238; in Singapore, 149; in South Korea, 128

methodology: field interviews, 170, 171, 218; and fieldwork, 65; sources, 48, 59–60, 156, 174; validity of Malaysia/Singapore comparison, 58, 64–68; validity of Philippines/South Korea comparison, 57–64

Mexico, coordination in, 9, 38–39, 68

MIC. See Malaysian Indian Congress (MIC)

middle class: in Philippines, 74, 78, 96–99; in South Korea, 106, 109, 113

military: defections, 3, 47, 73, 98, 102; in Philippines, 3, 73, 98, 99–100, 102; in Singapore, 217; in South Korea, 62, 116

Mitra, Ramon, 88

Mohammad Asri Muda, 139

Mohd Nor Bakhtiar, 204

Mohd Yunus Hasanuddin, 204

Moi, Daniel arap, 4–5

Moon Ik Hwan, 111

Morocco, co-optation of opposition in, 15

Muhamad Faisal bin Abdul Manap, 150

Muhyiddin Yassin, 142, 194, 234

Museveni, Yoweri, 50

mutual dependency: assumptions about, 19–20; elections table, 59; and information on party strength/weakness, 49–53; in Kenya, 19–20; in Malaysia, 59, 65, 156, 174, 177–80, 183–84, 186–92, 195–205; and perception of cross-voting behavior, 49, 51–53; in Philippines, 53, 57, 58–64, 74–75, 88–95, 103, 229; research implications, 69–70; role in

mutual dependency (*continued*)
formation of alliances, 21, 23, 24, 44, 48–53, 229–30; scholarship on, 25, 26; in Singapore, 65, 217, 218, 226; in South Korea, 58–64, 104, 105, 118–23, 128–29, 229–30; temporal fluctuations in, 133; as variable, 6

Nacionalista Party (Philippines), 88, 91
Nair, Devan, 139
Najib Razak, 142, 185, 186, 194, 195
names, coalition, 41
National Alliance for Constitutional Reform (South Korea), 111
National Citizens' Movement for Free Elections (NAMFREL) [Philippines], 75, 81, 98–99, 101, 102
National Coalition for a Democratic Constitution (South Korea), 113
National Council of Churches in the Philippines, 99
National Democratic Front (Philippines), 95
National Operations Council (Malaysia), 161
National Solidarity Party (NSP) [Singapore], 152, 153, 213–15, 219–21
National Unification Committee (NUC) [Philippines], 88–90, 92
Ndam Njoya, Adamou, 17
Neighborhood Committees (Singapore), 147
New Economic Policy (Malaysia), 161
New Korea Democratic Party (NKDP): defections from, 106, 112–13; increase in size and capabilities, 109–10; negotiations in, 118–23; unexpected gains by, 105, 106, 107–9, 120
New People's Army (NPA) [Philippines], 85–86, 100
"New Villages" (Malaysia), 136–37
Nik Aziz Nik Mat, 163
NKDP. *See* New Korea Democratic Party (NKDP)
NPA. *See* New People's Army (NPA) [Philippines]

NSP. *See* National Solidarity Party (NSP) [Singapore]
NUC. *See* National Unification Committee (NUC) [Philippines]
Nurul Izzah Anwar, 190–92

1MDB (1Malaysia Development Berhad) scandal, 142, 175, 194
Ongpin, Jaime, 88
Ong Ye Kung, 147
Onn Jaafar, 136, 139
Ople, Blas, 83
opposition alliances: assumptions in, 18–19; defining, 23–25; within democracies, 70, 235–36; formation theories, 17–20; and governance inexperience, 40; number of parties in, 56; as ordinal, 25, 43, 65; overview of challenges, 7–16, 32, 228; overview of successes and failures, 3–6; post-victory implications, 233–35; research implications, 25, 68–70, 230–33; role in democracy, 5, 7; scope conditions, 55–56; task overview, 5–6; terms, 241n4. *See also* campaign coordination; candidate coordination; mutual dependency; regime vulnerability; strength/weakness, party; temporality; voting behavior
opposition gains, unexpected: in Malaysia, 175, 185, 229; in Philippines, 74, 75, 77–78, 81–82, 87, 91, 98, 107; as regime vulnerability event, 22, 45; in Singapore, 208; in South Korea, 105, 106, 107–9, 120
Osmena, John, 91

PA. *See* People's Association (PA) [Singapore]
Padilla, Ambrosio, 88
Pakatan Harapan (PH) alliance [Malaysia], 158, 173–74, 175, 193–205, 229, 232–35
Pakatan Rakyat (PR) alliance, 158, 175, 185–93, 197, 229
Pan-Malayan Malay Congress, 136
PAP. *See* People's Action Party (PAP) [Singapore]

Park Chung Hee, 62, 104, 106, 112
Park Hyung Kyu, 111
Park Jong Chul, 106, 112, 113
parliamentary systems: coordination challenges in, 34, 39–40, 43, 65; in Malaysia and Singapore, 65–66, 134, 206, 207; and ordinal range of cooperation, 65; and post-election policy uncertainty, 39–40
Parti Amanah Negara (Amanah), 141, 142–44, 158, 175, 195–96, 200, 204. *See also* Pakatan Harapan (PH) alliance [Malaysia]
Partido Demokratiko Pilipino-Lakasng Bayan (PDP-Laban) [Philippines], 88, 91
Parti Gerakan Rakyat Malaysia. *See* Gerakan (Malaysia)
Parti Islam Se-Malaysia (PAS): Angkatan Perpaduan Ummah alliance (1990), 158, 175–78, 180; background on, 139, 143, 156, 157; Barisan Alternatif alliance (1999), 158, 175, 180–84; campaign coordination, 177–78; candidate coordination 1990 to 2018, 165–74, 233; and competition for Malay-Muslim voters, 195–96; co-optation of, 161, 193, 205; coordination, early, 163–65; election results, 10, 161, 162–63, 165, 184, 185, 193; expulsion from BN, 140, 158, 162; focus on Islam, 68, 139, 143, 163, 164, 165, 177–78, 183, 184, 188, 192, 193; as main opposition party, 162; membership increase, 181; newletter, 181; Pakatan Rakyat alliance (2013), 158, 175, 185–93; PAS Supporters Club, 139. *See also* Barisan Nasional (BN) [Malaysia]
Parti Keadilan Rakyat (PKR) [Malaysia]: alliance agreement, 170; background, 10, 141–42, 143, 158; Barisan Alternatif alliance (1999), 158, 175, 183–84; and candidate coordination, 168–70, 173, 182; and competition for Malay-Muslim voters, 195–96; in DAP's media, 187, 188, 189; election results, 185, 193; founding of, 141, 181, 200; internal conflicts, 234; logo use in 2018

election, 203–4; organizational growth of, 185–86; Pakatan Harapan alliance (2018), 158, 175, 193–205; Pakatan Rakyat alliance (2013), 158, 175, 185–93; resistance to Mahathir as PM candidate, 200, 201–2; role in DAP/PAS alliances, 170, 183–84
Parti Pribumi Bersatu Malaysia (PPBM): background, 141–42, 143, 158; and competition for Malay-Muslim voters, 195–97; formation of, 141–42, 194; Pakatan Harapan alliance (2018), 158, 173–74, 175, 193–205
Parti Sosialis Rakyat Malaya, 161
Party for Peace and Democracy (South Korea), 106
PAS. *See* Parti Islam Se-Malaysia (PAS)
patronage as challenge, 8, 97
PDP-Laban (Philippines), 88, 91
Pekemas (Malaysia), 161
People Power Revolution (Philippines), 3, 102, 106
People's Action Party (PAP) [Singapore]: background, 144–49, 153; dominance of, 67–68, 144–47, 153, 206, 207, 208, 209–11, 216, 217; election manipulation by, 15; election results, 219, 221; immigration policy, 223–24; structure of, 146; and succession, 146–47, 224–25; vulnerability in 2020 election, 222–27
People's Association (PA) [Singapore], 147
People's Front (PF) [Singapore], 211, 212
People's Power Party (PPP) [Singapore], 221, 226
People's Progressive Party (PPP) [Malaysia], 160–61
People's Voice (Singapore), 222
Perikatan Nasional (Malaysia), 234
PF. *See* People's Front (PF) [Singapore]
PH. *See* Pakatan Harapan (PH) alliance [Malaysia]
Philippines: boycotts in, 77, 81, 82, 101; campaign coordination in, 3, 75, 102–3; defections in, 3, 73, 74, 75, 76–77, 87, 98, 102; economy, 62–64, 74, 75, 80–81, 85, 87, 97, 100; effect on South Korea,

Philippines (*continued*)
105–8, 111, 115; election manipulation
in, 3, 73, 77, 78, 81, 102; elections table,
59; GDP, 63, 80; GNP, 80; martial law
declaration, 75, 76–77, 99; mutual
dependency in, 53, 57, 58–64, 74–75,
88–95, 103, 229; protests in, 3, 48, 62,
73–74, 75, 78–80, 96–97, 102; regime
vulnerability in, 3, 45, 48, 59, 62, 73–74,
76–87, 96–103; resources in, 64; role of
third-parties in, 53, 62, 74, 76, 85, 93–
94, 98, 99–102; timeline, 75; and US
relations, 53, 60–61, 74, 82, 83–87, 95–
96; validity of South Korea comparison, 57–64
Philippines, candidate coordination in:
and cross-party vote transfer, 74–75,
95–102, 103, 124; filing of joint candidacy, 3, 94; and mutual dependency, 53,
57, 58–64, 74–75, 88–95, 103, 229; and
negotiations, 74–75, 88–95; overview
of, 3, 57, 73–76; and role of third-
parties, 53, 62, 74, 76, 85, 93–94, 98,
99–102
Pimentel, Aquilino, Jr., 88, 91
PKMS. *See* Singapore Malay National
Organization (PKMS)
PKR. *See* Parti Keadilan Rakyat (PKR)
[Malaysia]
policy: implications for practioners, 237–
38; uncertainty of post-election, 39–40
polls and surveys: in Malaysia, 173, 194,
196; and party strength/weakness, 52–
53; and policy practioners' role, 237–38;
in South Korea, 121
poll watchers, in Philippines, 75, 81, 92,
98–99, 101, 102
PPBM. *See* Parti Pribumi Bersatu Malaysia (PPBM)
PPP. *See* People's Power Party (PPP) [Sin-
gapore]; People's Progressive Party
(PPP) [Malaysia]
PR. *See* Pakatan Rakyat (PR) alliance
presidential elections. *See* executive level
elections
Progress Singapore Party (PSP), 150, 151,
153, 155, 208, 224, 226, 227

protests and demonstrations: in Malaysia,
46, 141, 157, 175, 181, 186, 233–34, 237;
and middle class, 96–97, 106, 113; and
military defections, 47; in Philippines,
3, 48, 62, 73–74, 75, 78–80, 96–97, 102;
as regime vulnerability event, 21, 22, 45,
46, 47–48, 232; in Singapore, 48, 223–
24; in South Korea, 4, 56, 62, 105, 106,
110, 111, 112–13, 117, 122, 123, 127; violence and deaths in, 4, 106, 110, 111, 112,
113, 122, 123, 127
PSP. *See* Progress Singapore Party (PSP)
public endorsements, 41
punishment regime, 8

rallies in South Korea, 121–22, 125, 128
Raymond, Jose, 152
Razaleigh Hamzah, 141, 158, 167, 175–76,
180
RDP. *See* Reunification Democratic Party
(RDP) [South Korea]
Reagan, Ronald, 61, 83–87, 101, 114–17
Reformasi Movement (Malaysia), 141, 175,
181
Reform Party (RP) [Singapore], 152, 153,
221
regime vulnerability: acceleration of, 21–
22, 46; assessment challenges, 44–45;
assumptions about, 18–19; concessions
as sign of, 113–14; in elections table, 59;
event examples, 21, 45; in Malaysia, 45,
46, 59, 65, 156–57, 174–77, 180–82, 185–
86, 193–95; in Philippines, 62–64, 73–
74, 75, 76–87, 96–103; research implications, 69–70; role in alliance formation,
6, 17, 18–19, 21–22, 24, 44–48, 229, 230;
scholarship on, 25–26; sequences of,
21–22, 26, 45–48, 229, 232; in Singapore,
65, 216–17, 223–25; in South Korea, 45,
59, 62, 104–18, 128; and temporality, 26,
46, 133, 230–32
religious authorities: alternative media by,
101; and assessing mutual dependency,
53; role in PAS, 139; role in Philippines,
53, 62, 74, 76, 85, 93–94, 98, 99–102;
role in South Korea, 62, 105, 110, 111–12,
113, 116, 117–18, 122–23

repression: as challenge, 7, 15–16; of church workers in Philippines, 100, 101; and perceptions of regime vulnerability, 18, 44

Residents' Committees (Singapore), 147

resources: and candidate coordination, 36–37, 212, 215; as challenge, 8, 12, 56, 138, 228; and commitment to alliance promises, 14; in Philippines, 64, 91; as proxy for strength/weakness, 49; role in formation of alliances, 16–17; in South Korea, 64

Reunification Democratic Party (RDP) [South Korea]: defections from, 124; formation of, 106, 112–13; negotiations and lack of mutual dependency, 118–23; and uncertainty over vote transfer, 124–28

riots: in Malaysia, 140, 158, 161; in Singapore, 152

The Rocket, 179–80, 186, 187–92

Roh Tae Woo: concessions by, 113–14; declaration as candidate, 113; election results (1987), 4, 34, 105, 106; encouraging of single opposition candidate, 123; and US, 117

Roxas, Gerardo, 76–77

Roy, Jose, 91

RP. See Reform Party (RP) [Singapore]

S46. See Semangat 46 (S46) [Malaysia]

Salas, Rafael, 88

Salonga, Jovito, 88

sanctions, 17

Santiago, Charles, 200

SDA. See Singapore Democratic Alliance (SDA)

SDP. See Singapore Democratic Party (SDP)

security alliances with US: Philippines, 60–61, 83, 84, 95–96; South Korea, 60, 114, 115

self-censorship, 18, 44, 53

Semangat 46 (S46) [Malaysia]: Angkatan Perpaduan Ummah alliance (1990), 158, 175–78, 180; background, 141–42, 143, 158; Gagasan Rakyat alliance

(1990), 158, 175, 178–80; role in DAP/PAS alliances, 167, 233

SF. See Singaporeans First Party (SF)

Shanmugaratnam, Tharman, 224–25

Shultz, Stephen, 116

Sigur, Gaston, 61, 106, 115–16, 117

Sin, Jaime (Cardinal), 93–94, 99, 100–101, 102

Singapore: background on opposition parties, 149–53; boycotts in, 208, 210–11; break away from Malaysia, 158, 208, 210; and Covid-19, 221–22; defections in, 151, 152, 154; effect of 2018 Malaysia election on, 226; election manipulation in, 15, 145–46, 213, 214; election results, 219, 221; elections table, 59; "first dibs" rule, 207, 212–13, 227; GDP, 66; immigration as issue in, 150, 153, 200, 223–24; mutual dependency in, 65, 217, 218, 226; party system in, 133–34, 144–55; party table, 153; protests in, 48, 223–24; regime vulnerability in, 65, 216–17, 223–25; strength/weakness, party in, 59, 211, 213, 214–15; timeline, 208; valence focus, 67, 68, 134, 148–49; validity of comparison with Malaysia, 58, 64–68

Singapore, coordination in: campaign coordination, 147, 207, 221; campaign coordination, failures, 207, 215–21; candidate coordination, 206–15, 226–27, 229; candidate coordination failures, 207–9, 210–11, 214–15

Singaporeans First Party (SF), 152, 153, 221, 224

Singapore Democratic Alliance (SDA), 151–52, 153, 208, 219–21, 222

Singapore Democratic Party (SDP), 150–51, 153, 155, 218–19, 220, 227

Singapore Justice Party, 152, 219–21

Singapore Malay National Organization (PKMS), 152, 153, 219–21

Singapore People's Party (SPP), 151, 152, 153, 219–21

Singh, Karpal, 10, 184, 188, 189

Singh, Pritam, 150

single, nontransferable vote (SNTV) system, 11–12, 69

Siti Mariah Mahmud, 190, 191, 192
slogans, common, 41, 221
Slovakia, coordination in, 4
SNTV (single, nontransferable vote) system, 11–12, 69
social media in Malaysia, 181, 202–3
Solarz, Stephen J., 86, 87, 113–14
South Korea: concessions in, 4, 45, 105, 106, 111, 113–14, 118; constitutional changes, 111, 124; defections in, 106, 110, 112–13, 124; effect of Philippines regime change on, 105–8, 111, 115; election manipulation in, 56, 107, 108, 127–28, 129; GDP, 63; martial law declaration, 104, 106; mutual dependency in, 58–64, 104, 105, 118–23, 128–29, 229–30; and party strength perceptions, 59, 105; protests in, 4, 56, 62, 105, 106, 110, 111, 112–13, 117, 122, 123, 127; regime vulnerability in, 45, 59, 62, 104–18, 128; resources in, 64; timeline, 106; US relations, 60–61, 105; validity of comparison with Philippines, 57–64
South Korea, candidate coordination in: and cross-party voting uncertainty, 59, 105, 124–28; as failure, 3–4, 34, 57–58, 59, 104–5; and mutual dependency, 58–64, 104, 105, 118–23, 128–29, 229–30
South Korea, elections results: elections table, 59; 1984, 107; 1985, 108–9; 1987, 4, 105, 106, 129
Special Constitution Revision Committee (South Korea), 111
strategic entry problem, 11, 33
strength/weakness, party: attributes of, 49; in election table, 59; and ethnoreligious voting, 168–70; and geographic voting, 52, 168–70; and ideological coherence, 49; information on, 22, 23, 37, 49–55, 229; in Malaysia, 59, 157, 159–60, 162–63, 164, 167–71, 173; and mutual dependency, 49–53; in overview of challenges, 11; in Philippines, 64, 74–75, 88–95, 96, 229; resources as proxy for, 49; role in alliance formation, 11, 22–23, 37, 49–53; of ruling party, 63; in Singa-

pore, 59, 211, 213, 214–15; in South Korea, 59, 105, 118, 119–22, 129, 229–30
Suharto, 57
Sullivan, William H., 82
Syura Council (PAS), 139

Taiwan, democratization in, 57, 231
Tañada, Lorenzo, 88
Tan Cheng Bock, 151, 208, 224, 226
Tan Hwee Hua, 150
Tan Jee Say, 152, 224
Tanzania, alliance in, 13
temporality: and commitment to alliance promises, 13–14; and mutual dependency, 133; and regime vulnerability, 26, 46, 133, 230–32; and regime vulnerability in Malaysia, 64–65, 156; research implications, 230–33
Teo Chee Hean, 224
Teo Nie Ching, 190, 191
Teo You Yenn, 223
Thailand, repression in, 16
third parties: as information source, 52–53; role in Philippines, 53, 62, 74, 76, 85, 93–94, 98, 99–102; role in South Korea, 62, 105; role of, 17
T-shirts, 198, 199
Tunisia, coordination in, 5
Turkey: coordination in, 5, 17–18, 236; geographic voting in, 52

Uganda: coordination in, 50; repression in, 16
UMDU. See United Minjung (People's) Movement for Democracy and Unification (UMDU) [Korea]
UMNO. See United Malays National Organization (UMNO)
UNF. See United National Front (UNF) [Singapore]
UNIDO (United Nationalist Democratic Organization) [Philippines]: filing of joint candidacy, 3, 94; formation of, 76–77; strength of, 64, 88–95; unexpected gains by, 77–78, 81–82, 87, 91, 98. See also Laurel, Salvador

United Independents (Malaysia), 161
United Malays National Organization
(UMNO): and competition for Malay-
Muslim voters, 195–96; co-optation of
PAS, 193; defections from, 141–42, 158,
167, 175–76, 194; deregistration of, 175;
economic growth under, 164; election
results, 161, 193; first alliances, 137, 158;
as opposition, 233; purges, 181; role in
BN, 67, 134–36, 138, 143; and Singapore
Malay National Organization, 152. *See
also* Barisan Nasional (BN) [Malaysia]
United Minjung (People's) Movement for
Democracy and Unification (UMDU)
[Korea], 111–12, 113
United National Front (UNF) [Singa-
pore], 211, 219
United Nationalist Democratic Organization. *See* UNIDO (United Nationalist
Democratic Organization)
[Philippines]
United States: funding of NAMFREL, 98;
as information source, 53, 60;
-Singapore relations, 217
United States-Philippines relations: aid,
86; decline in support for Marcos, 53,
74, 82, 83–87, 90; historical relationship,
60–61; role in Aquino/Salvador negotiations, 94; and security alliance, 60–61,
83, 84, 95–96
United States–South Korea relations: historical relationship, 60–61; protests
against US support, 110; role in opposition, 105, 106, 114–17, 128; and security,
60, 114, 115; and trade, 114, 115, 116

Venezuela, coordination in, 4
Ver, Fabian, 98
violence and deaths: election violence, 47,
98; in South Korea protests, 4, 106, 110,
111, 112, 113, 122, 123, 127; at South Korea
rallies, 122, 125, 128
voting behavior: and candidate coordination risks, 37; and election manipulation, 47; and election violence, 47; past
election data on, 51–52; and regime
vulnerability, 18, 19, 229
voting behavior, cross-party: and ideological challenges, 10, 12, 38–40; in
Malaysia, 10, 163–64, 195–205, 229; and
perception of mutual dependency, 22,
49, 51–53; and Philippines, 74–75, 95–
102, 103, 124; uncertainty of in South
Korea, 59, 105, 124–28

Wamalwa, Kijana, 19–20
Wan Azizah Wan Ismail, 141, 181,
199
Weinberger, Casper, 83
Wolfowitz, Paul, 85
Wong, Lawrence, 147
Workers' Party (WP) [Singapore]: background on, 149–50, 153, 155; boycotts,
208; dispute with NSP, 213–15; election
gains, 208, 211; election results (2001),
221; lack of alliances, 219, 220; manifestos by, 150, 153; 1972 election, 211–12

Yemen, coordination in, 10
Yeo, George, 150
Yusof Rawa, 139, 163